D1104985

A More Perfect Union

A More Perfect Union
Holistic Worldviews and the
Transformation of American
Culture after World War II

Linda Sargent Wood

OXFORD
UNIVERSITY PRESS

2010

OXFORD
UNIVERSITY PRESS

Oxford University Press, Inc., publishes works that further
Oxford University's objective of excellence
in research, scholarship, and education.

Oxford   New York
Auckland   Cape Town   Dar es Salaam   Hong Kong   Karachi
Kuala Lumpur   Madrid   Melbourne   Mexico City   Nairobi
New Delhi   Shanghai   Taipei   Toronto

With offices in
Argentina   Austria   Brazil   Chile   Czech Republic   France   Greece
Guatemala   Hungary   Italy   Japan   Poland   Portugal   Singapore
South Korea   Switzerland   Thailand   Turkey   Ukraine   Vietnam

Published by Oxford University Press, Inc.
198 Madison Avenue, New York, New York 10016

www.oup.com

Library of Congress Cataloging-in-Publication Data
Wood, Linda Sargent.
A more perfect union: holistic worldviews and the transformation of American culture after
World War II / Linda Sargent Wood.
    p. cm.
Includes bibliographical references and index.
ISBN 978-0-19-537774-3
1. United States—Intellectual life—20th century. 2. United States—Civilization—1945–
3. Holism.   I. Title.
E169.12.W66 2010
973.91—dc22   2009041900

9 8 7 6 5 4 3 2 1

Printed in the United States of America
on acid-free paper

To Larry

Preface

A More Perfect Union contends that one of the most powerful visions to guide Americans between World War II and the mid-1970s was a holistic, communal, and often utopian worldview. This holistic perspective—a view that holds that reality can only be understood as a whole, can only be understood by focusing on relationships between the parts and the whole—emphasized unity, interdependencies, and integration. Holistic projects helped drive social reform, changed the ways many people understood themselves and their environment, and altered conceptions of science and religion. By the 1960s and 1970s, holistic sensibilities resounded throughout significant subsections of the culture with particular power.

To follow the story of this particular holistic sensibility, this book spotlights nature writer Rachel Carson, structural engineer R. Buckminster Fuller, civil rights leader Martin Luther King Jr., psychologist Abraham Maslow, Jesuit priest and paleontologist Pierre Teilhard de Chardin, and the Esalen Institute and demonstrates how they helped change the shape of American culture in the last half of the twentieth century. Each individual spoke to similar concerns and offered complementary answers. Troubled by what seemed to them a fragmented world, they chastised a science that led to atomic war and a government and economy that relied on military-industrial complexes. They balked at medical approaches that treated humans as parts, systems that compartmentalized life, and huge corporations that, in quest of profit, ignored the harm caused by their products. Some challenged accepted social codes, rebelling against hierarchical distinctions of race and sex. With zeal, each strove to create a better world, infusing their spiritual values and holistic sensibilities into some of the century's most powerful social movements. Though contested and controversial, their influence can be measured through their best-selling books; large turnouts at speeches, rallies, and marches; popular architectural designs; prominent academic work in journals and institutes; legal reforms; increases in the number of businesses offering holistic health; and changing spiritual practices and beliefs.

Throughout my exploration of this holistic moment, I have become indebted to many. I especially thank Jim Gilbert, my dissertation adviser, who helped me craft my study, provided a fruitful methodology, asked pointed questions, and offered unique and valuable insights about American culture. Conversations with him were always intellectually rich and wonderfully intriguing. My gratitude extends as well to many in the University of Maryland historical community who listened, read, and offered helpful critiques, including Isabelle Gournay, Alfred Moss, Robyn Muncy, and David Sicilia. I offer particular thanks to Ira Berlin, who not only employed me as a research assistant but also instructed me in countless ways about what it means to practice the historical craft. Thanks to my fellow graduate students, especially Shelley Sperry for the walks, talks, and many chapter readings. Graduate school would not have been so rich had I not walked through it with her.

I am also indebted to the University of Maryland for generous fellowships and travel grants, and to the archivists, librarians, and research specialists at Arizona State University, Brandeis University, Connecticut College, Georgetown University, Stanford University, the University of California, Santa Barbara, University of Maryland, Northern Arizona University, and Yale University. Thanks to John Ferry at the Estate of Buckminster Fuller for his help in finding pictures and important information. Thanks also to the Buckminster Fuller Institute, the Rachel Carson Council, and the many centers, institutes, organizations, and individuals who have put so many valuable resources on the Internet.

I offer my gratitude as well to Esalen cofounder Michael Murphy for an illuminating interview and helpful edits of my writing on the human potential center. I also appreciate the Esalen community who gave my husband, Leonard, and me a lovely introduction to the place in 1999. Walking the grounds of Esalen's lush landscape adds to its mystique. Including Daniel Bianchetta's picture of Esalen attendees performing t'ai chi in this book is a delight.

My appreciation extends to my colleagues and friends at Northern Arizona University and Arizona State University, particularly those who read and commented on all or part of the book: Rachel Fuchs, Brian Gratton, Gayle Gullet, Mark von Hagen, Dan Kain, Kyle Longley, George Lubick, Joan Miller, Catherine O'Donnell, Hava Samuelson, Adam Tompkins, and Tisa Wenger. I especially thank historians Paul Hirt and Rachel Koopmans for going the extra mile with me to read the manuscript at multiple stages and offer very insightful corrections, suggestions, and encouragement. My thanks also to historians Michael William Doyle, Maril Hazlett, Robert Johnston, and Michael Lumish, who offered helpful ideas on select pieces.

A version of the Esalen chapter appeared in the *Pacific Historical Review* 77 (August 2008); I greatly appreciate the editors and reviewers for their bountiful assistance. I offer special thanks to my editor, Nancy Toff, at Oxford University Press and the anonymous reviewers of my manuscript. Their invaluable suggestions and advice have helped me vastly improve the book. I also thank the Press's very helpful editorial staff.

In this book about community, I recognize that my one voice has truly been shaped by those around me. While any faults certainly remain my own, I am most grateful for the guidance, wisdom, and joys along the journey. My gratitude reaches beyond the professional help I have received to my family and friends. None of this would have been possible without the steadfast support of my parents, Jim and Alice Sargent. Their unconditional love, laughter, wisdom (and, yes, financial assistance) helped make this work possible. My father read each chapter carefully, asked key questions, and offered many helpful ideas. Exchanging our writings throughout the years has been a source of great joy, and this work is better because of his talents. In addition to my parents, Sharon, Larry, Lewis, Judy, Juliet, and many great friends reminded me that living a holistic life means balancing work with fun. A big thanks to Leonard, who has taken this journey with me from the beginning and made the pursuit of the beloved community well worth every step. I dedicate this book to my brother, Larry, whose creativity and unique eye on life cannot be matched.

Contents

A More Perfect Union

Introduction
Holistic Worldviews in the Long 1960s

Early in 1958, when snow blanketed the eastern seaboard and the days were cold and short, Rachel Carson opened a disturbing letter. Penned by Massachusetts's songbird lover Olga Owens Huckins, the note presented Carson with details of aerial sprayings of the chemical pesticide dichloro-diphenyl-trichloroethane (DDT) and its deadly results. Also enclosed was Huckins's letter to the editor of the *Boston Herald*, which read in part:

> The mosquito control plane flew over our small town last summer....The "harmless" shower bath killed seven of our lovely songbirds outright. We picked up three dead bodies the next morning right by the door. They were birds that had lived close to us, trusted us, and built their nests in our trees year after year. The next day three were scattered around the bird bath. (I had emptied it and scrubbed it after the spraying but YOU CAN NEVER KILL DDT.) On the following day one robin dropped suddenly from a branch in our woods. We were too heartsick to hunt for other corpses. All of these birds died horri-bly, and in the same way. Their bills were gaping open, and their splayed claws were drawn up to their breasts in agony.[1]

Carson sympathized and no doubt was moved by the story, but she needed no convincing. She had first started tracking poisons in the environment in 1938, expressing concern that human actions often upset the "balance of nature."[2] In 1945, after reading early test reports on the effects of DDT on wildlife, she queried *Reader's Digest* unsuccessfully about a possible article. And in 1958, when the mail carrier delivered Huckins's letter, Carson was engrossed in a lawsuit initiated by Long Island residents against the govern-ment. At issue was the U.S. Department of Agriculture's (USDA) aerial pesticide-spraying program to kill fire ants, gypsy moths, tent caterpillars, and mosquitoes. As she followed the trial, she grew agitated. "The more I learned about the use of pesticides the more appalled I became," she explained. "I realized that here was the material for a book. What I discovered was that everything which meant most to me as a naturalist was being threatened, and that nothing I could do would be more important."[3]

Four years later, Carson alarmed others when she published *Silent Spring.* Pointing to the interrelationships and interdependencies within an ecosystem, she warned that poisoning pests had consequences. Toxins intended to eliminate gnats and mosquitoes spread "from link to link of the food chain," until salmon and songbirds fall victim.[4] The book ignited a flurry of debate and activity, ultimately becoming one of the most powerful catalysts for the modern environmental movement.

The story of Rachel Carson is a familiar one, and her popularity persists today. Conservationists hail her as a hero; public schools bear her name; juvenile literature casts her as a role model; and college students study her books for their literary, scientific, and cultural value. Though her work still sparks debate, especially within the chemical and agricultural industries, she has become a cultural icon.[5]

So how do we explain Carson's success? More important, what does her story reveal about American culture? Certainly, as scholars have enumerated, the nature writer brandished considerable literary talent, understood her science, used reliable studies, and employed keen marketing skills. Sharp attacks against her sparked interest and spurred book sales. Contemporary debates swirled over wilderness preservation, dam construction, and nuclear test bomb fallout. Within this milieu, Carson made sense.[6] All these explanations, while accurate and important contributions to understanding the zoologist's achievement, focus on her chiefly as an environmentalist. Positioning her a little differently reveals another story. In this book, Carson remains a central player in the environmental movement, but she also serves as a guide to understanding a strong current in post–World War II American culture that can best be called "holistic."

Carson articulated a holistic worldview when she pronounced that the "earth's vegetation is part of a web of life."[7] The world was an indivisible community. "We cannot think of the living organism alone," she stated; "nor can we think of the physical environment as a separate entity."[8] She popularized this viewpoint when she declared that pesticides sprayed over croplands seep into groundwater and move throughout the ecosystem: "The problem of water pollution by pesticides can be understood only in context, as part of the whole to which it belongs." In this, she argued that all of earth's inhabitants survive through "a relation of interdependence and mutual benefit." Plants, animals, and the sea and land they occupy exist through mutual dependencies, and actions taken in one segment of the ecosystem have dramatic consequences elsewhere. In the "ecological web of life," the scientist explained, "nothing existed alone."[9]

This view contrasted sharply with reductionist positions held, for instance, by botanist Henry A. Gleason, who in 1926 argued for an individualistic, competitive perspective. Instead of finding harmony, balance, and associations in the world of nature, he found rivalries, constant change, and collections of strangers. Whereas Carson claimed that "nothing exists alone," Gleason countered that each "plant is a law unto itself." Summing up Gleason's outlook, environmental historian Donald Worster wrote, "We look for cooperation in nature and we find only competition. We look for organized wholes, and we can discover only loose atoms and fragments. We hope for order and discern only a mishmash of conjoining species, all seeking their own advantage in utter disregard of others."[10] Not Carson. She looked for and saw wholes. For her, life was more than a mere collection of individuated atoms. She found significance in the associations between parts—the relationships and points of convergence—within a system and the consequences of those relations upon the entire system.[11]

Carson never referred to herself as a holist; others, however, particularly environmental historians and ethicists, have. And the name fits.[12] It fits because it explains her view of the natural world and humanity's relationship with nature. It fits because her holism functioned as more than an ecological model. As a worldview and particular sensibility, it provided a framework, much like religion does for some, to organize knowledge, pass judgments, and offer ethical guidelines. Holism works as an intellectual framework that feeds the way people think, but it cannot be limited to the cognitive realm. Particular experiences, feelings, attitudes, and desires contribute to the shape, mood, tone, and tenor of holism. Taking into consideration not just the intellectual domain but also the emotional and experiential realms, we can describe holism as not only a worldview but also a particular sensibility.[13]

Holistic conceptions enabled Carson to map her world and chart change. In the shadow of the atomic bomb, in pesticide-dusted fields, in an atmosphere of superpower animosity and industrial profiteering—in short, in her technologically and scientifically advanced society—she questioned her culture's hierarchical, utilitarian relationship with the natural environment. Simultaneously, she attacked technological and chemical fixes that solved one problem but caused others. As she lobbed her assault upon her country's excesses, she used a holistic understanding of the world both to make her argument and to present an alternative approach. Hence, the naturalist provided her readers with a compelling vision that emphasized harmony, balance, community, and mutuality, and she struck a chord in American society that resonated with particular appeal.

The naturalist's message resounded, in part, because it communicated a sensibility that was not idiosyncratic. She joined a chorus of holists in her field and elsewhere who invoked holistic frameworks to comprehend the world, express individual needs, and enact social reform.[14] Making connections between spraying apple trees with chemicals and no birds singing, it turns out, was only one of the arenas where Americans embraced this train of thought.

This book contends that this holistic worldview, which in this era was markedly communal and often utopian, was one of the most powerful perspectives to direct Americans in the postwar period. Such understandings provided the intellectual underpinnings and emotional fervor for many of the great dreams that informed the era and fundamentally altered American history. During this period stretching from the 1940s to the 1970s and aptly called the long 1960s, holistic notions offered an ethical framework built on models of cooperation rather than conflict, on models of human beings as intrinsically valuable rather than instrumental cogs in the system.[15] This cooperative ethic helped drive social reform, changed the ways individuals understood themselves and their environment, guided plans for building a harmonious global community, and knit science and religion together. These holistic ideas, in turn, helped foster civil rights activism, counterculture expressions, environmentalism, feminism, humanistic psychology, holistic education, the holistic health movement, and changing understandings of spirituality.[16] In sum, postwar holists worked to unite what others separated and bring together what others treated separately: mind, body, and spirit; individuals and community; human beings and nature; nature and technology; science and religion; the material world and the sacred.

Viewing Carson as representative of this cultural mood and sensibility, beyond the practical fear of environmental hazards, helps explain why her words reverberated across society. At the same time, situating the nature writer more broadly provides understanding not only of modern environmentalism but of the wider contours of the post–World War II reform era.[17] Across an expansive cross section of the culture, communal visions that focused on interdependence, linkages, mutual support, integration, and whole systems flowered in vibrant hues. Those who planted such visions came from a medley of disciplines and sparked a variety of actions. Their philosophies became mechanisms for interpreting reality and tools for shaping reality.

This worldview, though certainly not the only viewpoint and sometimes not the dominant one, appealed, in part, because it made sense of life after World War II and in the midst of the Cold War. In the wake of totalitarian aggression, after concentration camps and the detonation of the atomic bomb inflicted unimaginable horror and pointed to troubling implications, people around the world faced a new terrain. Armistice agreements hardly settled things. What kind of world would be—could be—created in the war's aftermath?

For Americans, the international and domestic landscape after World War II brought celebration and alarm. Jubilation resounded in the streets with the news of Allied victory and fascism's defeat. With wartime restrictions lifted and new opportunities afoot, the country began an unprecedented period of economic expansion: living standards rose; college enrollments climbed; suburbs grew; home sales increased; and telephones and electricity reached rural communities. Political leaders focused on the United States' emergence from the war as the preponderant world power. Columnist Walter Lippmann summarized imperialist sentiments when he exclaimed in 1945, "What Rome was to the ancient world, what Great Britain has been to the modern world, America is to be to the world of tomorrow."[18] As *Time* publisher Henry Luce labeled it as he argued for an end to isolationism in 1941, this was the American Century.[19]

Yet, for all the revelry in material comforts and for all the arguments for exercising American hegemony, there were multiple discontents. This was an "age of contradictions," as historian Howard Brick found.[20] From the shadow of mushroom clouds to superpower divisions, blockades, and arms races to calamities and casualties in the Korean and Vietnam wars, men and women confronted an ambiguous and, for some, a dangerous world. Wars of independence in Southeast Asia and Africa, the dissolution of colonialism and the creation of new governments—some with unstable borders and shifting alliances—brought the potential for greater equality worldwide but also added to global uneasiness. Eleanor Roosevelt and others, hoping to prevent another world war, devoted themselves to making the fledgling United Nations a vehicle for easing geopolitical tensions. Scientists who worked on the Manhattan Project and regretted the use of the bombs on Japan forged the Federation of Atomic (later American) Scientists to advise public policy makers. On the home front, other concerns surfaced. Economic depression loomed large in the public's memory. McCarthyism suppressed civil liberties. Gender and labor relations, altered during wartime production and dislocation, remained contested ground. And racial discord persisted.

This world, with its contrasting satisfactions and discontents, produced a variety of responses. Returning soldiers claimed their benefits under the G.I. Bill of Rights and went to college, climbed the corporate ladder, and settled in suburbia. Television, soaring in popularity during the 1950s, offered a new medium of news and entertainment. Minority groups protested discrimination and agitated for change. Some explored the existentialism of Jean-Paul Sartre, the abstract expressionism of the New York school, the New Left politics of Herbert Marcuse, or the conservative politics of William F. Buckley. Others revived religious convictions. Billy Graham's crusades and Catholic bishop Fulton Sheen's television program *Life Is Worth Living* drew large crowds and viewers. Still others, the focus of this book, turned to holistic, communal understandings to promote a better life. Their cognitive maps of the world and their projects, in turn, served to change the contours of American society in deep and profound ways.

To demonstrate the power and reach of this outlook, I shine light on five influential people who embraced holistic ideas to make sense of their world and who helped craft and popularize holistic ideas and practices. In addition to Carson (1907–64), this book profiles structural engineer and futurist R. Buckminster Fuller (1895–1983); Baptist minister and civil rights leader Martin Luther King Jr. (1929–68); Jesuit priest and paleontologist Pierre Teilhard de Chardin (1881–1955); and humanistic psychologist and utopian Abraham Maslow (1908–70). The work concludes with an examination of the Esalen Institute, an educational center to foster human growth, which captured and spread this particular sensibility.

This small, yet suggestive, sampling of a broader cross section of American society serves to illuminate this holistic moment. These case studies have been deliberately chosen not as definitive renderings of holism or as an all-inclusive list but as influential representatives of holistic expressions in different parts of the human experience and in different fields of knowledge. Hence, while this is not a comprehensive digest or discussion of every postwar holistic idea or project, it is deliberately interdisciplinary, allowing for a richer, more diverse reading of the culture.

This posthole method provides a way to examine the depth and breadth of this particular phenomenon. At carefully selected junctures, I dig deep into a particular person's life and his or her respective discipline to examine holistic understandings and expressions. The results show that holism was part of a cultural revolution bent on improving society and how we inhabit this planet. From biology to the built environment, from psychology to sociology, from discussions of religion and philosophy to admonitions for civil rights and community involvement, these important people and their followers wielded holism, which had moral and political implications, to solve problems. Juxtaposing these individuals and their speeches, books, buildings, dreams, and campaigns reveals connections, concerns, and insights that would not be possible if one were to look at only one discipline or person. Congregating them highlights the fundamental role that holism played in the culture at midcentury.

The design of this book emulates the concept of holism. Each chapter focuses on one individual's vision, discipline, and influence. At the same time, each person is connected through a web of related concerns and interests to provide a broader view of American culture as a whole. Simultaneously, each chapter addresses constituent parts of the human experience: the natural and built environments; the individual (body, mind, and spirit); the human community; and the cosmos. In this way, each chapter illuminates how holistic ideas influenced different aspects of life. Carson speaks to the relationship between the human and the natural world. Fuller addresses the relationship between humanity and the built environment. Maslow addresses the individual psyche. King focuses on social relations. And

Teilhard points to the cosmic realm. The Esalen Institute brings these myriad expressions under one roof. In setting these individuals and projects side by side, the power of their optimistic communal visions becomes more evident, and events that first appear unrelated become more understandable. Each color in the kaleidoscope becomes a fundamental part of the whole.

I begin the story with Carson's release of *Silent Spring* in 1962, a year when more nuclear test bombs were detonated than any other year in history and shortly before the Cold War threatened to ignite in the Cuban missile crisis. This historical setting is important, as it shaped not only the zoologist's holistic understandings but others'. This initial chapter focuses our gaze on humanity's relationship with nature—our most essential relationship—and details Carson's formation of holism.

While Carson popularized her version of holism in books, articles, and campaigns for environmental protection, Buckminster Fuller created a more concrete manifestation of holism in the design of his geodesic dome. Held together in what he described as "synergetic" relation, each part relying on neighboring parts for stability, each part crucial to the creation of the whole, his geodesics served as colorful domiciles for counterculturalists, as well as spaces for fairs, military operations, scientific experiments, and sporting events. In other ways, too, Fuller expressed holistic underpinnings. Through his world maps, natural resource charts, World Game, and international connections, he championed global interdependencies and argued for equitable distribution of resources and global harmony. His ideas contributed to ongoing discussions in America about the place of the machine in the garden, and about the relationship connecting humanity, technology, and nature. For Fuller, who tried to emulate nature through his technological creations, both had a place in the modern landscape. Indeed, to account for his faith in technology and his love for nature, the technological wizard saw nature and technology as complementary parts of one whole. He formed his whole by naturalizing technology and technologizing nature. As the chapter on Fuller illustrates, the architect trumpeted his geodesic as both a natural system and a technological marvel. For him, in often vague and even mystical ways, the links between nature and technology made the machine organic.

Abraham Maslow was the only figure among those studied here to call himself a holist. In his influential book *Motivation and Personality*, he stated: "Holism is obviously true—after all, the cosmos is one and interrelated; any society is one and interrelated; any person is one and interrelated."[21] Inspired by Gestalt psychologist Max Wertheimer and anthropologist Ruth Benedict, Maslow crafted a psychology that focused on the healthy, whole, and "self-actualized" person. His work countered Freudian and behavioral psychology and linked him with others in the postwar era who were developing the field of humanistic psychology. As he concentrated on the development of the healthy individual, he imagined a future world of "self-actualized" individuals knit together in a "eupsychian" (psychologically whole) paradise. His writings influenced the practice of psychology and education, countercultural philosophies and practices, the Esalen Institute, business management, and the holistic health movement.

King's vision of a "beloved community" made another holistic declaration and testified to the redemptive power he placed in integration. "In a real sense all of life is interrelated," he contended, as he sought to unite race-divided America. "We are," he affirmed, "tied together in the single garment of destiny, caught in an inescapable network of mutuality."[22] This network of mutuality united all races and peoples and combated class and national divisions. Living in a day when racism abroad and at home was suspect, when decolonization opened up new political opportunities, and when American economic prosperity and legal changes created possibilities to wage war on poverty, the minister called for tighter bonds of cooperation between individuals and a more inclusive society. Recognizing our common humanity, he thought, promised healing and a worldwide "brotherhood" that was more than a sum of its parts or a negation of the customs of segregation. His notion of an organic society knit together in agape love, a beloved community built out of mutual respect for each person's dignity, expanded the work of others and helped initiate sweeping changes in America's political and social fabric. The 1963 March on Washington, for instance, led to the Civil Rights Act of 1964 and the Voting Rights Act of 1965. Seeing King as a holist, as a crusader for unity in a divided society, helps us understand him. His dominant metaphor, the "beloved community," spoke of union, reinforced notions of equality, and foretold a future of fraternity.

Holists did not stop with the physical universe. The web of life, according to Teilhard, connected spirit and matter, religion and science, faith and evolution. For his American followers, whether spiritual idealists or material scientists, this translated into a viable way of sustaining religious belief in an age of science, a welcome possibility for those who felt pulled both by their belief in the supernatural and by scientific reason. Merging Catholicism and Darwinism, Teilhard created a "religion of evolution." He envisioned an evolving universe progressing toward a place of unity, a mystical state that he called the "omega point." The priest postulated that everything had a part in the evolutionary process. Humanity, in particular, bore responsibility for "building the earth." Though distraught by two world wars, he imagined a "Cosmic Christ" drawing the world toward a place of greater unity and love. Teilhard voiced a communitarian spirituality and spoke in the language of holism, emphasizing "links," "mutual dependence," "cooperation," and "convergence." He articulated a whole that interlocked the universe. Everything was related to everything else in space and also in time.

In the 1960s, when his books were published posthumously, he gained a large American following. Especially for Catholics who did not want to abandon either their faith or science, Teilhard's synthesis was seminal. But the man's words spoke not only to priests like Thomas Berry but to writers like Flannery O'Connor and cosmologists like Brian Swimme. He also influenced communication theorist Marshall McLuhan, economist Kenneth Boulding, politician Albert Gore Jr., and many more. His inspirational message fed the human potential movement, including Esalen, and individuals who defied traditional religious classification, who saw themselves more as "spiritual," rather than "religious," and who chose to craft a very personalized faith. These believers—often identified with, though certainly not the sole province of, New Age spiritualities—borrowed ideas from a variety of belief systems and scientific findings. Outlining the contours of Teilhard's marriage of science and religion in this era of high scientific achievement and the attraction that many had for his mystical devotion and scientific expertise reveals that postwar America cannot be neatly divided into camps of the religious and the scientific.

From these singular expressions came movements, institutions, and associations that embodied and spread holistic understandings. The environmental movement gained members and political clout. Civil rights advocates pushed desegregation and changed economic, political, and social practices. Activists in these arenas and their organizations cannot be explained entirely by holism—just as other individuals and movements can never be defined by one element—but they often expressed themselves in holistic terms in striking ways. Racial integration, in significant ways, made a holistic declaration. Healing practitioners attended to a person's spiritual and emotional needs to achieve soundness of mind and body. Humanistic psychologists opened clinics designed to comprehend the "patient as a whole person, a unique and irreducible subject."[23] Teilhard's writings, the American Teilhard Association, the New Age movement, and *Zygon*—an academic journal yoking religion and science—broadcast the priest's views and inspired work in fields as diverse as architecture, computer science, ecology, paleontology, physics, and theology.

The Esalen Institute, located along the rugged Big Sur region of California's central coast, serves as one of the most tangible and intriguing centers for holistic thought and practices. Begun in 1962, this unconventional alternative to academia, corporate ladders, and suburban lifestyles offered a place to explore human capabilities. It reflected and shaped aspects of a 1960s counterculture that embraced and embodied this holistic moment. Esalen lectures and workshops promoted personal and social transformation through a holistic fusion of Eastern religion and Western science, cross-cultural exchanges, environmental responsibility, and an end to racism, sexism, and the Cold War. Attendees engaged in practices such as Gestalt therapy, massage, meditation, t'ai chi, and yoga to bring body, mind, and spirit into harmony. Ideas from each of the individuals discussed in this book influenced Esalen's development, and some spoke at the center. Profiling how and why founders Michael Murphy and Richard Price started Esalen and charting the institute's history demonstrates some, though certainly not all, of the ways holistic thinking penetrated American life and contributed to discussions about human nature and relationships between man, woman, nature, and technology. It also signals one of the ways that a holistic synthesis of Eastern and Western thought influenced the transformation of spiritual belief and practice in this era and provides evidence that holism was one avenue for religion's continuing presence in a scientific age.

By the 1970s, holistic conceptions reverberated throughout significant subsections of the culture with particular power and holistic practices moved from a marginal status in the 1940s to a more central place in the culture. When NASA started sending photos back to earth from space in 1965, Fuller and others, particularly his colleagues in the alternative technology branch of the environmental movement, had visual support for seeing the earth as whole, beautiful, and everyone and everything on it as intricately connected to its sustainability.[24] In 1970, when historic numbers gathered on the mall in Washington, D.C., to celebrate the first "Earth Day," environmentalists spoke of "ecology," "ecosystems," and global harmony and admonished the vast audience to think globally and act locally. This crowd thought of the world—from sea to soil to sky—as one united, interconnected community. One college student described the period as a time when an entire generation was "seeing, thinking, feeling wholes."[25]

Yet, while holism continued to attract followers into the twenty-first century, even by the 1970s the sensibility had shifted to reflect a much more individualistic era. Competing visions, the rise of a new conservatism, the coming of age of the baby boomers, political assassinations and corruption, economic downturn, and violent confrontations at home and abroad blocked full realization of these communal hopes. Hence, this tale of holism is neither one of complete triumph nor of complete declension. Nonetheless, holists made substantial contributions that shaped the American experience. Their ideas continued to ripple throughout society, capturing imaginations and motivating action. Holistic beliefs about the individual, society, and nature translated into practical, political results. In less tangible though still important ways, holistic notions sparked new understandings of the body and health care, initiated revisions in scientific paradigms, and contributed to changing beliefs and practices that affected Catholics, Protestants, and individual spiritual seekers. Holism marked American culture in deep and surprising ways.

While this work tracks the story of holism in the postwar era, I should emphasize that this was not the first cycling of this constellation of ideas and that prior expressions influenced holistic projects in the long 1960s. The word "holism" was coined in 1926 by the South African statesman General Jan Christiaan Smuts to reflect his interest in the captivating elements of holism in evolution, philosophy, and psychology. One of those interests, Gestalt psychology, was especially grounded in holistic, antireductionistic thought.[26] *Gestalt*, in German, means "pattern" or "unified whole." Gestalt psychologists claimed that the mind perceives reality in terms of *gestalten*, or wholes. People, they contended, do not understand experience in a piecemeal fashion but rather in organizational wholes. When we perceive a pattern, solve a problem, answer a riddle, we exclaim, "Aha!" We see the whole. Christian von Ehrenfels (1859–1932) laid the groundwork for Gestalt psychology by explaining that a melody is composed of musical notes, yet it is more than a collection of notes. It follows a distinct form. If the notes are rearranged, the melody is lost. Hence, the melody is a whole that is more than the sum of its parts.[27] Wertheimer and other Gestalt psychologists, as we shall see in the chapter on Maslow, voiced adherence to organic wholes and the interdependencies of the parts, influencing other holists, such as Ruth Benedict, Frederick Perls, Maslow, and Smuts. But holism was not unique to this era either.

Smuts derived the word from the ancient Greek word *holos*, meaning "whole." *Holos* abounded in the writings of Plato, Aristotle, Hippocrates, and Paul, often conveying a holistic meaning. Plato, in *Dialogues*, critiqued medicinal practices that did not treat the "whole" patient, and he quoted favorably from Hippocrates, who wrote that "the nature even of the body can only be understood as a whole."[28] Aristotle wrote what has become today's common understanding of holism in the *Metaphysics*: "The whole is more than the sum of its parts." The apostle Paul used the term in his biblical letters to express that the person should be viewed as wholly integrated in spirit, body, and mind, linking his ontology with other New Testament passages that referred to wholeness of life in terms of salvation and sanctification. In this way, he united holiness with wholeness. Other peoples, in diverse regions and times, utilized holistic philosophies. Medieval European philosophers employed holistic conceptions to explain life as a "great chain of being." Hildegard of Bingen, a twelfth-century mystic and patron saint of the twentieth-century New Age movement, developed a holistic theology of immanence, exclaiming, "O Holy Spirit, you are the mighty way in which everything that is in the heavens, on the earth, and under the earth, is penetrated with connectedness, penetrated with relatedness." Human beings, in synergetic relation with God and a fundamental part of this organic whole, were, she professed, "co-creators with God in everything we do."[29] In India, too, holistic expressions were manifest in

Vedanta philosophy and Hindu culture. One only needs to think of the yin and the yang as complementary visions of the whole in Chinese thought to see holistic ties. (By the end of the twentieth century, in fact, the symbol for yin and yang became a popular trademark of holistic enterprises in the United States, hinting at some of the power of Eastern thought on postwar American culture, especially after Congress revamped immigration laws in 1965 and opened the doors to greater numbers of Asian peoples.)

As the many appropriations of holism in various disciplines and times suggest, the concept of holism, like other intellectual constructs and sensibilities, is malleable.[30] Across time and space, individuals and groups invented, borrowed, and reclaimed holistic understandings for their own purposes, manipulating the sensibility to fit multiple agendas. The twentieth century alone contains many manifestations. Alternative or complementary medicine, for example, has viewed the person (emotional, mental, physical, and spiritual) and the person's environment as a whole in the diagnosis and treatment of disease.[31] In philosophy, semantic holists have argued that meaning can only be derived from the context of the language as a whole. The parts—syllables, words, sentences—are derivative.[32] In biology, theoretical biologist Ludwig Bertalanffy (1901–72), father of general systems theory, applied a holistic approach by focusing on the whole organism and the integration of its parts. The systems model became a guiding paradigm for a variety of disciplines, from the sciences and social sciences to corporate management and public administration. The ecosystem, which posits that the organism continuously interacts with its environment, reflects this approach.[33] Cybernetics studies, especially under the hand of Norbert Wiener, employed another systems methodology, using mathematical feedback theories and self-organizing assumptions that were foundational for computer designers and some psychologists.[34]

Social and political theories have, at times, also reflected organic, holistic thinking. Sociologist Émile Durkheim's view of society as an organic whole is one example. Socialism is another. Even as it focuses on the uneven distribution of power among the classes, socialist theory prioritizes the communal whole. In 1914 Vladimir Lenin wrote, "Everything is connected to everything else."[35] Totalitarianism, in its demand for subservience by all members to the centralized state, reveals how holism may be appropriated for ill. Adolf Hitler's vision of a superior Aryan race and his ideal of a unified world legitimized in his eyes the subordination of the one for the many, the sacrifice of some for the good of the whole. His manipulation of holism, in stark contrast with other versions, demonstrates the idea's pliability and dangers.

In American history, holistic thought has infused sundry utopian experiments and reform impulses from the romantic movement in the nineteenth century to the conservationists of the twentieth century. While responding to unique concerns of their particular generation, each of these, in turn, informed post–World War II expressions. Comparisons between Margaret Fuller, editor of the transcendentalist journal *Dial*, and her grandnephew R. Buckminster Fuller hint at more than generational differences. Other twentieth-century holists also found their nineteenth-century ancestors inspirational to the extent that many parallels can be drawn between the eras. Both borrowed from organic models of nature; presumed connectedness, unity, and harmony with nature; and catered to pantheistic religious conceptions or, at least, a belief in divine immanence rather than transcendence. In multiple ways, as we shall see, the postwar holistic moment owed much to the romantics of the antebellum era.

Twentieth-century figures concerned about human relationships with nature have also articulated holistic ideas. Conservationist John Muir summed up his view in a statement frequently quoted by later environmentalists and sustainability experts: "When we try to pick out anything by itself, we find it hitched to everything else in the Universe."[36] Naturalist Joseph Krutch's early laments about science, rationality, and the modern condition turned more hopeful and more pantheistic after he read Thoreau and escaped into nature. His books on Arizona's desert ecology make plain his holistic lens.[37] Scientist Aldo Leopold found human beings connected to the land in inseparable ways. He defined community as more than a union of people by including flora and fauna, soil and water. In his well-known land ethic, he argued, "A thing is right when it tends to preserve the integrity, stability, and beauty of the biotic community. It is wrong when it tends otherwise."[38]

In these and other instances, individuals and groups bent and employed holistic understandings for their own purposes. In this way, holism is, to borrow from historian James Gilbert's lexicon, an "episodic notion," an idea that rises and falls at varying historical intervals. "Democracy" and "republicanism" serve as examples. These terms convey "broadly held ideas" with several definable characteristics, but they often "present themselves as puzzles whose meaning may not be immediately apparent." Consequently, they "require a degree of decoding to grasp their larger implications" and must be "constantly redefined in terms of context, intent, and reference."[39]

Holism fits this pattern. Cyclically, it has come in and out of favor. We can broadly define its characteristics, and yet its literal meaning is slippery. It loses exactness if we fail to consider who shaped it and what purpose it served. To read holism's significance and discern how its articulations worked in post–World War II America, it must be decoded. Like a puzzle, it must be deciphered. This book is thus an investigation into mid-twentieth-century American culture, employing holism as the entry point. In answering how holistic mind-sets were formed and to what end they were enacted, it reveals key understandings about individuals and important insights about the postwar generation.

Tracing the production of each holistic representation illuminates the amazing plasticity of this episodic notion as it was reworked to meet competing agendas and venues. Probing each rendition unveils how each of these individuals wrestled with common problems and interjected their ideas into relevant conversations of the day.[40] Maslow's holism, for instance, bestowed personal meaning, gave him a means for discussing social change, and countered the reductionistic, mechanistic approaches inherent in behavioral and Freudian psychology. King's holism had two pivot points: affirming the dignity of the individual, whether black, white, red, or brown, and caring for the collective well-being of society. His reliance on a social gospel that addressed body, mind, and spirit and his upholding of America's ideal of equality provided him with the platform to demand an end to discrimination, poverty, and war. Seeing the ways these individuals fashioned the concept to meet their needs not only reveals that holism was in the air but also highlights some of the ways that a culture adapts, modifies, reforms, and rejuvenates itself.

As a recurring phenomenon that owes much to prior articulations and also bends to the winds of its own era, holism emerged in the 1960s as both an old idea and yet as something distinct. As I explored the ebb and flow of this moment, three important ongoing conversations in American culture surfaced, each helping to define this particular manifestation of holism. The first conversation centered on the relationships concerning human beings, the natural environment, and technology; the second on the relationship between the individual and community; and the third on the relationships between religion, science, and technology. Within their highly scientific and increasingly global world, a world that sometimes left individuals feeling estranged from nature, overwhelmed by the size and complexity of urban communities, and vulnerable to technological disasters, each holist in this study struggled to understand the place, importance, and role of the human being in the modern, corporate world, grappled with tensions between the individual and society, and delved into questions about the relationship between religion and science. They confronted similar questions: In a highly advanced industrial society, what is the nature of humanity? In the urban and suburban landscape where most Americans lived, what role did nature have in people's lives? How can the world of nature be reconciled with a scientific, technological age? Can it? How could one assert individual rights and achieve social equality and harmony? Finally, what is the place of religion in a scientific age? Can the two be reconciled? Holists in the 1960s posited answers to these questions. They wrote prescriptions for societal harmony, made space for technology while preserving a harmonious relationship with nature, and adapted their faith to fit an increasingly scientific world.

In offering answers, holists did not respond to their world with angst and turmoil. Rather, they expressed optimism. Communal visions illustrated this. King declared, "The end is reconciliation; the end is redemption; the end is the creation of the beloved community."[41] Teilhard endeavored to move all toward an "Omega Point" of universal love. Maslow envisioned a world of self-actualized, fully integrated, healthy people. Carson pushed for the cultivation of a bucolic garden untainted by pesticide dust or atomic fallout, and Fuller wrote a manual for a smoothly operating "spaceship earth." To each, connections and unity were paramount. Breaking down barriers and living in harmony with other Americans, other nations, the natural world, indeed, even with the planet, was their utopian vision.

These visions of community varied, however, in fundamental ways. When, for instance, it came to questions about technology's role in American society and about relationships between nature and technology—questions that were central, though far from new, to American culture at midcentury—these holists did not offer a unified response. Instead, they reflected a long-seated ambivalence. Technologically, this was an age that presented frightening challenges to some and exhilarating possibilities to others. America's long debate about the machine in the garden raged again. For Carson, technology, coupled with capitalists' quest for profit, often intruded in harmful ways upon the landscape. Human irresponsibility initiated a chain of destruction. In contrast to the harmony and balance she perceived in the world of nature, she saw atomic fallout, cancer-causing chemicals, and poor soil management. Modernity's march appeared destined to destroy the bucolic, spiritual landscape she idealized. Conversely, Fuller thought technology offered salvation. Human inventions, particularly those that used nature as a guide, could provide solutions to housing shortages, unequal resource distribution, and other problems plaguing humanity. As an early voice in sustainability discussions, he saw technology as a harbinger for maintaining life on this planet. Moreover, by harnessing the machine, the garden could be made better, and people could enjoy greater freedom, security, and happiness. Teilhard, likewise, embraced technological change as a path to a brighter future. His followers argued the priest's ideas presaged the invention of the World Wide Web.[42]

Communitarian ideals did not always fare well in broader cultural conversations and decisions, especially as holists confronted the deep ethos of individualism within American culture. Hardly diminished after World War II, this ethos found expression among those who trumpeted independence, liberty, and self-expression. Offering a sharp critique of American life in the 1950s, individualists from across the political spectrum interpreted interdependence as conformity and decried what they perceived to be a herd mentality. German exile Herbert Marcuse described America as "one-dimensional" and monotonous.[43] Anti-Communist McCarthyites feared anything akin to communal solidarity that smacked to them of Marxism. Others—some of whom were Communists, many of whom were not—concluded that loyalty oaths at universities, anti-Communist purges of unions, Hollywood blacklists, and actions taken by the House Committee on Un-American Activities were a direct infringement on constitutional rights and individual liberties. Sill others expressed indignation at the corporate world and what appeared to them as the diminishment of the individual employee. William H. Whyte's *Organization Man* (1956) surmised that middle management workers were becoming an unthinking mass caught in "group think" and ideals of "togetherness." Instead of exerting an independent voice, they succumbed to "the togetherness of the whole." Security, stability, cooperation, and group priorities took precedence over individual expression. It was more important to get along than to ruffle feathers. The larger community took priority.[44] Sociologist David Riesman's *Lonely Crowd* (1950) articulated similar concerns. Conformity, a fear of being abnormal, and an unwillingness to stand apart or voice an unconventional opinion characterized Americans, he thought, during the 1950s. Unlike "traditional" preindustrial community types, and unlike "inner-directed" persons of the nineteenth century, "outer-directed" folks of the 1950s followed the crowd and made modern mass society possible. Playwright Arthur Miller, short-story writer John Cheever, novelist Sloan Wilson, sociologist C. Wright Mills, and others supported Whyte's and Riesman's critiques.[45]

Holists were sensitive to many of these admonitions and reproofs. Perhaps ironically, many of them lived a very individualistic lifestyle and blasted conventionality. This was true of Buckminster Fuller, in particular. Nonetheless, holists argued that societies could foster individual expression and simultaneously form a united whole that was harmonious, equitable, and just. They emphasized unity and interdependencies and celebrated what they interpreted as the oneness and interrelated nature of life. Their utopian projects were designed to make this possible. Setting holism within the debate over individual and communitarian values helps explain this impulse as one that was bent toward consensus, yearned for integration, and favored concord.

Situating this particular moment when holism flourished within this tension between the one and the many helps explain it. To historicize this debate, it should be remembered that individualistic and communalistic impulses have been two strong traditions in American culture. The United States inscribed a reverence for individual rights and freedoms into its constitutional foundation. Civil liberties formed a cornerstone of American identity, even though practice did not always live up to the ideal. Turnerian conceptions of the American character as embodying "rugged individualism" and myths about "frontier pioneers," "lone cowboys," and "self-made men" contributed to these individualist ideals.[46] Concurrently, even before the Declaration of Independence, some British immigrants committed themselves to communal values. Massachusetts Bay Colony leader John

Winthrop, in his "Modell of Christian Charity," set forth a vision of society that favored "the good of the whole." To be "a city on a hill," the English Puritan immigrants "must be knit together in this work as one man, we must entertain each other in brotherly affection, we must be willing to abridge ourselves of our superfluities for the supply of others' necessities, we must delight in each other, mourn together, labor and suffer together, always having before our eyes our Commission and Community in the work."[47]

Other religious sects, political societies, and countercultural groups scrambled from colonial times to the present to erect their own "city on a hill," their own distinct utopias. Sometimes this resulted in tangible unions, such as Brook Farm, the Oneida Community, and Shaker societies. Transcendentalism, Fourierism, Christianity, and other outlooks formed the basis for these groups. Communitarian values and priorities have been evident in any number of additional projects. Reform movements, addressing issues of slavery, women's suffrage, labor interests, temperance, urban crowding, poor sanitation, and other concerns, articulated a social ethic and demanded social cooperation.[48]

Postwar holism, though never abandoning American ideals of individual rights and freedoms, sits within this expansive communal tradition. Indeed, many holistic ideals forwarded in the 1960s owed much to communal ventures in the past, whether the transcendentalists of Brook Farm, the Bohemians and Communist sympathizers of Greenwich Village, or the communal values of indigenous populations and the African American church.[49]

As they built on these and other communal traditions, holists hoped to form a more perfect union. This was part of the appeal of the call for equality and democratic change in the 1960s. King's vision of community promised union of the races; Carson's offered harmony between human beings and the natural world; Fuller's, Teilhard's, and Maslow's assured the dawning of a new age. Hence, holistic projects not only were a reaction to the Cold War and the man in the gray flannel suit but also were extensions of earlier calls for communal oneness and alternative road maps to developing a society where cooperation rather than conflict defined international relations, where equality marked political and economic activities, where self-actualization and environmental sustainability were possible. In a time of nuclear anxiety, holistic, communitarian visions flourished, no doubt aided by the era's unprecedented economic expansion and not yet stained by the suspicion, cynicism, and distrust that marked American life in the wake of political assassinations, the Gulf of Tonkin attacks on Vietnam, Watergate, energy crises, abusive drug use, and strident cultural wars. Especially in the 1950s and 1960s, belief in the human potential and societal wholeness informed communitarian notions.

Within this democratic, capitalistic, scientific society, 1960s holists frequently addressed the role of technology and religion. Indeed, there could be no serious expression of holism in postwar America without reckoning with the interplay of religion, science, and technology. Not surprisingly, holists did not divorce nature or religion from science or society but looked for ways to reconcile them. Postwar communal dreams were infused with spirituality. For Martin Luther King Jr., Christianity defined his conception of social solidarity. In ways not dissimilar from John Winthrop, King's beloved community stood on biblical injunctions to serve one another in brotherly love. Each person, he believed, should bear in mind the interests of others. King's notion of equality was far different from Winthrop's hierarchical one, but each relied on biblical injunctions to form the beloved community. Other holists also relied on religious precepts. Teilhard built his holism on a mystical interpretation of Catholicism, and Maslow, though a self-proclaimed atheist, drew on Jewish concepts of justice, as well as Buddhist understandings of selflessness. Carson borrowed from her Presbyterian roots, and both she and Fuller linked their holistic philosophies to Unitarianism and transcendentalism. Esalen, attracting faiths of East and West, became an experimental hothouse for germinating a variety of religious hybrids.

In these and other expressions, holists combined the physical and the metaphysical. When they gazed at nature, they perceived the embodiment of the spiritual realm, and when they looked for the sacred, they found it in nature. Consequently, they crafted holistic perspectives filled with spiritual significance and inserted their opinions in the ongoing, vibrant conversation concerning the place of religion in a scientific culture.

This conversation took place within the heyday of science and technology. Scientists solved age-old problems, and inventors produced time-saving machines, new technological tools, and materials to make life easier. New penicillin and sulfa drugs performed miraculous cures; the new chemical compound DDT, doused in liberal measure on lice-infested soldiers, saved lives during the war and came to the rescue of pest-fighting farmers; aeronautic engineers catapulted America into a place of air and space supremacy. This was a period of high scientific achievement and prestige, and scientists took advantage of their privileged rank. To a remarkable extent, they attached themselves to government and educational enterprises and exerted unprecedented power. Still, as scientists parlayed their good favor into more control, they came under greater scrutiny.

Significant questions arose about the role, values, and dominance of a developing scientific priesthood. In the decades after World War II, news of scientists' involvement in Hitler's euthanasia programs—freezing, sterilization, and neurological experiments, for example—revivified Mary Shelley's Frankensteinian vision of science. Reports from Germany probably provided the most shock value, but other factors also raised suspicion. The high degree of specialization required to be a practitioner of science distanced scientists from nonscientists. Especially in the world of physics, scientists who mastered complex theories about quarks and neutrinos spoke a special language and commanded an elite position. This could be an uncomfortable position for scientists, who found their esoteric knowledge and privileged status sometimes made it difficult to communicate with lay audiences, and elicited some public wariness, even fear. For amateurs, limited access to this sophisticated world provoked doubt. More misgivings surfaced as the public learned of secret alliances between scientists and government officials.[50]

The creation and deployment of the atomic bomb demonstrated with horrifying drama the use of scientific knowledge in war and cast a pall over the physicist in the white lab coat. Physicists wrestled with this heightened level of public fear and distrust, as Paul Boyer documents in *By the Bomb's Early Light*. Manhattan Project scientist Louis Ridenour claimed that the atomic bomb had "entirely transformed lay thinking regarding science....[People] are beginning to hate and fear [it]. They feel...that scientists are somehow warmongers." Raymond Fosdick, president of the Rockefeller Foundation, expressed this transformation in November 1945: "Science is the search for truth....It springs from the noblest attribute of the human spirit. But...this same search for truth...has brought our civilization to the brink of destruction."[51] As Americans and Russians continued to use science and technology for military gain—developing the nuclear bomb, technologically sophisticated satellite equipment, U-2 spy plane reconnaissance, and intercontinental ballistic missiles, for example—individuals, including President Dwight Eisenhower, questioned the growth of the military-industrial complex.[52]

Using nuclear energy for peaceful gain also came under criticism. Those who dreamed "of vast power and plenty made possible by atomic energy," wrote Richard M. Fagley in a 1945 issue of *Christianity and Crisis*, appeared myopic. "How distorted is our vision to see so easily the vista of mechanical progress in this Atomic Age, and to fail to see the greed, pride, and fear in ourselves which have now brought us to the doorstep of doom!" As disgusted as Carson with the pursuit of nuclear technology, Lewis Mumford called for a moratorium on atomic-energy research in 1948: "We have reached a point in history where the unchecked pursuit of truth, without regard to its social consequences, will bring to a swift end the pursuit of truth, by wiping out the very civilization that has favored it."[53]

Positivism, mechanistic thinking, reductionism, and Enlightenment rationality—much of which can be seen as the opposite of holistic thinking—also came under harsh review during this era. According to two of the best-known critics of Western society, Theodor Adorno and Max Horkheimer, Enlightenment epistemology and scientific practices lacked moral grounding and rationalized control of nature and people.[54] Carson, Fuller, and Maslow—and to some extent King and Teilhard—agreed. Reductionistic thinking, Carson argued, ushered in a world that was exploitive and fraught with danger. An authoritarian penchant to dominate nature led to a science that created poisonous "fallout," whether instigated by a desire to kill human beings or insects. Maslow, too, rebelled against science's instrumentalist, "mechanomorphic" rationality.

Such anxieties about the role and value of science fed American religious culture, which did not fade in light of science's advance. Notwithstanding the predictions of Enlightenment thinkers and secularization and modernization theorists, Americans did not become more secular as scientific knowledge increased. Instead, they maintained religious traditions and adapted new ones. They did so in the second half of the twentieth century, as they had done throughout their history, by reconfiguring and revitalizing their beliefs.[55] Postwar holists who were both scientists and people of faith provided several routes for Americans to do so.

Instead of opting for science over religion as positivists had, or religion over science as some evangelicals did, many postwar holists merged tenets and constructed cosmologies that reflected both. At the same time they sought to enlarge human understanding through scientific knowledge, they adjusted science to meet their humanistic beliefs, values, and ethics. Each figure in this study crafted a perspective that was filled with spiritual meaning and contributed to the vibrant conversation concerning the place of religion in a scientific society. Especially for the paleontologist who remained a priest, creating a "religion of evolution" made space for both faith and science, and Catholics, New Age worshipers, and Esalen participants found this synthesis specially appealing. Of course, the holistic mixes offered did not appeal to everyone. Certainly some East-West experiments alienated traditional Christians, and many of the liberal holistic reforms found opposition from conservative fundamentalists. Still, paying attention to the allure of holistic frameworks at this time helps explain how a cross section of believers maintained strong religious allegiance and a core commitment to scientific principles.

To miss this holistic *mentalité* would discount vital aspects of American life and lead to only partial explanations of the period's events. Yet, while declaring holism's importance, I do not mean to suggest that holism explains everything about any one person, nor do I presume that holism singularly defined the era. People and history defy such simplicity. Rather, in calling this a key period for holistic thinking and action, I seek to capture—as students of the Enlightenment, romanticism, or modernism have done for their eras—a broad framework, sentiment, mood, and intellectual configuration.[56] Historians have offered labels for the post–World War II period: Howard Brick found an "age of contradiction"; James Farrell identified a personalist thread through the sixties; Samuel P. Hays made the environmental movement and "quality of life" ethic the central component; James Patterson called it the "rights revolution"; Elaine Tyler May identified it as a culture of "containment."[57] Historians have also traced conservative values throughout this period and shown that the rise of Presidents Ronald Reagan and George W. Bush owed much to William F. Buckley, Barry Goldwater, and others in the long 1960s. Religious historians note the steady rise of fundamentalism and the evangelical Right.[58] These were all important strands of American life. So, too, was holism. In significant and illuminating ways it was a strong impulse—and not just a countercultural beat— reverberating through disciplines and among a variety of people. Thus, this book aims to add to our understanding of one way that Americans negotiated life after World War II and to illuminate the intellectual synergy among the most powerful social reforms of the twentieth century.

However compelling holism may be in any of its enactments, this discussion is not about the truth of holism.[59] Rather, this book focuses on the historical forces that shaped holistic expressions, how these articulations influenced people and events, and what this reveals about the era. It explores how individuals and groups reclaimed and invented holistic understandings and applied them to a variety of contexts, manipulating the idea to fit multiple purposes. Putting individuals and conversations together reveals the ubiquity of holistic tropes in postwar culture. The idiom was pervasive. Consensus-building and communitarian currents surged through many discussions and shaped the activities of civil rights activists, cosmologists, environmentalists, "hippies," humanistic psychologists, structural engineers, and a wide variety of religious believers. Historian of religion Martin E. Marty wrote that after Pearl Harbor and the entry of the United States into World War II, America's religious community found a vocabulary of consensus. In contrast to the "noise of conflict" that had marked the 1920s and 1930s, words like "consensus, dialogue, ecumenism, interfaith, church unity, integration, collegiality, conciliarism, merger" and phrases such as " 'global village,' 'spaceship earth,' 'the American century,' 'world federalism' " formed the vocabulary of the religious.[60] As the pages of this book reveal, this vocabulary also permeated the physical sciences, psychology, engineering, environmentalism, the civil rights movement, and many other aspects of American society and culture. Seeing these literatures in dialogue with one another and the many projects these intellectuals forged makes it apparent that holism was not only a sign of something manifest in one particular arena but a signpost pointing the way to a well-developed cultural mood—a language for understanding an age and a tool for grappling with its problems.

Rachel Carson at Woods Hole, Massachusetts, 1951. *Courtesy of the Lear Center for Special Collections and Archives, Connecticut College*

1

The Natural Environment
Rachel Carson's Web of Life

Before Rachel Carson, marine biologist and nature writer, shocked the world with her book *Silent Spring* in 1962, she was internationally known for her sympathetic characterizations of nature. In three best-selling books on the sea and articles in *Atlantic Monthly, Reader's Digest, Science Digest*, and numerous conservation publications, the author described the genesis of "Mother Sea," detailed wind and wave patterns, described how volcanic eruptions created islands, and explained new scientific findings.[1] Her writings tugged at human sympathies and were "as readable," one reviewer wrote, "as a first-class adventure story."[2] In her first book, *Under the Sea Wind* (1941), she personified the migration, food, and mating habits of "Rynchops" the black skimmer; "Silverbar" and "Blackfoot," the sanderling couple; and "Scomber," the mackerel. She also wrote dramatically about the 200-mile journey of "Anguilla," the eel, from riverbed to ocean abyss. For each reader, she hoped to cultivate "a deeper appreciation of nature" and "make animals in woods or waters, where they live, as alive to others as they are to me."[3] In all, Carson imagined a nature that was awe-inspiring and enchanting, resilient, containing within it the power to endure tumults; it was not a nature "red, in tooth and claw" but harmonious, balanced, filled with beauty, mystery, and wonder.[4]

By 1958, however, her construction of nature as indomitable, enduring, and steadfast was crumbling. No longer able to ignore synthetic pesticides and atomic tests, she wondered what the earth's future was if human beings continued down a technological path of destruction. Alarmed, she shifted her attention to human actions and pondered cataclysmic possibilities. "Of course, in pre-*Sputnik* days," she explained in a letter to her good friend Dorothy Freeman, "it was easy to dismiss so much as science-fiction fantasies. Now the most farfetched schemes seem entirely possible of achievement.

And man seems actually likely to take into his hands—ill-prepared as he is psychologically—many of the functions of 'God.'" She suggested that her once comforting thoughts about nature "began to be affected soon after atomic science was firmly established." Before this she tried to believe "that much of Nature was forever beyond the tampering reach of man."[5] She was content to ponder earth's origins, research the cranial nerves of reptiles, and write on the sea's "brine-drenched seaweed," "gnome-like shrimps," and "spine-studded urchins."[6] Her world consisted of natural phenomena that occurred long before or were far removed from human touch. But after allowing herself to "open my eyes" to chemical and atomic poisoning, she stared in horror. "I feel ill with a distress that has nothing to do with my cold," she wrote.[7] Now, the possibility of the earth's annihilation because of human action seemed entirely possible.

The problem Carson confronted in that terrifying moment in 1958 involved, as she phrased it, the "subject of man's relationship to his environment."[8] Following a train of environmental thinking voiced by John Muir and other conservationists, the scientist explained that contemporary attitudes toward nature coupled with technology's unintended consequences disturbed nature's equilibrium.[9] In her postwar world, she fixed her gaze on the "contaminated rubbish . . . of the atomic age."[10] She questioned sending machines into space, exploding atomic bombs, and spraying chemicals on crops. Such actions appeared to be arrogant folly and acts of human plunder. In anguish, she migrated from her position as lyricist of the sea to take up the role of scolding prophet, drawing attention to "ugly facts" and demonstrations of ruin.[11] After World War II, after widespread DDT use, it was as if Carson suddenly got to the third chapter of Genesis and saw Eden fall. She spent the last six years of her life trying to recover the Garden.

In 1962, Carson delivered her jeremiad *Silent Spring*, an assault on excessive pesticide use and a tale about the pride of "man" and the fall of the earth.[12] Telling her story through a prism of death, she disclosed the hazards of synthetic chemicals, chastised the chemical industry for pursuing dollars at nature's expense, chided agriculturists for single-crop farming, and berated government officials for spraying too many compounds over croplands and roadsides.[13] Continuing this behavior, she claimed, would lead to a spring where no birds chirped, no chicks hatched, and a strange shadow of death hovered everywhere. Thus, her early writings on the sea may be understood as descriptions of the Garden *before* the Fall. *Silent Spring*, in contrast, chronicled the Fall, and in the tradition of the American jeremiad, she, like a Puritan minister, called for repentance, humility, and change. Only her lamentation summoned social rather than individual salvation, and instead of drawing authority from the Bible, she drew on her conception of ecological holism.

Examining how this holist wrestled with humanity's connection with the natural world—this most basic of all human relationships—is a good place to begin an exploration of holism in postwar America. The subjects Carson addressed and the questions she asked placed her within important cultural, political, and scientific conversations. Discussions resurrected old questions about the machine in the garden and reflected common concerns during the Cold War. As a popularizer of ecological holism, Carson helped people see relationships between the whole and the parts.

Like other holists, the zoologist subscribed to a sensibility that emphasized unity, community, and interdependence. Nature was democratic, a series of interdependent relationships between equally valued parts in a balanced and harmonious ecosystem.[14] "The earth's vegetation is part of a web of life," the ecologist declared, "in which there are intimate and essential relations between plants and the earth, between plants and other plants, between plants and animals."[15] She believed that the world was designed to be orderly, not chaotic, and she explored how the relationships within her organically whole universe either worked for the health, balance, and harmony of all or faltered, spreading havoc throughout the system. This was ecology to her; this was, as she put it, "the intricate web of life whose interwoven strands lead from microbes to man."[16] Hence, to solve problems such as pollution, Carson stated, we "need to see the problem as a whole" instead of focusing on a single event. "We must never forget the wholeness of that relationship. We cannot think of the living organism alone; nor can we think of the physical environment as a separate entity."[17]

Describing nature as a web of relations with interconnecting parts helped Carson and her audience make sense of humanity's relationship with nature in a highly industrialized, capitalistic society. For America's growing urban and suburban populations, Carson's books on the sea in the 1950s introduced many to the world of nature. In *Silent Spring*, the nature writer helped her audiences focus on one of the problems she considered most fundamental for her day: human-made poisons. And she explained, in very clear language, why these were hazardous. Chemicals used to banish pests from the household or sprayed to produce a worm-free apple were problematic because of the damage they caused throughout the environment. "The problem of water pollution by pesticides can be understood only in context, as part of the whole to which it belongs," the ecologist explained. "For each of us," she wrote, "this is a problem of ecology, of interrelationships, of interdependence." If we poison insects, the poison travels. "We spray our elms and the following springs are silent of robin song, not because we sprayed the robins directly but because the poison traveled, step by step, through the now familiar elm leaf-earthworm-robin cycle." She made clear that these poisons were "chemicals born of the Industrial Age."[18] By pointing to industrialization as the root of these problems, she did not limit her attack to one part of the system. Instead, she leveled it at her entire industrialized, technological society.

At the same time, Carson's holistic frame was personal. The strands connecting "microbes to man" were not an abstract expression for her. They signaled concrete demonstrations of health and illness. To her, nature was intricately connected to the human body, and she was quick to correlate sickness or health to the environment.[19] *Silent Spring* contains multiple references to chemical poisoning and cancer. She quoted experts from the National Cancer Institute and cited studies to warn "that polluted waterways may carry a cancer hazard." She blamed the insecticide endrin for the deaths of large numbers of fish and cattle, then pointed to a sad human case of a "normal, healthy infant" who came into contact with endrin and "became little more than a vegetable." She linked chemical sprays to the deaths of farmers, a college student studying ants, a homemaker, a cotton field worker, and two cousins working at a farm cooperative in Czechoslovakia.[20] In these and other depictions of the human body's links to the environment, Carson contributed to what historian Maril Hazlett has identified as an "ecological turn" in American society, one that "began in people's growing experience or recognition of their bodies as ecological entities." For Carson and many who read her work, "humans and nature were inseparable."[21] Because she labored on *Silent Spring* while battling her own breast cancer, the connections she made between the body and the environment also contained a personal edge. Cancer took her life two years after the book was published.

To craft her holism, the writer borrowed concepts from her education and personal experience. She relied on the nature-study movement, Presbyterian religion, transcendentalism, and especially ecology. The paradigm she developed was not unique; rather, it was emblematic of romantics and ecologists in the nineteenth century, as well as naturalists and conservationists in the twentieth. What the eloquent and ingenious scientist did, however, was to popularize the paradigm. She made it accessible and understandable to her readers, situating it within the atomic age and using it to critique her society and spur environmental reform. Before 1962, few Americans thought in terms of ecosystems or contemplated how actions in one part of an ecosystem influenced another. *Silent Spring* changed that. The holistic frame Carson employed to cast her story helped her do so. As such, she becomes a window onto this holistic moment. This chapter details how Carson constructed and communicated her holism and suggests some of the ways this holistic perspective influenced a generation.

Born in 1907, Carson developed her admiration for nature in the woods and wetlands of her childhood home in western Pennsylvania's Allegheny hills. The third child of Robert and Maria Carson may have been drawn to the outdoors on her own, but it was her nature-loving, Christian mother and the nature-study movement that nurtured her interest. Maria read books written by popular nature writers Mabel Osgood Wright and Olive Thorne Miller. She enjoyed bird watching, learning about wild creatures, and imparting such knowledge to her children. An amateur naturalist and Presbyterian, Maria Carson was representative of many in the early twentieth-century nature-study movement. To this largely Protestant, white, middle-class, educated group, nature was holy. "If God created the earth," reasoned Cornell University professor and leading nature-study advocate Liberty Hyde Bailey, "so is the earth hallowed...so must we deal with it devotedly and with care that we do not despoil it."[22] This moral imperative, coupled with natural history lessons, made followers more than passive bird-watchers, engaging them in natural habitat stewardship and preservation.

All this was not lost on Rachel Carson, who as a child was "happiest," she recalled, "with wild birds and creatures as companions."[23] She read natural history readers, written for elementary students by Bailey and his colleague Anna Comstock, then conducted outdoor activities with her mother to detect God's design. And she wrote her own stories, first publishing at the age of eleven in St. Nicholas, a children's magazine. Years later, Carson created her own nature-study book, A Sense of Wonder, to help adults introduce children to life out of doors. Recounting experiences with her grandnephew Roger, she suggested games and activities to help children "drink in the beauty, and think and wonder at the meaning of what you see." Her wish, like Bailey's and Comstock's, was to instill an awe for nature "so indestructible that it would last throughout life, as an unfailing antidote against boredom and disenchantments of later years, the sterile preoccupation with things that are artificial, the alienation from the sources of our strength."[24] Writing in the shadow of the atomic bomb, Carson may have had a greater sense of alienation and urgency than her predecessors, but this only strengthened her commitment to nature-study principles.

Throughout her life, and despite her shy personality and penchant for a quiet, private life, Carson ardently defended nature. She used her position at the U.S. Bureau of Fisheries (the U.S. Fish and Wildlife Service after 1940) to champion naturalist concerns, arguing frequently as she did in the publication Conservation in Action in the 1940s: "Wildlife, like other forms of natural wealth, must be vigorously protected."[25] She devoted her free time to conservation-minded activities, too, joining the Wilderness Society, Audubon Society, and Nature Conservancy. As a member of the Washington, D.C., Audubon chapter, she edited its magazine, contributed book reviews, and served on committees. In the 1950s, she spearheaded the Nature Conservancy's efforts to save a section of Maine's coast, and she protested the damming of Colorado's Echo Park, one of the formative battles in the emergence of the modern environmental movement. Carson's concern for natural habitats and resistance to human domination of nature set her apart from multiple-use conservation, which benefited economic concerns and transformed wilderness spaces. Although she was a longtime supporter of most federal conservation policies, her sympathies increasingly swung more toward the other side of the conservation movement—wilderness and wildlife preservation.[26] None of these actions, however, compared with her activism against pesticides. On this topic especially, she overcame her reserve and sent letters to Congress and newspaper editors, spoke at legislative hearings, appeared in television documentaries, and lobbied the U.S. Agricultural Department and local county agents to restrict chemical use.

Carson's defense of nature had a religious grounding. Baptized and confirmed a Presbyterian, she attended Sunday school regularly as a child. Calvinist doctrines affirmed a view of nature as both beautiful but tainted, and human beings as wondrous but fallen. Accordingly, the human-nature relationship was fraught with problems; sinful human beings bore the blame for earth's tainted condition. Outside of church, this lover of literature was likely reminded of this construction of nature as both sacred and fallen through the poetry of Puritan Anne Bradstreet, the sermons of Jonathan Edwards, or the political discourse of Abraham Lincoln. It was a familiar current running throughout American culture. She heard it from Bailey, too, who in his book *Holy Earth* proclaimed nature's wonder at the same time he moaned, "The ground was cursed for Adam's sin....The whole creation groaneth and travaileth in pain."[27] Both Carson's sense of wonder and her lamentations about human transgressions fall within this tradition.

Like many contemporaries and holists of this period, the zoologist accepted evolution, blending her religion with science to understand her world. At one point Carson's mother reminded her that God created the world. "Yes," Rachel agreed, "and General Motors created her Oldsmobile, but *how* is the question."[28] To a critic who accused her of slighting God in her book *The Sea around Us* (1951), Carson explained her acceptance of evolution "as the most logical one that has ever been put forward to explain the development of living creatures on this earth." But, she continued, she saw "absolutely no conflict between a belief in evolution and a belief in God the creator." Evolution, she thought, "is the method by which God created, and is still creating, life on earth. And it is a method so marvelously conceived that to study it in detail is to increase... one's reverence and awe both for the Creator and the process."[29]

Combining scientific understandings and religion did not come easy, and the answer she gave her critic sounded more assured than what she sometimes felt. Confiding again to her friend Freeman, she expressed serious doubts: "Of course, part of my trouble is finding anything definite I can really feel is true." Despite uncertainty, two things were certain. First, she thought the earth was a sacred and wondrous work of God, writing that "there is a great and mysterious force that we don't, and perhaps never can understand"; second, she believed that "a large share of what's wrong with the world is man's towering arrogance—in a universe that surely ought to impose humility, and reverence."[30]

Carson's mixture of beliefs aligned her with liberal Protestants who adapted their beliefs to science. She also fell within a current of spiritual belief in America that religious historian Catherine Albanese has identified as "nature religion."[31] Explaining her faith, she suggested that in "contemplating 'the exceeding beauty of the earth,'" people could find "calmness and courage." For the nature lover, earthly beauty provided spiritual sustenance: "For there is symbolic as well as actual beauty in the migration of birds; in the ebb and flow of the tides; in the folded bud ready for the spring. There is something infinitely healing in these repeated refrains of nature— the assurance that dawn comes after night, and spring after winter."[32] She believed that nature had the power to heal not only the individual but also the society she diagnosed as diseased: "Mankind has gone very far into an artificial world of his own creation.... But I believe that the more clearly we can focus our attention on the wonders and realities of the universe about us, the less taste we shall have for destruction."[33] Nature had the power to heal itself and resume its balance and harmony, she contended. It also had the power to heal human beings, if only they would listen. Her faith wavered, however, as she discussed some of the devastating consequences of pesticides on birds with biologists at Patuxent Research Refuge in Laurel, Maryland. This research and other scientific reports she read made her question nature's ability to recover, and she increasingly called on human beings to reverse course.

The scientist's nature spirituality had roots in Christian reverence for creation and natural history, but it primarily relied on her readings of American romantics. She attended Protestant services but also signaled her identification with the religion of transcendentalists by asking a Unitarian pastor to conduct her funeral services.[34] Henry David Thoreau's *Journal* rested on her nightstand.[35] She patterned her books after his and the works of other romantics who enthralled her with their descriptions of nature's beauty and the seasons' rhythms. She most appreciated writings that could spark an affinity with the nonhuman. As historian Donald Fleming argued, Thoreau set the standard for this style of romantic writing through his literary strategy of "imaginative identification with other animals as they lived to a tempo of their own, keyed to a world of signals to be urgently heeded." Carson followed.[36] Along with Thoreau, Henry Beston captured her heart with his book *The Outermost House.* His record of his yearlong sojourn of Thoreauvian solitude on Cape Cod was, to Carson, "written with great simplicity and beauty, and with a feeling for the great rhythms of nature."[37] Undoubtedly she envied his year at the sea's edge, too. Not one for small talk or crowds, she felt more at home in nature—especially the seaside—than in society.

Like other transcendentalists who valued solitude, nature was Carson's refuge from human troubles, a place for healing and self-discovery, best enjoyed alone, away from the presence of other human beings. Such leanings prompted both an extreme individualism and a belief in communal oneness. Nature, to the transcendentalist, was at once a source of solitude and self-rejuvenation and a place for self-abnegation where one could become part and parcel with everything else.[38] This paradoxical stance suited her personality perfectly. It also conformed to her Christian roots, which underscored individual salvation and self-denial.

Borrowing from these varying traditions, the twentieth-century romantic read human beings as fundamentally one with nature, not above nature, not superior to nature, not lords over nature. She stood in agreement with Thoreau, Emerson, and other transcendentalists who found that human beings could best be understood as members of the natural terrain. "I wish," Thoreau penned, "to regard man as an inhabitant, or a part and parcel of Nature, rather than as a member of society."[39] Carson echoed Thoreau, though she employed a more strident tone: "Man, far from being the overlord of all creation, is himself part of nature, subject to the same cosmic forces that control all other life. Man's future welfare and probably even his survival depend upon his learning to live in harmony, rather than in combat, with these forces."[40] She may have been influenced here as well by Liberty Hyde Bailey's nonanthropocentric view. "The living creation is not exclusively man-centered: it is biocentric," he said. "We can claim no gross superiority and no isolated self-importance. If we are parts in the evolution, and if the universe," he surmised, "is not made merely as a . . . theatre for man, so do we lose our cosmic selfishness. . . . This is the philosophy of the oneness in nature and the unity in living things."[41] This essentially equal relationship defined Carson's holism.

A career in the sciences further strengthened Carson's nonanthropomorphic views and solidified her holistic stance. Though Carson started college as an English major, Mary Scott Skinker's biology course led her to switch fields. In 1929, after graduating from Pennsylvania College for Women (later renamed Chatham College), she spent the summer on fellowship at the Marine Biological Laboratory at Woods Hole, Massachusetts. Though long enchanted by the ocean, this was the first time she stood on its shores. That fall, she began her master's degree in zoology at Johns Hopkins University. Upon completion, she taught courses at Johns Hopkins and the University of Maryland, and in 1935 she became one of the first women scientists employed by the Bureau of Fisheries. She started as a radio script writer and rose to chief editor for service publications. At night, she wrote articles and books about nature. After seventeen years, royalties from her second book, *The Sea around Us*, allowed her to quit her government job. In July 1951, the book was published; by November, 100,000 copies had sold. Translated into forty languages, it appeared on the *New York Times* bestseller list for a record eighty-six weeks.

Before addressing the ways that science shaped Carson's holism, it is important to pause and recognize that for her holism was not simply an intellectual construct but an approach to life that followed a particular tone and sentiment. Hence, as with the others presented in this study, this scientist's holistic attitude, reference point, and creations were shaped by personal and emotional factors, contemporary events (national and international), and rational explanations. Her turn to nature for refuge and salvation, the desire to see equanimity between human beings and the environment, the satisfaction found in an ecological explanation of life were shaped by a world that was anything but melodious. In contrast to the harmony and balance she read into the natural sphere, she confronted atomic fallout, chemicals, and spaceships; family and health problems created other obstacles. Constructing a whole and welcoming natural space no doubt appealed to her, at least in part, because of her encumbered and troubled life.

Family pressures escalated when she was in her twenties, and for the rest of her life, obligations to her parents and siblings inhibited personal options.[42] When she moved to Maryland to attend Johns Hopkins, her family followed and became increasingly dependent upon her. Due to ill health, her father failed to provide enough for the family. Her brother helped infrequently, and her diabetic sister was too sick to hold a job, so Rachel taught part-time and submitted articles for publication to try to make ends meet. When her father died, she assumed sole financial responsibility for her mother, her sister, and her sister's two daughters. Her sister's early death in 1937 ensured that Rachel would be the primary provider for her two nieces.[43] Finding employment during the Great Depression was not an easy task for anyone, but especially not for a woman seeking a career in the sciences. After failing to obtain an academic position, she took a temporary post with the Bureau of Fisheries in Washington. A year later the job became permanent, but it was not a research position as she would have liked, and she still needed to supplement her salary with freelance work. Though Maria Carson remained her daughter's steadfast confidante and though the two shared much—they lived and vacationed together, followed like pursuits, and expressed similar values—the close bonds could be restricting. Maria's continual presence, strong opinions, and illnesses kept Rachel from exploring career and relationship possibilities. She never married, nor did she socialize much. As one of her biographers stated, "It is probably an under-statement to say that Maria never urged Rachel to marry."[44] Whether or not Rachel was interested in marriage is dubious, but her mother still shaped her choice of associates, male and female.[45]

Her health and family troubles imposed additional burdens and impeded her work. When one of her nieces, Marjorie, had an affair with a married man in the 1950s and became pregnant—a source of great emotional dis-tress for Rachel and Maria and something they tried to hide from even their closest friends—Rachel provided financial and emotional support. When Marjorie died from complications of diabetes at age thirty, Rachel, at forty-nine, adopted her son Roger. By 1958, when she revealed her fears that sci-entists and superpowers were usurping the "functions of God," she was facing additional hardships. Her mother, ailing after a stroke, died later that year, and parenting proved overwhelming. Roger demanded attention, caused trouble at school, and fell ill frequently. Finally, as her calendar filled with more and more speaking engagements and writing commitments, her own health deteriorated with what she called a "catalogue of illnesses."[46] These included an ulcer, breast cancer, heart disease, and crippling arthri-tis. Misdiagnosis, evasive and dishonest answers from her doctor, a radical mastectomy, chemotherapy, radiation, and a host of painful complications added to her suffering and ultimately ended her life at the age of fifty-six.[47]

In the face of these tribulations, nature tendered solace. In this respect, her holistic construction of life provided not only an abstract intellectual strategy for interweaving the human and the environment but also a way for her to map her own psychological terrain. In a letter explaining her sea tales, she suggested that her words "give us a little better perspective on human problems. They are stories of things that have been going on for countless thousands of years. They are as ageless as sun and rain, or as the sea itself. The relentless struggle for survival in the sea epitomizes the struggle of all earthly life, human and non-human."[48] More than any other place, the ocean's shores and deep abyss gave her a sense of satisfaction and meaning. She kept a cottage on Maine's coast that was as important to her as Walden Pond was to Thoreau. That she elected to spend her time at this rugged, rela-tively isolated setting instead of at Ocean City, Rehoboth, or another popular seaboard resort close to D.C. was not surprising. She lived in devotion to nature with the seashore as her temple.[49] Though conversant with the world through her writing, she removed herself as often as possible from her audi-ence and retreated to the sea and to the company of a few good friends.

The sea, too, affected the construction of her organic views of nature. It was, to her, "the great mother of life," a landscape of cosmic dimensions, holding "the ultimate mystery of Life itself," as well as "plain and inescap-able truths" revealed through science. It represented timelessness and durability. It was the birthplace of everything—an "all-providing, all-embrac-ing mother," a womb, producing in its "warm saltiness" the "mysterious and wonderful stuff called protoplasm." And it was the end of all things: "For all at last return to the sea—to Oceanus, the ocean river, like the ever-flowing stream of time, the beginning and the end."[50]

That Carson read the sea as female and maternal is not surprising. With metaphors of motherhood, she personified the sea in terms of her most meaningful relationships. Her closest friends were all women, from her mother to her teacher Mary Skinker to her literary agent, Marie Rodell, to her compatriot in the pesticide battle, Marjorie Spock, to her most intimate friend, Dorothy Freeman.[51] Each of these female companions held a mean-ingful place in Carson's life. Each was instructive and offered satisfying friendships. In their warmth and hospitality, they could be seen as analo-gous to her presentations of nature.

The naturalist did not adopt traditional interpretations of nature or female as passive.[52] Instead, she rewrote both as vibrant actors. Nature, she liked to think, was in control. She endowed it with healing and nurturing capacities, as well as forceful and powerful qualities. Her oceanic descriptions revealed a busy world, teeming with creatures in dramatic play. Advocating a "new and more dynamic concept" about the deep, dark reaches of the ocean, she explained in the introduction to the 1961 edition of *The Sea around Us* that "even a decade or so ago it was the fashion to speak of the abyss as a place of eternal calm." But that "picture is rapidly being replaced by one that shows the deep sea as a place of movement and change, an idea that is far more exciting and that possesses deep significance for some of the most pressing problems of our time [dumping nuclear wastes into the ocean]."[53]

The message of her science, nature writing, and life called for a revised scientific outlook and democratic reforms in science and society. Women, she felt, ought to be more active and equal partners in society's affairs, and all—male and female—had a significant role in the societal ecosystem. At least some of her readers understood the social implications, as feminism took lessons from this ecological lens to inform the burgeoning field of femi-nist science and the women's movement of the 1960s and 1970s. Ecofeminist scholars employed some of the same constructs of nature as organic, not mechanistic, and humanity as part and parcel of the larger whole to inform scientific research.[54] Blending prescribed and assumed notions of what it meant to call nature feminine and what it meant to be female—also nascent expressions of later ecofeminist and Gaia thought—she contributed, though perhaps not intentionally, to the women's liberation movement. While never claiming a feminist identity, she strove to compete on equal ground with male peers and enjoy advantages afforded men. She pursued scientific stud-ies, carved out an independent writing career, and supported her family.[55]

Certainly, she had strong female role models, and it is clear from early writings that she valued strong, career-minded women. In her short story "The Golden Apple," she poked fun at pathetic female characters who relied on dull and foolish men; she questioned why women could not make their own way in life.[56] Years later, she was bemused by those who expressed surprise that a woman could write about science. She laughed at those who, if they accepted her sex, expected her to be a "tall, oversize, Amazon-type female" and were surprised when they found the opposite.[57] Pleased to step onto science's male terrain, she gleefully announced that she had sometimes "shattered precedent" and defied traditions.[58] Once, after some cajoling, she won her way aboard a research vessel formerly reserved for men. On another occasion, she persuaded a Fish and Wildlife Service agent to take her and another woman into the Everglade swamps, something he initially protested because of their sex.

While much may be made of Carson's multiple subtexts on the sea, nature, and life, the fundamental grounding of any subject she took up was ecological holism, and it is to that we now turn. The earth, she wrote, was an "intricate fabric of life by which one creature is linked with another, and each with its surroundings." Often sentimental in tone, the author relied on a romantic epistemology of intuition and empirical science. "To understand the shore, it is not enough to catalogue its life," she explained in *The Edge of the Sea* (1955). "True understanding demands intuitive comprehension of the whole life.... I have tried to interpret the shore in terms of that essential unity that binds life to the earth."[59] To decode the "unity that binds," the scientist used the tools of ecology. German zoologist Ernst Haeckel (1834–1919) coined "ecology" in 1886 to mean "the science of relations between organisms and their environment."[60] An ecologist, Haeckel surmised, should study the links between organisms and their surroundings, examining their context, life cycle, and energy flows. Carson, in her embrace of this approach, made ecology a household word.

Haeckel took his lead from Charles Darwin (1809–82), who bound plants and animals that were seemingly unrelated in "a web of complex relations." In one example in *The Origin of Species*, Darwin linked the disappearance of red clover and bees in England to a low cat population. Fewer cats triggered an abundance of mice. An abundance of mice prompted more destruction of bees' combs and nests, which, in turn, resulted in fewer bees and minimal clover fertilization. Hence the population of cats was linked to the number of red clover blooms.[61] Fascinated by such relationships, Haeckel called for a new science to study Darwin's system: ecology.

As an ecologist in Darwin's wake, Carson united one species to another, drawing lines of association. For example, similar to Darwin's correlation of cat, mouse, bee, and clover bud, she, in 1962, detailed the symbiosis between the Western sage, grouse, and antelope, which seemed "made for each other." Their destinies intertwined; the sage provides food and shelters nests and young. Grouse behavior also contributed; the birds' mating dances "loosen the soil beneath and around the sage," allowing grasses to spring up and grow. The grasses, in turn, offer food for antelope after winter snows.[62] While stressing the beauty of such symbiotic relationships, the scientist believed that the world evolved according to a "Struggle for Life," as Darwin phrased it.[63] Struggle, she believed, was part of the natural order. But, unlike for Darwin, struggle was not her focus. What it produced was, for the fight was the path to harmony. Plants and animals might battle through a "long period of trial and error," but the strife produced "a natural system in perfect balance."[64] Thus, she described a holistic synergy that emphasized community and compatibility over individualism and discord.[65]

Carson's vision contrasted sharply with America's capitalistic ideology. She denied a market rationale that placed a premium on individual self-interests and allowed for the exploitation of nature, values she found to be commonplace in the chemical industry she deplored: "No such humility marks the booming 'weed killer' business of the present day, in which soaring sales and expanding uses mark the production of plant-killing chemicals."[66] Instead, she stressed mutuality. In this way, she revisited the nineteenth-century argument between those who interpreted Darwinism in Spencerian terms and those who articulated a Darwinism that emphasized organic unity. Clearly she shunned the individualistic, all-against-all view of Herbert Spencer. Her notions instead paralleled Darwin's organismic side, found, for example, in a poetic passage at the close of *The Origin of Species*:

> It is interesting to contemplate a tangled bank, clothed with many plants of many kinds, with birds singing on the bushes, with various insects flitting about, and with worms crawling through the damp earth, and to reflect that these elaborately constructed forms, so different from each other, and dependent upon each other in so complex a manner, have all been produced by laws acting around us.... There is grandeur in this view of life, with its several powers, having been originally breathed by the Creator into a few forms or into one; and that, whilst this planet has gone cycling on according to the fixed law of gravity, from so simple a beginning endless forms most beautiful and most wonderful have been, and are being evolved.[67]

A century later, Carson celebrated the earth's wondrous forms and reiterated time and again Darwin's themes of connectedness. One passage in *Silent Spring* described the activities of earthworms, mammals, and a "horde of minute but ceaselessly toiling creatures"—bacteria, fungi, insects, lichen, and mosses—that "work their creative magic" in the soil. She then exclaimed that the "soil community, then, consists of a web of interwoven lives, each in some way related to the others—the living creatures depending on the soil, but the soil in turn a vital element of the earth only so long as this community within it flourishes."[68]

For both Darwin and Carson, nature was largely imagined apart from humanity. His tangled bank, which could be a description of England's countryside, contained no human, just as her sea seldom harbored a person. Of course, Darwin did contemplate the human species as he pondered its origins, but he did not confront in the 1850s what Carson would be forced to address in the 1950s. He never imagined that tourism might destroy his Galápagos Islands or that atomic fallout might wreak havoc with the processes he called "natural selection." Yet, even while he did not focus on the impact of human beings in nature, others, somewhat ironically, used his ideas to justify a market economy that ushered in the world that Carson so opposed.

Though distanced by historical contingencies, Darwinian thought profoundly influenced Carson. She also owed much to her contemporary scientists who subscribed to a holistic model. Individuals such as Frederick E. Clements, Charles Elton, Eugene and Howard Odum, Victor Shelford, and Alister Hardy—researchers in different fields of ecology from plants to animals to ecosystem studies—were important to her work, and they all held holistic assumptions in the 1930s, 1940s, and 1950s. Each prioritized community and equilibrium over individualism and disturbance. The zoologist Charles Elton, for example, emphasized each member's function in relation to the whole; he stressed cooperation between members and system interdependence, and he explained the structure in terms of producers and consumers within the food chain.[69]

This holistic model echoed eighteenth-century Arcadian visions and nineteenth-century romantic ideas and was a response, especially in the twentieth century, to hierarchical notions and reductionism.[70] Communalists argued against an epistemology of simple dissection and asserted that examinations of individual organisms alone did not lead to satisfactory explanations of reality. As historian Donald Worster notes, ecologists such as Frederic Clements labored under a communal view of nature and stressed whole-systems thinking. Though not without challenge, this paradigm guided the field during Carson's career.[71] To highlight the importance of the holistic view, one might contrast it not only with reductionism but also with models of disequilibrium that ordered biological research in the last decades of the century. Particularly in the 1970s, biologists beheld a nature in which disturbance, not harmony, individualism, not community, and heterogeneity, not homogeneity, were the norms.[72] But this postmodernist view was not Carson's.

To communicate her communalistic vision, she chose to structure her books around ecological communities and not focus exclusively on individual organisms. She relied on the "web of life" metaphor that Darwin and others had used.[73] She also engaged contemporary ecological ideas, such as the "ecosystem," a term coined by Arthur Tansley in 1935 to equate nature to an energy system. Eugene Odum popularized the notion in ecology textbooks, starting in the 1950s. Odum explained that organisms depended on one another and on the inanimate elements of the physical environment. Together they formed a tightly knit community, not random, atomized selves. Each part worked together for the whole.[74]

Carson used the notion of the ecosystem in similar fashion to illustrate how she understood nature's order. She described habitats that mammals, birds, insects, and microscopic organisms shared and charted the feeding, preying, and mating behavior of different species. In each depiction she returned to the central message of holistic ecology: everything was related to everything else, and all contributed to the whole. This too was the vision that she carried into *Silent Spring*, and she used it effectively to explain her new focus on pesticide abuse.

By the late 1950s, when the naturalist expressed her anger with atomic science to Dorothy Freeman, the Cold War had risen to a fever pitch.[75] The Berlin Wall divided East and West, Russians downed a U.S. U-2 spy plane, and soon the Cuban missile crisis would bring the world to near disaster. Clouds of radioactive test material poisoned fishermen in the Pacific and livestock in Nevada; scientists and legislators discussed nuclear war; science fiction stories explored atomic catastrophes; and American consumers learned that radioactive materials had infected milk products and pesticides had contaminated cranberries.[76] Meanwhile, widespread chemical spraying continued.

Carson made her complaint public in 1961 in a new foreword to *The Sea around Us*, where she argued against oceanic dumping of radioactive byproducts. Again, she stated that she used to think that, even though "man's record as a steward of the natural resources of the earth has been a discouraging one," the oceans were "beyond man's ability to change and to despoil. But this belief, unfortunately, has proved to be naïve." She explained that "unlocking the secrets of the atom" posed a "frightening problem—what to do with the most dangerous materials that have ever existed in all the earth's history, the byproducts of atomic fission." Discarding "these lethal substances" at sea, however, was not permissible; it opened the possibility of "rendering the earth uninhabitable."[77] Carson read the situation through the eyes of ecological holism and appealed to human self-interests. Transporting radioactive wastes was "only part of the problem. The concentration and distribution of radioisotopes by marine life may possibly have even greater importance from the standpoint of human hazard." Plants absorb wastes, and poisons move through the food chain.[78]

Nuclear fallout was not her only fear. Certainly her deteriorating health, cancer treatments, thoughts of her approaching death, and her concerns for

Roger brought other anxieties. In addition, she felt increasing distress about her society's use of pesticides. She first started tracking natural poisons in the environment in 1938. In 1945, after reading early test reports on the effects of the pesticide DDT on wildlife, she queried *Reader's Digest* unsuccessfully about a possible article.[79] Her interest stirred again in January 1958 when she opened a letter from Olga Owens Huckins, a Massachusetts songbird lover. Huckins presented details of the U.S. Department of Agriculture's (USDA) aerial sprayings of DDT over private lands, including her bird sanctuary. She lambasted the USDA for showering poisons that killed her songbirds, vanquished bees, grasshoppers, and other insects, and left only large numbers of mosquitoes. Huckins asked for help to prevent future sprayings. Sympathetic, Carson sent information, made phone calls, and began writing her own impassioned letters.[80]

Huckins's request came at the same time that others enlisted Carson's help. Irston Barnes, president of the D.C. Audubon Society, recruited her in the fall of 1957 to help him get USDA pesticide policy reports, and several Long Island residents, including Marjorie Spock, solicited her help in a lawsuit they had initiated against the government. At issue was the USDA's program to kill fire ants, gypsy moths, tent caterpillars, and mosquitoes. The New York citizens knew they faced a Goliath, but they were upset that officials had sprayed DDT on their private property. They called experts and mounted evidence to argue the detrimental effects of chemical poisons. Still, they lost. Following each day's proceedings of the trial and fully engrossed in the controversy, Carson grew agitated. "The more I learned about the use of pesticides the more appalled I became," she exclaimed. "I realized that here was the material for a book. What I discovered was that everything which meant most to me as a naturalist was being threatened, and that nothing I could do would be more important."[81]

Silent Spring picked up where her sea trilogy left off. "Nature" remained her protagonist. She spoke of the environment with reverence; persisted in viewing nature as a "vast web of life"; and reiterated the "balance of nature,...a complex, precise, and highly integrated system of relationships between living things which cannot safely be ignored any more than the law of gravity can be defied with impunity by a man perched on the edge of a cliff."[82] Several of her biographers have emphasized this connection.[83] And she did too: "In each of my books I have tried to say that all the life of the planet is inter-related, that each species has its own ties to others, and that all are related to the earth. This is the theme of *The Sea around Us* and the other sea books, and it is also the message of *Silent Spring*."[84]

Still, while the ecological web of life did provide an immutable framework, much had changed. Her tone shifted. Her writing became more threatening, her message more pointed. And she changed her focus. In her

sea stories, Carson employed the web metaphor to show healthy connections. Now the web cast a net of physical sickness and spiritual decay.
Instead of describing the effects of eons of time in the sea's physical formation or tracking the flight of sanderlings from Nova Scotia to South America,
she directed her attention toward human beings. Appreciating birds, trees,
mackerel, and sea winds became insufficient. Now she implored others to
look at how harmful their own deeds were. In *Silent Spring*, the holistic
metaphor became her weapon. From the mundane realm of leaves, earthworms, and robins, she detected physical and metaphysical loss: spray pesticides, and springtime will yield no songbirds. Upset the web of life, she
threatened, and behold a web of death.

Of course, as her conservationist activities testified, she had been alarmed
about human conduct before, and she had occasionally noted that human
beings hurt themselves when they harmed the planet. "Mankind has gone
very far into an artificial world of his own creation. He has sought to insulate
himself, in his cities of steel and concrete, from the realities of earth and
water and the growing seed," she exclaimed in 1962 when receiving the
John Burroughs Writer of the Year Award. "Intoxicated with a sense of his
own power," she continued, "he seems to be going farther and farther into
more experiments for the destruction of himself and his world."[85] But, while
Carson had noticed human beings, she had fixed her gaze at nature.
Previously, if human beings appeared at all, they played the antagonist.
They were instruments of ruin, "uneasy trespassers."[86] In *The Sea around
Us*, she wrote of man as an antihero, a "destroyer on the oceanic islands."
Seldom, she said, has "man...set foot on an island that he has not brought
about disastrous changes. He has destroyed environments by cutting, clear-
ing, and burning; he has brought with him as a chance associate the nefarious rat; and almost invariably he has turned loose upon the islands a whole
Noah's Ark of goats, hogs, cattle, dogs, cats, and other non-native animals as
well as plants." As a result, the "black night of extinction has fallen"; quoting
an islander, she wrote that "the quietness of death reigns where all was
melody."[87]

Associating man and rat was undoubtedly deliberate. To her, "men,"
like the "nefarious rat," were insensitive interlopers who disrupted
nature's "delicately balanced relationship."[88] Like most nature writers
before her, she understood human beings—and perhaps she meant
"males"—to be, as nineteenth-century conservationist George Perkins
Marsh put it, the "disturbing agent."[89] But where she only shook her
finger at human beings occasionally before 1958, she now gave them the
full fury of her wrath.

Throughout *Silent Spring*, originally and tellingly titled "Man against the
Earth," she argued that human actions led to contamination, disease, mutation,

and extinction. "As man proceeds toward his announced goal of the conquest of nature," she contended, "he has written a depressing record of destruction, directed not only against the earth he inhabits but against the life that shares it with him."[90] Her plot was simple: human beings were at "war against nature."[91] And in the role of antihero, human beings displayed terrifying might. "Only within the moment of time represented by the present century has one species—man—acquired significant power to alter the nature of his world," she warned. Since World War II, "this power has not only increased to one of disturbing magnitude but has changed in character." The shift occurred with "the chain of evil" unleashed upon the earth by "sinister" chemicals and "the unnatural creation of man's tampering with the atom."[92]

She especially faulted "control people"—scientists, government officials, and chemical industrialists—for failing to see the whole picture or to act democratically. "This is an era of specialists," she charged, "each of whom sees his own problem and is unaware of or intolerant of the larger frame into which it fits."[93] "Temporarily entrusted with power," these "authoritarians" set off a "wave of death that spreads out, like ripples when a pebble is dropped into a still pond."[94] In their zeal to dominate nature, industrial specialists subjected people to poisons "without their consent and often without their knowledge."[95] Though she refrained from championing animal rights in this passage, she also believed that these authoritarians robbed nonhumans of their rights as well.[96]

Possibly, she associated "control people" with males and subtly suggested that men more than women should be blamed for the problems she outlined. Though she never condemned males explicitly, and though it was still customary in the 1950s and 1960s to use "mankind," "men," and male pronouns as generic references for all humanity, Carson's language appeared at times to be distinctly gendered. Her writing patterns associated men with arrogance, destruction, aggression, manipulation, and dominance. Couple this with her gendering of the sea as female, her fondness for female companionship, her overt links with women and nurture, and her holism bears a decidedly feminine cast. Taking a gendered approach in a speech to women journalists in 1954, she stressed the importance of "women to realize that the world of today threatens to destroy much of that beauty that has immense power to bring us a healing release from tension." She surmised: "Women have a greater intuitive understanding of such things."[97]

Regardless of her gendered understandings, it is clear that her style shifted in the last six years of her life and that she perceived contemporary pesticide use as uncivilized: "As crude a weapon as the cave man's club, the chemical barrage has been hurled against the fabric of life." And "practitioners of chemical control," she argued "have brought to their task no 'highminded orientation,' no humility before the vast forces with which they tamper." This "control of nature," she exclaimed, emanated from "arrogance born of the Neanderthal age of biology and philosophy, when it was supposed that nature exists for the convenience of man." This was an attitude from the "Stone Age of science," she explained. "It is our alarming misfortune that so primitive a science has armed itself with the most modern and terrible weapons, and that in turning them against the insects it has also turned them against the earth."[98]

Thus, *Silent Spring* took on a different character from her previous works. It was more than a depiction of food chains and mating habits, more than an exposé on pesticides. Instead, she derided her society for its scientific conceit, grievous inventions, and hubris. In this denouncement, she posed a countercultural attack on "our modern way of life."[99]

Somewhat ironically, it was at this point where she cried hubris and shook her finger at her society—the point where she lamented anthropocentrism—that she herself turned to anthropocentric Christianity to help make sense of the situation and persuade her audiences. In particular, she used the Puritan doctrine of human depravity and the tale of the Fall to explain why the earth and human beings were off balance. The preface to *Silent Spring* boldly announced her argument, serving as a prime example of how she conceived her whole. "A Fable for Tomorrow" begins in an everyday village "where all life seemed to live in harmony with its surroundings." "Prosperous farms" surrounded the town, and all inhabitants hummed in perfect serenity. In summer, wildlife scampered, birds chirped, and people fished. In autumn, maple and oak trees "flamed and flickered" in a "blaze of color." In winter, "countless birds came to feed on the berries and on the seed heads of the dried weeds rising above the snow."[100]

All was well until a "strange blight crept over the area." Death—sent as if by an "evil spell"—visited the place. "Cattle and sheep sickened and died." Maladies, sicknesses, and a mysterious hush fell upon the land. "Everywhere was a shadow of death." Where mornings once greeted people with the "dawn chorus of robins, catbirds, doves, jays, wrens, and scores of other bird voices there was now no sound; only silence lay over the fields and woods and marsh." Winter lingered. "The few birds seen anywhere were moribund; they trembled violently and could not fly." No chicks broke out of their shell, no piglets survived, no bees droned around the apple trees. "It was a spring without voices."

Explaining the nightmare, Carson disclosed that "no witchcraft, no enemy action had silenced the rebirth of new life in this stricken world." Instead, her version of the Fall was up-to-date. Alluding to atomic rain, she reported "a white granular powder" had dusted roofs and lawns. An earlier draft was more explicit. The residue resembled the white shower that had blanketed the unfortunate crew of a Japanese tuna fishing boat, the *Lucky Dragon*, on

March 1, 1954. These fishermen had sailed close to Bikini Island when the U.S. detonated a powerful thermonuclear test weapon. The bomb's ash rained on them for hours; all grew ill, and Kuboyama, the radioman, eventually died.[101] If readers still did not make the connection, the next pages made the point directly by comparing atomic fallout to strontium 90, the radioactive isotope. Each initiated, she wrote, a "chain of poisoning and death."[102]

The apple may have transmogrified into a bomb in her tale, but the story was familiar to many Americans, and it gave her message cultural resonance. The source of evil lay at human feet. Human pride and irresponsibility caused calamity. Setting her fable within a cyclical view of life, the zoologist stressed the rhythm of the seasons, both plant and animal life. When the life cycle functioned smoothly, the connections promoted health and wholeness: "All life [lived] in harmony with its surroundings." But when one link in the chain broke down, the entire system malfunctioned.[103] The fall from Eden was initiated then by human hands, hands that failed to recognize their humble part in the overall system. Recovering the garden could only come by learning how to share and act in cooperation within nature's community. Hence, in Carson's whole, humans were the problem, but they were also the solution.

Silent Spring aimed to frighten. Carson hoped to awaken, startle, and change her neighbors. Just as Calvinist Jonathan Edwards designed his sermon "Sinners in the Hands of an Angry God" to trigger weeping and wailing, so she crafted her dirge to initiate repentance. Nature was glorious and the human a violent intruder. "Nature has introduced great variety into the landscape," she wrote with conviction, "but man has displayed a passion for simplifying it. Thus he undoes the built-in checks and balances."[104] To redeem the whole, and recover her Eden, she offered an anthropocentric solution and called upon human beings to change their attitudes and initiate actions to restore earth's balance. The earth could be saved, but only if human beings acted quickly. Farmers could arrest wrongful practices with diversified farming methods. Entomologists could aid farmers and consumers by applying biological, not chemical, solutions to achieve insect management.[105] Government regulations could prevent toxic chemical levels in food and provide instructions on safe insecticide use. And the public could educate itself, lobby for environmental protection, and heed ecological needs.

Although Carson entreated Americans to stop exploiting and destroying natural habitats, she was not what one might call a "zoo ecologist."[106] She never advocated controlling nature in the sense that a zookeeper marks, measures, and regulates every aspect of an animal's environment. Instead, she preferred to focus on the beauty of natural habitats undisturbed by human industry. Nor was she an "earth manager," intent on using the earth for maximum production, as some of her contemporary ecologists did.

Assuredly, some earth-friendly practices might prove to be an antimarket move.[107] Still, her activism on behalf of nature was not a strictly hands-off approach either. She wanted to control human actions, through regulations and legislation. Indeed, her organic conceptions of the earth affected her moral stance. If one adopts a notion of the earth as living, active, and alive, then how we treat it calls for different moral considerations than if we think of the world as an inanimate machine. For Carson, these assumptions prompted a basic questioning of science, industrialization, and modern life and a reassessment of utilitarian and anthropocentric ethical frameworks.[108] In this Carson followed Aldo Leopold's moral reasoning that human actions are right when they preserve the balance of the biotic community and wrong when they disturb its integrity.[109]

True to the form of the jeremiad, then, *Silent Spring* was not devoid of hope. She prescribed a return to the balance she believed was the natural order of things. Still, Carson acted in the 1960s with urgency and anger, perhaps because she knew that her own death from cancer was imminent, and perhaps because she grew less confident in human compliance. Struggling to weave human beings into her holistic web, she implored Americans to step down from their self-created thrones, raise their regard for the planet, and refrain from abuse. She repeated these ideas in her speeches, imploring Congress and ordinary citizens, and she employed the new power of television to reach large audiences, appearing in 1963 on *CBS Reports*.[110] In her last public address, she cautioned that in "this atomic age," and "in spite of our rather boastful talk about progress...we are beginning to wonder whether our power to change the face of nature should not have been tempered with wisdom for our own good, and with a greater sense of responsibility." Again, she returned to her main theme: "Man does not live apart from the world; he lives in the midst of a complex, dynamic interplay of physical, chemical, and biological forces, and between himself and this environment there are continuing, never-ending interactions."[111] By imagining the human in "a complex, dynamic, interplay" with nature, the ecologist tried to create for herself a whole and seamless world.

Had her life not been cut short, Carson would have likely extended her holistic argument to other arenas she thought needed reforming. Even while she kept a narrow focus in her fight against pesticides, she realized the logical implications of her holistic argument. Her attack on her society and her call for an alternative path had a much broader focus than chemicals and atomic fallout: she was challenging, as she put it, her "modern way of life." Two examples illustrate this. First, Carson, always concerned about animal welfare and a strong believer in democratic values, began at the end of her life to quietly embrace the fledgling animal rights movement. After meeting Animal Welfare Institute president Christine Stevens in 1959, she used her pen to discourage animal cruelty by pointing to the holistic links between human beings and animals. She did so in an introduction to a high school biology pamphlet, in letters to Congress demanding an end to inhumane lab experiments, and in the preface to Ruth Harrison's book on livestock production, *Animal Machines*.[112]

Second, in drawing a close connection between human beings and nature, the ecologist helped change American conceptions of the body and wellness. Carson's understanding of the human body as intimately connected to nature coupled with her own grave medical problems gave her a different perspective on health care than was conventional in the 1950s and 1960s. It led her to question traditional medical practices and made her more open to alternative therapies. As her biographer Linda Lear emphasized, her illnesses sharpened "the moral dimension of [her] social critique" as she realized the limited time she had left.[113] Moreover, her treatment, especially the fact that initially she was not told the truth about her cancer and not given the option for radiation or other remedies when the cancer was first detected, dismayed her.[114] Though wary of associations with "food faddists" and quacks (she guarded her private life so as to not give her enemies any reason to dismiss her message), Carson consulted with endocrinologist Morton Biskind, a researcher of the effects of DDT on human beings and animals in the 1940s and 1950s. He recommended a nutritional therapy program of bioflavinoids.[115] She also found assistance from her friend Marjorie Spock (sister of pediatrician Benjamin Spock). The two met during the Long Island lawsuit against pesticide spraying, shared an interest in organic farming and natural medicines, and held similar worldviews.

A Waldorf teacher, Spock was a follower of Rudolf Steiner, an Austrian philosopher (1861–1925) who established the Anthroposophical Society to advance his views of education and health. Steiner's holistic philosophy blended scientific and mystical thought, as well as practical programs such as Waldorf education, which emphasized teaching the "whole child." Anthroposophical medicine combined anatomy, biochemistry, and physiology with homeopathy, naturopathy, and biodynamic agriculture, a nonchemical farming method.[116] It was out of concern for her own biodynamic garden that Spock first protested pesticide spraying, and it was out of concern for her friend's health that Spock sent Carson organic foods and advice. She referred her to other doctors sympathetic with anthroposophy, "when the specialists don't work the necessary magic." She also sent reports that linked cancer to a host of problems: "In the view of these researchers, cancer is a disease of the entire person, not of cells, which merely reflect at last an underlying disorder of the whole organism."[117]

In turn, Carson made her own health recommendations to her friend Beverly Knecht, confessing her disquiet with modern medicine. She suggested a vitamin regime as a supplement to the medical "specialist's treatments [which] were only temporarily helpful, and the same could be said of the antibiotics he prescribed." Carson explained that she put herself on large quantities of vitamin C and found improvement.[118] At the end of the 1960s, Linus Pauling did the same and then began public promotion of the vitamin in the 1970s, much to the consternation of fellow scientists.[119]

Though she never campaigned for holistic health practices, Carson, in drawing a close connection between human beings and nature, helped change American conceptions of the body and wellness. As Maril Hazlett has noted, she "used ecology to define people's homes, gardens, and health as part of the natural world" and depicted "humans as ecological creatures, their bodies physically entwined with their surroundings."[120] This paralleled the works of other 1960s holists who expanded holistic connections between nature and people (body, mind, and emotion). For instance, Pierre Teilhard de Chardin fundamentally linked human spirituality with the natural world, and Abraham Maslow simultaneously spoke about the human person as a whole, linking psychological well-being with physical and environmental health.

Americans first confronted Carson's exposé in serialized form in the *New Yorker* beginning in June 1962. The magazine brought the holistic web of life and the issue of pesticides to countless homes, which explains one reason Carson's message reached the public domain so quickly. Even before the second issue reached mailboxes, readers had penned scores of letters to the author, congressional representatives, other government officials, and newspapers, expressing a mixture of alarm and disbelief. Some called for an end to DDT. Others thought she exaggerated. When her book came out in September, it shot to the top of the *New York Times* best-seller list and provoked more controversy. Agriculturalists, chemical engineers, conservationists, gardeners, housewives, naturalists, public officials, and scientists alternately critiqued the work, debated its science, and discussed its merits. Those who challenged her conclusions accused her of misrepresenting scientific studies and ignoring the miraculous, lifesaving benefits of DDT in war-ravaged Europe. Some ridiculed her as a hysterical female infatuated with cats and wildlife.[121] One horticulturalist found *Silent Spring* to be "more poisonous than the pesticides she condemns."[122] Conservationists countered, calling her a Harriet Beecher Stowe writing an *Uncle Tom's Cabin* for nature. Supreme Court justice William O. Douglas praised her book as "the most important chronicle of this century for the human race."[123]

Soon the conversation went worldwide, as the book was translated into twelve languages in the first year. In June 1963, Netherlands plant specialist C. J. Briejèr wrote Carson, "The hurricane you unchained is now over us. The chemical industry is furious and so are several chemical-minded scientists."[124] Other countries faced similar debates. In the United States, television newscasts and specials addressed the pesticide issue, and in May 1963, President Kennedy's Science Advisory Committee issued a report largely agreeing with Carson's findings.[125] The debate broadened to other environmental concerns such as pollution, population growth, and nuclear energy production. Congress acted, passing legislation that changed government policy, industrial actions, scientific development, and individual lifestyles. Legislation included the Clean Air Act (1970), Clean Water Act (1972), Safe Drinking Water Act (1974), Endangered Species Act (1973), and Toxic Substances Control Act (1976). The Environmental Protection Agency monitored compliance. On the grassroots level, membership rolls in the Sierra Club expanded, record numbers gathered across the nation for the first Earth Day in 1970, and new groups such as Environmental Action (1970), Friends of the Earth, Greenpeace, and Earth First! began.[126]

In addition to playing a major role in the modern environmental movement, Carson should be credited for her pivotal role in popularizing a holistic mind-set in postwar America. By explaining that actions undertaken in one area of an ecosystem had an impact on another, she helped others see the globe as a complex web of relations. This holistic *mentalité* was, in ways, more sweeping than actions taken. While it became popular to declare oneself an environmentalist and commonplace to recognize that no one part of an ecosystem existed alone, not all—indeed not even a majority in the 1960s—were willing to recycle, stop spraying insecticides to rid their houses of ants and roaches, or give up other technological advantages of the modern world. Furthermore, not all regulations that Carson's book stirred Congress to pass were equally enforced. Neither did businesses fully comply. The chemical industry continued to produce synthetic chemicals, with some companies moving production to other countries where regulations were minimal. In the early years of the twenty-first century, pollution, though controlled in some significant ways, still presented problems, and the world emitted carbon dioxide at record levels.

Despite America's mixed environmental record, Carson's message was not lost on the public. Her holistic logic had an immediate impact, in both elite and popular circles. It resounded in the halls of Congress, where she lobbied after the printing of *Silent Spring*, and captured the attention of ordinary citizens. From there, the message spread. In the world of comics, for example, Charles Schultz, the creator of *Peanuts* and a fan of Carson's work, used his talent to celebrate her vision; he made Carson a role model for his character "Lucy."[127] In March 1963, another cartoonist, J. W. Taylor, conveyed Carson's holistic message in the pages of *Punch*.

Others also caught her holistic vision. "Carson's main point," one Virginian wrote a few months after the book was released, "is that the entire

"This is the dog that bit the cat that killed the rat that ate the malt that came from the grain that Jack sprayed."

J. W. Taylor in *Punch Magazine* (March 6, 1963). *Reproduced with permission of Punch Ltd. www.punch.co.uk*

life processes, the 'web of life,' are still but poorly understood; the myriad, intertwining and incredibly interdependent relationships, from the inorganic nutrients, the soil bacteria, and on through the long chain of living forms that include the human animal and the lowliest worms, are something that science has hardly touched yet." Then he echoed the scientist's holistic frame: "We just do not know the final result of suddenly disrupting these processes which have evolved so slowly to their present state; we should be cautious about fooling with something we do not yet understand, the ecology of which we are a part."[128] David Brower, a lifelong environmentalist and executive director of the Sierra Club from 1952 to 1969, credited Carson with changing his perspective, too: "She removed a veil that had concealed from me...what the life force consists of, and how interrelated are all of us who share in it." Before reading the *New Yorker* chapters of *Silent Spring*, he had failed, he said, to see the interconnections between the parts and the whole: "For the first time I began to understand that some of the essential building blocks of life were the same in people as they were in the lesser creatures people decided to kill with poison. It was amazing that so simple a truth had escaped so many—until Rachel Carson caught it."[129] He passed the message on through his environmental activism, including the founding of a worldwide environmental network Friends of the Earth.

As explained on the Web site of the David Brower Center at the University of California, Berkeley, he "created a legacy of activism that made the environmental movement not only a part of our day-to-day lives, but a way for us to engage the world around us as an interconnected, integrated whole."[130]

As Brower indicated, before *Silent Spring*, few people outside biological circles used the word "ecology." Few examined the consequences of their action in terms of its bearing on an entire ecosystem. Few interpreted the natural landscape and all its various inhabitants and resources as a web of interconnected parts. After *Silent Spring*, the story changed as people caught the holistic conceptualization. Scholarly articles in biology, Gaia science, deep ecology, and ecofeminism explicitly stating holistic assumptions, as well as widespread environmental messages carrying a holistic ring, attest to this.[131] When environmentalists celebrated Earth Day, they spoke of global harmony and helped spread the communitarian ecological message that the earth is finite, fragile, intrinsically valuable, and one small community. Many pointed to the first photographs from outer space at the end of the 1960s to bolster such assertions. Buckminster Fuller wrote a popular manual to care for "spaceship earth." Legislators reinforced, through additional regulatory laws, the need for human beings to do their part in sustaining the planet. Biologist Barry Commoner developed his own laws of ecology shortly after Earth Day. The first law, in Carsonian fashion, declared a holistic assumption that "everything is connected to everything else."[132] And, as we shall see in the chapter on Esalen, workshops by Brower, historian Lynn White, and British philosopher and interpreter of Buddhism Alan Watts taught that human beings were part and parcel of everything else.

Articulating a holistic perspective of the environment proved to be an ingenious move, for holism resonated in many places throughout postwar culture. It made Carson's work immediately accessible, even to those who disagreed, and it helped convey the significance of her words. This is not to imply that Carson, by embracing a holistic worldview, insincerely manipulated holism to sell her ideas. Certainly, she genuinely expressed her conviction that holism was America's answer and alternative to Cold War technology gone awry. In sum, her work shows some of the ways that ideas are embedded within culture and how they reflect and inflect the historical moment. In this way, she signified an important cultural consciousness within American society during her day.

Finally, Carson spoke to the alienation many felt with modernity and contributed to the changing views and growth of American spirituality in this era. Her romantic and mystical perception of nature coupled with her confidence in science typifies this holistic moment. She represented a large group of individuals both within and without the modern environmental movement who followed what Catherine Albanese, William Cronon, and

Thomas Dunlap have called a natural religion. While not new to American life, the melding of nature and spirituality has been a defining part of a large segment of the modern environmental movement. In wrestling with the tension between science and religion, between materialism and mysticism, environmentalists have not turned their back on either. Rather, environmentalism, as William Cronon stated, has been successful at "embracing a materialist vision consistent with modern science at the same time that it finds deep spiritual meaning at the heart of a material universe that might otherwise seem soulless. In its holism, its communitarianism, its vision of the sacred, and in the claims of individual and collective moral responsibility that it derives from the intersection of these other values, environmentalism goes a long way toward imagining what a 'natural religion' might look like in the modern world."[133]

Carson's egalitarian and communal holism illustrates how one individual used holistic conceptions to make sense of her world and further her agenda. This sensibility permeated the environmental movement, contributed to changed perceptions of the human body, and altered understandings of humanity's relationship with the earth. It heightened social reform in other arenas as well, for her approach was broad and could be promiscuously applied. The next pages will show how others created and used a holistic paradigm to further their own enterprises. Beyond ecology, and across the broad terrain of American culture, individuals in disparate fields were seeing wholes, too. Buckminster Fuller Jr., whose representation of holism became one of the defining marks of 1960s architecture, was one of those individuals. It is to Fuller and his geodesic dome that we now turn.

Buckminster Fuller working at Black Mountain College, c. 1948. *Reproduced with permission of R. Buckminster Fuller Estate*

2

The Built Environment
Buckminster Fuller's Spaceship Earth

On July 24, 1959, Soviet premier Nikita S. Khrushchev met U.S. vice president Richard M. Nixon in Moscow's Sokolniki Park to recognize the opening of the American National Exhibition, a grand exposition showcasing U.S. technology. Before they discussed washing machines in the now famous "kitchen debate," they paused in front of a large, round, gold-anodized building, measuring 200 feet in diameter and standing 78 feet high.[1] Called a "geodesic dome" by its designer, Richard Buckminster Fuller (1895–1983), the structure did not look like other domes. It bore little resemblance to the Kremlin's five distinctive onion-shaped domes a short distance away. Nor did it look like the Pantheon, Saint Basil's, Saint Paul's Cathedral, or the U.S. Capitol. Rather, it boasted little outside ornamentation, employed twentieth-century prefabricated materials, relied on new engineering principles, and appeared peculiarly modern. Like the biomorphic shapes swimming through a painting by Salvador Dalí or Joan Miró, the dome called to mind aberrant images of nature, resembling an overgrown, mutated turtle or, as one fairgoer said, a "giant, gilded armadillo shell." The building also evoked images of a technological cast. The mathematical name "geodesic" (meaning the shortest line between two points on a spherical surface) contributed to a scientific reading, and the use of aluminum suggested an industrial form. It could serve as a modern manufacturing plant.[2] Other interpretations of the dome pervaded the public mind as well. Space-age iconography popularized in science fiction films linked geodesics and flying saucers. Closer to reality, yet more horrifying, the dome assumed the shape of a mushroom cloud, that distinguishing emblem of the nuclear age.

Fuller's geodesic became one of the defining architectural marks of the postwar world, a symbol of this holistic age. Erected on every continent, including Antarctica, the geodesic enthralled people with its strange

Buckminster Fuller at Sokolniki Dome, American National Exhibition in
Moscow, 1959. *Reproduced with permission of R. Buckminster Fuller Estate*

aesthetics and practicality. In 1964, *Time* claimed God's signature was on
patent number 2,682,235. That same year, numerous companies took out
licenses to build the dome, including fifty different U.S. companies. By the
1990s, several hundred thousand domes functioned as auditoriums, aviar-
ies, banks, churches, exposition halls, greenhouses, homes, industrial
plants, military sheds, planetariums, playground equipment, radomes, and
sports arenas. Strikingly different from the International Style architecture
of tall, straight, hard-edged, flat lines that developed in the 1920s and 1930s
and characterized city skylines, his spheres typified the organic art and
architecture that characterized American aesthetics in the atomic era. It
made an organic statement in its shape, in its construction—each part relied
on neighboring parts to create the entirety—and in the designer's conception of it. To Fuller, the geodesic's technology and nature were complementary parts of one whole.[3]

Domes became Fuller's most famous work, but this was not his only
creation or central concern. Distraught about inadequate housing, ineffi-
cient designs, and wealth and power discrepancies, he hoped, through his
"comprehensive anticipatory design science," to create efficient technologies, better allocation of resources, and a more sustainable planet. Contrary

to Rachel Carson and other holists, he did not focus on changing people. Instead, he employed whole-systems thinking to manipulate the built environment. His many creations included houses, world maps, synergetic geometry, elaborate charts of natural resources, and a problem-solving World Game to make the world work for everyone's total enjoyment. To spread his ideas, he lectured, participated in cultural exchanges, and published articles and twenty-five books on ecological design, education, mathematics, and utopian thoughts.

Many scientists dismissed Fuller as a quack and a wild-eyed maverick. Critics condemned him for speaking absurdities, inventing words, twisting sentences, and peppering his speech with gibberish and jargon. These accusations were not without substance. He was not a trained architect or scientist, instead relying on haphazard readings, intuition, observations of nature, and self-promotion. At times he was blatantly wrong, confusing chemical facts, misunderstanding physics, misinterpreting geometric principles, and dismissing the mathematical notion of pi (π). Though he invented himself as a type of Robin Hood offering salvation to a world held captive by "pirate politicians," he often made a comedic or egomaniacal impression. Counterculture historian Theodore Roszak, who occasionally found himself on the same stage as Fuller, found the designer pretentious and full of exaggerations: "I would not have been surprised to hear him announce that he had invented a better tree."[4]

In spite of his idiosyncrasies and fantastic ideas such as placing a clear dome over a two-mile section of Manhattan—or perhaps because of them— Fuller captivated people. Living in Greenwich Village in the 1930s, he frequented Romany Marie's popular bohemian salon and entertained artists with futuristic ramblings. From the 1920s to the 1940s, in what he called his Dymaxion period, Fuller designed innovative houses and cars, created world maps, taught at Black Mountain College, and worked for *Fortune* and *Life* magazines. In the 1950s, he lectured at architectural schools and produced exhibition domes and military housing for the government; in the 1960s and 1970s, college students and counterculture environmentalists made him a cult figure, attending his marathon lectures, playing World Game, and building domes from kits ordered from the *Whole Earth Catalog*. Stewart Brand, the *Catalog*'s founder, credited Fuller with "electrifying" counterculturalists and inspiring the *Catalog*'s genesis.[5] Architectural critic M. W. Newman called him a "messiah of technology, advance man for utopia, and a radiant force."[6]

At the end of his life in 1983, a long list of accolades followed Fuller's name, including nearly fifty honorary degrees, and architectural, civic, corporate, military, religious, and union awards. He held the Charles Eliot Norton Professorship in Poetry at Harvard University (1962–63); the United Nations twice awarded him the Planetary Citizen Award (1975 and 1977); he was nominated for the Nobel Peace Prize (1969); and President Ronald Reagan conferred on him the Medal of Freedom (1983).[7] In 1985, two scientists named the sixty-atom carbon molecule, C_{60}, the Buckminsterfullerine or "Buckyball" because it reminded them of the Montreal Exposition biosphere.[8] Continuation of the Buckminster Fuller Institute, dome building, World Game workshops, book sales, exhibits, and Internet sites into the twenty-first century testifies to his ongoing influence. Perhaps most important, Fuller's focus on whole systems and the connections between the parts and the whole supplied a seedbed for ecological design, alternative technology developments, and sustainability initiatives.

Fuller's success sprang from his ability to speak, however strangely, to current architectural, political, and social problems and to offer optimistic answers that helped people imagine a better world and sustainable future. Disgusted with military ventures, Cold War rivalries, and unjust resource allocation, he condemned specialization that took one's gaze off the big picture and argued for a more comprehensive approach. Like others with fertile imaginations, the engineer often acted outside conventional circles, generated innovative designs, and suggested alternative ways of living. Still utilitarian, he promoted mass production and the use of new materials as a solution to global housing, food, and energy shortages. He believed technology, if modeled after patterns seen in nature, could guarantee progress.

Articulating these views placed him squarely within the long debate about the role of technology in nature and society. Since setting foot on American soil, European religious leaders, politicians, and travel writers interpreted the continent as an oasis of possibility, a refuge from corrupt civilization, and a wilderness ripe for cultivation. Fed by classical notions of the pastoral in Virgil's Arcadia and biblical stories of the Garden of Eden, ideas of nature as bucolic, peaceful, and regenerative informed myths about the American Revolution; served as a bedrock for Jeffersonian democracy; sparked utopian communities; stoked westward expansion; inspired nineteenth-century landscape painters such as Frederic Church, Winslow Homer, and Thomas Moran; and nourished interpretations of American exceptionalism. As American studies scholar Henry Nash Smith revealed, the "pastoral ideal" fertilized imaginations and ordered lifestyles, values, and meanings for multiple Americans.[9]

While not the only view of nature to inform the nation's consciousness, the "myth of the garden" has played a useful and dominant role. Consequently, this romantic notion has affected American perceptions of technology and fueled debates about technology's value. If the land is a garden, does technology belong? Will human constructions destroy the pastoral refuge? The desire for both and the resulting tension between pastoral appeal and technological desire have formed one of the central contradictions of American life. Striving for a "middle ground," as scholar Leo Marx explained,

Americans yearned for a place where the fruits of technology might be enjoyed without ill effects, where nature and art, country and city, wild and cultivated might coexist. Accordingly, one of the distinguishing features of American culture has been its continual espousal of pastoralism while becoming thoroughly technological.[10]

Technological power—forcefully demonstrated in August 1945 with the dropping of atomic bombs on Hiroshima and Nagasaki—complicated this picture and fueled the debate. Some, confident of human ingenuity, sought more mechanical fixes and forged stronger links between government officials and scientists. Others expressed skepticism. Historian Lewis Mumford feared the loss of humanism in science and lost confidence in a story of progress. Ray Bradbury's science fiction reinforced such anxieties. So did the terrifying film classic *Them!* (1954) in which fallout from an atomic bomb test in New Mexico transmogrified ants into giant, hostile, human-eating creatures. An entomologist in the movie made the message explicit when he explained that humans crossed a boundary in developing the atomic bomb. Nevil Shute's *On the Beach* (1957 book; 1959 film) continued this theme as it dramatized the end of the world through radiation. Shute began his novel with the detonation of atomic bombs in America and England, then traced the menacing reach of nuclear fallout as air currents carried the deadly poison to the Southern Hemisphere. Released about the same time as *Silent Spring*, the two works not only engendered fear but also reinforced global interconnectedness.

It is within this dialogue that Fuller preached his technological gospel and attempted to craft his own "middle ground." Divorcing himself from those who saw the machine as aberrant, alien, and apocalyptic, he promoted technology as a force for progress and might be likened to futurist thinkers John Cage, Marshall McLuhan, and Pierre Teilhard de Chardin.[11] In contrast with Jacques Ellul's claim that technology enslaved human beings, Fuller contended that machines freed people to devote themselves to higher ambitions. Though distraught over industrialization's land desecration and an outspoken critic of scientific "weaponry," he did not think natural beauty had to be forfeited in a modern, technologically endowed society. If it was modeled after nature and used for environmental preservation and "livingry," not "killingry," he figured technology would be humanity's salvation, the answer to hunger, sickness, and shelter needs. The good life on "spaceship earth" depended on forward, comprehensive thinking, improved design, and better gizmos.[12] Building better machines for the garden was therefore the best way to assure global progress.

To account for his faith in technology and nature, he merged the two. He formed this whole by naturalizing technology and technologizing nature. To naturalize the machine, the engineer designed inventions by looking to nature as a guide. He found patterns everywhere, in cells, plants, and

natural phenomena such as when a pebble is dropped into a pond and pro-
duces a circle of waves. He then applied the patterns he saw to his creations.
But he took this even further. Good technology, he reasoned, not only mimicked nature; it became a part of nature; it extended nature. His comments
on the geodesic dome, as we shall see, especially illustrated these assumptions. By aligning technology with nature, Fuller stripped the technological
world of its foreignness and made it less threatening. In ways, he reen-
chanted it. At the same time, he united these two domains by technologizing nature, suggesting, for example, that the globe was one vast machine.
"Spaceship earth," he argued, was an "integrally designed machine."[13]
     Fuller defined nature in these ways by combining two old metaphors.
First, he asserted that nature could be read as a book. Within nature thus
apprehended, human beings could discern the laws and patterns of the universe, apply them to technological fixes, and create a better built environment. Second, he reclaimed the metaphor of nature as a machine in
somewhat the same fashion as Enlightenment thinkers had done, only in his
day, he replaced the Deist's metaphor of the clock with the metaphor of the
spacecraft.[14] To understand how he formed this holistic marriage of technology and nature, it is useful to follow his life's trajectory. Like other holists, his
conceptualizations were marked by personal, as well as cultural factors.
     In 1895, Richard Buckminster Fuller Sr. and his wife, Carolyn Wolcott
Andrews, welcomed Richard Buckminster Jr. (Bucky), their second child
of four, into their well-to-do Milton, Massachusetts, home. Both parents
descended from British immigrants. Ancestor Timothy Fuller was
Massachusetts's delegate to the Federal Constitutional Assembly. Bucky's
father broke the family's Harvard-trained lawyer tradition to become a merchant, making frequent voyages to India and South America. His death in
1910, after a series of debilitating strokes, was the first of several traumatic
experiences for his young son. Lacking a steady income, the family struggled
financially. Bucky still attended a prestigious high school but felt ashamed
that he could not keep pace with his wealthy friends' acquisitions. He also
felt rebuffed by teachers, who labeled him an impertinent troublemaker.[15]
     Bear Island in Maine's Penobscot Bay became his sanctuary. Purchased
by his maternal grandmother in 1904 for summer vacations, the island
offered a natural playground and experimental arena. Here, Fuller's fascination with nature and the mechanical coalesced. As a young boy, he rowed a
boat four miles round trip to another island for the mail. To expedite the trip,
he invented what he called his "first teleologic design invention," a "mechanical jelly fish." Noting the design of the fish as it moved through the water, he
copied the action and produced a boat of greater speed and ease.[16]
     For most of his life, he made yearly island visits. Despite a love of tech-
nology, he kept the place rustic, refusing to install a telephone, running
water, or electricity.[17] It was his "Walden Pond," and, like Thoreau and

Thoreau's disciple Rachel Carson, he wanted to keep it wild. The family constructed houses on the island, however, and later he erected a dome. He contended that periodic retreats to this natural terrain helped him conceive more technologically advanced designs. It also provided an annual escape from the futuristic world he advocated.

Fuller entered Harvard in 1913 but did not last. To his dismay, all the social clubs rejected him, and a broken knee barred him from football. He also failed academically. Twice, Harvard expelled him for raucous behavior. After the university first "fired" him, as he phrased it, he apprenticed in a cotton mill machinery plant.[18] After his second expulsion in 1915, he moved to New York City and worked for the meatpacking house Armour and Company, one of the first companies to use the assembly line. This experience likely influenced Fuller's later push to mass-produce houses. At the same time, he developed an aversion for specialization, trying instead to focus on the big picture, interconnections, interdisciplinarity or "omnidirectionality," as he called it, and a more whole-systems epistemological approach. When World War I commenced, he joined the navy and continued his pragmatic education. In the service, he demonstrated his design skills by creating a lifesaving device to rescue pilots who crashed their planes at sea.[19]

The accretion of these experiences—from design experiments on Bear Island, to Harvard "demotions," to industrial work and military service—set him on an innovative path. But it was not until he lost a daughter and experienced more "ejections from the Establishment" that he deliberately created an unconventional lifestyle and experimented with unorthodox designs. In 1917, Fuller married Anne Hewlett, the daughter of architect James Monroe Hewlett. A year later Alexandra was born, but she soon developed spinal meningitis and infantile paralysis. In 1922, pneumonia ended her life. Angry, frustrated, and depressed, Fuller blamed her demise on their inadequate environment. He determined to build better houses.[20] In that same year, he and his father-in-law founded the Stockade Building System. Fuller's move into housing was likely also spurred by his wife, who had taken classes in design, and her father's invention of a new building brick. Regardless of the impetus, Fuller credited his architectural career to his belief that progress came from transforming the environment, not people, which he deemed impossible. He hoped to build better "instruments, tools, or other devices" to increase the "technical advantage of man over environmental circumstance."[21] How much he thought about renovating the built environment in 1922 is unclear. More likely he arrived at these conclusions gradually and then retold his life experiences in this way. What is unambiguous at this point was Fuller's reliance on alcohol, parties, and women to ease his pain.

According to his carefully crafted autobiography, the year 1927 was pivotal. This, he commonly announced, was the year he reached bottom. His daughter's death and business failures led him to contemplate suicide. By this time, he, Anne, and their second daughter, Allegra, had moved to Chicago and were living in poverty. Despite constructing more than 200 buildings, the company never turned a profit. When Hewlett pulled out in 1927, the board fired Fuller. Believing construction codes and society's "dogmas" had thrust him into "an enormous pinch-point of pain," the unsuccessful businessman took a late night walk along the shore of Lake Michigan with the intent of throwing himself into the cold waters.[22] Instead, he claimed an epiphany: "You do not have the right to eliminate yourself. You do not belong to you. You belong to the universe. The significance of you will forever remain obscure to you, but you may assume that you are fulfilling your significance if you apply yourself to converting all your experience to the highest advantage of others." He "vowed to do my own thinking, instead of trying to accommodate everyone else's opinions."[23] And with that he plunged not into the water but into a period of introspection.

For the next year, he hardly spoke, while he crafted an individualistic philosophy. "The individual can take initiatives without anyone's permission," he asserted.[24] He later wrote in his poem "No More Secondhand God" (1940) that individuals do not have to follow "legislative code, not proclamation law, not academic dogma, nor ecclesiastic canon." He explained, "All organized religions of the past were inherently developed as beliefs and credits in 'second hand' information." Instead he called for "an entirely new era" in which human beings relied on their own ideas, integrity, and intuition and experienced God firsthand through "direct experience."[25]

Of course, Fuller did not cultivate his thoughts in isolation. He read widely, and he changed with the twentieth century. As indicated by his love of efficiency and faith in progress, he was a product of the Progressive Era. He developed his design science views in the 1920s, at the height of Taylorism and the technocracy movement, which contended that scientific experts, engineers, and technicians were best prepared to solve world problems and called for a reordering of American society based on scientific management and technical efficiency.[26] Fuller's early houses particularly reflected the machine age, but whole-systems thinking best describes his work overall. Especially in his ruminations about spaceship earth, he leaned upon the work of holistic biologist Ludwig von Bertalanffy's general system's theory, which rejected a reductionistic approach in favor of a more organismic one.[27] In architecture, Fuller mirrored twentieth-century shifts toward an organic form. His domes may be compared to the architectural organicism of Frank Lloyd Wright and Wright's student Paolo Soleri, both of whom wed natural and built environments.[28] When Fuller and his family moved back to New York in 1929, frequent visits to Greenwich Village brought him into daily contact with artists like architect Isamu Noguchi, who became a friend and collaborator. In form, Noguchi and other nature-

inspired artists such as sculptor Ray Eames and abstract expressionist painters Willem de Kooning and Jackson Pollock revealed a fascination with
biomorphic patterns, undulating curves, and amoeba-like shapes. The geodesic dome adhered to this same morphology. In materials, too, Fuller followed postwar trends in using new plastics and molded plywood technology.
In sum, Fuller's technological, whole-systems, organic philosophy had long
and multiple roots. Not attributing his ideas to other people, however,
helped him cultivate his maverick mystique.

To feed his unconventionality, he refused to find employment, deciding
instead to put his trust in nature. "Nature," he surmised, "never 'fails.'
Nature complies with her own laws. *Nature is the law.*"[29] If he lived by
nature's laws, he reasoned, his family would survive. Hence he turned "to
the invention and development of physical artifacts to reform the environment. . . . It became obvious that if I worked always and only for all humanity, I would be optimally effective. I'd be doing what nature wanted me to do,
and nature literally would support me."[30] He explained that once "released
from the idea of earning a living," he felt free to question, read, introspect,
and imagine. He started with questions about the existence of a higher
power and came to the conclusion that a "Greater Intellect" or "Greater
Integrity" guided the universe. Fuller developed a notion of the world as a
unified system and studied the Book of Nature for its basic structures.
Learning principles and patterns that undergirded Earth's system, he presumed, would provide the basis for him to design superior technologies to
aid humanity. Conceiving of a God of Greater Integrity and nature as "an
orderliness of interactive, exceptionless principles" gave him purpose, solace, and a sense of wholeness. The name he gave his deity suggests this. "To
integrate" means to unify or make whole by bringing the parts together.
"Greater Integrity" thus signaled a God of wholeness.

Though peculiarly expressed, the designer's religious notions and ideas
about nature were not so unusual. He was a Unitarian-Universalist who
kept his New England Brahmin family's sensibilities. Like his great-aunt,
Margaret Fuller, the transcendentalist and coeditor of the *Dial* with Ralph
Waldo Emerson, he espoused romanticism's epistemology of intuition even
while he worked in design science. He wrote: "Intuition is our contact
between conscious and subconscious. It's your subconscious that suddenly
comes through and lets you know 'this is something important to be thought
about.' It's intuition that is constantly opening doors of thought."[31] His ideas
also ran analogous to naturalists who looked to nature for lessons or even to
1920s expatriate writers and 1940s and 1950s Beat poets disturbed by
America's political path. Hence, Fuller's ability to attract a crowd before and
after World War II testified not only to his unique expressions but also to
the fact that his message addressed important cultural questions and resonated within a significant segment of American society. He belonged within

a crowd that questioned the status quo: iconoclastic writers, bohemian artists, and counterculturalists. Untethered from social customs, he found his
authority in nature. His biomorphic, organic architecture sprung out of an
affiliation with the natural world.

From his epiphany at Lake Michigan's shoreline and reflective study,
Fuller developed confidence and purpose. This reinforced both his individualistic side and his commitment to community. While he vowed to work
independently (something he succeeded in doing only marginally, as he
regularly collaborated with a variety of students, design engineers, architects, and artists), he determined to apply his "inventory of experiences to
the solving of problems that affect everyone aboard planet Earth." He reasoned, "Each one of us is born of two, and we really belong to each other."[32]
Describing the moment years later, he said, "In 1927 I made a bargain with
myself that I'd discover the principles operative in the universe and turn
them over to my fellow men."[33] To do this, he purposed to discover, invent,
and test. If his designs worked, then he figured he was following "nature's
coordinate system."[34] To reflect his experimental attitude, he called himself
"Guinea Pig B" ("B" for "Bucky"). His experiments led eventually to the
geodesic dome, his highest architectural achievement. While the geodesic
epitomizes his holistic merging of nature and technology, it only came
about after he designed other energy-efficient buildings and machines,
developed his own mathematical system, and created a cartographical representation of his "one world," utopian philosophy.

His first "Guinea Pig B" experiments began in the 1920s and built upon
his experience in construction, a logical choice, as Fuller found more potential in changing the world through technological innovation than he did in
anything else. He declared himself to be apolitical and contended that design
science promised more than politicians could. In one of his later books, he
wrote: "I was convinced in 1927 that humanity's most fundamental survival
problems could never be solved by politics."[35] His political animosities
began a couple years earlier when he knocked heads with Chicago's building regulators and escalated as the United States ratcheted up its Cold War
military-industrial complex. To the delight of some in the 1960s, he eventually denounced politicians as "pirates," suggesting they squandered capital,
fought needlessly, and distributed resources unfairly.[36] "All the politician
can do regarding the problem [of overpopulation and resource allocation],"
he charged, "is to take a fraction of that inadequate ratio of supply from one
group and apply it to another without changing the over-all ratio."[37]

To improve human life, the designer started imagining technologically
sophisticated, hexagonal homes at the end of the 1920s. The traditional
square house, he thought, was a static embodiment of old thinking. To
modernize, he built the "4D house" ("4D" for "fourth dimension"). John
McHale, an artist, sociologist, and Fuller's colleague at the University of

Southern Illinois, Carbondale, explained that Fuller used 4D symbolically as a "reference to 'time' in relativity theory, a sort of (4th) extension of physical dimension."[38] His strange, circular abode branded him a visionary. As much machine as domicile, the aluminum structure hung from a central support mast and was stabilized by cables. It generated its own power by converting wastes into usable energy and recycled its own water. The house had central climate control and built-in laborsaving utilities: automatic laundry machines that cleaned, dried, folded, and rehung garments; washers that cleaned, dried, and reshelved dishes; and compressed vacuum units.[39]

Chicagoans first saw the strange design in the windows of Marshall Field's department store. Advertising agents used the house to display a new line of modern furniture. Field's public relations people renamed it "Dymaxion House" to reflect Fuller's ideas and draw customers. They coined the term by splicing the words "dynamic" and "maximum" to the scientific term "ion." Giving his house a scientific-sounding name appealed to Fuller, who adopted it to communicate a philosophy of "doing more with less."[40] This was his twist on the Bauhaus architect Ludwig Mies van der Rohe's axiom that "less is more." Dymaxion, to Fuller, was synonymous with efficiency or, in his words, "maximal gain of advantage of performance from minimal energy input."[41] According to architectural critic Hugh Aldersey-Williams, Fuller appropriated the word to explain an invention that "extracted the best performance from available technology."[42]

The Dymaxion House fulfilled another modern architect's maxim to create a "machine for living" but perhaps to an extent that Le Corbusier (Charles-Édouard Jeanneret) never imagined. Le Corbusier, one of the founders of the International Style in architecture, wrote in 1923 that a "house is a machine for living in" to describe his "Citrohan house" project. "Citrohan," a play on the French automaker's name of Citroën, reflected the architect's belief that industrial function should be represented in its form and that houses, like cars, could be standardized, mass-produced, and serviceable.[43] Fuller, though not schooled in architecture or a member of Le Corbusier's elite circle, shared his contemporary's industrial spirit. To Fuller, the house was a machine and a step toward building a "one-town" global society. Intent on providing efficient homes for all, he proposed mass-producing houses for global distribution. To show how to deliver a fully constructed house to any location, he drew a series of sketches. First, a helicopter airlifted the assembled building to the site, where workers had prepared a crater (his instructions called for exploding a bomb to make the hole). Then, the helicopter lowered the building's mast into the opening, and ground crews stabilized the home.[44]

Eventually the designer used his "doing more with less" adage to call for societal reform and wise, efficient use of natural resources. In the 1920s, he began to create an "Inventory of World Resources, Human Trends and

Buckminster Fuller with 4D Dymaxion House Exhibit, Marshall Field
department store, Chicago, 1929. *Reproduced with permission of*
R. Buckminster Fuller Estate

Needs." He became part of a widening circle of Americans, Rachel Carson
included, who developed a holistic awareness that industrialization and
energy consumption had implications beyond economic efficiency. Fuller's
conservationism, in concert with Carson's, proved influential during the
1960s when concerned scientists, environmentalists, and ordinary citizens
pointed to wasteful consumption and connected capitalistic and materialistic values with environmental pollution, blight, and human health hazards.
Both addressed problems in a holistic way, though Carson represented an
environmental voice more skeptical of modernism.

Hatred of waste and inefficiency coupled with a love for proficient technologies placed Fuller in the population debate of the 1960s. When environmentalists revived eighteenth-century Malthusian ideas, Fuller scoffed. He
dismissed Stanford biologist Paul Ehrlich's claims that the world's resources
could not meet the growing population's needs. In his popular book *The
Population Bomb* (1968), Ehrlich called for immediate population control to
help avert widespread starvation and death in the 1970s and 1980s.[45] Fuller
denied this dark prognostication. The population explosion was a "myth."
The problem, he thought, was distribution, not population. The answer was

improved housing, resource allocation, and technologies. Living standards around the world could rise, and the "have-nots" could join the "haves."[46]

By the time Fuller debated Ehrlich, he had spent his life inventing energy-savings devices. In his 1930s Dymaxion phase, he designed several efficiency tools for living. His Dymaxion Bathroom was a one-piece aluminum fixture, with its own "fog gun," an economical showerhead using a mixture of 90 percent air and 10 percent water. His Dymaxion Car ran on three wheels, had front-wheel drive with rear-wheel steering, and registered forty to fifty miles per gallon. The car looked like a flying fish, so he made the fish his logo, a symbol for the merging of the mechanical and natural. Making the fish fly communicated Fuller's love of speed and progress.[47] These creations brought the inventor recognition, but the news was not always positive. His demonstration car flipped and killed its driver. The American Institute of Architects (AIA) dismissed the Dymaxion House in 1929, calling it machinery, not architecture. When Fuller offered to give proprietary rights for his house patents to the AIA, the institute damned prefabrication and registered a sharp rebuke, going on record to say it was "inherently opposed to any peas-in-a-pod-like, reproducible designs."[48]

What architects found distasteful, the U.S. Army found practical. In World War II, Fuller manufactured and sold his Dymaxion Deployment Units (DDUs), a strange, grain bin–looking shelter, to the government for military housing. In 1946 he tried to convert these units into civilian residences. The DDU became the "Wichita House," a circular, aluminum unit so named because production was to take place in Kansas. The prefabricated structure contained laborsaving tools, including motorized closets. An illustrated article in *Fortune* magazine publicized the house, and Fuller was flooded with 37,000 unsolicited letters from hopeful, though soon disappointed, purchasers. Beech Aircraft Company planned to mass-produce 20,000 a year, but Fuller tussled with financers and builders and the project failed. One prototype became the family home of investor William Graham, but it was Levittown tract homes, not Wichita Houses, that soon dominated suburban landscapes. Graham's home was refurbished in the 1990s and exhibited in the Henry Ford Museum in Dearborn, Michigan.[49]

Folding up his DDU project, Fuller delved into another introspective research period. This time he focused on mathematics, world maps, and the geodesic dome. Each of these activities related to the other, and each made his holistic sensibility evident. First, in mathematics, Fuller was sure that geometry held the key to understanding "nature's coordinate system." Euclidian geometry, however, failed to satisfy him. Fuller wanted everything in simple wholes. Nature, he asserted, knew no fractions. So he invented his own mathematical system and called it "energetic-synergetic geometry." To do so, he focused on spherical geometry rather than plane geometry, an important decision that later factored into his dome's design, since it was out of the notion of great circles, triangles, and tetrahedrons that he developed his tension-based geodesics.[50] Four crucial terms—"synergy," "energetic," "synergetic," and "tensegrity"—helped him describe his system. While this is not a treatise on his mathematics, a short summary is important to explain his holism and geodesic construction.

First, Fuller equated synergy and holism. In his book *Ideas and Integrities*, he defined synergy as "the unique behavior of whole systems unpredicted by behavior of their respective sub-systems." To explain, he pointed to the alloy of chrome, nickel, and steel. The alloy's tensile strength (durability of a material when stretched) was far greater than that of the individual components.[51] Thus, the whole was greater than the sum of its parts. Abraham Maslow and Gestalt psychologists were equally attracted to the concept of "synergy," and one can find its use in other fields as well. Christian theologians used "synergy" to refer to a belief that sinners worked with God to bring salvation. Physicians employed the word to describe muscles acting in concert to move an object, and they spoke of the synergistic value of ingesting two or three drugs together to receive a greater benefit. Neurophysiologist Charles Scott Sherrington, in 1906, used the concept to explain that all parts of the nervous system are connected; no part acts without affecting other parts. He called this a "synergy of reflexes—a holographic ensemble of interrelated and embedded scales of activity." Fuller contributed to contemporary understandings of synergy by referring to it as a combined effort to achieve a result that is greater than that from any individual effort. Applying it to geometry, as architect Lindy Roy concluded, Fuller "saw the potential for a new generative geometry, able to deal with the integration and inter-activity of elements." Fuller stated that he wanted a mathematics that explained the "whole of experience and knowledge" rather than "specialized isolations."[52]

"Energetic" referred to his conception of the universe as one great energy field and the planet as a "spinning, cosmos-zooming earth ball." The "world seems at rest," he explained, but it is really moving at an amazing velocity.[53] Inspired by Einstein's theories of time and space, he tried to design his geometry to capture motion, something more than straight two-dimensional lines and curves. "Synergetic," a combination of "synergy" and "energetic," referred to the integration of energy in a system.[54] "Tensegrity" evolved from his understanding of synergy, tensile strength, and geometric shapes. To erect buildings, engineers historically relied on tension and compression. To make a lighter weight structure, Fuller and his students concentrated on holding materials together in tension. The formations that resulted became known as "tensegrities" (tensional integrities) because they relied on continuous tension to stand. His geometry gained few adherents, but his reliance upon tension became a very useful architectural concept. It solved long-standing difficulties of creating large-span buildings, allowing him to create the geodesic and others to patent similar structures.

While the designer worked on his Dymaxion creations and then on mathematics, he also engaged in mapmaking; indeed, his interest in spherical geometry stemmed from his interest in maps. His cartographic renderings are important to this story for numerous reasons. They helped Fuller create his dome and illuminated how he imagined the earth as one united whole. When he designed his World Game, his maps also served as useful tools to assess problems and chart solutions.

Standardized Mercator projection maps vexed Fuller because of their distortions. Translating the spherical surface of the earth to a flat plane amplified and warped land masses. Greenland, for instance, is much smaller than depicted. To solve that problem, Fuller created the "Dymaxion Air-Ocean World Map," which he made public in the March 1943 issue of *Life* magazine. The eighteen-page article included a cutout of the map's separable triangles and instructions for assembling one's own. *Life* called the map "pure invention," but readers responded enthusiastically, and the issue sold a record-breaking three million copies.[55] As a manipulable, the map could be laid out flat or folded into a global shape. Internet sites later animated the map, showing how it could form a ball or a plane.[56] There was no up, down, north, south, east, or west. The parts could be rearranged to give any region—or no region—center stage, thus highlighting different perspectives and interests. To encourage thinking of the globe as one comprehensive whole, the "Dymaxion World Map" could be arranged to line up the continents and showcase one stream of land. Conversely, his "One-Ocean World Map" highlighted the interconnectedness of the earth's water by showing it as one united body, dispelling assumptions of oceans as separate and isolated. Antarctica sat in the middle of this map, while the other land masses framed the ocean.

Eventually Fuller used maps to address sustainability, resource distribution, and international relations, as we will see, but now the focus remains on his dome creation. Observing the great circle routes sailors traveled to circumnavigate the world, he noted that these paths traced the shortest distances between two points on the globe: they were, by definition, geodesics. Always interested in doing "more with less," the designer liked to say these routes involved the least investment of time and energy, an efficiency he hoped to emulate in his structures. He further observed that these routes crossed to form triangles. He mimicked this in a structural design by joining together a network of great circles. At every place the circles intersected, he bolted them together. "When I had worked out my three-way great circle grid of perfect triangles for the map," he explained, "I realized that it would be possible to make a spherical structure or dome." To make sure that the building held its shape, he joined the triangles together with tension bands, which worked to distribute the load evenly to "all parts of the structure." Consequently, he named the design "Geodesic Structure because of its employment of great circle geometry."[57]

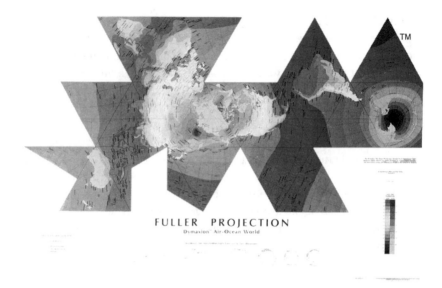

FULLER PROJECTION
Dymaxion Air-Ocean World

Dymaxion Air-Ocean World Map. *Reproduced with permission of R. Buckminster Fuller Estate*

Fuller's first dome failed. While he was an artist-in-residence with musician John Cage and dancer Merce Cunningham at the avant-garde Black Mountain College in 1948, he and his students tried to erect a fifty-foot-diameter dome. For a brief moment the construction of Venetian blind strips, fastened together with bolts, swelled to form a sphere. In the next second, it sagged, succumbing to gravity. Fuller jokingly referred to it from then on as his "flopahedron" or "supine dome." The next year—after working with Chicago Institute students, refining his mathematics, and switching to a sturdier material—he returned to Black Mountain and tried again. This time the experiment did not flop.[58]

From the experimental realm of Black Mountain, Fuller turned to the government to sell his dome. In 1949, he perched a geodesic frame in the Pentagon's courtyard and touted the utility of these cheap, practical structures. The government became one of his best customers, ensuring the dome a part in the Cold War. The Defense Department commissioned domes for weather installations; the air force and Marine Corps used geodesics for sheltering men and equipment.[59] The Commerce Department and State Department purchased geodesics for world's fairs. Starting in 1956, administrators, frantic to exhibit at the Jeshyn Fair in Kabul, Afghanistan, and compete with the massive exhibit buildings of China and Russia, commissioned Fuller to produce a dome in two months. He did so in one month and at minimal cost. To the delight of Afghanis, the dome resembled ancient Afghan yurts, though Fuller's dome was made of aluminum and plastic-coated nylon instead of saplings and sheepskins. At the fair's end, the dome was dismantled and flown to trade shows in Thailand and Japan. Other designers contributed similar buildings in this time of grand world exposi-tions. Cornell researcher Walter Bird helped develop pneumatic domes, and in the 1960s, his whale-shaped structure traveled the globe as the exhibit building for the U.S. Atomic Energy Commission's "Atoms for Peace" proj-ect.[60] Other Fuller domes housed expositions in Burma, India, Italy, Morocco, Poland, Tunisia, and Turkey. At the Milan Triennale in 1954 and 1957, Fuller won the "Gran Premio" architecture prize.[61] The Geodesic Pavilion at Expo 67 in Montreal gained Fuller the prestigious architectural design award from the American Institute of Architects—the group that had spurned him earlier.

The U.S. government found geodesics to be functional and practical. Outside government, geodesics also proved useful. In 1953, the engineer built his first commercial dome atop the Ford building in Dearborn, Michigan, and gained international attention. He placed a dome over the inner court of Ford's giant gear-shaped building—an appropriate represen-tation of the modern machine age—to help the company commemorate its fiftieth anniversary.[62] In doing so, he managed to solve an age-old engineering challenge: how to put a dome on a fairly weak foundation without causing the base's collapse. Because the edifice was not strong enough to support the weight of a conventional radial rib steel frame, he devised a geodesic structure that weighed about 8.5 tons, a mere fraction of the 160 tons that Ford's engineers estimated a dome that size would weigh. His dome, so lightweight that he initially attached the translucent polyester fiberglass material to aluminum spars with cellophane tape, amazed engineers world-wide. It did have a fatal flaw, however. It leaked. When workers tried to seal sections in 1962, fire engulfed the rotunda and reduced it to ashes.[63]

Despite leakage, geodesics were highly practical. Formerly, large-diame-ter domes relied on a double layer of support to achieve strength and stabil-ity. Many of these were visually arresting for their beautiful crisscrossed joints and complicated trusses, but the volume of material needed made them heavy and costly. Hence, most domes were reserved for cathedrals and buildings where expense was not a factor.[64] Fuller managed to defy both cost and weight. In 1958, the Union Tank Car Company constructed one in which to repair its railroad cars. This Louisiana building was the largest clear-span building for the time, measuring 384 feet in diameter. "When we developed the first geodesic dome," Fuller noted, "the two largest domes in the world were St. Peter's and the Pantheon. St. Peter's is around 30,000 tons...the first geodesic dome of 150 feet came out at 30 tons—a 1000th the weight of St. Peter's."[65] The top of a 200-foot-diameter dome, such as the Sokolniki Exhibit sphere, weighed only about 1,000 pounds. A helicopter lifted the huge Union Tank dome.[66]

Discarding classic architectural principles and materials made Fuller's domes different and earned him a place in architectural history. Nineteenth-century architects and engineers had already tested older construction techniques and experimented with new designs and materials. Crystal palaces, cast-iron buildings, and octagonal houses in the nineteenth century by Francois-Joseph Bélanger, Joseph Paxton, and Orson Fowler and glass architecture by Bruno Taut in the twentieth century anticipated but did not achieve Fuller's lightweight marvels.[67] Though Fuller was the first to patent the geodesic, Walter Bauersfeld was first to assemble one in Jena, Germany, in 1922. How much, if any, influence Bauersfeld had on Fuller is unclear. While Fuller knew of Bauersfeld, he did not acknowledge his predecessor. That was hardly surprising. He rarely attributed ideas to anyone else.[68]

The uniqueness of the geodesic was in the design. It did not employ heavy vaults or flying buttresses. It did not rely on compression from the walls to support the roof. Instead, the dome depended on balanced tension between the parts to form the whole. Joining multiple tetrahedrons (a poly-hedron with four triangular faces) together in tension yields a spherical shape. With this basic scheme, Fuller created all sorts of geodesics.[69] The tensile strength of interlocking triangles gave the geodesic its shape and lift. If pressure was applied at any one point, the stress was transmitted through-out the whole, allowing for a very strong construction. To demonstrate, Fuller erected a thirty-foot dome at one of the world's windiest location, the top of New Hampshire's Mount Washington. The dome stood without dam-age against nearly 200 mile-per-hour winds in trial and remained standing for nearly two years before scientists dismantled it. This dome served as the prototype for numerous radomes (to house radar equipment) around the world. The U.S. Air Force installed the first of many radomes above the Arctic Circle in 1954 for its first distant early warning (DEW) line for defense against nuclear attack.[70] One dome of wood and plastic survived Hurricane Carol in 1954 with minimal damage.[71]

Relying on tension rather than compression allowed Fuller to create a dome that defied older standards. New materials—aluminum, plastic, fiber-glass, steel, and cardboard—made it possible to erect inexpensive, light-weight buildings. The materials he employed varied according to function, design, and region. The U.S. Marine Corps domes of lightweight aluminum and plastic could be transported by helicopter. Paperboard served as the main cover for the 1954 Milan Triennale Gran Premio dome. The Monsanto Chemical Company sandwiched Styrofoam between layers of kraft paper to make an insulated dome for use in either the very hot tropics or the cold tundra of the Arctic.[72] Individuals in Asia utilized bamboo. Using materi-als indigenous to the region and equipped with easy-to-read directions, geodesic models were easily exportable. The domes were practical, efficient, cost-effective, strong, easy to transport, and made for quick assembly. For example, a few Afghans, assisted by one of Fuller's engineers and color-coded pieces, assembled the Kabul dome in forty-eight hours. But the structure was not simply utilitarian. Although U.S. government officials may have been attracted to the dome chiefly for its pragmatic value, it also gave them a chance to boast of one of America's great technological wonders—an important value to Cold War warriors intent on proving superiority of culture and technological expertise as well as military strength. Richard Nixon's meeting with Nikita Khrushchev under the shadow of the Sokolniki dome illustrates this well. The size of the dome communicated power and grandeur. They worked as a space to sell U.S. technology.

Though Fuller trumpeted the dome's functional qualities, what is most intriguing for this study is the way that the geodesic exemplified the designer's conviction that nature and technology were one. Some domes illustrated this more than others. For instance, he perched his restaurant dome on a hill in the old fishing village of Woods Hole, Massachusetts, not far from Woods Hole Oceanographic Institution, where Carson conducted studies. This geodesic did not sparkle and shine like exposition domes; it did not dominate the landscape or call attention to itself. Rather, the airy, clear-walled sphere made of wood and plastic merged with the environment, akin to Frank Lloyd Wright's organic architecture. Customers sat beneath a grove of trees with only a thin, translucent veil between them and the elements. This dome leaked, too, so sometimes diners probably felt as though nothing had come between them and the elements. Still, instead of symbolizing technological power, it nestled within nature.

Clear-skinned domes and futuristic designs broadcast Fuller's belief that technology could improve human life and nature. The Montreal pavilion regulated the environment. As he explained, "From the inside there will be uninterrupted visual contact with the exterior world. The sun and moon will shine in the landscape, and the sky will be completely visible, but the unpleasant effects of climate, heat, dust, bugs, glare, etc. will be modulated by the skin to provide a Garden of Eden interior."[73] In the 1960s and 1970s, he proposed doming cities and megastructures for environmental and social advantage. His "Old Man River" plan of 1971 to revitalize the poor, largely African American, highly industrialized East St. Louis called for building a self-contained city under a half-mile-diameter dome. With others, he aimed to forge new community partnerships, alleviate class and racial tensions, and make the area more environmentally friendly. Other projects called for other city domes; the development of underwater islands to serve as bases for oceanographic exploration, oil drillers, or submarines; and floating cities off Japan's coast.[74] All failed as practical endeavors but succeeded in utopian fashion, to spark novel thinking and smaller community projects. Walt Disney's Epcot

Woods Hole Restaurant, Woods Hole, Massachusetts. *Reproduced with permission of R. Buckminster Fuller Estate*

Center, short for Experimental Prototype Community of Tomorrow, promoted sustainability by using the geodesic (and naming it Spaceship Earth) to showcase new technologies and discuss the community of tomorrow.

In the naming of his domes, Fuller signaled his desire to link technology with nature or even, in a vague, mystical way, to make technology become nature. He called some domes "Garden of Eden." Other appellations made the connection between nature and technology more explicit: "Fly's Eye," "Skybreak," "Climatron," and "La Biosphère." In these domes, the machine was not only in the garden; they became the garden.

As architectural historian John Hix noted, Fuller's love for thin-skinned enclosures revealed his mystical and utopian attitudes.[75] This was evident in Fuller's 1967 discussion of his Montreal dome. Geodesics could do "spectacular" things, he said. "I haven't let much of it be visible except that anyone looking at the geodesic dome in Montreal saw a very beautiful piece of mechanics.... there were curtains that could articulate by photosynthesis and so forth, could let light in and out." To control the temperature of his clear-skinned dome, he installed light sensors that raised and lowered

shades. Then he suggested that the mechanical aspects of the dome mimicked the functioning of the human being and dreamed of a more sophisticated dome: "It is possible, as our own human skin, all of our pores, all of
the cells organize, so that some are photo-sensitive and some are sound-
sensitive, and they're heat-sensitive, and it would be perfectly possible to
create a geodesic of a very high frequency where each of these pores could
be circular tangencies of the same size. One could be a screen, others breathing air, others letting light in, and the whole thing could articulate just as
sensitively as a human being's skin."[76]

Continuing to make meaning from his domes, Fuller attempted to make
his structures "emulate the structuring of the universe." He tried to copy the
atom's shape and energy, what he described as "the compound curvature
trussing of the atom's dynamic structure," in the geodesic. The dome
"employs [this force] for the first time in a man-made structure."[77] With an
intriguing twist, then, he translated the shape and dynamic of the atom—
synonymous with weaponry in the 1950s—into "livingry," a shelter for
habitation and protection.

In multiple ways, Fuller described the dome as a metaphor for and an
embodiment of nature. It was a technological marvel—an energy field dis-
playing maximum efficiency—as well as a representation of the way that he
read the natural world. Again, these were not separate domains to him. As
one critic remarked, the geodesic was "much more than an image; it was a
living, breathing, throbbing piece of nature, so perfect, so efficient, and so
'organic.' "[78]

These conclusions become even more apparent when the dome's relationship to the earth is considered. Some hugged the earth; others seemed
to float. Initially, his curvilinear inventions were hemispheric. Many sat on
the ground. Others, such as the Ford rotunda, sat atop a foundation, like
earlier church domes that were separated from earth by a base. And some,
like Montreal's dome, became a complete sphere. Fuller's keen interest in
world resources, his global perspective, and his society's ongoing exploration in space may have contributed to this evolution. In some of his imaginative drawings, planet-looking domes defied gravity. His "cloud nine"
sketches showed round ball-like buildings floating just above the earth's
surface.[79]

Regardless of the domes' shape, the technological wizard, in rather
remarkable ways, maintained that he had welded the mechanical to the natural so that dome and earth united to form one whole. He understood one
definition for the term "geodesic" to mean "half," and he called his domes
"the upper or enclosing surface of a hemisphere (geodesic)." The bottom
hemisphere, he thought, was the earth. Furthermore, these two halves were
fundamentally linked through compression and tension. When he applied
for his geodesic dome patent, he wrote that his configuration is "a frame of

generally spherical form in which the main structural elements are interconnected in a geodesic pattern of approximate great circle arcs intersecting
to form a three-way grid."[80] He drew lines to show these interconnections,
but the lines did not simply connect one part of the dome to another. They
connected the dome to the earth. In discussing the way a geodesic works, he
explained compound curvatures, stresses, and outward thrusting as an
"omnidirectional process." "In the case of a geodesic structure representing
a portion of a sphere," he added, "the functions of the balance of the sphere
are rendered by the earth, which tends to complete the spherical structure
by stress extension with the earth." In his plans to enclose cities in "water
floatable enclosures," he again asserted the "earth completes the sphere."[81]
The two balanced one another.

Linking technology to nature formed the heart of his holism. The geodesic dome—a whole unit with each part bearing its share of weight, each part
relying on its neighboring part for stability, each part crucial to the whole—
was a concrete form of his abstract holistic hopes. The fact that the whole
was expressed only when all parts pulled together to make the dome rise
expressed his holistic notions about the interrelations or, in Fuller's lexicon,
the "synergy" of all things. In sum, his domes were a practical space and a
philosophical musing.

Fuller advertised dome houses by living in one with Anne from 1960 to
1971 in Carbondale, Illinois. He made the design public through talks and
articles published in Fortune, Newsweek, and Time. Popular Science published
plans for his "sun dome" in May 1966, showing how almost anyone could
build a thin wooden dome with a clear vinyl skin stapled to it. And many
did. By 1970, more than 80,000 blueprints had sold.[82] Handbooks assisted
amateur builders. In 1970, Domebook 1, published by West Coast dome
builders, hit the market, followed in 1971 by Domebook 2.[83] These do-it-yourself instruction books offered multiple variations to the basic dome and
encouraged each builder to personalize his or her shelter. Soon, dome kits
could be purchased around the world. The builder did not have to read;
color-coded pieces enabled assemblage. In the twenty-first century, the
Internet offered a plethora of designs. Counterculturalists became the biggest consumer of dome houses, but before examining those connections, it
is important to review Fuller's Geoscope, global politics, and World Game,
as they also drew those who wanted an alternative to the Cold War ethos.

Time spent building and promoting geodesics did not deter Fuller's
global interests. To the contrary. In 1951, Fuller built a miniature earth
dome—a twenty-foot-diameter sphere—with Cornell University students
and named it the "Geoscope." It was, as one of his biographers described it,
a "hybrid of the geodesic dome and the Dymaxion Map." Students painted
the wooden edifice blue to depict water and affixed Dymaxion Map sections
for continents. He delighted in comparing photographs of the earth with

the Geoscope and in using it to think about global relations.[84] Connecting his maps and domes illustrated the link he made between the mechanical/ organic configuration of the globe and its politics. In these artifacts, he declared his conviction that the world was one synergetic whole.

Maps are, as political and cultural theorists explain, abstracts that may be used as *models of* or *models for* something, be it a tangible, objective reality or a vision. Fuller's maps fell into the second category. Through them, he called for the development of a peaceful, equitable international community and smoothly operating spaceship earth. He named his domes "world-around structures" to fit his global vision of "one world town."[85] Just as each part of his dome relied on its neighboring part for stability, so he felt that each part of the earth was crucial to the whole. By joining the dome and globe to form the Geoscope, he could depict his global village.

Fuller's whole-world lens offered ways of reconceptualizing life in the midst of the tumultuous twentieth century. At odds with those who declared this the "American Century" and articulated a Cold War containment ethos, he declared his passion for global unity. To combat imperialism and promote peace, he stressed connections. "We can see by experiment with this map," he wrote, quoting the poet of imperialism Rudyard Kipling, why one "laughs at the suggestion that '*East is East and West is West and never the twain shall meet.*'" Manipulating the map so that the North Pole sat in the center allowed one to see countries in close relation to one another. Later, he concluded, "The old east/west, north/south separations, with each nation looking out for itself, are no longer valid. The fragmentation of the world into nations that was logical yesterday . . . is no longer valid or socio-economically tenable." Instead, he promoted a holistic outlook: "We have not been seeing our Spaceship Earth as an integrally-designed machine which to be persistently successful must be comprehended and serviced in total." To see in total and meet the needs of all meant a decentering of the Northern Hemisphere: "No longer need the American continents, for instance, with only twelve per cent of the world population, occupy relentlessly the central and non-distorted portion of the world map, assigning fifty-two per cent of the world's population to an insignificant, fragmented, and distorted Asiatic borderline position."[86] Such statements resonated with growing numbers in the 1960s. NASA's photographs of the earth, taken in the 1960s and 1970s, especially shots of a whole earth floating in space, reinforced Fuller's global, holistic perspective. They altered human perceptions of their place in the world and encouraged readings of the earth as one "global village," as Marshall McLuhan phrased it (McLuhan's conception was influenced by Teilhard's global ideas).[87]

Conceptualizing the world as one unitary whole affected Fuller's politics; he preferred to see himself as a world citizen and a champion for global peace. He insisted that he represent himself and not America at the U.S.

National Exhibit in the Soviet Union in 1959. He also participated in nongovernmental cultural exchanges organized by *Saturday Review* editor Norman Cousins. The Dartmouth Conference, as it came to be known, was designed to bridge differences with the Russians, especially after an American U-2 spy plane was shot down over Russia in May 1960. The first of these citizen-to-citizen talks began in October 1960 at Dartmouth College and continued for forty years. Fuller joined Cousins and other prominent citizens from both countries, including Marian Anderson, Zbigniew Brzezinski, John Kenneth Galbraith, Alexander Korneichuk, James Michener, and David Rockefeller, at several of these conferences, held at various locations in the United States and Russia.[88]

In his most popular book, *Operation Manual for Spaceship Earth* (1963), Fuller criticized politicians and promoted global reallocation of wealth, labor, and resources. Later books such as *Utopia or Oblivion* and *Critical Path* made his utopian dreams more explicit and called for more global engagement. In his projects, he tried to work cross-culturally. He traveled to Asia frequently and met with Asian leaders, including India's Jawaharlal Nehru and his daughter, Indira Gandhi. In 1969 he delivered the Jawaharlal Nehru Memorial Lecture in New Delhi, and in 1983 he coauthored a book with scholar Anwar Dil. In their collaborative venture, the authors attempted to represent East and West not as opposites but as symmetrical and complementary.[89] Optimistic that the world could be united, he predicted that by the end of the century "the word 'nation' is going to be...obsolete."[90] In its place, one spaceship earth would suffice. If he saw a mushroom cloud as an impetus for his designs, it was not as a symbol of destructive power meant to evoke fear. Rather, it signaled that the world was bound together by that terrifying act in such a way that made survival paramount.

Of all his creations, probably nothing promoted his message better than his World Game. Already using maps to discuss humanity's relationship with the earth and each other, he called on people in the 1960s to focus on environmental, population, energy, and other concerns through a set of simulated exercises. An antidote to Cold War military games and an interdisciplinary, constructivist approach to education, World Game began as part of Southern Illinois University's core curriculum in 1961. Students used Fuller's resource inventory, geometry, and maps to pose practical, sustainable solutions to world problems. The motto read: "To make the world work in the shortest possible time through spontaneous cooperation without ecological offense or the disadvantage of anyone." From there, people played the game in various venues, from small workshops to large conferences. In 1967, when NASA announced plans to collect data via remote sensing planes and satellites, Fuller presented his organizational tools at a Senate committee, White House meetings, and a United Nations conference.[91]

Until a massive heart attack ended his life in 1983, Fuller continued to press others to create sustainable options for spaceship earth. His followers did as well. Workshop leader Gene Youngblood wrote articles promoting World Game for the *Los Angeles Free Press*, *Earth Times*, and *Whole Earth Catalog*.[92] Fuller and another workshop leader, Medard Gabel, cofounded the World Game Institute in 1972 to gather and disseminate information. Gabel became the executive director, created more simulations, and published *Energy, Earth, and Everyone: A Global Strategy for Spaceship Earth*. In 1996, the institute recorded data from every country on "mineral and agricultural resources, literacy levels, human rights records, soil conditions, medical facilities, average incomes, environmental problems, and life expectancies."[93]

Spreading his message of technological salvation, sustainability, and global unity through architecture, cartography, cultural exchanges, writings, lectures, and the World Game, Fuller attracted students, futurist thinkers, and artists who used, modified, expanded, and promoted his holistic approach. He especially drew a host of countercultural environmentalists and ecological design architects, many of whom made up the burgeoning alternative (or appropriate) technologies (AT) movement. This group read his books and attended his lectures. Moreover, these individuals joined with him to achieve similar objectives. The structural engineer's comprehensive design science, as historian Andrew Kirk explained in his study of countercultural environmentalists, attracted and required "flexible holistic thinkers who cast their nets wide in the sea of science, design, and mathematics." One of those individuals, J. Baldwin, first heard Fuller describe his interdisciplinary method, design ethics, and vision of an interconnected world in 1955. Fuller's words set the architectural student on a lifetime of experimentation that put Baldwin at the front of the ecological design revolution and connected him with Stewart Brand and others in the AT movement. Baldwin worked with Fuller on a variety of projects and served as an editor for the *Catalog*.[94]

Sharing Fuller's technological enthusiasm and holistic sensibility, Brand began the *Whole Earth Catalog* in 1968 to showcase books, machines, tools, and any number of products to help people grow personally, live more self-sufficiently, and act in an eco-friendly way. Amid product details and ordering information, Brand scattered mini-essays promoting whole-systems thinking and holistic practices. Like Fuller, he believed that giving individuals access to tools for living could empower individuals and save the planet. Human action as a saving force was something Rachel Carson only reluctantly concluded. Brand, on the other hand, enthusiastically proclaimed, "We are as gods, and might as well get good at it."[95]

Fuller, Baldwin, Brand, and others congregated around a "nexus of ideas about nature, New Urbanism, technology, and quality of life that offered a different path toward ecological harmony" than conservationists in the Sierra Club and Wilderness Society, who made wilderness the ideal and who looked askance at modernity. This new breed of counterculture environmentalists held some things in common with other counterculturalists and environmentalists. They took seriously the dangerous consequences of some technological innovations, questioned their complex capitalistic society, and identified social ills. Many detested nuclear proliferation and military conquest, American consumerism, tract housing, highway mazes, gridlocked traffic, and fast-food dining that fed the military-industrial complex and the suburban-industrial complex.[96] But this strain of environmentalists, akin with Fuller, argued that the problem was not technology per se or overpopulation or resource scarcity. Consequently, they rejected a return to preindustrial life. Instead of throwing the machine out of the garden, they created and adopted what they hoped were appropriate technologies for contemporary life and a sustainable planet. They reasoned, as Kirk notes, that "technology used amorally created the social and environmental problems of industrial capitalism; therefore, technology used morally and ecologically could create a revolution toward a utopian future."[97]

Especially in the Southwest, with its libertarian ethic, dry climate, abundant sunshine, and wide-open spaces, whole-systems thought and alternative technologies became popular. In New Mexico, Arizona, and California, designer Steve Baer, solar architect Peter Van Dresser, *Shelter* author and publisher Lloyd Kahn, and *Septic Tank Practices* author and another *Whole Earth* editor Peter Warshall created ecologically friendly housing designs, alternative energy sources, recycling machines, and household waste and conservation systems. These pragmatists created practical tools for living, with goals of making a light footprint upon the earth. Fuller's "doing more with less philosophy" fed this circle, as did the ideas of others, including British economist E. F. Schumacher, whose book *Small Is Beautiful* (1973) called for more local, adaptive, and wise use technology in order to promote a more just distribution of resources and environmental stewardship. Schumacher and other AT advocates denounced large, centralized, corporate economic and political structures as impersonal. Instead, they sought to humanize technology by making it smaller, local, and accountable to those it served. Concurrently, they advocated a more holistic lifestyle of self-reliance, home production, do-it-yourself technologies, and neighborly care. The *Whole Earth Catalog* served a group hungry for how-to manuals, do-it-yourself kits, low-technology skills, and self-care health books. Here were tools for just about anything, including how to put a roof over one's head.[98]

Domes became one of the emblematic symbols of the appropriate technologies and countercultural movements, and Drop City, Colorado, became one of the first places to adopt the circular home as the norm. This hippie artist commune in southeastern Colorado, as historian Timothy Miller explained, "brought together most of the themes of its predecessor communities—anarchy, pacifism, sexual freedom, drugs, open membership, art—and wrapped them in an exuberance and an architecture that trumpeted the coming of a new communal era." The commune's name originated from the art practiced by founders Clark Richert and Gene and Jo Ann Bernofsky, who met in Lawrence, Kansas, in 1961. After painting rocks, they dropped them from an upstairs window onto the street below and watched reactions. In 1965, they traveled west and for $450 purchased seven acres outside of Trinidad, Colorado, to pursue art on a large environmental canvas. Soon after, they heard Fuller discuss his dome in Boulder. Inspired, the impoverished threesome scavenged for resources and built two domes. Steve Baer, a practiced Zome (his version of the dome) builder from Albuquerque, joined them. With salvaged car parts and other materials, they built several more domes to house an increasing population.[99]

Domes symbolized efficiency and promoted a more sustainable, environmentally friendly world. Hence, Drop City dwellers lived Fuller's revolution by design, as Richert noted: "Like Fuller, we were interested in the new, alternative technologies—solar energy, wind energy, and recycling."[100] In 1967, a pleased Fuller gave Drop City his Dymaxion Innovative and Economic Housing construction award. Before the commune disappeared in 1973, the artists, with media attention, popularized the dome.

While easy assembly and affordability made these domes practical, the dome shape, complete with Fuller's philosophical underpinnings, made them a countercultural symbol. For Drop City dropouts and *Whole Earth* consumers, domes, in form and function, communicated an antimaterialistic, antiestablishment, and back-to-nature ethic. Counterculturalists used these circular spaces to make a philosophical, even spiritual statement. At odds with society's boundaries and "square" living, nonconformists rejected rectilinear ramblers and their accompanying white-picket fences marking the parameters of square lots. Communal architecture critic Doug Dahlin noted that dome inhabitants "hate square rooms." Drop City member Bill Voyd agreed; the dome refuted the common house, where "corners constrict the mind." Unlike rectangular Levittown houses, the circular construction suggested a communitarian, often romantic, and sometimes utopian ethic. "Domes are advanced," John Curl, a three-year resident of Drop City, wrote in his memoir. "All these rectangles make our heads into boxes." Domes free up "your inner harmonies." In this, countercultural dome dwellers made a holistic declaration, and as historian James Farrell has observed, "In the Age of the Organization Man,... an age when bureaucracies specialized and divided people functionally and hierarchically, holistic informality was an attraction for many people."[101]

These communitarian ethics echoed nineteenth-century ideas and architectural spaces. Orson Fowler designed octagonal houses, churches, and schools. His book *The Octagon House: A Home for All* went through nine printings. By the Civil War, hundreds of octagon homes had been erected in forty states.[102] At the Oneida Community, members crafted a song to articulate their philosophy: "We have built us a dome / On our beautiful plantation / And we all have one home / And one family relation." One hundred years later, the spirit of one, the search for a whole life and communal solidarity was captured, with much merriment and satire, at another communal experiment started in California by some of Ken Kesey's Merry Pranksters. Hog Farm members occasionally hit the road to proselytize for commune life, exhibiting in Dadaist fashion the countercultural lifestyle. Portable domes, along with music and slides, helped them communicate the practicalities of alternative living. One of their songs harkened back to the Oneida Community: "We built a big dome (a domelette next to what we're into now) out of rubber hose, wooden dowels, and this enormous yellow parachute, under which we would gather in circles and search for our center."[103]

Fuller's ideas reached beyond the counterculture to influence academics and social reformers for decades. At the end of the 1960s, a new generation of architects, including the Paris group Utopie, employed Fuller's principles to design pneumatic forms and nontraditional, efficient structures.[104] In 1993, Justiceville/Homeless USA, a nonprofit organization led by Ted Hayes with some assistance from Jamie Snyder, Fuller's grandson, created a village of twenty "omnispheres" in downtown Los Angeles to aid homeless people.[105] Peter Pearce, a former student of Fuller's, helped engineer Biosphere Two near Tucson, Arizona, a closed ecological system. The complex, complete with two geodesics, reflected Fuller's environmental design ideas.[106] Design science gained renewed interest in the first decade of the twenty-first century as an increasing number of news reports highlighted shrinking supplies of oil, coal, and other natural resources. Scientific studies on global warming further raised the alarm level. Concerned about the planet's sustainability yet excited about the power of technology to usher in a better world, scientists, designers, environmentalists, and everyday citizens dedicated themselves to creating concrete, efficient solutions to address transportation issues, health concerns, poverty, and political turmoil. The Buckminster Fuller Institute promoted action. In 2007, it initiated an annual contest with a cash prize of $100,000 to "support the development and implementation of a solution with significant potential to solve the world's most pressing problems in the shortest possible time while enhancing the Earth's ecological integrity."[107]

From cartography to mathematics to geodesic domes, Fuller communicated his whole-systems thinking and belief that technology and nature were two halves of one whole. His ideas and inventions—from the government to the counterculture, from banks to sporting arenas, from Epcot to the Biosphere—found wide play in the culture. To those concerned about social equity, fair housing, and sustainability, he provided a way for keeping technology and the garden.

The technological dilemma was one of the central problems that holists Fuller and Rachel Carson grappled with after World War II, with each hoping to integrate a fractured world of promise and danger. But they interpreted nature and technology with different eyes, and the solutions they proposed varied tremendously. Consequently, their holistic responses to mid-twentieth-century problems were equally diverse. Carson's vision ran more in line with the nineteenth-century writer Henry Adams, who contended that machines intruded upon the landscape, disturbed its bucolic appeal, ravaged its natural wonders, and initiated a fatal chain of events.[108] Carson argued that technology, coupled with human greed, overuse, ignorance, and American corporate capitalism—especially manifest in the chemical industry—caused all sorts of terrible repercussions that ultimately would destroy the garden. Fuller agreed that human beings had not always been wise with technology, and he faulted waste in the capitalistic system, but his "middle ground" presented a more sanguine picture. He happily placed the machine in the garden. Design science "would enable humankind to live better and in closer harmony with nature."[109] Thus, while she hummed a holism in the minor key, he trumpeted tunes of progress. She looked back, he looked forward; she warned of disaster, he anticipated success.

Despite these differences, both found receptive audiences. Indeed, diverse shades of holism contributed to the success of this worldview, as each held unique appeal. As the next pages reveal, Martin Luther King Jr. added to holism's power. His message of integration echoed some of the same problems Carson and Fuller addressed and attracted some of the same people. But the crises King confronted also gave his holistic oratory a distinctive ring that beckoned different crowds. His communitarian ethic addressed social inequities, fractured relations, histories of oppression, and unfulfilled ideals at the same time it communicated the possibility of a beloved community.

Martin Luther King Jr. at press conference, Gracie Mansion, New York City, July 30, 1964. *World Telegram and Sun* photo by Dick DeMarsico. *Courtesy of Library of Congress, LC-USZ62-122988*

3

The Social World

Martin Luther King Jr.'s Beloved Community

In the middle of the summer of 1962, Baptist minister and civil rights leader Martin Luther King Jr. went before the National Press Club in Washington, D.C., to explain the pursuit of his beloved community. His values, he announced, were America's values. His quest for equality and justice was the same as that inscribed in the Declaration of Independence and U.S. Constitution. Already well known for his leadership role in the Montgomery bus boycott, freedom marches, and nonviolent philosophy for social change, he announced then and a year later at the March on Washington that he was "simply seeking to bring into full realization the American dream." This dream, promised to African Americans a hundred years earlier by Abraham Lincoln in the Emancipation Proclamation, foretold an "equality of opportunity, of privilege and property widely distributed." Achieving this, the preacher declared, would create "a land where men no longer argue that the color of a man's skin determines the content of his character...where every man will respect the dignity and worth of human personality." In that day, "the jangling discords of our nation will be transformed into a beautiful symphony of brotherhood."[1]

The brotherhood King imagined followed a holistic score; its lyrics anticipated a day of individual wholeness and communal oneness. Grappling with troubles that divided individuals from their community, he sought a more perfect union. Like W. E. B. DuBois, the Baptist preacher thought that "the problem of the Twentieth Century is the problem of the color-line." Racism, King said, was "the hound of hell which dogs the tracks of our civilization."[2] The root of this evil, he claimed, was "man's hostility to man," manifested primarily in racism, poverty, and war.[3] To end these injustices, he trumpeted individual dignity and argued that all should be brought into the fold of American life, given equal access to earning a just wage, and assured the power of the vote. To exact these practical realities, he articulated a communitarian ethic that linked the good of the individual with the good of the whole. His vision inspired others to conceive and nurture a community knit together in brotherly love; a community that esteemed all members as valuable; a community that promoted the full functioning of its citizens; a community not fragmented into classes or races but united as one. In all his marches, petitions, sermons, sit-ins, speeches, and voter registration drives, the goal was the same: "the end is reconciliation; the end is redemption; the end is the creation of the beloved community." In this, King's holism fed yearnings for equality and nurtured communitarian visions that balanced individual rights against social responsibilities.[4] Like the hymn of the civil rights movement, "We Shall Overcome," the beloved community forecast a day of triumph against the ills that alienated and segregated one from another.

King presented his vision of a world interconnected and interdependent at the National Press Club during the same year, 1962, that countless Americans first read Carson's *Silent Spring*. Though addressing different problems, their messages sprang out of a similar organic framework. Like the zoologist, the establishment of the minister's beloved community rested upon a holistic perspective. "All life," he proclaimed, "is interrelated. All men are caught in an inescapable network of mutuality, tied in a single garment of destiny."[5] The difference was that while Carson imagined food chains and connections between wind, water, and soil, he focused on human beings of every stripe—black, brown, red, white, and yellow; rich and poor—united by love and bound together by bonds of mutuality. She employed her holism to fight the chemical industry; he used his rendition to combat economic, political, and social institutions that perpetuated racism, materialism, and militarism. She spoke to the relationship between human beings and their environment; he addressed relations between the individual and the community. Prompted to action by discrimination and poverty at home, decolonization and war abroad, King called for tighter bonds between individuals, within societies, and across national boundaries. He promised racial healing and a brotherhood that was more than a sum of its parts, more than a negation of the customs of segregation. In his hands, holistic interpretations of social and political relations reinforced American ideals of equality, invigorated the hopes of minorities and the impoverished, and united a diverse score of people worldwide in the pursuit of an ideal community.

The tale of King's march toward freedom has been told many times.[6] But few have interpreted his work in holistic terms. Instead, most have compartmentalized his life to fit within the civil rights movement. This is certainly important, but when we take a broader view of the man, we see that his thoughts and actions emanated from an organic understanding of life and that this holistic vantage point linked him with others, both within and without the civil rights movement. Like Buckminster Fuller, for example, he saw humanity connected as one, not separated by race, class, or national boundaries. For both, the earth was a global village.

Identifying King as a holist is not simply adding another category; rather, it is to locate him within the context of American society after World War II and to demonstrate practical ways that holistic ideas penetrated the culture. In his hands, holism became a powerful political tool to persuade and unite people. Just as Carson's employment of the "web of life" captured her audiences and instigated change, so too King's evocation of the "beloved community" stirred Americans to overcome toxic racial ideologies, dismantle segregation, and make significant strides toward ending disparities.[7] Envisioning a more harmonious whole and pushing for a more communitarian ethos proved to be one important catalyst for action.

King's vision and oratorical skills sparked significant social reform, but he did not act alone, and his vision was not the only option. He was but one in a long history of civil rights activists. He depended on the crucial involvement, organizational skills, and insights of contemporary leaders such as Ralph Abernathy, Ella Baker, Fannie Lou Hamer, John L. Lewis, Thurgood Marshall, A. J. Muste, Bayard Rustin, and Roy Wilkins. He acted in concert with countless foot soldiers, black and white, male and female, southern and northern, in such organizations as the National Association for the Advancement of Colored People (NAACP), the Congress of Racial Equality (CORE), and the Southern Christian Leadership Conference (SCLC). Different visions and strategies informed the work of those who defied segregationist practices throughout American history, and some actions were more successful at times than others. In the 1950s and throughout most of the 1960s, the integrationist model was particularly effectual in changing social and political policies, as well as the hearts and minds of many white people. Again, King, though certainly the most influential communicator, had help in crafting and spreading this organic philosophy. He borrowed heavily from black and white folk preachers, including whole sections and themes from the sermons of C. L. Franklin, Harry Emerson Fosdick, and J. Wallace Hamilton, as King scholar Keith Miller ably demonstrates. Indeed, as Miller shows, King's blending of black and white traditions gave him added authority among both whites and blacks. In addition, his inner circle shared strategies, helped draft speeches, and protested and faced jail time together. Jointly these people, sharing a communalistic perspective, achieved reforms of national significance.[8] Though the enactment of the dream fell

short, its holistic ideals marked society in lasting ways, demonstrating yet
another arena in which holism resonated in America's long 1960s.

As the chapters on Carson and Fuller have done, this discussion traces
King's formation and dissemination of his worldview. Beginning with his
family and strong church ties, King drew on the African American Baptist
tradition, the Social Gospel, neoorthodoxy, personalist theology, and nonviolent strategies to forge his holistic faith. Through his experiences as pastor
and civil rights leader, he refined his faith to meet contemporary needs. He
married a like-minded woman, Coretta Scott (1953), and served as the pastor of Baptist churches in Montgomery, Alabama (1954–60), and Atlanta
(1960–68). The Montgomery bus boycott in 1955 and 1956 lifted him into a
leadership position and tutored him in nonviolent strategies for social
change. As he witnessed the end of colonialism, traveling to Ghana in 1957
and India in 1959, he sharpened his holistic understandings and global
communitarian ethic. Until his assassination in 1968, he articulated holistic
ideals and applied them to projects for integration and peace. In total, his
holistic frame functioned as an interpretive lens and motivating force. We
turn now to those formative moments.

King's worldview was grounded in the love and security he learned at his
Atlanta family's hearth and church pulpit. Born in 1929 to a family of preachers, he inherited a Christianity that recognized individual dignity, the importance of community support, and the ideals of love and justice. In his world,
church and family were intertwined. He was the son, grandson, and great-
grandson of preachers. His brother was a preacher, and so was his father's
brother. His mother and grandmother participated in church programs,
choirs, and prayer meetings. The church, King recognized, was his second
home. He did not have much choice but to enter the ministry. Growing up
in a close, disciplined, religious, and patriarchal family, he enjoyed a secure,
loving childhood. His father, a stern, self-confident, and charismatic soul,
gave and expected much. He believed his family setting helped him to imagine a loving God and to be more optimistic than pessimistic about human
nature.[9] It also predisposed him to a holism that rested on a communitarian
ethic and the kindness of a benevolent God.[10]

A keen sense of justice shaped his holism, too. As theologian Benjamin
Mays has stated, African Americans have historically turned to God either
for help "to endure hardship, suffer pain, and withstand maladjustment" or
for motivation "to eliminate the source of the ills they suffer." King fell especially into the second tradition. The minister felt, as historian Clayborne
Carson has noted, compelled to combat his society's inequities.[11] In this,
King followed his forefathers. Few records remain of his great-grandfa-
ther, but census and church accounts of Shiloh Baptist Church in Greene
County, Georgia, indicate that Willis Williams, a slave to a prosperous

planter, was "an old slavery time preacher" and "exhorter" before the Civil War.[12] His son Adam Daniel (A. D.) emulated his father by playing minister to children in his community, preaching at animal funerals and leading shouts. In 1893, A. D. left sharecropping to preach in Atlanta—just as King Sr. would do years later. In the city, Williams took over the 13-member Ebenezer Baptist Church and increased the membership to 900. In 1926, King Sr. married Williams's daughter and served as Ebenezer's minister after Williams died. This was the same Ebenezer that King Jr. copastored with his father from 1960 until 1968. Each made Ebenezer one of the most politically active and influential churches in Atlanta.

Williams and King Sr. pushed for social change long before King Jr. took center stage. They did so in black organizations and interracial groups, within and without Christian circles, locally and nationally. Each participated in protests against segregation, economic discrimination, and political disenfranchisement. Each held leadership positions in Atlanta's branch of the NAACP; Williams, in 1917, petitioned the school board for better education for black children. He helped defeat the board of education's plan to end seventh-grade classes for blacks so that a new junior high school might be built for whites. After he became chapter president, he led a successful voter registration campaign and toppled a referendum that would have disproportionately allocated funds to white schools.[13] King Sr. regularly defied segregation's rules, rode whites-only elevators, and disregarded discriminatory store policies. When leading the NAACP chapter, he championed voter rights and equalization of teachers' salaries. In the pulpit, he preached a social gospel and urged fellow ministers to do the same: "The Church is to touch every phase of the community life. We are to do something about the broken-hearted, poor, unemployed, the captive, the blind, and the bruised."[14] This social gospel, so essential to his elders, became King Jr.'s.

The young man learned the social gospel from women, too. Though denied pastoral roles, black females traditionally sustained the church with committee work, outreach, and volunteer networks. His mother and grandmother operated in these capacities to make Ebenezer a powerful social force. Jennie Williams led the missionary society and participated in local and national Baptist women conventions. Alberta King contributed to the musical and spiritual life of Ebenezer.[15] Coretta Scott King strengthened her husband's commitment to a social Christianity with her faith and fight against racism. Before marrying in 1953, she held membership in civil rights organizations and the Progressive Party. Being denied a teaching position because of the color of her skin strengthened her activist spirit. After marriage, she joined her husband in the Montgomery boycott rallies and singing at marches.[16] This was a family, then, that embraced a version of Christianity that spoke to the material and spiritual—to the whole of life.

By attending Christian colleges, becoming a minister, and speaking for the underprivileged, King Jr. declared allegiance to his family's belief system.

King's engagement in the religious life of the black Baptist church must not be minimized. It is key to understanding his theology, crucial to comprehending his social vision, and central to his holistic sensibilities. Early scholarship on King highlighted his academic achievements and noted his intellectual debts to white theologians and philosophers. More recent studies have provided an important corrective, pointing to the fundamental role of the black church. Clayborne Carson wrote that King "acquired his basic convictions through daily immersion in the life of Ebenezer." Theologian James H. Cone agreed; the minister was "a product of the black church.... The most significant circumstances that shaped King's theology, in my judgment, were the oppression of black people and the liberating message of the black church."[17]

Whereas he actively participated in the church throughout his life, King was not without questions, and working out his theology took time. He eventually discarded more fundamentalist aspects of Baptist doctrine while retaining belief in a personal God, the dignity of the individual, and the importance of social commitments. "From the age of thirteen on doubts began to spring forth unrelentingly," he confessed. By fifteen, when he began his education at Atlanta's Morehouse College, he wondered whether the bodily resurrection of Jesus was true. As an undergraduate, many Sunday school lessons fell by the wayside: "It was at this period that the shackles of fundamentalism were removed from my body."[18] Like other twentieth-century holists, he could not square scientific facts with biblical fundamentalism, and so he abandoned a literal interpretation of the Bible.[19] He wondered how religion could accommodate, intellectually and emotionally, scientific findings and modernity, but his questions did not sidetrack his spirituality. Instead, he welcomed scientific contributions; investigated alternative interpretations; embraced ideas from multiple perspectives in America, Asia, and Europe; and developed answers that supported his faith and social reform impulses. Throughout, the teachings of his faith-filled family and church conditioned him, as Professor of Religion and African American Studies Cornel West has noted, to accept, reject, or modify ideas he encountered.[20]

Education strengthened King's social vision in several ways. At Morehouse (1944–48), where he acquired a sociology degree, at Crozer Theological Seminary (1948–51), where he gained a divinity degree, and at Boston University (1951–55), where he earned a doctorate in systematic theology, he studied under many socially engaged intellectuals. Morehouse president and longtime family friend Benjamin Mays modeled political participation and a liberal faith, galvanizing, in turn, King's commitment to a socially relevant Christianity. King also credited Henry David Thoreau, Mahatma Gandhi, Walter Rauschenbusch, Reinhold Niebuhr, L. Harold DeWolf, and Edgar Sheffield Brightman as influential on his religious and social thought.[21] Of those he read at Crozer, Rauschenbusch proved to be one of the most influential, leaving, King said, "an indelible imprint on my thinking by giving me a theological basis for the social concern which had already grown up in me as a result of my early experiences."[22]

Known for his role in the Social Gospel movement, Baptist theologian Rauschenbusch (1861–1918) spread his progressive vision and liberal theology through well-known books such as *Christianity and the Social Crisis* (1907) and *A Theology for the Social Gospel* (1917). Believing human beings were essentially good, he laid the problem of evil at society's feet. Living at a time of high immigration, industrialization, and urbanization, he was concerned about squalid living conditions, unfair labor practices, unjust wages, and poor working conditions. Instead of waiting for heaven, he called for social reform in this world. Only a community-oriented religion based on love, cooperation, and the spiritual and physical care of each neighbor could right the wrongs of the capitalistic system and usher in the kingdom of God on earth.[23]

Though he later faulted Rauschenbusch for promoting "a superficial optimism concerning man's nature" and for "identifying the Kingdom of God with a particular social and economic system," King's vision of the beloved community owed much to Rauschenbusch's Social Gospel. Rauschenbusch buttressed the socially vibrant Christianity of King's family and church, affirming that a religion devoid of social concern was not worth holding. King praised Rauschenbusch for preaching a gospel that "deals with the whole man—not only his soul but his body; not only his spiritual well-being but his material well-being." King added that any religion that "professes concern for the souls of men and is not equally concerned about the slums that damn them, the economic conditions that strangle them, and the social conditions that cripple them is a spiritually moribund religion."[24] Hence, King's rendering of the gospel made a holistic contention that the gospel addressed body, mind, and spirit. It did not end with the soul; it did not stop with spiritual salvation. Furthermore, his holism yoked the welfare of the individual to the health of the community.

Caring for both the total human and the collective well-being became his holistic pivot points. Material concerns without spiritual insight, for which he criticized Marx, were as bankrupt in his eyes as spiritual matters ignorant of physical needs, something for which he condemned the white church. He later mocked the "pious irrelevancies and sanctimonious trivialities" of white Christians who did little to ameliorate social inequities. Instead of acting as a "thermostat" and setting the opinions of society, many white ministers, to his dismay, acted more like a "thermometer," maintaining, pathetically and passively, the social climate.[25]

Rauschenbusch's liberalism ultimately failed to satisfy King fully. He felt it did not address the problem of evil sufficiently. Specifically, he thought Rauschenbusch's espousal of humanity's essential goodness flew in the face of America's vicious racism. Born in Atlanta at the height of Jim Crow, King knew the segregated system well. He lived in a black neighborhood, attended black schools, joined a black church, drank from "colored" drinking fountains, and sat—or stood if whites needed seats—in the back of the bus. He dared not play in a public park, swim in a public pool, eat at a downtown lunch counter, or step into a white theater. He observed his parents' troubles, too. He was with his father when King Sr. asked for a pair of shoes in a department store and was told by a clerk to go to the back for service. King Sr. marched out, muttering, "I don't care how long I have to live with this system, I will never accept it." On another day, when a policeman stopped his father for a traffic violation, the officer referred to King Sr. as a "boy." His father snapped back that he was not a boy but a man and that he would not listen if his manhood was not acknowledged. The child also learned the power—both legal and vigilante—of the system he and his father hated. He watched the Ku Klux Klan beat a black person, and he walked near areas where whites lynched blacks. Like his father, he said he could never adjust to the black and white divide, "partly because the separate was always unequal, and partly because the very idea of separation did something to my sense of dignity and self-respect." To illustrate, he called to mind a train ride: "The first time that I was seated behind a curtain in a dining car I felt as if the curtain had been dropped on my selfhood." The segregated system was to him cruel, "rationally inexplicable and morally unjustifiable."[26]

By the time King was reading Rauschenbusch, America's apartheid system was more than a half century old. And the paradox within American history that Jim Crow rested upon was older still. From its inception, the United States espoused equality as an ideal but rejected its full implementation in practice.[27] In 1944, Swedish sociologist Gunnar Myrdal highlighted this disparity in his groundbreaking study, *An American Dilemma.*[28] Though King occasionally referred to the Myrdal report, he and other African Americans needed no survey to convince them of the discord they felt between abstract political theory and action. They knew racism firsthand in Atlanta's separate facilities, on Mississippi's farms, and in Chicago's slums. When King described a man "whose children are being plagued by rats and roaches, whose wife is robbed daily at overpriced ghetto food stores, who himself is working for about two-thirds the pay of a white person doing a similar job and with similar skills," African Americans recognized the universality of his story; they knew the teenage boys who experienced "life as a madhouse of violence and degradation."[29] As he stated in 1962, "Only a Negro can understand the social leprosy that segregation inflicts upon him. The suppressed fears and resentments, and the expressed anxieties and sensitivities make each day of life a turmoil.... He is shackled in his waking moments to tiptoe stance, never quite knowing what to expect next."[30]

No doubt King's thoughts about human depravity were reinforced during his studies by international and personal events as well as other theological perspectives. News of the atrocities of World War II, colonial uprisings, the nuclear arms race, and the Cold War exposed humanity's inhumanity. And in a much more limited yet personal way, he was reminded again of injustice at Crozer when a student pointed a gun at him and when he was refused service at a tavern. Readings in neoorthodox theology also cast doubt on liberalism's sanguine assumptions. Particularly as voiced by theologian Reinhold Niebuhr in such books as *Moral Man and Immoral Society* (1932), this Christian realist view stressed humanity's sinful nature and excoriated the idea of progress. Niebuhr's books impressed King, who wrote: "While I still believed in man's potential for good, Niebuhr made me realize his potential for evil as well. Moreover, Niebuhr helped me to recognize the complexity of man's social involvement and the glaring reality of collective evil."[31]

Disabuse of the idea of innate goodness by personal experiences, the black church's teaching, historical and contemporary events, and Niebuhr's theology did not translate into pessimism. Rather, King reconciled liberalism and neoorthodoxy by maintaining an emphasis on sin and the need for repentance at the same time that he affirmed the possibility of goodness and the potential for social progress. Thinking it best to avoid extremes, he asserted in a 1949 college paper that "man is neither good nor bad by nature, but has potentialities for either."[32] Again, the racism he experienced coupled with the eschatological hope of justice percolating through black theology helped him arrive at these conclusions.

While both the Social Gospel and neoorthodoxy contributed to King's worldview, neither gave him the solid foundation to build his beloved community. But personalism did. As he expressed it, the personalist philosophy triggered "two convictions: it gave me metaphysical and philosophical grounding for the idea of a personal God, and it gave me a metaphysical basis for the dignity of all human personality."[33] From these guiding principles, he came to think in holistic terms of the world as an interlocking system of unique, valuable, worthy, rational persons. Each person was related to another. Each—black and white, rich and poor—was an integral part of the community, important as individuals and vital to the organic whole. This is what the preacher imagined when he exclaimed all were interrelated, when he explained that human beings are "caught in an inescapable network of mutuality; tied in a single garment of destiny." In significant ways, personalism, in conjunction with the faith of his fathers, shaped his vision of the beloved community and affected his fight for civil rights, economic justice, and world peace. Because of its critical importance for King's thought, it requires unpacking both as a general philosophical system and for how it was given expression in the American experience. Personalism, it turns out, helps elucidate this 1960s holistic moment.

Coined by Walt Whitman in 1868, personalism has long roots, reaching back to the humanitarian philosophies of Kant, Hegel, Pascal, and a variety of Greek philosophers, including Protagorus. It rests on the assumption, as King put it, "that the clue to the meaning of ultimate reality is found in personality."[34] Some branches of personalism have emphasized the spiritual and communitarian view of the person. For example, in the 1930s, French Catholic intellectuals Emmanuel Mounier, Jacques Maritain, and others articulated a theistic personalism. Revolting against both capitalism and communism, they suggested that people had intrinsic value because they were created in God's image; they were ends in themselves, fulfilled through community. As ends and not means, people did not owe allegiance to the state; instead, the political community existed for the growth of whole persons.

Echoing these views, American personalists at midcentury scorned cultural forces they perceived as depersonalizing. Repelled by the Holocaust, nuclear arms races, and an atomistic view of individuals, they espoused a communitarian ethic that prioritized individual worth and spoke to matters of conscience, ethics, morality, and human will. Personalists such as Dorothy Day, Allen Ginsberg, Peter Maurin, A. J. Muste, and Bayard Rustin resisted institutions, organizations, and factories that regarded human beings as mere cogs in an assembly line. Rather, personalists conceived of human beings as worthy because of their intrinsic, rather than their utilitarian, value.[35] King was one of these personalists. In *Where Do We Go from Here* (1967), he wrote, "We must rapidly begin the shift from a 'thing'-oriented society to a 'person'-oriented society. When machines and computers, profit motives and property rights are considered more important than people, the giant triplets of racism, materialism, and militarism are incapable of being conquered."[36] The converse, he believed, was also true. When people are treated as ends in themselves, as persons with dignity rather than impersonal pegs in a system or puppets of a government, then injustices could be overcome and community made possible.

American personalism owed much of its development to Methodists at Boston University in the 1950s. Certainly King did. Two leading proponents, Edgar S. Brightman and Harold DeWolf, served as King's doctoral advisers.[37] By graduation, personalist theology became the anchor of his holism, securing his belief in a personal God, the whole person, reconciliation between peoples, and social solidarity.

One part of King's anchor focused on relationships between human beings and the deity. The second addressed relationships between human beings. Boston personalists such as Borden Parker Bowne asserted that God was personal, rational, and loving. He defined personhood as conscious and self-identifying.[38] Given this, personalists further posited that human beings could enjoy relationship with God. Brightman argued that rationality and consciousness made personal interactions and community possible; the universe was an "interacting system of persons" that is "social and interpersonal."[39] Albert Knudson concurred but added that human fellowship with God would be impossible "without freedom and intelligence." Communion, he said, "can exist only between beings that know each other and take an emotional and volitional attitude toward each other." God, Knudson thought, had "a heart and will" and was "responsive to human need."[40] This allowed for communion. This logic appealed to King. Indeed, he liked Knudson's logic so much that he lifted the passage and put it in his dissertation. This and other acts of plagiarism in his speeches and sermons have been duly noted by King scholars. Without condoning the practice, such reliance on the words and ideas of others further substantiates the assertion that holistic thinking emphasizing the whole person and the linkages between individual and community was not an idiosyncratic expression but rather a part of a wider sensibility.[41]

Holding the theological position that God was "a personal spirit immanent in nature and in the value structure of the universe," King distanced himself from several contemporary Christian theologians.[42] He found Karl Barth's notion of God as "wholly other" too removed from personal experience. His dissertation on the theology of Paul Tillich and Henry Nelson Wieman revealed his disdain for transcendent, impersonal definitions of God. Tillich argued that "the ground of being" was the source of all; Wieman posited that God was a process. Neither wished to define the divine in human terms. Instead, they scorned personalism's anthropocentrism. "We [should] not allow our wishes and needs to shape our idea of God," Wieman contended. The very idea of personality limited God.[43] King disagreed. Tillich's and Wieman's reasoning rested, he thought, "on a false conception of the nature of personality." Granting personhood does not bind God or make God human. "It is certainly true that human personality is limited," he wrote, "but personality as such involves no necessary limitation. It means simply self-consciousness and self-direction." Hence, he concluded that personality in complete and perfect form was realized in God and that the conception of God as personal does not imply any limitation.[44]

In essence, King had no trouble locating God within human terms. Instead, he found Tillich's and Wieman's theology lacking. How, he wondered, could one worship such an abstract God? How could one call on

Barth's "wholly other" or Tillich's "ground of being" for help in the midst of daily trials? To King, if one relinquished the personhood of God, then with it went a rational and loving God. God, "responsive to the deepest yearnings of the human heart," must possess "feeling and will." He (to King, God was decisively male—another anthropomorphizing characteristic) was intricately involved in human history. In a college exam, he wrote that this did not mean that God was so immanent as to be a part of nature, as pantheists conjectured.[45] God was behind and in the process, not "an unconscious process devoid of any true purpose," as he understood Wieman to be saying, or "an impersonal absolute devoid of life," as he understood Tillich to be saying.[46]

Personalist theology appealed to King, in part, because it described the God of African American Christianity. To have embraced Tillich's "ground of being" or Barth's "wholly other," he would have had to distance himself from the God of black theology, a God of triumph who actively comforted the oppressed.[47] Personalism fit with the black church's idea of a personal relationship with Jesus Christ. Cornel West explained: "The Christocentric language of the black church—of Jesus as the bright and morning star against the backdrop of the pitch darkness of the night, as water in dry places, a companion in loneliness, a doctor to the sick, a rock in a wearied land—exemplifies the intimate and dependent personal relationship between God and individual and between God and a world-forsaken people."[48] From the standpoint of many black churchgoers, religion was deeply personal, experientially real, and intellectually satisfying. "Martin believed all his life that God is both infinite and personal," Coretta Scott King wrote, "a loving Father who strives for good against the evil that exists in the universe."[49]

While he committed himself intellectually to a personal God, his faith became, as he put it, "more than a metaphysical category" when his family's life was threatened.[50] In the second month of the Montgomery bus boycott, King had what he termed his "kitchen experience." Things were going well until white people began making angry phone calls to his home. On January 27, 1956, the minister endured yet another: "Nigger, we are tired of you and your mess now, and if you aren't out of this town in three days, we're going to blow your brains out and blow up your house." King rose from bed and went to the kitchen table to pray: "Lord, I'm down here trying to do what's right.... But Lord, I must confess that I'm weak." Then he heard an "inner voice" exhorting him: "Martin Luther, stand up for righteousness. Stand up for justice. Stand up for truth. And lo I will be with you, even until the end of the world."[51] At this point Baptist sermons and personalist theology became personal. He felt affirmed, partnered with the supernatural, united in a mission of justice and love. Bearing witness to his faith, he declared later that he was "convinced that the universe is under the control of a loving purpose and that in the struggle for righteousness man has cosmic companionship."[52] This experience sustained him through more threats in Montgomery and dangers elsewhere. It helped him make sense of himself and others in a world that denied African Americans equality, dignity, and full personhood; it strengthened him as a leader; and it underscored the promise that he was one significant part of a divine whole.[53]

Through this kitchen experience, church teachings, and personalist theology, King formulated his belief that a vertical relationship between God and human beings was possible. This was the first component in the creation of his whole. The second, horizontal part of his communal ethos centered on relationships between human beings. Again, personalism aided his construction. Personalists stressed not only God's personhood but also human personality. DeWolf especially emphasized human dignity, rationality, freedom, and responsibility. While he acknowledged human transgressions, he rejected the doctrine of total depravity, saying if that were so, no individual would reach out for redemption or goodness.[54] Instead, in their spiritual nature and personality, human beings were godlike.[55] King agreed that all were created in God's image: "Every human being has etched in his personality the indelible stamp of the Creator."[56]

Again, personalism corresponded with the black church. The institution, a creative political and communal creation of a people in bondage, traditionally offered African Americans a profound sense of self and personhood despite the "social death"—to borrow sociologist Orlando Patterson's phrase—that white society imposed.[57] In the hands of slaves and freed blacks, the doctrine of the *imago Dei* had served as a powerful weapon of defiance. It countered the message of masters and segregationists.[58]

The consequences of personalism on the development of King's holistic interpretation of the world were profound. With this, he had the makings of his beloved community. Through personalism, he concluded that people were interlocked in relationships one to another. King agreed with Brightman, who stated that "the universe was an interacting system of persons.... Reality is social or interpersonal." He also concurred with Bowne, who wrote that reality is "an organic whole."[59] For all three, society was a whole made up of persons, and each person was an integral member of the community.

While Davis, DeWolf, Brightman, and other personalists had affirmed community and promoted the creation of a loving and cooperative brotherhood, it was King who applied it directly to social reform. Carrying with him the black church's focus on oppression, he was quick to recognize personalism's power in addressing human depravity and the racial divide.[60] Because human beings are created in God's image and all receive their value from their "relatedness to God," all are equal, he told a church conference in 1962. "The worth of an individual does not lie in the measure of his intellect, his racial origin, or his social position." Given this, he declared, "'whiteness' and 'blackness' pass away as determinants in a relationship, and 'son' and 'Brother' are substituted."[61] As King scholar John Ansbro explained, King's readiness to ascribe special value to all persons gave his message added weight. The preacher decreed: "Segregation stands diametrically opposed to the principle of the sacredness of human personality. It debases personality."[62] He reiterated this as he marched for civil rights. By acknowledging one another's personhood, he believed people could move "toward a world of brotherhood, cooperation and peace," and society could establish "true brotherhood, true integration, true person-to-person relationships."[63]

Comparing King's idealization of the beloved community with Rachel Carson's communal ideals indicates how differently holism could be marked in terms of gender. Unlike her feminine holism, he imagined a masculine community; his holistic construct—a "brotherhood" of believers submitted to the "fatherhood" of God—was largely patriarchal. Though he found equality between the sexes when quoting the biblical passage "In Christ, there is neither male nor female," and though he spoke of all having inherent worth, his message was inconsistent.[64] Focused on racism, he was blind to the discrimination women faced and contributed to it by adopting a doctrine of separate and unequal spheres. Raised in a male-centered home, he accepted a standard of male superiority. Women, though important, should play subordinate roles. His mother worked outside of the limelight. As a pastor and civil rights leader, he called on men and women for committee work, prayer circles, marches, and boycott work, but he elevated men to positions of authority while keeping women, including his wife, in the background. Women received his praise as "resourceful," "persevering," "caring and strong," but his inadequate recognition of female civil rights leaders such as Ella Baker and Fannie Lou Hamer testified to his belief that women should not wield too much power.[65]

This patriarchal perspective ultimately compromised his democratic rhetoric and distorted his vision of social equality. It is clear that King's sympathies resided more heavily with the black male's struggle for respect than with the plight of black women. Troubled by society's emasculation and infantilization of African American men physically, economically, socially, and politically, he lamented the affront on black men's sense of dignity. Under slavery and segregation, he mourned, the black man was never able to be a man. Ending segregation and restoring a sense of personhood would allow black men status, privilege, and power.[66] Thus, he promoted equality and affirmed black masculinity, but he did little to address inequities between male and female. Though his holism was limited, others borrowed from his formulation of the beloved community. In the latter decades of the twentieth century, womanist theology strove to correct his inequities, just as feminists labored to right social discrimination more broadly. Finding hope in the doctrine of *imago Dei* and King's organic frame, yet troubled by his patriarchal assumptions, Katie Cannon and Jacqueline Grant, for example, championed the personhood of black women in the same fashion that King did for black men.[67]

By the time King accepted a pastoral call to Montgomery, Alabama, in 1954, his dissertation was nearing completion and his holistic Christianity was fairly well established. As he put his holistic ideas into action, he modified and sharpened his thoughts. At the same time, he honed his preaching, mastering black folk oratorical traditions and blending in some language, themes, and patterns of white liberal sermons. He responded to and learned from fellow church members and activists, the civil rights movement's successes and challenges, and national and international events. Indeed, he became one part of a whole host of activities, and these in turn shaped who he was. "For Martin Luther King to be the Martin Luther King he was," Juanita Abernathy, Ralph Abernathy's wife, contended, "there had to be a whole lot of little folk...to give him the impetus." Or as Ella Baker poignantly asserted, "The movement made Martin."[68] The timing was perfect, too. He preached his first sermon as pastor at Dexter Avenue Baptist Church in the same month the U.S. Supreme Court declared segregation in public schools unconstitutional, the culmination of years of legal wrangling and lobbying by the NAACP. He joined the local NAACP and soon assumed a leadership role in a yearlong boycott of Montgomery's buses. Concurrently, independence movements around the world rejected oppressive colonial rule; it was a time of worldwide revolution.

The Montgomery bus boycott (December 5, 1955–December 21, 1956) positioned King for his national role in the civil rights movement. It gave him a leadership position, as E. D. Nixon noted, and a fledgling grassroots movement. Years of resistance readied Montgomery's black community for revolt against Jim Crow. The local NAACP was active, as were other civil rights groups. Before Rosa Parks, the forty-two-year-old seamstress and NAACP activist, denied her bus seat to a white man and took her case to the U.S. Supreme Court, others had acted with similar defiance, and boycott schemes swirled within the community. On March 2, 1955, fifteen-year-old Claudette Colvin was arrested, convicted, and placed on probation for refusing to give up her seat, claiming that "she was just as good as any white person."[69] In October of the same year, teenager Mary Louise Smith failed to move to a different bus seat and was taken into custody. When Parks was arrested on Thursday, December 1, 1955, she, with the encouragement of NAACP activist E. D. Nixon, challenged the law. Nixon, English professor Jo Ann Robinson, and other leaders began to organize a boycott. Mimeographed flyers, an orchestrated voice from church pulpits, and newspaper coverage spread the word so effectively that very few African Americans rode the buses on December 5. That day, the black community created the Montgomery Improvement Association, elected King as president, and held a mass meeting. Strengthened by King's oratory to act with love and for justice, the audience of thousands voted with a cheer to continue the boycott. For the next year, with encouragement from a team of dynamic leaders including Nixon, Ralph Abernathy, Rufus Lewis, and King, black people walked, hitchhiked, carpooled, shared taxis, and acquired rides from white employers. They stayed off the buses while Parks's case rose through the court system. Acting in concert, Montgomery protesters demonstrated a strong, communitarian ethic, and by the end of 1956 the U.S. Supreme Court found Alabama's bus segregation laws unconstitutional.

As the Montgomery boycott unfolded, King developed a nonviolent philosophy that was at once harmonious with the activism of his family, the black social gospel, and his personalistic, communitarian ethic. Gandhi's practice of satyagraha and conversations with American practitioners of peaceful strategies further convinced King that methods of nonviolence could be effective. "*Satya*," King approvingly noted, "is truth which equals love, and *agraha* is force; *Satyagraha*, therefore, means truth force or love force." This fit with King's belief that love, mounted with truth, could usher in justice.[70] Howard University president Mordecai Johnson initially spurred King's interest in Gandhi and freedom movements abroad. World War II conscientious objectors Bayard Rustin and Glenn Smiley tutored him in nonviolence practices and helped pioneer the mass Montgomery protests.[71] Later A. Philip Randolph, founder of the Brotherhood of Sleeping Car Porters, deepened King's commitment to nonviolence. So did lawyer, pacifist, and civil rights worker Harris Wofford, who with his wife wrote *India Afire*, a book about Gandhi's independence movement and how such strategies could spur civil rights in America.[72]

Though King initially expressed hesitation about the boycott, he assumed essential responsibilities. His rhetoric, moral convictions, and holistic vision provided courage and understanding. His call for self-respect and some-bodiness empowered people. His demand to sacrifice self-interest for the good of the community stimulated action. For example, when he solicited the Reverend Benjamin Simms to use leadership skills, he appealed to his communal sense, "We need you, Brother B. J., don't fail us" and "Do it for me and your people."[73] The good of the community to him extended to whites as well, and he framed the contest as a fight not of black over white but as justice over injustice. His practical ability to work with a variety of people, listen to individual needs, and raise money to make the boycott work also helped. At the same time, his sense of history and intimate knowledge of the longings of a people too long downtrodden helped him communicate that the time had come for changing the social fabric. Situating the boycott within a worldwide struggle for freedom also gave it greater significance. In the process, he helped unite the black community and drew white people into the fold; hence, Montgomery's boycott worked as a demonstration of the beloved community in action. In his vital role, he was one among many. Each individual depended on another for its success. Each bore a part for the good of the whole. As historian Stewart Burns recognized, the "boycott carried forward and consummated the communitarian lifeblood of the African American freedom struggle"; then it "served for a decade as the model community movement."[74]

Catapulted forward by Montgomery's success, the civil rights movement pushed across the south, with King at the forefront. In January 1957, he accepted the chairmanship of the newly formed Southern Christian Leadership Conference, and for the next eleven years, he translated his holistic vision of a beloved community into a social movement for civil rights, economic empowerment, and international accord. Throngs of people embraced the dream. He drew widespread praise in 1963 when he spoke to well over 200,000 people at the Lincoln Memorial, and he won international approval the next year when he won the Nobel Peace Prize. The movement gained power with President Lyndon B. Johnson's signing of the 1964 Civil Rights Act, which forbade discrimination in employment and public accommodations based on race, religion, national origin, or sex. A year later, following additional petitions, demonstrations, and the bloody march from Selma to Montgomery, Alabama, Congress acted again, and President Johnson signed the Voting Rights Act. When he did, he articulated the holistic cry for a beloved community, echoing King's language that this was not a black or white problem but an American problem; hence, all were responsible for overcoming racism's legacy. This act banned literacy tests and other discriminatory provisions used to disenfranchise minorities. The results were dramatic. Between 1964 and 1968, the percentage of black people who were registered to vote shot from 7 to 59 percent, causing dramatic shifts in the political configuration of the South. White Democrats contributed to this shift as well by leaving the party.[75] Broadening his message and campaign, King spoke out against the country's economic disparities and military actions. He delivered his last speech in Memphis, Tennessee, on April 3, 1968. The next day, at the Lorraine Motel, white segregationist James Earl Ray fired his rifle and ended King's life.[76] The civil rights activist was thirty-nine years old. In some of his final words, he alerted people to the threats he faced, while reminding them of his communal values: "I've seen the promised land. I may not get there with you. But I want you to know tonight, that we, as a people, will get to the promised land."[77]

As he fought for an integrated community fully congruous with his democratic ideals, King gave his holism concrete form. Paying attention to the ways he applied his holistic ideas to fighting racism, poverty, and militarism, as noted in several examples in the following, highlights how his organic philosophy empowered his message. In one speech after another, in sermons and protest cries, he articulated a communitarian ethic, teaching and inspiring others. He followed this with communal, nonviolent protests. He saluted individual worth—no matter the color—and then fused one to another in community. He argued that slavery, segregation, and racism had broken individuals and fractured communities; he insisted love, mutuality, equality, and integration could heal people and unite the whole. In doing so, he spoke to multiple audiences.

To Montgomery's black community in 1956, the preacher decried the enervating reality of slavery and segregation that had dehumanized and debilitated African Americans and called for a new identity that trumpeted self-worth. From "1619 when the first Negro slaves landed on the shores of this nation," and through the centuries of slavery, "the Negro was treated in a very inhuman fashion. He was a thing to be used, not a person to be respected. He was merely a depersonalized cog in a vast plantation machine." Slave owners knew this, he said, as calling slaves "hands" indicated. The "hand" serves a job; that is its purpose. "The only concern is performance, not well being." After slavery, treating "men as means rather than ends" continued. Jim Crow's "separate-but-equal" laws "led to a strict enforcement of the 'separate,' with hardly the slightest attempt to abide by the 'equal.'" As a result of this history, King exclaimed, many blacks "lost faith in themselves," taking on an identity of "nobodiness." They had come to feel that "perhaps they were less than human." But humans, he argued, were not things. They were intrinsically valuable. Consequently, the minister strove to instill a sense of "somebodiness," a "new self-respect and a new sense of dignity" in the bosom of the black person in Montgomery and later in the bosom of people of color everywhere.[78]

King acknowledged the value of white people, too. "God loves all of His children," he declared, "every man, from a bass black to a treble white, is significant on God's keyboard."[79] Moreover, segregation also injured white people. At a church conference in Nashville in 1962, he found oppressive behavior wrong because treating human beings "as anything less than a person of sacred worth, the image of God is abused in him and consequently and proportionately lost by those who inflict the abuse." Those who battered the dignity of one person forfeited a portion of their own worth in the transaction. Borrowing from Jewish theologian Martin Buber, he contended segregation substitutes an "I-it" relationship for an "I-thou" relationship. But "man is not a thing," shouted King, and he must not be treated as "an animated tool but as a person sacred in himself. To do otherwise is to depersonalize the potential person and to desecrate what he is."[80] In his last Sunday sermon, delivered in 1968 at the National Cathedral in Washington, D.C., he proclaimed, "Every man is an heir to a legacy of dignity and worth." Then he argued, as he had before, that those who denied the dignity of others also lost. Under Jim Crow, white people were also diminished. Societies built on racial inequities were abhorrent not only because they trampled the oppressed but also because prejudicial actions turned back upon the tyrant. Segregation locked oppressed and oppressors together as one. Acts of bondage and discriminatory practices damaged black people, marred white people, and wounded the entire community: "the disease of racism permeates and poisons a whole body politic."[81]

In affirming the worth and connectedness of all persons, he wrote a prescription he hoped would heal the disease of racism. If Americans accepted the "somebodiness" of blacks and the "somebodiness" of whites, according mutual respect to all, then he felt his dream had a chance. "Only by establishing a truly integrated society can we return to the Negro the quality of 'thouness' which is due because of the nature of his being."[82] This "I-Thou" relationship pushed his communitarian ethic. Individual personhood was only possible through relationships with others: "My personality can only be fulfilled in the context of community," he wrote in his 1958 biography.[83] This is one of the reasons he placed such a high premium on community, which he defined as "the mutually cooperative and voluntary venture of man to assume a semblance of responsibility for his brother."[84] Thus, if a person was isolated or denied dignity, the individual and the whole were compromised. Conversely, building one another up helped each realize his or her potential and strengthened the whole.

King read the problem holistically because he saw the world and community relations holistically. Repeatedly, he referred to ties that bound individuals, families, races, classes, communities, and nations. In his 1963 letter to white clergymen from the Birmingham jail, he declared: "I am cognizant of the interrelatedness of all communities and states. . . . Injustice anywhere is a threat to justice everywhere. We are caught in an inescapable network of mutuality, tied in a single garment of destiny. Whatever affects one directly affects all indirectly."[85] To this common refrain, he often added favorite lines from the poet John Donne: "No man is an island entire of itself. Every man is a piece of the continent—a part of the main."[86] Later he used the same reasoning to fault black separatism, saying that "the weakness of Black Power is its failure to see that the black man needs the white man and the white man needs the black man." He continued, "The problem is that in the search for wholeness all too many Negroes seek to embrace only one side of their natures," to identify with Africa or America. But, he said, there could

be no separate way to fulfillment. "We are bound together in a single garment of destiny. The language, the cultural patterns, the music, the material
prosperity and even the food of America are an amalgam of black and
white."[87] On multiple occasions, he explained that if the interconnections
between the individual parts of society were broken, if the institutions people created were maladjusted, then society as a whole was a "broken community." The universe, he wrote in 1958, was so interconnected and human
beings so intertwined, so integrated into one whole, that "to the degree that
I harm my brother, no matter what he is doing to me, to that extent I am
harming myself."[88] Malcolm X and others disagreed, but for much of the
1960s, King's communal vision prevailed.

    This integrationist ethic was grounded in love and justice and made tan-
gible through nonviolent actions. Americanizing the principle of satyagraha,
King spoke in the language of Christianity, borrowing from black students
of Gandhi such as Howard University professor William Stuart Nelson and
white liberal preachers Hamilton and Fosdick.[89] Specifically, he called on
people to practice *agape*, a Greek word for love that he translated as "understanding, redeeming good will for all men." Agape, to him, relied on "the
fact that all life is interrelated." It "makes no distinction between friends
and enemy." This "love in action" made his beloved community work as a
harmonious collective: "*Agape* is love seeking to preserve and create community. It is insistence on community even when one seeks to break it.
Agape is a willingness to go to any length to restore community. It is a willingness to forgive, not seven times, but seventy times seven to restore community."[90] He demanded an agape life. People were the parts, then, that
made up his whole, and love was the social glue that held people together.
To initiate change and promote justice, love was also the tool. Application of
his approach and widespread media attention confirmed its power. For
instance, when news broadcasts in May 1963 rolled footage of Birmingham
police commissioner Eugene "Bull" Connor's force attacking nonviolent
civil rights demonstrators—men, women, and children—with cattle prods,
clubs, dogs, and high-pressure fire hoses, white segregationists, not black
protesters, drew national anger.

    The demands of King's agape love called for revolutionary changes to the
status quo. His dominant metaphor, the "beloved community," spoke of
union, reinforced notions of equality, and forecast a future of fraternity not
only across racial lines but across class lines. To meet the needs of all members in the community and end poverty, he contended there must be equal
access to education and jobs and a more just allocation of wealth. "I have the
audacity to believe," he declared in his 1964 Nobel Peace Prize acceptance
speech, "that peoples everywhere can have three meals a day for their bodies, education and culture for their minds, and dignity, equality and free-

dom for their spirits."[91] No doubt King's concern for the impoverished grew as he traveled. In a trip across the Mississippi Delta in 1962, poor black people recounted for him police brutality and economic hardships: "How sobering it was to meet people who work only six months in the year and whose annual income averaged $500 to $600."[92] In 1968, he described the inadequate and squalid situations impoverished black people confronted: rat-infested apartments in Newark and Harlem, and Mississippi children without shoes and families picking berries and catching rabbits to scrape together an existence.[93]

To end discriminatory practices and show that black people merited equal treatment, pay, and access to power, he made a holistic case by pointing to the critical role African Americans had played in the country's history. The fate of black people, he revealed, "is bound up with the destiny of America—we built it for two centuries without wages, we made cotton king, we built our homes and homes for our masters and suffered injustice and humiliation—but out of a bottomless vitality continued to live and grow."[94] The orator's language was shrewd. Not only did his words speak his desire for "wholeness" in the political body—a wholeness that could only come by righting the wrongs of the past done to the nation's "troubled soul"—but the metaphors that he chose carried particular meaning in a society that had enslaved blacks and expropriated their labor to make cotton king. The "single garment of destiny," fashioned from cotton raised by slaves, united blacks and whites economically, socially, politically, and spiritually. They were, hence, cloaked together (in the political economy of King Cotton) in "an inescapable network of mutuality." And now by employing his logic in what could be read as a veiled threat, he declared, "we will continue to insist that right be done." The aim of the "American racial revolution," he said, "has been a revolution to 'get in' rather than overthrow. We want our share in the American economy, the housing market, the educational system and the social opportunities"[95]—in other words, all the institutions that King Cotton had built.

In the "revolution to get in," King pushed for economic equity by working with President Johnson on his War on Poverty and by linking hands with civil rights groups, labor unions, and religious associations that lobbied on behalf of the poor. In his speech at the March on Washington for Jobs and Freedom in 1963, he reminded Americans that "the Negro lives on a lonely island of poverty in the midst of a vast ocean of material prosperity."[96] When he traveled to riot-torn Watts in Los Angeles in 1965, he explained the violence, without condoning it, as pent-up rage against squalid, slum life.[97] In 1966, to shine a light on black people's plight, he lobbied for an end to housing discrimination and unfair hiring practices while he and his family lived in a Chicago ghetto. He called for a guaranteed family income and open housing programs, and he threatened national boycotts. When he was assassinated, he was focusing attention on the plight of Memphis sanitation workers, a segment of the city's unorganized labor force, and planning a Poor People's March to Washington to demand economic justice.

As King moved across the country, uttering speeches, delivering sermons, leading rallies, he used the same holistic language and the same holistic arguments. His call for the beloved community was consistent, his language effective, his logic compelling. Crowds grew larger; media attention increased; politicians acted. His message worked; it attracted others and was repeated in action, word, and song. Still it did not win the hearts of everyone. Spotlighting poverty and proposing programs to share the wealth made enemies just as his policies of integration had. King withstood accusations of communism, endured J. Edgar Hoover's FBI wiretaps, and suffered the wrath of Senator Strom Thurmond and Governor George C. Wallace. Conservative evangelical preacher Jerry Falwell delivered a sermon in Lynchburg, Virginia, in March 1965, questioning "the sincerity and non-violent intentions of Dr. Martin Luther King, Jr., Mr. James Farmer, and others, who are known to have left-wing associations."[98] Opposition to King only increased as the preacher raised his voice against the Vietnam War.[99]

King's pacifism serves as yet another demonstration of how he harnessed holistic notions to address problems. Though he did not begin to attack President Johnson's war in Asia until 1965, his ethic of nonviolence had never been limited to civil rights work. In his book *Stride toward Freedom* (1958) and again in *The Christian Century* (1960), King warned of the "threat of being plunged into the abyss of nuclear annihilation." The Cold War convinced him that "the potential destructiveness of modern weapons of war totally rules out the possibility of war ever serving again as a negative good." Now, he declared, "when sputniks dash through outer space and guided ballistic missiles are carving highways of death in the stratosphere," the church must demand "an end to the arms race."[100] Around this same time, he joined the pacifist group Fellowship of Reconciliation, called for a nuclear test moratorium with an interdenominational group of ministers, and signed his name to newspaper statements issued by the Committee for a Sane Nuclear Policy. In 1960, King declared, "It is very nice to drink milk at an unsegregated lunch counter—but not when there is strontium 90 in it." To demonstrate her own antipathies, Coretta Scott King joined Women Strike for Peace. As James Farrell noted, the two tackled "racism and militarism with a consistent social ethics based on the worth of persons."[101]

In the last years of his life King became more fervent in his identification with the Vietnamese. In 1965, he called for the end of U.S. bombing of North Vietnam. In 1966, he spoke at a joint news conference with the Vietnamese Buddhist religious leader Thich Nhat Hanh, comparing Vietnamese and

African American struggles. King had been influenced by Nhat Hanh, who had written King a year before to clarify the self-immolation of Buddhist priests in Saigon. These actions were affirmations of life, not political protests, Nhat Hanh wrote; the immolations aimed at "moving the hearts of the oppressors and calling the attention of the world to the suffering endured by the Vietnamese." King empathized. In 1967, he nominated Nhat Hanh for the Nobel Peace Prize.[102] By this point, his opposition to the Vietnam War was clear. King called it a "senseless, unjust war." He found American actions criminal, oppressive, imperialistic, and arrogant. He condemned the country's violent assaults, disproportionate dependency on black and poor soldiers, and diversion of funds away from the Great Society. "A few years ago," he cried, "there was a shining moment in that struggle. It seemed as if there was a real promise of hope for the poor, both black and white, through the poverty program....Then came the buildup in Vietnam, and I watched the program broken and eviscerated as if it were some idle plaything of a society gone mad on war."[103]

As he trudged on in his fight for justice, he employed the same logic to combat poverty and militarism as he had to confront racism. His defense of impoverished people focused on the institutional fabric that locked the destitute in a never-ending cycle of poverty. His critique of war centered on humanitarian relations. In each judgment, he linked oppressed to oppressor, neighbor to neighbor. He drew chains of association between cities, nations, and races. He did not think in isolated groups. In his "Christmas Sermon on Peace," delivered first at Ebenezer Baptist Church and then aired on radio on Christmas Eve 1967, the pastor pled for an ecumenical world perspective: "As nations and individuals, we are interdependent....This is the way our universe is structured, this is its interrelated quality."[104] Several times he described the poverty he encountered in India, detailing the lack of food, housing, and medical care. "Can we in America stand idly by and not be concerned?" he asked. "No! Because the destiny of the United States is tied up with the destiny of India and every other nation."[105] Social obligations did not stop at the nation's shores. His opposition to the Vietnam War rested on this same logic. Beginning with his belief in the "sacredness of human personality," he told his audiences that despite Cold War divisions over ideology and political systems, "the Vietnamese are our brothers, the Russians are our brothers, the Chinese are our brothers; and one day we've got to sit down together at the table of brotherhood." All were one. Thus, militarism and exploitation were wrong.[106]

Though he often described his dream in nationalistic terms, King's vision was global. In 1967, he wrote that "the crisis we face is international in scope. In fact, it is inseparable from an international emergency which involves the poor, the dispossessed, and the exploited of the whole world."

When he died, he had been, as he phrased it, beginning to "planetize [his] movement for social justice."[107] His social Christianity spoke to issues of poverty, class, and material well-being for the person, for nations, and for the world. Hence, like Rachel Carson and Buckminster Fuller, his holism did not stop at national boundaries.

The "world is geographically one," King declared. We are "witnessing in our day the birth of a new age, with a new structure of freedom and justice." As such he asked people to "rise above the narrow confines of our individualistic concerns to the broader concerns of all humanity. The new world is a world of geographical togetherness." He rebuked notions of isolationism. Nations, like individuals, were not islands, and so "We must all learn to live together, or we will be forced to die together." This was true, he thought, particularly in his age of science and technology. The "world of geographical togetherness" had been aided by science that "has been able to dwarf distance and place time in chains." Sounding in many ways like Fuller, he thought of the world as "a neighborhood." But, instead of looking at technological fixes to make the one-world town better; King focused on morality and spirituality as the key to the "neighborhood" becoming "a brotherhood." For him, it was all a "single process." He argued, "Whatever affects one directly affects all indirectly. We are all links in the great chain of humanity."[108] In his beloved community where national boundaries and racial categories melted away, King united inhabitants, no matter the race, no matter the class, no matter the continent.

In the end, though he never gave up on America, he pledged allegiance to the world. Especially after receiving the Nobel Peace Prize, he believed he was obliged to work for the "brotherhood of man" worldwide. The prize was a "calling that takes me beyond national allegiances." Expressing disdain for the "madness" of American military intervention in Vietnam, he distanced himself from American actions. Instead, he felt a global commitment to "speak for the weak, for the voiceless, for victims of our nation and for those it calls enemy."[109]

His reading of the world as one interconnected, interdependent whole was consistent with his theology and reinforced by dramatic global shifts. When he was born in 1929, most African and Asian nations were under colonial rule. By 1960, more than thirty African and Asian nations had overthrown European rule. He called it "a new age" in 1957 when he and others celebrated the birth of Ghana, the first African power to gain independence from colonial domination. It appeared to be a "world-wide freedom revolution," and, like others, he saw the destinies of black persons in Atlanta, Birmingham, and Chicago as inextricably tied to those in Calcutta and Johannesburg.[110] Decolonization contributed to his ideas of integration, the mark of his holistic society, as something he understood in global terms. No quest for freedom was isolated. Instead, he read the whole as one united expression of "the old order of colonialism and imperialism passing away and the new order of freedom and justice coming into being."[111]

Other events also presaged his global outlook. He thought that he lived in a "new age" brought on by a "triple revolution" in human rights, technology, and weaponry. Because of changes in these arenas, he imagined it necessary to "develop a world perspective."[112] One needed to abandon isolationist tendencies and think globally. Planes, communication tools, and other technological innovations shrank distance and time. Atomic weapons and Cold War competition threatened total disaster, but, as he stated in his Nobel Prize acceptance speech, he "refused to accept the cynical notion that nation after nation must spiral down a militaristic stairway into the hell of thermonuclear destruction."[113] Instead it was a time for a reorientation. Postwar events—the Double V Campaign (victory against racism abroad and at home); the integration of the army; the migration of blacks from South to North; the Supreme Court decision overturning the "separate but equal" doctrine; and more—also upset conceptions of race and promised changes to the status quo.

The minister read these shifts and challenges as opportunities. The world, he surmised, needed a new map. Quoting philosopher Alfred North Whitehead, King declared, "'We live in a day...when civilization is shifting its basic outlook; a major turning point in history where the presuppositions on which society is structured are being analyzed, sharply challenged, and profoundly changed.'"[114] He presumed his holistic order would provide a new map of morality, charting the path to a better future. In this he called on personalist theology and the traditions of the African American church, but he did not dismiss the contributions that science could also add. Science and religion were not "rivals," he said. "They are complementary." Science prevents religion from "crippling irrationalism and paralyzing obscurantism," and religion keeps science from "materialism and moral nihilism."[115] Both could help create the beloved community.

In ways, there was little that was new about King's vision of the beloved community. Philosopher Josiah Royce used the phrase before him, and Christians had long used the "kingdom of God" in similar manner. Certainly, a long tradition in the African American community had also issued this same cry for justice and brotherhood. Neither was he unique in expressing ideals of equality and justice. As he admitted, student demonstrators "have taken the whole nation back to those great wells of democracy which were dug deep by the Founding Fathers in the formulation of the Constitution and the Declaration of Independence."[116]

Still King configured and reshaped African American Christianity to fit the particular experiences of the postwar era and he did so within a holistic frame that had great appeal. He articulated in speech and action a strong communitarian ethos. His amalgam of peoples into one single global garment contributed in significant ways to the holistic, communitarian, and utopian impulse that beat throughout the long 1960s. His push for a beloved community marked by equality, justice, and peace served the civil rights movement and complemented the era's kaleidoscope of holistic representations. He linked hands with those both within and without the black church who forwarded a similar worldview. Randolph and Rustin, for example, planned the March on Washington in 1963 and an earlier rally at the Lincoln Monument in 1957 in such a way as to evoke a sense of *communitas* and political commitment. According to journalist Lerone Bennett, they succeeded. The march was "a moment in time when they were one." The music of contralto Marian Anderson and gospel singer Mahalia Jackson at the March on Washington in 1963 reinforced this call to unity. Music, especially the gospel and folk songs that were so fundamental to the movement, inspired hope and spiritual community. The rallies and marches, the collective act of singing, the call-and-response, and the songs chosen—"We Shall Overcome," "He's Got the Whole World in His Hands," "This Little Light of Mine"—fostered communal feelings and carried a communal message.[117]

Embracing a robust humanitarian and communitarian personalism, King joined with those who made individual dignity and social cooperation central to work not only in civil rights but in humanistic psychology, the Catholic Workers Movement, the peace movement, the Beat generation, and the counterculture. With psychologists Abraham Maslow, Carl Rogers, and Rollo May and many connected to Esalen, he focused on the wholeness—the somebodiness—of individuals and to the building of healthy relationships between individuals. In similar ways, Beat poet Kenneth Rexroth intertwined the individual and community in holistic accord in declaring:

> A community of love is
> A community of mutual
> Indwelling, in which each member
> Realizes his total
> Liability for the whole.[118]

Barbara Deming, editor of the humanistic journal *Liberation*, explained her protests for peace by saying that nonviolence "always tries to dramatize the words of St. Paul, 'We are members one of another.'...and act out the truth that all men are kin to one another.'" This "love-for-more-than-one" might be a "sympathy and compassion that might befit a beloved community."[119]

This was a time when holistic ideas thrived in post–World War organizational actions, in songs and speeches. Holistic sensibilities infused the United Nations, the Peace Corps, and the World Council of Churches. John

F. Kennedy's inaugural address spoke to many when he implored American citizens to "ask not what your country can do for you" but "what you can do for your country," and world citizens to "ask not what America could do for you, but what together we can do for the freedom of man."[120] Within this milieu, King's dream resonated, and during much of the 1960s it thrived.

These communal values continued to pulse within the culture into the 1970s, but they grew fainter after King's and Robert F. Kennedy's assassinations in 1968, the debacle of the Vietnam War, Watergate, the conservative backlash, and the energy crisis. Integrationist ideas grew fainter still with the growth of the Black Power movement, which Malcolm X, Stokely Carmichael, Huey Newton, Bobby Seale, and others began in the 1960s as a revolutionary engine for change. Advocates for Black Power rejected integration, seeing it as an assimilationist program, as a dismissal of black culture and a whitening of black identity. They championed black nationalism, political power, and cultural values. The black arts movement and the beginning of African American studies forwarded the shift from whole-cloth integrationist programs to emphasize cultural identity. Despite disillusionment and disappointments, shifting strategies, changing ideologies, and a resurgence of individualism, elements of King's moral vision and legacy continued into the twenty-first century.

Each person in this study called on religious understandings to ground his or her holistic worldview. Certainly, this was true of King. He wed his social actions to the Social Gospel of the black church and personalistic theology. He made faith central to his fight for civil rights and quest for the beloved community. "There is," he contended, "a creative force in this universe that works to bring the disconnected aspects of reality into a harmonious whole."[121] It was similarly true of the next subject in this study, Jesuit priest and paleontologist Pierre Teilhard de Chardin. Both made explicit their reliance on religion. Concurrently, these holists embraced and critiqued the modern world and their scientific age. At times, they adapted their faith to meet current scientific realities and paradigms. At other times, they held science to their moral standards. Certainly King's critique of atomic warfare signaled such a stance. As the preacher and the priest forwarded their spiritual, communal, and global perspectives of life, they advanced different agendas and seized the imagination of different audiences. King was Protestant, and Teilhard Catholic; King thought more of the here and now, and Teilhard pondered long geologic epochs and vast stretches of space; King was practical, and Teilhard abstract; King worked within the political realm, and Teilhard stayed within scientific and priestly communities. Despite these differences, each in their unique way developed a holistic vision that upheld religion after World War II, and each made their visions especially relevant to the 1960s generation.

Pierre Teilhard de Chardin on a picnic in China, 1936. *Courtesy of Georgetown University Library*

4

Cosmic Dimensions
Pierre Teilhard de Chardin's Omega Point

When French Jesuit priest and paleontologist Pierre Teilhard de Chardin (1881–1955) sailed from Peking to Seattle in the winter of 1937, then traveled cross-country to attend a scientific symposium in Philadelphia, all seemed perfectly normal. On the way, he stopped at Chicago's Field Museum to show a reconstructed skull of "Peking Man" (*Sinanthropus pekinensis*). As a member of the team that had unearthed fossil remains of this prehistoric human in 1931, he delighted in talking about the find. At the Philadelphia conference, he presented evidence that "Peking Man" used fire and tools, and he visited with Yale scientist Helmut de Terra and other distinguished paleontologists. From there, he went to Villanova University to receive the Mendel Medal for his scientific contributions. That is when his trip turned sour. In his acceptance speech, he strayed from scientific statements to declare his belief that evolution was God's ongoing creative act, that all was converging into one complete, harmonious whole. When a curious *New York Times* reporter cornered him after the meeting, Teilhard elaborated, making clear his allegiance to evolutionary science. The next day, newspapers across the country carried stories bearing the headline: "Jesuit Who Believes Man Descended from Apes." While Americans expressed intrigue, the Vatican roared disapproval. Hostile to evolutionary science at this point, church officials had already commanded him to speak only on strictly scientific topics and had even gone so far as to exile him to China to lessen his influence. Boston College planned to give him an award a few days later, but Jesuit administrators, fearful of association, abruptly withdrew the honor. This only fed interest, however, and soon Americans knew Teilhard as the evolution priest.[1]

This fracas over Teilhard's views exposed American fascination with both religion and science. Just a decade before Teilhard revealed his beliefs at

Villanova, Tennessee's famous Scopes trial, pitting evolutionists against creationists, had captivated the country. Science emerged the victor in Tennessee, and many modernists predicted science's rise and religion's demise. But the issue was hardly resolved, as Teilhard's comments elicited in 1937 and as school boards' wrestling over science curricula in the coming decades revealed. Neither scientists nor religious figures have ceded authority, and Americans have continued to show allegiance to both. Hence, the relationship between religion and science has been a complicated one. Sometimes, as witnessed in the Scopes trial or more recent controversies over right-to-die legislation and stem cell research, competing worldviews, conflicting agendas, bitter skirmishes, and overt hostility characterized debates. At other times, religious and scientific people have kept to their separate spheres, each preoccupied with dissimilar agendas, indifferent to the work of the other. At yet other moments, the story line has been one of cooperation and mutual engagement. Teilhard's merging of Catholicism and evolution fits this last account. Indeed, shining the light on his synthesis and its acceptance among significant circles in American society reveals some of the tenacity with which Americans have held both religion and science. It also indicates yet another way holism was bent, used, and practiced during this era.

Though Teilhard regularly traveled to the United States to attend conferences, study geologic sites, and arrange liaisons between Chinese and American institutions after 1937, and though he lived his last years in New York City, he spent most of his life in other parts of the world. He gained a Jesuit education in France and England, becoming a priest in 1911 and earning his doctorate from Paris's Sorbonne University in 1922. During these years, he also taught science in Egypt, participated in scientific digs, and served as a medic in World War I. Before making his first expedition to China in 1923, he taught at the Catholic Institute in Paris. By that time, acceptance of evolution and doubts about original sin had brought him to the Vatican's attention. Finding his ideas problematic, officials sent him to China. From 1926 through World War II, he pursued paleontological work in China and around the world. He also wrote mystical pieces in pursuit of a new spirituality that fit his science and the contemporary world, including *The Phenomenon of Man; Christianity and Evolution; Mass on the World; Building the Earth; Science and Christ*, and *Toward the Future.*[2] After the war, he made research trips to South Africa and lived in Jesuit houses in Paris, then in New York City. He died in 1955.

Because of the church's moratorium on his theological writings, Americans did not have an opportunity to fully engage Teilhard's evolutionary faith until the 1960s. He had circulated manuscripts surreptitiously, but his message did not reach a wide audience until supporters published his works. *The Phenomenon of Man*, which examined the process of evolution and human dignity, came first. The book was translated into English in 1959, and by 1961 more than 50,000 copies had sold in the United States alone.[3]

Reaction to Teilhard was mixed. Religious fundamentalists found his evolutionary views anathema. Scientists faulted him for trying to sneak God back into the evolutionary process. Paleontologist George Gaylord Simpson dismissed Teilhard's science as mystical.[4] Some found Teilhard's neologisms—"Christogenesis," "hominization," "personalization," "spiritualization," and "noosphere"—off-putting, even bizarre. Still others celebrated his vision. Evolutionary biologist Julian Huxley, son of Darwinian Thomas Huxley, wrote the forward to the English translation of *The Phenomenon of Man*, finding it a "remarkable work" by a "distinguished paleontologist" who "helped define...our own nature, the general evolutionary process, and our place and role in it."[5] Geneticist Theodosius Dobzhansky echoed the praise, and rocket scientist Wernher von Braun found Teilhard's cosmology "the most promising bridge between science and religion."[6] One twenty-one-year-old medic serving in Vietnam who "stumbled upon *Building the Earth*" declared "it most astounding and such a spiritual up-lifting venture that I felt the need to go out and announce to the whole world of the writing of this brilliant and humble Jesuit priest."[7] By 1970, numerous Catholics applauded his work, and Catholic universities regularly assigned Teilhard for graduate readings.[8]

In less formal ways, others imbibed and spread Teilhardian thought, too: communication theorist Marshall McLuhan, economist Kenneth Boulding, mathematician Ralph Abraham, physicist John Barrow, and Vice President Albert Gore applied the priest's vision to their own work. So did New Age religious proponents. In these and other ways Teilhard's ideas wound their way into American culture.

This chapter details the evolution of Teilhard's holism, how it satisfied him personally, how he used it to fulfill his longing to understand his world both scientifically and spiritually, and how it spoke to a significant subsection of Americans. The key to understanding why his ideas resonated in so many corners centers on his holistic amalgamation. When Americans picked up *The Phenomenon of Man*, it sounded some of the same themes they read in *Silent Spring*, saw in the geodesic, and heard in King's dream. His marriage of science and faith trumpeted human significance, knit one to another in community, and spoke optimistically of the future. To a nation reluctant to part with a spiritual cosmology and unsettled over Darwinian notions, the Jesuit created a conciliatory "religion of evolution," which kept God in the picture using older arguments by design but also updated religious answers consistent with scientific knowledge.[9] His organismic ideas proved attractive to many in the long 1960s who wanted an alternative to reductionistic, dualistic, mechanistic evolutionary views. It satisfied many who were looking for ways to reconnect with nature and one another, who wanted to revitalize and make personal the spiritual part of life, and who hoped to tame, humanize, and spiritualize science. The next section details how this person born into a Catholic family in France became both a scientist and a priest.

The fourth of eleven children, Pierre Teilhard developed his lifelong fascination with both religion and science at home in France's central province of Auvergne. His mother, Berthe-Adèle de Dompierre d'Hormoy, a devotee to the cult of the Sacred Heart of Jesus, taught the children their catechism and maintained a strict household. Emmanuel Teilhard de Chardin, one of the region's largest landholders, ran his estates, fished, hunted, and studied natural history. He read field magazines, joined naturalist societies, and amassed a considerable collection of birds, insects, plants, and stones. The volcanic hills surrounding their farmhouse offered much to explore. When the young Pierre walked in them, he carried with him his father's intrigue with natural history and his mother's mystical passion.

Like Carson, Teilhard spent his childhood out of doors; but unlike the ecologist, who named wildflowers and turned her ear to songbirds, he burrowed himself in the hard, gray world of rocks. In his lava-worn environment, he collected pieces of flint. Solid objects mesmerized him. Of all the mineral, metal, and shale he pocketed, nothing seemed more immutable than iron. Nothing was "harder, heavier, tougher, more durable than this marvelous substance," he later wrote. "I withdrew into the contemplation, the possession, into the so relished existence, of my 'Iron God.'" Thus began his love affair with the material world and the spiritual value he found within it. Recalling his early attraction, he said, "I was certainly not more than six or seven years old, when I began to feel myself drawn by Matter—or, more correctly, by something which 'shone' at the heart of Matter."[10] Within matter, he thought, lay clues to essential truths.

His formal education began at an elite Jesuit institution that trained boys in the natural sciences. At eighteen, he joined the Jesuit order and was ordained in 1911. His training, part of which took place on the English Isle of Jersey, prepared him in priestly and scientific matters.[11] The island, ideal for geologic exploration, seemed especially made for one intrigued with rocks and sediment. The jagged shoreline and the sea's crushing waves inspired him. While there, he wrote three scientific papers on the island's geology, mineralogy, and tectonics as well as a monograph on the land's structure.[12] Through such publications, he and other Jesuits helped make the Jersey house an important center for geologic and archaeological research.

Exhilarated by his surroundings, impressed with the force of wind and waves, Teilhard also used his time on the island to cultivate his theological views and mystical beliefs about the spiritual qualities within the material world. To his thinking, God was both immanent and transcendent, pulsing through nature and yet separate from nature. In later essays, he described God as "vibrant in the ether; and through the ether he makes his way into the very marrow of my material substance. Through Him, all bodies come together, exert influence upon one another and sustain one another in the unity of the all-embracing sphere."[13] His organic description of the earth resembled Buckminster Fuller's description of his geodesic. Each focused on the relationship between the parts and the whole, the "influence upon one another" to achieve the "unity of the all-embracing sphere."

Blending spirit and matter, God and nature, Teilhard flirted with pantheism. In "The Spiritual Power of Matter," he greeted the inanimate with a personal voice: "Blessed be you, harsh matter, barren soil, stubborn rock.... Blessed be you, perilous matter, violent sea, untameable passion."[14] Ultimately, he rejected these pantheistic leanings, the belief that *all is God*, and settled instead on panentheism, the doctrine that *all is in God*.[15] This subtle yet crucial theological distinction allowed him a God that was both transcendent and immanent, a God that was in all but not equivalent to all. For him God was personal and not, as he put it, the "Formless" deity of "Hindu poets and mystics."[16] He, like King, worshiped a living personality, not, he said, a "faceless organism, a diffuse humanity,—an *Impersonal*."[17] Though maintaining a personal and transcendent God in the present, Teilhard eventually subscribed to a teleological vision of future union between God and the world. He supposed, though the evolutionary process, that the world was moving forward and rising up to God. He called this the "divinization" of the earth and moved closer to an immanent view, perhaps more influenced than he cared to think not only by his scientific work but also by his travels and life in the East.[18]

Teilhard left his island studies, traveling to Egypt in 1905 to assume a post at a Jesuit high school in Cairo. When he was not teaching physics and chemistry, he walked the desert paths of early Christian ascetics; visited the pyramids, Sphinx, and archaeological museums; explored Arab mosques and markets; and traveled the Nile. "This was the East," he wrote later. "I caught glimpses of it, and drank it in avidly."[19] As he explored, he began to develop a global perspective, albeit one centered on the natural habitat. He was, he explained, "under the attraction of [Egypt's] light, its vegetation, its fauna and its deserts."[20] He learned more by attending meetings at the Institute of Egyptology, making a scientific expedition into the desert area of El Faiyum, and conducting weekly excavations of local flora. He shared his results in scientific articles, and one of the sea fossils he found was subsequently named *Teilhardi* by the French Geological Society.

After three years, the young man moved to "Ore Place," a Jesuit house in Hastings, England, and resumed his priestly studies. Sussex Weald, a large forested region with layers of soils from several geologic eras, was close by and presented itself as a perfect laboratory. Except for the change in location, little appeared different in the way Teilhard lived. Here, as in France, Jersey, and Egypt, he dug, prayed, uncovered fossils, said his rosary, analyzed finds, and perused his Bible. Yet all was not the same.

In the 1890s, conservative Pope Leo XIII revived medieval Scholasticism, especially the teachings of Thomas Aquinas. Some Catholics resisted, contending that the deductive methods of Scholasticism could not match the inductive reasoning of modern science or that biblical literalism could sufficiently address modernism, German historicism, and higher biblical criticism. Progressive American Catholics were among those who challenged the pope's antimodern, antiscientific views, setting in motion a somewhat antagonistic relationship between the Vatican and the American church for the first half of the twentieth century.[21] Not until Pope John XXIII and the Second Vatican Council (1962–65) did the church accommodate an evolutionary, modern perspective. Until then, the Vatican's position set the stage for what became an ongoing battle between the church and Teilhard. Similarly, Vatican II opened more people to Teilhard's ideas, about the same time his books were hitting bookstores.[22]

When Teilhard entered Ore Place, Jesuits heeded Vatican dictates and taught Scholasticism. At first Teilhard adhered. Under Jesuit sway most of his life, he sidelined beliefs about inanimate matter and abided by Thomistic doctrines. In 1908, he affirmed a papal decree condemning modernism, and as late as 1911, he published a piece denouncing evolution.[23] But the man who spent his spare time in Sussex Weald with hammer and magnifying glass in tow was not at ease. Intent on producing good science, he questioned Scholasticism's static, dualistic categories and gradually shifted perspectives. Indeed, he swung so far that instead of reviling evolution, he began to embrace it as "magical," little knowing how much this would cost him.

Teilhard's shift to evolutionary thinking bears scrutiny, as it profoundly affected his holistic perspective. Combining science and Christianity, he developed an evolutionary argument of design that did three things. First, it kept God in the picture; second, it discarded dualism; third, it provided a scientific explanation for his theological views that matter was related to spirit. His ideas were somewhat akin to nineteenth-century naturalist William Paley's watchmaker argument that complex living things must have been designed by an outside force. But while Paley, working before Charles Darwin, saw the world as static, Teilhard saw it as dynamic and ever changing. Unlike Darwin, however, Teilhard surmised that God drove evolution. The goal was the harmonic unification of everything, matter and spirit.

Describing his switch to evolutionary thinking as a conversion experience, Teilhard recalled that "the magic word 'evolution'" hung with him "like a tune: which was to me like an unsatisfied hunger, like a promise held out to me, like a summons to be answered."[24] While he described the call as irresistible and mystical—"whence it came I cannot say"—he was reading

Henri Bergson's newly published *Creative Evolution* (1911).[25] Bergson, a French philosopher, accepted evolution but rejected materialistic or mechanistic interpretations. Instead, he constructed an organic, metaphysical explanation for the evolutionary process. A force in nature, which Bergson called the "élan vital," caused the development of new and more complex systems and initiated, among other things, the evolution of instinct and human perception. This vital, driving force—vitalism—was mysterious, unable to be explained by science. Teilhard judged Bergson's work "brilliant" but downplayed its influence on his own thinking, saying its only effect "was to provide fuel at just the right moment, and very briefly, for a fire that was already consuming my heart and mind."[26] Bergson likely did more than that. After reading the book, Teilhard switched from belief in a "static Cosmos" to "Cosmogenesis," his term for an evolving universe.[27] In any case, Bergson became a foil for Teilhard to explain his own ideas.

Though enamored with Bergson's integration of physical and metaphysical elements, Teilhard only partially agreed with Bergson's conclusions. He rejected his élan vital. Instead of an impersonal force guiding evolution, the priest looked to his "Cosmic Christ": "God is at work within life. He helps it, raises it up, gives it the impulse that drives it along, the appetite that attracts it, the growth that transforms it. I can feel God, touch Him, 'live' Him in the deep biological current that runs through my soul."[28] To explain a God that was fully engaged in the ongoing evolutionary process and make known his mystical beliefs (beliefs that estranged, attracted, or puzzled people), Teilhard likened the deity to a "circle of energy," an "active force" that sets the world ablaze and transforms all. The "Divine" was "for me the form, the consistence and the properties of an ENERGY, of a FIRE." This energy propelled change. The image of fire, a recurring metaphor in the priest's writings, signaled both his belief that God was fully involved in the transformative process and Teilhard's passionate personality. The trope also reflected a twentieth-century fascination with energy; from Bergson to Einstein to New Age seekers, many perceived the world as an energy field.[29] Here, Teilhard used fire to explain his relationship with the divine: "It is not in the form of a ray of light or of a tenuous matter, but as fire that I desire you; and it was as fire that I felt your presence, in the intuition of my first contact." Creation was not, he said, "a far-distant, instantaneous act which happened long ago." Instead, "creation has never stopped. The creative act is one huge continual gesture, drawn out over the totality of time. It is still going on."[30] Hence, Teilhard kept God in the picture but divorced himself from static interpretations of creation.

In another way, Teilhard set himself apart from his contemporary. Bergson suggested that the evolutionary process brought divergence, diversity, and disequilibrium. Teilhard found the opposite. He postulated that evolution pursued a path of "creative union," "convergence," and "confluence."

According to this teleological vision, the earth was progressing into a unified, harmonious whole (the Omega Point).[31] This drive to union or wholeness is fundamental to understanding Teilhard's holistic cosmology. It revealed his organic perspective, synthesized religion and scientific notions, and made a holistic claim that everything in the universe was being amalgamated into one integrated whole. As Teilhardian scholar and *Zygon* editor Philip Hefner concluded, the unification process "is central to Teilhard's thinking, representing as it does a dimension of his near obsession for unity. It is impossible to overemphasize its centrality in his vision."[32]

Convergence gave Teilhard a scientific hypothesis for his monistic childhood beliefs about spirit and matter. He proposed that matter was in various stages of becoming spirit. They were not two different entities. Everything, according to the scientist, was part matter and part spirit. Everything had a "without" (an outer physical part) and a "within" (an inner spiritual part). To explain the evolution of human beings, he argued that at the core of inorganic material, there existed a tiny seed of consciousness. Through the course of evolution, the seed grew and progressed in an "irreversible process," guided as it was by the hand of God. Gradually it materialized in full consciousness in the human form. Moreover, he said, everything, matter and spirit, living and inanimate, was a part of one forward, spiritualizing process. All was the same cosmic stuff in different stages, and all was rising toward a "progressive spiritualization of Matter." The universe, he believed, was "falling—falling forwards—in the direction of Spirit." Matter was being "metamorphosed into Psyche.... Spirit was by no means the enemy or the opposite pole of the Tangibility which I was seeking to attain: rather was it its very heart."[33]

As he concluded in his autobiography, aptly titled *The Heart of Matter* (1950), this tiny core—the metaphysical within the physical—was what he had been searching for as a boy. The tangible he had sought in iron was really spirit—the heart of matter. Rocks and other matter contained the "Absolute in the form of the Tangible," he said. Within them lies "a sort of universal root or matrix of beings." In his own abstruse way, he kept the initial site of his holism—that God of iron he idolized in his youth—holy. "I no longer doubted but that the supreme happiness I had formerly looked for in 'Iron' was to be found only in Spirit." In total, he chose to prioritize spirit as did his church, but he never privileged spirit by renouncing matter or by separating spirit from matter as many Christian mystics had done. To him, it was the same. It was one. In this way, he interpreted evolution as a progression of all into one organic whole.[34]

As he described his evolutionary, monistic view in his autobiography, he explained his earlier ambivalence over dualism: "My education and my religion had always led me obediently to accept—without much reflection, it is true—a fundamental heterogeneity between Matter and Spirit, between

Body and Soul, between Unconscious and Conscious." Yet for the boy who loved rocks, who saw something spiritual in matter, and for the young priest in training who flirted with pantheism on the Isle of Jersey, dualism never appealed. Monism did. "You can well imagine," he wrote, "how strong was my inner feeling of release and expansion when I took my first still hesitant steps into an 'evolutive' Universe." At this point, he "saw that the dualism in which I had hitherto been enclosed was disappearing like the mist before the rising sun." Now, Teilhard surmised that "Matter and Spirit: these were no longer two things, but two *states* or two aspects of one and the same cosmic Stuff."[35] Released, he no longer felt pulled between the stuff of science and the otherworldliness of spirit. He could dig fossils and pray. For the rest of his life he did just that, announcing at old age: "The truth is that even at the peak of my spiritual trajectory I was never to feel at home unless immersed in an Ocean of Matter." Monism, thus, brought him inner "release and expansion" and created a sense of personal wholeness. By "seeing the Sense of Consistence" between these two worlds of matter and spirit, he was "led to the awakening and expansion of a dominant and triumphant Sense of the Whole."[36]

In many ways, Teilhard's evolving, monistic, converging whole corresponded with twentieth-century notions of a universe in constant flux, but his teleological thrust set him apart from other scientists. The younger paleontologist Stephen Jay Gould recounted an evolutionary story of blind chance, pitiless indifference, conflict, and anguish. Other secular evolutionists agreed, supposing any God of evolutionary theory would be "capricious, cruel, arbitrary, wasteful, careless and totally unconcerned with the welfare of his creations"—a far cry from Teilhard's benevolent architect.[37]

The priest's evolutionary ideas complemented his theology and gave him certitude of a future day of organic harmony between God, human beings, and the material world. His holism rested on experiences, too. World War I, close relationships with women, and world travels fed his yearnings for universal oneness and reinforced the importance of community. We will see in the next section that Teilhard, like other holists whose views became popular in the 1960s, came to think an individual's full potential could only be realized through community. Again, communal values infused this particular holistic moment.

After his ordination in 1911, he moved to Paris to take classes in geology and paleontology at the Catholic Institute and to work as a research student for Marcellin Boule, a specialist of Neanderthal man at the Museum of Natural History.[38] Teilhard analyzed fossils and became fascinated with primate and human brain development. In 1913, he joined prehistorian Abbé Henri Breuil on an expedition in Spain's Pyrenees. By December 1914, however, instead of digging for fossils, the priest was digging trenches and working as a stretcher-bearer in World War I. He joined the war as a medical orderly, not, as one might suppose, a chaplain. He opted to work alongside soldiers and repeatedly refused promotion beyond the rank of corporal. He also resisted an assignment to Vichy and instead went to the front as a stretcher-bearer. For four years he moved with his regiment, composed largely of North African Zouaves and sharpshooters, to the main battles of the war. In 1919, he exited decorated but unscathed.

Though he bore no battle wounds, he was marked by the engagement. In contrast to the American novelist Ernest Hemingway, who left World War I psychologically scarred and feeling he was doomed to inhabit "burned-over wastelands," the priest, ever the mystical optimist, dreamed not of wastelands but of utopian fields of communal harmony. While his journal mingled expressions of fear with passionate declarations for life, he read the war as a prelude to union. Testifying to his infatuation with the world, his words, far from bleak, were celebratory, even rapturous.[39] After experiencing the Battle of Ypres in 1915, he wrote "that life is beautiful, in the grimmest circumstances—when you can see God, ever-present, in them."[40]

Reading Édouard Schuré's Les Grands Initiés, a book about mystics, contributed to his reading of the war. He began having visions of the world as one. Perhaps these apparitions served as a psychological defense against the horrific displays of death, destruction, and disease confronting the soldiers daily. At the devastating Battle of Verdun, he escaped the brutalities of warfare by falling into a trance. He imagined Christ's heart was a circle of fire and energy, emanating throughout the earth, radiating through matter, and circumscribing the universe. Writing about it later, he described his Cosmic Christ as universal, immanent, and transcendent; Christ was "the Centre at which all things meet."[41] In his holistic understanding of the "organic unity of the total Christ," he believed that humanity was being drawn into oneness with God.[42] New Testament readings, particularly Paul's statements that "in [Christ] all things hold together" and "Christ is all, and in all" confirmed this to him.[43] He wrote that Christ was "the Instrument, the Centre, the End, of the whole of animate and material creation."[44] Feeling God's presence through visions and finding support for his notions of wholeness through biblical readings emboldened his holistic theological views and evolutionary theories. The world was one, and the evolutionary process was a positive, forward power for good.

Again, oneness did not mean nirvana. In essays written during the war, he still rejected pantheism, still asserted that the divine was "at once transcendent and immanent.... God cannot in any way be intermixed with or lost in the participated being which he sustains and animates and holds together, but he is at the birth, and the growth and the final term of things. Everything lives, and everything is raised up—everything in consequence is one—in Him and through Him." Importantly, this meant, to him, the growth of individual personality—not its loss as expected in a pantheistic world—and it indicated fulfillment of human personality through companionship with a "God, who is as immense and all-embracing as matter, and at the same time as warm and intimate as a soul...an Infinite that knows and attracts and loves."[45]

Similar to King, Teilhard embraced a God who was personal and communal; he considered each individual unique but judged that none was an island. In his essay "The Universal Element," he wrote that we think of a person as a "natural, complete, unit," as "an independent reality, co-terminous with itself, separable *in its identity* from other souls," but this was "most inaccurate." Instead, none "can attain his full personality, his full significance, his full determination, except within the general design of the world." The individual knows itself only in and through community, or, as he phrased it, "individual aspirations can be fulfilled in the realization of the whole."[46] This, too, corresponded with King, and it did as well with Maslow. Each holist's articulation reinforced the other; each emphasized the one-ness of the person and the importance of community in the fulfillment of an individual's potential.

Teilhard, again like King, remained a Christian because he thought Christianity was "the only collective stream of living thought saving and promoting the idea of a *Personal Whole* in the world."[47] In the essay "Cosmic Life," he detailed what he meant by this "personal whole" and the network of relations within it. Humanity, he believed, was a collective unit or, at least, was on its way to becoming so. The church (the body of Christ) was an organic representation of the whole. Each individual, each part of the whole, was related to Christ, the "head"; each had value; and each was mutually dependent upon another for the functioning of the whole. Organic commu-nion grows out of this relationship between the parts and the divine: "Like particles immersed in one and the same spiritual fluid, souls cannot think or pray or act or move, without waves being produced, even by the most insignificant among them, which set the others in motion." Interdependent relationships bound one to the other to form "one solid whole." Hence, the priest explained, the "Communion of Saints is held together in the hallowed unity of a physically organized Whole; and this Whole—more absolute than the individuals over which it has dominion, in as much as the elements penetrate into and subsist in God as a *function* of Him and *not as isolated particles*—this Whole is the Body of Christ."[48]

Daily exchanges in an internationally mixed regiment influenced Teilhard's understanding of what this whole looked like. He had already broadened his worldview by teaching in Egypt. Now, in war, he deepened his universalistic views. Though discouraged by the "difference in language and the gulf that separates" North Africans and French, and likely harbor-ing some racialist attitudes commonly held at the time, he nonetheless anticipated global accord. At one point, he gazed at "an audience of

Senegalese, Martiniquans, Somalis, Annamites, Tunisians and French" and surmised that one good outcome of war is that it allied a diversity of people; he hoped that "among other results of the war, will be that of mixing and welding together the peoples of the earth."[49]

His wartime optimism may be attributed to his positive nature, his belief that life had purpose, and the sense of community he felt. Even as a violent war raged, and even though he lost two brothers in battle, he saw human beings ascending to a place of "final harmony" without "conflicts and cleavages." In that final day, he wrote, "suffering and mischance and gloom will no longer disfigure the regenerated cosmos.... every false or reprehensible relationship, all physical and moral evil, all the evil part of the world, will have disappeared."[50] He hated war, but out of bad could come good. Camaraderie brought solace, a dim foreshadowing of future unity and harmony in Christ. He applied this interpretation to the next war, too. Even atomic warfare did not escape this optimistic reading.[51]

As the preceding passages reveal, Teilhard spoke in the language of holism. He wrote of "links," "mutual dependence," "mutual interdependence," "co-operation," "interrelations," and finally of "convergence," "unity," and "wholes." He articulated a vision that interlocked all. Everything was related to everything else in space and time. Given his evolutionary perspective and paleontological work, he thought in terms of eons rather than years. He concluded that "each one of us is perforce linked by all the material, organic and psychic strands of his being to all that surrounds him. Not only is he caught up in a network, he is carried along, too, by a stream."[52]

The war's male setting reinforced his belief in unity, solidarity, and community. He found comfort in and gave encouragement to soldiers, all in a familiar setting for the priest. From his boarding school days, he lived in a communal brotherhood. But his vision of community was only framed in part by men; women and cultural notions of femininity also played a significant role. Initially, his mystical mother and devout sisters, especially Françoise and Guigite, along with church teachings on Mary shaped his gendered understandings. Each inspired spiritual sentiments, and accordingly, he associated women with a higher, spiritual realm. In addition, Teilhard forged a number of close, personal, and highly intellectual relationships with women, the first of which was with his cousin Marguerite Teilhard-Chambon. Playmates as children, the two became reacquainted before the war and enjoyed long conversations and lengthy letters throughout their lives. One of his biographers said, "It is beyond doubt that Marguerite was the first great love of Teilhard's life." But she would not be the last.[53]

When he returned to Paris after the war in 1919, he continued his studies, gaining certificates in geology, botany, and zoology. By 1920, he commenced his doctoral research in France on mammals of the Lower Eocene. During this time, he met frequently with his cousin and other women, including those who challenged his traditional notions and gave him a more cosmopolitan outlook. Leontine Zanta, the first French woman to gain a doctorate in philosophy, played a leading role in the development of French feminism and engaged him in conversations about the rights of women. Teilhard frequented philosophical discussions in her salon, and the two corresponded long after he left the city.[54] About the same time, he supervised the scientific work of an American student, Ida Treat. She was an atheist and Communist, and the two clashed frequently. Nonetheless, passionate debate led to mutual respect. She opened his mind to new political persuasions and helped him see the world from an atheist's eyes. He entrusted his difficulties with the church to her and became emotionally attached. They, too, remained steadfast friends and correspondents. These women helped him develop a communal perspective that granted women respect, if not full equality. The most intimate female relationship Teilhard enjoyed came when he met the American sculptress Lucile Swan in China. Their deep conversations and rich correspondence speak of mutual admiration and love.[55]

Though intimate in friendship, he remained faithful to his vow of celibacy. Even with Swan, who hoped for more, he made the church his first priority. He interpreted his side of these relationships as a "general, half-worshipping, homage which sprang from the depths of my being and was paid to those women whose warmth and charm have been absorbed, drop by drop, into the life-blood of my most cherished ideas."[56] Part of his idealization of femininity stemmed from his resolute commitment to his vows. By making these women, at least to some degree, representatives of an idealized spiritual energy, he could more easily keep his physical distance while developing deep attachments intellectually, emotionally, and spiritually.

He read masculine and feminine as complementary parts of a universal whole. Carrying his culture's patriarchal notions, he associated femininity with emotions but did not see this as inferior. Rather, this was essential to the development of the whole person, and he argued that men—priests included—would be remiss without the feminine. There was "no road to spiritual maturity or plenitude except through some 'emotional' influence....No man at all can dispense with the Feminine, any more than he can dispense with light, or oxygen, or vitamins." The feminine also figured into his understanding of the evolutionary process. He saw the "Universal Feminine" as a "unitive" force in the cosmos, an energy that worked to unite all into one.[57] In a 1919 poem, he also made the feminine the drawing force in the creation of his whole.[58] Of course, he had already delegated this unifying force to his Cosmic Christ, but perhaps there was room for both.

In 1922, Teilhard defended his dissertation and continued what became a highly successful scientific career. Upon graduation, he became a professor at the Catholic Institute in Paris and was elected president of the

Geological Society of France. His first visit to China came in 1923, at the invitation of fellow Jesuit and scientist Émile Licent. The two conducted an expedition along the Yellow River to western Mongolia.[59] The dig produced such remarkable fruit, yielding about 500 kilos of ancient stones for analysis and an abundance of perfectly preserved animal fossils, that Teilhard postponed his return home. He studied the material at the Jesuit museum in Tientsin and undertook another excavation.

While in China, the priest, keenly interested in the purpose of life, speculated as much about the future as he pondered the earth's past. In the summer of 1923, he drafted a letter to his colleague Abbé Breuil stating that though "absorbed" by Mongolia's "museum of antique specimens (zoological and ethnological)," he was more intrigued in "the future of things" rather than this "slice of the past."[60] He began to examine places he visited in terms of the evolutionary time line and signs of progress. In doing so, he adhered to common racial theories. He surmised that Asia was behind the West in its development. Mongolia seemed "an empty reservoir," he wrote in the same letter. That fall in another letter to Breuil, he made clear his Western bias: "To see Central Asia with an assured and confident eye, you must see it at dusk when the sun, taking with it all the glory of the Far East, sinks behind the mountains of the west, to rise on our western civilization."[61]

He modified his ethnocentric attitudes later, but during the twenty years he lived in the East, he never learned to speak Chinese proficiently, and the evolutionary schema he developed betrayed a Eurocentric bias. The British scientist Joseph Needham noted this prejudice. He chastised Teilhard for his assessment of China as "Neolithic" and the idea that "during historic time the principal axis of anthropogenesis passed through the west." To write this, Needham thought, perpetuated "a vulgar error still capable of doing great harm."[62]

Teilhard's views on nationality and race were complicated by his international travels, friendships, world wars, assumptions of universal oneness, and belief that one day there would be no notion of separate races. "Sooner or later, the unification of the human race is bound to come, and if the world wishes to survive there must be an end to racial conflict."[63] Repulsed later by Adolf Hitler's National Socialism, he denounced racism as a form of extreme isolationism and individualism that worked against the formation of the whole. The "doctrine that there are a few select and chosen races" was "insidious."[64] Instead, he imagined a future that promised "a fusion of races leading directly to the establishment not only of a common language, but of a common morality and common ideals…a community of effort and struggle for the same objectives."[65]

During this initial visit to China and in subsequent years, the priest associated with people of many nationalities. At scientific gatherings in Peking he met American, Chinese, English, French, Russian, and Swedish scientists who had created a number of important scientific institutions in China. They often gathered on Sundays to socialize. His friend, fellow Jesuit and scientist Pierre Leroy, remembered: "I was greatly struck myself at these meetings by Père Teilhard's winning manner. Buoyant and vivacious... the life and soul of our gatherings."[66] This community increased his world perspective.

The priest—kind, gregarious, and open to many—was not easy to label. "The world is round," he liked to say, "so that friendship may circle it."[67] Any prejudice he harbored did not seem to dampen his influence with the Chinese. Instead, troubles surfaced with his French colleagues. When Teilhard, in 1929, accepted a position with the Chinese Geological Survey working under the directorship of Chinese geologist Wong Wen-hao and Canadian Davidson Black, his fellow Jesuit scientist Licent grew disgruntled with him, accusing him of becoming a "coolie" and going over to the Chinese side. Protective of the museum he had established at Tientsin, Licent viewed their work as belonging to the French. Teilhard believed scientific knowledge belonged to no nation but was the property of all.[68]

In sum, this was not simply the case of an imperialist in a foreign land. Though proud of his French roots and never fully able to discard some racialist notions, Teilhard adopted, through his science, religion, and friendships, a more global position. As early as 1926, he saw himself as a world citizen: "I would like to express the thoughts of a man who, having finally penetrated the partitions and ceilings of little countries, little coteries, little sects, rises above all these categories and finds himself a child and citizen of the Earth."[69] Thirty more years of crisscrossing the oceans and continents augmented his globalism.

He went to China for science, but, of course, he explored the spiritual, too. Through his daily routine of mass and prayer, fellowship with priests, obedience to his order, and constant pursuit of a consecrated life, he revealed himself as a man of the cloth, wholly committed to his religion. He compared his China experiences to time in war. In both, his "pan-Christic" mysticism permeated everything. He felt "communion with God" and saw Christ as "a fire with the power to penetrate all things."[70] On Mongolia's outer reaches in 1923, living in the midst of rocks, fossilized animals, and scientific gear, he penned "Mass on the World," shaping it to align with the segments of the Catholic Mass: consecration, adoration, and communion. Lacking the elements of bread and wine, he offered up the world, giving praise to a Christ both of spirit and as "incarnate Being in the world of matter." Hence, he reiterated his monistic and evolutionary themes.[71]

In 1924, Teilhard sailed back to Paris to teach at the Catholic Institute. But teaching was not enough. He desired a larger forum "to make myself heard." He told a friend, "I seem to have, deep inside myself, something that needs to emerge and be disseminated: a certain enthusiastic vision of the immensity and promise of the World."[72] He longed to set others "afire" and did, judging by the large following he began to amass. The Vatican, however, did not join the throng. Indeed, the Catholic prelacy pitched water at any fire he tried to ignite.

Almost as soon as he set foot in France, his superiors brought him in for questioning. Earlier, he had written about his "serious difficulty in retaining the former representation of original sin." Science allowed little room for Adam or the Garden of Eden.[73] By 1924, his writings landed in the hands of papal authorities, sparking anger. This was not the first time officials interrogated him. Before Teilhard took his final vows, church superiors reviewed his writings. Befuddled by his strange lexicon, they struggled to discern his meaning. Was he a pantheist? An evolutionist? Though unsettled, they granted approval.[74] This time, censors were less forgiving. They demanded he sign a statement of silence on original sin. He balked, only agreeing not to proselytize. A year later, his superiors ordered him to stop teaching, sign six propositions, and return to China. He obeyed, and there he remained, save mostly scientific trips, until 1946.[75]

Though deeply disappointed by the church's reprimand, he still felt compelled to share his mystical thoughts on paper. "'If I didn't write,' he told Leroy, 'I would be a traitor.'"[76] In 1926, he drafted *The Divine Milieu*. Finding a "divine milieu"—a center of divine action—in the midst of despair, he told Ida Treat, provided an "outlet."[77] Through his writing, he remade his trials into spiritual opportunities and masked his pains. Seeking to make his world whole, he found comfort in forgetting self and focusing on Christ. "To adore," he wrote in *Divine Milieu*, "means to lose oneself in the unfathomable, to plunge into the inexhaustible, to find peace in the incorruptible, to be absorbed in defined immensity, to offer oneself to the fire."[78] But instead of bringing peace, the manuscript produced more frustrations. When he sent it to Jesuit headquarters in Lyon for publication, several priests read and commended the work. Everything looked favorable until an official sent it to Rome for one final reading. Papal referees rejected publication. Teilhard reworked the text numerous times, trusting that one day it would please his superiors, but it never did. Not until two years after his death did it reach the printing press, and then without official church sanction. Still from 1927 to 1957, this work and other essays passed privately from hand to hand.

Covertly circulating his writings was just one of the strategies Teilhard resorted to in order to assure an audience. Repeatedly, he circumvented his orders. He spoke whenever possible, asked for publication rights numerous times, and traveled to Rome to entreat officials. Finally, in 1951, when he conceded that the church never would lift the ban, he designated his friend Jeanne Mortier his literary executive so she might publish his work after he died. Between 1955 and 1976, she carried out his wishes, publishing thirteen volumes of his censored writings.

Throughout this contentious relationship, he remained a Jesuit, fully expecting he could convince his superiors his work was inspired. Every time the church refused publication, he stubbornly knocked again at the Vatican door. Though sometimes despairing, he consoled himself by thinking this was his cross to bear.[79] His friends said he resisted bitterness, and while this may have been true, he did not shy from criticism. In 1929 he judged the church severely, contending it was "drifting in a backwater of abstract theology, of a sacramentalism whose standard is quantity rather than quality." He believed it had lost touch, "confined to a little artificial world of ritualism, of religious practices, of pious extravagancies, which is completely cut off from the true current of reality." Because of church actions, "the progress of Christian truth has, one might almost say, come to a halt."[80] For that reason, he announced he was "reshaping a New Christ in conformity with a New Universe."[81] He hoped to throw off the "God of the old Cosmos" and establish the "God of the new Cosmogenesis." He prayed that the "universal Presence" would "spring forth in a blaze that is at once Diaphany and Fire."[82] His desire for a reincarnate Christianity was revolutionary, he knew, and that is perhaps one reason he revisited the image of fire. It would take a conflagration, he thought, to change the Vatican.

While banishment to China effectively squelched dissemination of the priest's religious views during his lifetime, it advanced his scientific work. This was partly due to his international scientific community, which accepted Darwinian notions and applauded Teilhard's scientific exactitude and astute observations.[83] China alone presented him with a vast terrain for his geologic work. As soon as he returned in 1926, he set out on an expedition with Licent. They crossed Shansi and Kansu provinces and traveled close to Tibet. This proved one of many treks he made, exploring areas never before examined by geologists. Discoveries only elevated his position, and soon he gained an international reputation, attended prestigious conferences, and participated in multiple excavations. A yearly itinerary in the 1930s might take him to Mongolia, Paris, Hong Kong, San Francisco, Cairo, Rangoon, Calcutta, Philadelphia, and London. In 1935, for example, he joined Yale and Cambridge scientists to study the Pleistocene era in the hopes of making geologic connections between India and China. He then traveled to the site where, in the late nineteenth century, Java Man had been found. By the time he died, he had collaborated with scientists around the world and authored more than 200 scientific articles.[84]

As Teilhard practiced science, traveled, and wrote mystical pieces in the 1930s and 1940s, he refined and extended his holistic perspective, as demonstrated by the development of his interdisciplinary science and optimistic evolutionary schema. In both he tried to see life from a broad perspective and to infuse hope in people that life had purpose and meaning, that the world was moving forward toward one united, loving end. As we will see, his assessment of the twentieth century contributed to his understanding, but first we turn to his creation of a science that treated life as a whole and the universe as interconnected.[85] True to his holistic leanings, Teilhard urged not only a synthesis between religion and science but a broad, synthetic, transdisciplinary science. This conformed to his worldview, training, and circumstances. Certainly his work required him to be conversant and practiced in many fields. Often one of only two or three scientists on an exploration, he worked simultaneously as biologist, botanist, geologist, geographer, and paleontologist.

Beginning in the 1920s, Teilhard advanced a holistic science of the "biosphere," a term coined by geologist Edward Suess in 1875. Teilhard's notion of the biosphere as the totality of all living things developed in conversation with philosopher of science Édouard Le Roy and Russian geologist Vladimir Vernadsky. Fed by evolutionary thinking, the three did much to promote looking at the earth as a whole system.[86] Teilhard, who like Buckminster Fuller resisted overspecialization, called for "tackling the study of the earth in a more radical and comprehensive fashion, and for looking at it as a whole, endowed with specifically terrestrial, mechanical, physical, and chemical properties…instead of burying our noses in a detailed study of the action of very limited causes, which influence only very limited parts of the earth."[87] Working in China during the midst of an exciting period of paleontological studies prompted further thinking of the earth as one whole. The "most decisive event" came in the 1930s, when he and others uncovered Peking Man (who actually turned out to be a woman).[88] Teilhard affectionately called her "Nelly," and it was her reconstructed skull he carried to America in 1937. Nelly's bones called for analysis. The geologic age of the fossils eventually led Teilhard and other scientists to think more synthetically and to reinterpret the Quaternary period in the Far East. This prompted additional investigations, some of which took him to India, Burma, and Java. Numerous publications on these data contributed to his international stature and gave him a forum for advocating a conceptual framework to interpret data and significance. Eventually he framed a new discipline that was decidedly holistic and called it "geobiology."

"Geobiology" incorporated several branches of knowledge: biology, paleontology, and geography. According to Teilhardian scholar Lodovico Galleni, geobiologists "examine together the development in time of certain phyletic branches (the field of paleontology) with the geographic dispersal of living forms (the field of biogeography), and do all of this on a vast, continental scale."[89] Teilhard thought this "science of the biosphere" explained nature's interdependencies: "Life taken as a whole, forms a single system bound to the surface of the earth; a system whose elements, in whatever order of association they may be considered, are not simply thrown together and moulded upon one another like grains of sand, but are organically interdependent." The earth's crust or "organic sheet, which is spread over the whole surface, . . . is in fact chemically the most active 'sphere' of our planet" and cannot be separated from the earth it covers. The aim, he stated, was to study "all of the organic links of every description that are recognizable between living beings considered *in their totality as a single closed system*. And, secondly, the study of the physico-chemical links by which the birth and development of this living envelope are bound up with the history of the planet."[90] To promote this method, he and Pierre Leroy started the Institute of Geobiology, produced a geobiological world map, and published the journal *Geobiologia*.[91]

Teilhard's notion of a "living" earth was not new to him. Plato said that the cosmos was "a living creature, one and visible, containing within itself all living creatures which are by nature akin to itself." In total it was "endowed with soul and reason."[92] Alexander von Humboldt, a pioneer in ecological biology, looked for harmonies in nature and felt that an organic wholeness unified nature.[93] At the end of the twentieth century, conceptualizations of the earth as a live phenomenon again played a powerful role in American culture, feeding work in deep ecology and ecofeminism and contributing to the continued and creative interlocking of religion and science through the Gaia hypothesis and New Age religion.[94] Placing Teilhard's ideas alongside these cultural expressions helps explain American receptivity to the priest's holistic writings.

Thinking about geobiology occurred while Teilhard wrote his mystical essays and while the world endured the rise of fascism and war. Japan's conquest of Asia and Germany's march through Europe brought unprecedented devastation in two places he knew best: China and France. When France surrendered to Hitler in 1940, he wept openly, crying out, "I don't understand."[95] Still, he tried to reconcile this to his more sanguine views. "It is much too early," he wrote a French friend, "to appreciate the magnitude of the collapse, and chiefly the span of the impending changes. But one thing is sufficiently clear. It should be absurd to decide that the world is definitely lost or bad." He hoped it would lead to spiritual renewal and a "mutual form of love, based on the consciousness of a common Something (or rather Somebody) into which all together we converge." Probing "how a new Man may rise out of the crisis," he emphasized that the "absurd" response would be hopelessness.[96] He saw instead an opportunity for community—not as commanded by fascism or communism, which led to "the most appalling linkage in chains," robbed the individual of personality, and turned "him into a gadget or slave," but as forged out of "a mutual form of love" that respected personhood.[97] Here we see Teilhard's personalism aligned with King's.

The priest rejected totalitarianism for the same reason he had abandoned pantheism. Both, he thought, failed to recognize individual personhood. Community was important, but never should the individual be sacrificed for the whole. "Union differentiates," he thought, meaning that even as people form a collective whole, they are still differentiated one from another and free to develop unique personalities: "In every organized whole the parts perfect and fulfill themselves. By failing to grasp this universal law of union, so many kinds of pantheism have led us astray to the worship of a great Whole in which individuals were supposed to become lost like a drop of water, dissolved like a grain of salt, in the sea."[98] As he had determined in World War I, his was a personal whole.

From 1937 to 1940, Teilhard wrote *The Phenomenon of Man*, a synthesis of his holistic framework, a defense of the human, and an attempt to explain a world at war. Always interested in determining where the world was in the evolutionary path, he tried to place current events in geologic time. Living through two world wars, he wrote, "A great many internal and external portents (political and social upheaval, moral and religious unease) have caused us all to feel, more or less confusedly, that something tremendous is at present taking place in the world. But what is it?"[99] In answer, *The Phenomenon of Man* declared that human beings had significance and that the future held promise. Teilhard hoped that his "half-scientific, half-religious faith" would inspire others. He wrote a friend that he understood the current pessimism and cynicism, but he believed that "something has to be said (or at least *prepared*: who would listen these days?) clearly and strongly *for* Man." After "the storm is over," he thought his book might provide "some constructive hope.... In spite of all these troubles, I am always more convinced that the present crisis is for the birth of a new world. I should like it if my book would be ready (and allowed) for publication just when the fight is over."[100] Though publication came later, it was this more than any other writing of his that resonated with Americans in the 1960s, when social reform and the building of beloved community appeared possible and imminent.

The book presented an evolutionary story of "complexification." We have already seen how Teilhard believed that matter was gradually being transformed into spirit. In this work, he developed this idea and emphasized human significance and community. From atoms and molecules to plants and animals, from the very simple to the highly organized, the world developed along a scale of complexity. Gradually, the unfolding of more advanced nervous systems led to a fully conscious human being. He called the point where matter was "humanified" and human beings appeared "hominization." Human beings were "ultra-complex" creatures and an amazing phenomenon; "the coveted fruit that all things work to produce, in which all is summed up and fulfilled, in which all finds joy and pride, is mankind."[101]

Though, biologically speaking, the "human as reconstructed by science today is an animal like the others," there is "something entirely different" about humankind. In fact, the human phenomenon was of "supreme importance." What made human beings so special? Self-consciousness. The "superiority of the human over the animal" rested on the "central phenomenon of *reflection*" or "the power acquired by a consciousness of turning in on itself...to know *itself*; no longer only to know, but to know that it knows."[102] Thus, the goal of complexification was "a rise toward Consciousness."[103] The human, who evolved from tiny seeds of consciousness within the material world, was the apex of creation. So far.

As important as the human being was, it was not the final goal. Teilhard anticipated the birth of a yet higher consciousness as human beings converged, working together as one to form an even better world. (Recall his debate with Bergson. Instead of divergence, Teilhard saw things converging forward, uniting into one with his Cosmic Christ.) He identified this evolutionary stage as "collectivization" or "socialization," believing that through social cooperation and powerful technological systems of communication, human beings were creating a new collective life, one that would ensure "not only survival, but *superlife*."[104] This new collective life required a collective brain—a "brain of brains."[105] The world, moving as one organic whole, had already progressed from the geosphere, when the world existed materially, to the biosphere, when the earth was able to support life. "And now, like a germ of life in the dimensions of the planet," he wrote, "the thinking layer is developing and intertwining its fibers over its whole expanse."[106] He said it "germinated in [his] mind" during World War I when a diversity of men from many nations fought together. He felt a psychic energy from the collective group that seemed to have its own organic integrity. "This envelope was not only conscious but thinking...the essence or rather the very Soul of the Earth."[107] Teilhard named this new layer the "noosphere." Just as "biosphere" denoted the totality of the earth's surface that supports ecological systems, so "noosphere," from the Greek word *noos*—for mind or reason—meant "the terrestrial sphere of thinking substance." (Later, some equated the noosphere with the World Wide Web.)

Now that human beings had become conscious of their own evolution, the scientist suggested that they, working collectively in the noosphere, could join with the unitive force, Christ, and move evolution to a stage of final harmony—a beloved community that he called the Omega Point.[108] The problem was that many did not understand the significance of the human being and so persisted in engaging in war, hatred, racism, and animosity. His mission, he felt, was to awaken his fellows: "The true summons of the cosmos is a call consciously to share in the great work that goes on within it."[109] We must, he contended, "build the universe," grow in love, and converge in harmony with God and each other.[110]

Hence, Teilhard's world was one organic whole, not stagnant, but in the process of becoming something greater. Sarah Appleton-Weber, a Teilhardian scholar, described his understanding of the "collective reality" as "more than the sum-total of its parts. It has a mysterious unity and active power in itself—a birth, unfolding, and a passing." Teilhard believed there were "no isolated 'things' in the world. There are only elements of a whole in process." Those who fail to see this unified whole saw reality as fragmented and absurd.[111] It was this fragmentation, manifested in fear and despair, that he sought to counter. This was why he wanted to update Christianity, making it speak to contemporary science.

For a few years, Teilhard made the Jesuit house in Paris home. He tried to get *The Phenomenon of Man* past Catholic censors, traveling to Rome to petition personally. Again the answer was no. In frustration, he wrote Swan, "Those people in Rome are living on another planet!" To another correspondent, he cried, "If only Rome would start to doubt herself at last, a little."[112] Though critical, and sometimes despondent, he remained resolute. In 1951, he wrote a superior that despite the rejections, he felt "more indissolubly bound to the hierarchical Church and to the Christ of the Gospel than ever before in my life. Never has Christ seemed to me more real, more personal or more immense." He "resolved to remain a 'child of obedience.'"[113]

Though an embarrassment to the Vatican, Teilhard enjoyed acclaim. In 1947, France made him an officer of the Legion of Honor, praising him for his scientific accomplishments, "which have won the highest standing for him in international scientific circles."[114] Other recognitions included memberships in the London Linnaean Society and the French Institute of Science. Amid the honors, Teilhard was in demand as a speaker. "If you want to fill an auditorium," a student chaplain declared, "all you have to do is advertise that you have Teilhard or Jean-Paul Sartre."[115] All this was too much for the church. Though close to seventy, Teilhard could not stay in France. But where to go? After a heart attack in 1947, strenuous work was out of the question. Returning to China after the Communist Revolution in 1949 was impossible. So he used his international connections to secure a position in New York with the Wenner-Gren Foundation of Anthropological Research. Given his many American friends, this was logical, and so from 1951 to his death on Easter Sunday of 1955, he resided in a tiny Jesuit room that looked out on a neon-lit wall of the Copacabana nightclub.

Despite his faithfulness, the church never granted his writings the *nihil obstat* (an attestation that "nothing stands in the way"), which would have declared them doctrinally and morally just. Threatened by his growing status in Catholic and scientific circles, it not only forbade publication but warned others about his heretical thoughts. The encyclical *Humani Generis* (1950) implicitly denounced his evolutionary ideas by affirming Scholasticism, prioritizing scripture over fossils, spurning evolutionists for seeking novelty, and warning all to be cautious of science. As if addressing Teilhard himself, Pope Pius XII contended, "Some imprudently and indiscreetly hold that evolution, which has not been fully proved even in the domain of natural sciences, explains the origin of all things, and audaciously support the monistic and pantheistic opinions that the world is in continual evolution."[116] If that was not enough, Rome decreed a *monitum* in 1962 that admonished priests, bishops, and seminaries to be wary of Teilhard's ideas. In 1967, Thomistic philosopher Jacques Maritain, concerned about the positive response to Teilhard's works in the 1960s, called Teilhard's ideas a "theology-fiction" filled with "confused ideas, a mystico-philosophical imagery, and a whole emotional commotion of huge illusory hopes which a good many men of good faith are ready to accept as a genuinely exalting intellectual synthesis and a new theology." Instead, Maritain concluded, Teilhard's theology was nothing less than "Christianity upside down, so that it is no longer rooted in the Trinity and the Redemption but in the evolving Cosmos." Using Cold War communist fears, he said it was one thing for Marx and Engels to turn Hegel on his head; it is another matter to twist Christianity.[117]

Despite such warnings, many embraced and dispersed Teilhard's ideas. In 1961, Cardinal Maurice Feltin of France called Teilhard's philosophy a wonderful "global vision of the universe wherein matter and spirit, body and soul, nature and supernature, science and faith find their unity in Christ."[118] That same year, writer Flannery O'Connor showed her attraction to Teilhard's evolutionary concepts in a short story entitled "Everything That Rises Must Converge."[119] Novelist Thornton Wilder, politicians Sargent Shriver, Mario Cuomo, Harris Wofford, and others were captivated with Teilhard's global understandings. Secretary-general of the United Nations U Thant (1961–71) agreed with his internationalism, saying, "The age of nations is past. It remains for us now, if we do not wish to perish, to set aside the ancient prejudice and build the earth."[120]

Representing diverse disciplines and often holistic in their thinking, other individuals also credited the priest. Architect Paolo Soleri found in Teilhard a philosophy and an esthetic of beauty and applied it to Arcosanti, his Arizona organic megastructure.[121] Economist Kenneth Boulding, who, like Buckminster Fuller, spoke of "spaceship earth," used Teilhard's concept of the "noosphere" to convey his ideas about the earth's economy.[122] In their history of the "anthropic principle"—the notion that some sort of intelligent design guided the direction of the universe and paved the way for the evolution of human life—physicists John Barrow and Frank Tipler pointed to Teilhard. Adherents of the anthropic principle argue that conditions at the beginning of the universe were ideal for the evolution of human life, hence affirming the notion that the world was made for human beings. This revivification of the argument by design posited that some sort of intelligence orchestrated these conditions.[123] Marshall McLuhan, a Catholic convert, communication theorist, and popularizer of the notion that the "medium is the message," found Teilhard persuasive, too. McLuhan's phrase "the global village" was his translation of "noosphere." Fearful of his academic colleagues and the church, he scarcely mentioned Teilhard in his footnotes, but he did describe the global village as "the Christian concept of the mystical body—all men as members of the body of Christ—this becomes technologically a fact under electronic conditions." He believed television could facilitate the convergence of all peoples; had he not died in 1980, he likely would have been excited about the possibilities of the Internet, too.[124] Ralph Abraham, Frank Jas, and Willard Russell were. They dedicated their manual *The Web Empowerment Book* (1995) to Teilhard, believing that the priest predicted the Internet when he proposed his idea of the noosphere and when he spoke about technology's power to improve the "interconnections of the global brain." The Web, they hoped, would promote a more democratic, sane, and beautiful universe.[125]

Beginning in the 1960s, two organizations, the American Teilhard de Chardin Association and the Institute on Religion in an Age of Science (IRAS), were particularly effective vehicles for disseminating the priest's thought in America. Fordham University became a center for Teilhard studies as early as 1960. As interest grew, scholars and laypeople first established an institute, then incorporated as the Teilhard Association in 1967. Prominent members included anthropologist Margaret Mead, philosopher Ewert Cousins, scientists Loren Eiseley and George Barbour, and cultural historian and Catholic priest Thomas Berry. The group spread Teilhard's ideas through conferences, books, and the journal *Teilhard Studies*. Berry, one of the most vocal proponents, developed a holistic philosophy from Teilhard's theories and Rachel Carson's environmental ethics.[126] One zealous Episcopalian member urged people to "read, mark, learn and inwardly digest" his writings. Monthly lectures in 1963 drew more than 600 individuals. Members, according to the association's historian, "testified with deep feeling to the insight Teilhard had given them into the religion they had all but abandoned because they could not reconcile it with modern scientific views of the world. It was a period of high excitement, of hope that a new world-view synthesizing religion and science would bring a breakthrough of the greatest importance."[127] IRAS also discussed Teilhard's ideas. As one of many organizations intent on maintaining faith in an age of science, IRAS founded the academic journal *Zygon* in 1966.[128] "Zygon," meaning "yoke" in Greek, expressed Teilhardian-like hopes of harnessing religion and science. Journal editors dedicated entire issues to him and published numerous other articles referencing his work.[129]

The priest's religio-scientific views also wove their way into school curricula once thought settled in the *Scopes* case. In 1973, biology professor and

Catholic sister Julia Van Denack advocated using Teilhard's theories to teach biology in the *American Biology Teacher*. "With the controversy over evolution and creation still not resolved in some classrooms," she argued, "it might be profitable" to teach the Teilhardian synthesis.[130] Geneticist Theodosius Dobzhansky, a member of the Teilhard Association, agreed in a 1972 address to teachers. Teilhard, he told them, helped communicate "that evolution is God's method of creation."[131]

Though some Catholic conservatives sided with Jacques Maritain (who was very critical of post–Vatican II reforms) over Sister Van Denack, many American Catholics began to take a more liberal stance. And so did the Vatican. By 1981, Rome moved to "rehabilitate" Teilhard, praising his contributions and character. In 1987, Pope John Paul II called a conference on the relationship between science and religion to bring more integration between the two.[132] These changes, in turn, facilitated greater receptivity to Teilhard.

Teilhard's popularity within Catholic circles may be attributed in large measure to a revival of American Catholicism in the 1960s. Though the church had earlier disappointed progressive Catholics with its antimodernist stance and lost the allegiance of a significant number of young members, Vatican II, the election of a Catholic president in the United States, renewed papal interest in social reform, and liberation theology reversed the decline. Throughout the last half of the century, Catholics grew in influence, wealth, and organizational power to become the largest denomination in America. Many renewed their faith and rededicated themselves to spiritual participation in the church and society. They turned to the mystical writings of such individuals as Trappist monk Thomas Merton, who appealed as much for his spiritual mediations as for his critiques of materialism and militarism. Lay participation increased in Catholic education, service-learning programs, the Catholic Worker movement, and civil rights reform.[133] For many, Teilhard's call to rebuild the earth made sense. It fit, too, with King's plea for the beloved community.

Catholics who revived spiritual interests in the 1960s were not alone. Jews, Protestants, and others did so also. In addition, some began to develop what scholars have identified as a highly personalized, eclectic spirituality. Those who crafted this new spirituality blended beliefs, traditions, and practices from multiple sources: Christian, Jewish, Hindu, Buddhist, and Native religions.[134] The New Age movement does not represent all within this new spirituality (it was much too individual and fragmented for any one vision), but it was significant. The movement is also significant in the story of holism, for some aspects of New Age spirituality captured Teilhard's holistic ideas and illustrate some of the ways his ideas filtered into the culture. New Age seekers emphasized interconnections between mind, body, and spirit; stressed harmony; and drew lines of association between people and nature. The "key to New Age thinking is holism," Ted Peters asserted, "that is, the attempt to overcome modern dualisms such as the split between science and spirit, ideas and feelings, male and female, rich and poor, humanity and nature."[135] In reaction to their world, Peters explained, drawing on Thomas Berry and cosmologist Brian Swimme, New Age believers have looked to the universe to fashion a new metanarrative.[136]

Marilyn Ferguson, a student of the New Age movement, described it as an "Aquarian conspiracy," a loosely knit network uniting to bring about a "global shift in consciousness" and a New Age of love, light, positive energy, global spirituality, and consciousness.[137] Such hopes resembled Teilhard's evolution of convergence (a popular word among this group). Drawing also on astrology, New Age believers conjectured the earth was moving out of the age of Pisces, a dark and violent period, and into the age of Aquarius, a place of harmony, sympathy, and understanding. The musical *Hair* (1960) captured such hopes in the song "Dawning of the Age of Aquarius." The rock band Fifth Dimension made the lyrics popular as it sang "harmony and understanding/Sympathy and trust abounding...And the mind's true liberation/Aquarius."[138]

Ferguson interviewed 185 New Age leaders to find out who had most influenced them. Teilhard came in first, ahead of Carl Jung, Aldous Huxley, Thomas Merton, Werner Erhard, and Maharishi Yogi.[139] Ursula King, a theology scholar and former president of Britain's Teilhard Association, confirmed these findings: "Teilhard was really a pioneer of what is today called 'new age thinking,' one of the early observers of our planet Earth who clearly saw its need for a profound transformation, for an entirely new culture which cannot come about without a new spirituality."[140]

Two of the most important New Age leaders include American Teilhard Association members Robert Muller, a former assistant secretary-general of the United Nations, and psychologist Jean Huston. Muller thought "that much of what I have observed in the world bears out the all-encompassing, global forward-looking philosophy of Teilhard." His observations came from his UN activities and his World War II experience as a Belgian refugee, resister, and prisoner. He believed "future peace, justice, fulfillment, happiness and harmony on this planet will not depend on world government but on divine or cosmic government." Humanity "must seek and apply the 'natural,' 'evolutionary,' 'divine,' 'universal' or 'cosmic' laws which must rule our journey in the cosmos."[141] In addition to delivering speeches, Muller constructed a "global core curriculum" that emphasized evolution and spirituality and included such titles as "Toward a World Religion for the New Age," "Teaching the Gaia Hypothesis," "Education in the New Age," and "Whole Brain Teaching." Captivated by Teilhard's vision but more promiscuous in drawing from all the world's religions, Muller is representative of the New Age movement.[142]

Muller often shared the platform with Huston. Former president of the Association for Humanistic Psychology, Huston introduced Teilhard to "the Human Potential Movement, the Omega Institute and different New Age workshops."[143] The Omega Institute for Holistic Studies, a wellness center begun in 1977, took its name from Teilhard's Omega Point.[144] In 1983, Huston predicted that "in our lifetime we will see the rise of essentially a New World Religion.... I believe a new spiritual *system* will emerge."[145] For Muller, Huston, and others, Teilhard inspired. Human beings, they agreed, were significant actors in the evolutionary process, determiners of the future.[146] Together humanity held the power of ushering in a *new age*.

The human potential movement, including the Esalen Institute, as we will see in the following chapters, became a forum for new spiritualities, including some aspects of the New Age movement. As Walt Anderson noted, Esalen's early years were infused with a "kind of spirituality...that harmonized with the themes of self-actualization, human potentiality, and transformation; it saw the coming cultural change as an awakening, a new phase in human evolution. There was much talk of evolution in the seminars; the source most often cited was not Darwin, with his bleak notions of survival of the fittest, but the scientist-theologian Teilhard de Chardin, with his ideas of the onward-and-upward spiraling of the human spirit."[147] Before we turn our attention to Esalen, however, we need to explore another intellectual who contributed to this holistic sensibility. Humanistic psychologist Abraham Maslow helped spark the growth of the human potential movement, holistic health, and late twentieth-century spirituality. He, too, would figure prominently in the early years of the Esalen Institute.

Abraham Maslow. *Courtesy of Robert D. Farber University Archives and Special Collections, Brandeis University*

5

The Psychological Realm
Abraham Maslow's Self-Actualized Individuals and Eupsychian Community

Holism after World War II was about imagined communities. Rachel Carson connected human beings to an ecosystem of elm leaves, earthworms, and robins to create an idyllic web of life. Structural engineer Buckminster Fuller envisioned a highly efficient built environment that yielded greater individual happiness, social harmony, and global sustainability. Martin Luther King Jr. dedicated himself to the formation of a "beloved community," marked by interracial and economic equality and peaceful internationalism. Pierre Teilhard de Chardin, in a creative amalgamation of Catholicism and evolution, wrote of a final day of love and brotherhood as the "Omega Point."

Abraham Maslow was no different. Though he is best known as one of the founders of humanistic psychology and a proponent of "individual growth," his holism had a strong communitarian thrust. Hand in hand with his hope to foster "self-actualized" people—his expression for emotionally healthy, fully integrated, and self-fulfilled individuals—he dreamed of the establishment of democratic, just, and peaceful societies and "construction of the One Good World."[1] He called his utopia "eupsychia" (pronounced, he said, "yew-sigh-key-a").[2] Hence, in understanding his psychology, community was fundamental. Differences existed between Maslow and the other holists in this study, but, like the rest, he fashioned a holism that pieced his fragmented world together as one and helped him imagine a new age. Though no Pollyanna, he did, in ways, rival the others as the most utopian.

Maslow claimed that his vision of eupsychia began to jell in the days following Japan's attack on Pearl Harbor. As he was driving home one day, a "poor, pathetic parade" crossed before him at an intersection. "Boy scouts and fat people and old uniforms and a flag and someone playing a flute off-key" formed a ragged patriotic procession and symbolized to him a world in disarray. His tears began to flow. As he recalled: "I felt we didn't understand—not Hitler, nor the Germans, nor Stalin, nor the Communists." Hence, instead of responding to this lack of understanding with military might, Maslow called for psychological enlightenment. He claimed "a vision of a peace table, with people sitting around it, talking about human nature and hatred and war and peace and brotherhood," and determined "that the rest of my life must be devoted to discovering a psychology for the peace table.... I wanted to prove that human beings are capable of something grander than war and prejudice and hatred."[3]

In a 1968 interview, the psychologist contended that this epiphanic moment—or "peak experience," as he termed such happenings—forever altered his work: "I gave up everything I was fascinated with in a selfish way around 1941. I felt I must try to save the world and to prevent these horrible wars and this awful hatred and prejudice."[4] The problem, he thought, was that psychologists had yet to identify why some people behaved aggressively and why others followed. What motivated human beings to act the way they did? Why were some malicious and some kind?[5] Convinced that psychology could provide the answers, he dedicated himself to the study of human motivation and ushering in a eupsychian world.

Of course, other students of the mind—most notably, psychoanalyst Sigmund Freud—had confronted problems of motive, development, and aggression. And Maslow borrowed from them. He subscribed to some Freudian ideas, but not all. Instead of adopting Freud's pessimistic stance, Maslow chose to see the grander side of human nature. Instead of placing human beings in a struggle between id, ego, and superego, he focused on human potential, integrity, and peak experiences. Instead of setting up the individual in opposition to society as Freud described the relationship in *Civilization and Its Discontents*, Maslow saw symbiosis. Finally, rather than denigrating religion as illusionary, he regarded transcendental experiences as legitimate and potentially healthy expressions. Like Freud, he was a child of science, but unlike Freud, he made room for the mystical.

This chapter examines Maslow's formation and employment of holism and suggests that he embraced this perspective to make whole his particular sense of reality, fashion a more humanistic science, and design a more harmonious world. It does so by highlighting pivotal childhood moments as a Jewish boy in New York City in the early years of the twentieth century and by tracking his intellectual journey from behaviorism as an undergraduate in the 1920s to Freudian and Adlerian theories in his doctoral studies on monkeys in the early 1930s to Gestalt psychology and humanistic psychology by 1940. Throughout his career, Maslow labored as an academic researcher, exploring human sexuality, then human motivation, peak experiences, creativity, mysticism, and community. After a postdoctoral fellowship at Columbia University from 1935 to 1937, he joined the faculty at Brooklyn College, staying until 1951, when he was called to start the Department of Psychology at the newly established Brandeis University. Eighteen years later he left Massachusetts to take a writing fellowship with Saga Corporation in Menlo Park, California. There he died in 1970.

As he told it, the beginning of World War II was his turning point, and surely it was key to understanding his holistic paradigm and psychology. Totalitarian aggression in the East and West, the Jewish Holocaust, and atomic weaponry marked him and his generation, changing his conception of life and making him long for a more secure and whole world. But his hope for "setting the table for peace" also was driven by personal crises, dissatisfaction with reductionistic science, and optimistic belief in the human potential.

Maslow captivated other psychologists and members of the public at large. In doing so, he made a substantial contribution to this holistic sensibility. Through his numerous writings, chiefly his best-selling books *Motivation and Personality* (1954) and *The Psychology of Being* (1962), his teaching, professional activities, business consulting, speeches, and widespread popularity, Maslow shaped the work of academic and clinical psychologists, corporate leaders, counterculturalists, feminists, social reformers, and the general public. In the 1950s, he, along with James Bugental, Erich Fromm, Rollo May, and Carl Rogers, took a leading role in crafting humanistic psychology, a field grounded in holistic thought. Their talk of personal and social transformation (often intertwined and treated together) fed American optimism in Kennedy's New Frontier and Johnson's Great Society, as well as multiple visions by social reformers and counterculturalists. Before discussing the ways his holistic ideas influenced others, we turn first to a more in-depth look at the forces that drew him to a holistic worldview.

Maslow's childhood was neither happy nor promising. Born in 1908 to a lower-class Jewish immigrant couple in New York City, he endured scorn from his mother and emotional and physical distance from his father. He witnessed bitter fights between his parents and encountered rejection, ridicule, and anti-Semitism at school. At twenty-four, he wrote in his diary: "My childhood and boyhood were miserably unhappy. In retrospect, it seemed so dark and sad a period that I wonder how I accepted it so unquestioningly. I can find no single glimpse of happiness in all my memories."[6]

His mother, Rose, left an especially bitter impression on him, the eldest of seven children. He remembered her as controlling, cruel, ignorant, superstitious, and frightful, recounting stories of her padlocking the refrigerator door, allowing her children food when she deemed it necessary. When she granted a meal, she denied her oldest select pieces of meat, reserving them for the younger children. Frequently, Rose ridiculed her son. And sometimes, she displayed an uncontrollable anger. On one occasion, just after purchasing several classic 78 rpm records, Abe spread his purchases on the living room floor to admire them. Rose walked in and commanded him to pick them up. When he failed to act promptly, she crushed the records with her heels. Another day, Abe brought home two abandoned kittens. He hid them in the basement, but his mother heard their meows and found her son feeding them milk. Enraged that he dared to bring animals home and furious that he was using her dishes as drinking bowls, she whipped the kittens against the basement wall and bashed their heads until they were dead.

Never forgetting or forgiving his mother, despite years of psychoanalysis, he scorned everything about her, rejecting "her physical appearance, world view and values." Once started, he spewed forth a long list of animosities: "her stinginess, her total selfishness, her lack of love for anyone else in the world—even her own husband and children—her narcissism, her Negro prejudice, her exploitation of anyone, her assumption that anyone was wrong who disagreed with her, her lack of friends, her sloppiness and dirtiness, her lack of family feeling for her own parents and siblings, her primitive animal-like care for herself and her body alone."[7] His siblings minimized his stories and protested his public disclosures, but they were unable to silence him. As the oldest, his experience was probably somewhat different from theirs. Perhaps, too, he exaggerated. The divorce of his parents after he left for college testified, however, to at least some strain in the household. Despite attempts to overcome his intense hatred, Maslow never visited his mother after he left home. When she died, he refused to attend her funeral. If Maslow wanted to describe someone who was not a "self-actualizer," this negative account of his mother did the job. Perhaps that was part of his aim.

Using his mother as a foil, he imagined himself the opposite. And according to many colleagues and friends, he succeeded. Most described him as a thoughtful, optimistic, warm, and personable man, a loving husband, and a devoted father. Some even found him too kind. Anthropologist Gregory Bateson thought Maslow suspiciously generous, recalling, "He was always so *good*."[8] Others accused him of arrogance and obstinacy. Brooklyn College faculty members denied him a promotion every year for nine years, citing conceit and an inability to be a team player. And while his Brooklyn students adored him, many at Brandeis found him aloof. The fact that he worked best alone and refused to bow to any person, system, or school of thought did not help. Even relationships with mentors, many of whom he admired, ended uncomfortably. Sometimes, as with Alfred Adler, his tutors withdrew when Maslow began to express his own ideas. This may say as much about Adler and others as it does about Maslow, but Maslow's cool confidence in his own intellect could be offensive. He perceived himself as superior (even while he privately wrestled with feelings of insecurity). Though smug, he often disarmed people with his enthusiasm, positive outlook, and fatherly heart.

Not only did he seek to make himself the opposite of the mother he described, but his humanistic psychology was likewise motivated by abhorrence of her. One of his colleagues at Brandeis described Maslow's work as a quest for "that germ of goodness" in the human, "to describe it, and show us how it should be developed."[9] In some respects, his project was personal: he was searching for the germ of goodness within himself to dispel his hurt childhood feelings. But it also became the mark of his philosophy. Maslow, in his own self-analysis, thought that his "utopianism, ethical stress, humanism, stress on kindness, love, friendship, and all the rest" stemmed from "having no mother-love." Indeed, he felt that "the whole thrust of my life philosophy and all my research and theorizing also has its roots in a hatred for and revulsion against everything she stood for."[10] He said he started forging his worldview by questioning and rejecting Rose's superstitions. When he misbehaved, she threatened that God would "strike [him] down." Strangely, he took her literally and tested her statements. One day she told him that if he climbed through the window, he would not grow. "So I climbed through the window and then checked my growth."[11] This childhood response may have given him courage to play the maverick whenever he thought his ideas superior.

Hatred for his mother and her superstitions prompted early disdain for religion and contributed to a holism that was somewhat different from that of others in this study. The little religious training he received did nothing to instill faith either. Though his parents did not practice Judaism, they did insist on his bar mitzvah. This proved a disaster. In the ceremony, when he had to turn to Rose and say, "My dear mother, to whom I owe my life, and to whom I owe my upbringing," he burst into tears. Instead of finishing, he ran from the synagogue podium, nauseated.[12] Uttering such words, he contended, would have been hypocritical.

Anti-Semitism added to his sadness. To cope—and to satisfy his intellectual curiosity—he escaped into a world of books: "I used to get up out of my house before anyone else and go to the library and stand at [its] doors until it opened."[13] To reach the library, he had to walk through non-Jewish territory. If he was detected, anti-Semitic gangs cursed and chased him, pitching rocks at his skinny frame. At elementary school, classmates mocked him, and he overheard teachers speak derisively of him as "that smart Jew."[14] This, coupled with his precociousness, made him feel like a "freak with two heads."[15] To protect himself, he tried to join a Jewish gang. He failed miserably, for, unlike his mother, he could not execute cats. Initiates proved their worthiness by flinging rocks at girls and stoning cats. Unable to perform, he was left to fend for himself. In response to these childhood events, the boy renounced God.

Atheism, humanism, and naturalism became the psychologist's foundation. "Man *can* solve his problems by his own strength," he conjectured in 1944. "He doesn't have to fly to God. He can look within himself for all sorts of potentialities, strength and goodness."[16] Later, as he listened to his research subjects describe mystical experiences, he backed down from a purely empiricist approach. He started reading Buddhist, Christian, and Taoist texts and called transcendent encounters "peak experiences," comparing them to philosopher William James's descriptions of religious expression. These moments, Maslow surmised, gave people a "feeling of great ecstasy and wonder and awe" and altered daily life.[17] To explain these transformative moments, the psychologist dissociated them from religion: "They do not necessarily imply any supernatural concepts. They are well within the realm of nature, and can be investigated in an entirely naturalistic way."[18] He eventually concluded that human beings needed transcendent encounters. Without them, "we get sick, violent, and nihilistic or else hopeless and apathetic. We need something 'bigger than we are' to be awed by and to commit ourselves to in a new, naturalistic, empirical, non-churchly sense, perhaps as Thoreau and Whitman, William James and John Dewey did."[19] Coupled with his lifelong commitment to science, the psychologist's naturalistic faith proved to be another holist's creative amalgamation of the tangible and transcendent. It was, yet again, a fusion of naturalistic religion and science in postwar America.

Despite Maslow's cheerless childhood, he found solace in books and friendship with his cousin Will, and at about the age of twenty, joy surprised him in two fundamental ways. First, he fell in love with his cousin Bertha; second, he discovered the psychology of John B. Watson, the noted behaviorist. Life began, he declared, when he met Bertha, and in 1928, to the dismay of his parents, they married. Life also began when he encountered three of Watson's seminal essays.[20] While his love for Bertha was lifelong, his enchantment with behaviorism faded. Still, Maslow's attraction to Watson solidified his métier and revealed what motivated the young man.

As an undergraduate, Maslow dabbled in numerous fields. Initially, he "thought 'Phooey!'" with psychology, too, but when he read Watson at the Forty-second Street Library in 1927, he ran out "in high excitement and exhilaration, danced down 5th Ave., jumping and shouting."[21] It is not hard to see why Watson's words excited him. By this point Maslow, in step with his father and cousin Will, identified with socialism. He counted Norman Thomas,

Upton Sinclair, and Eugene Debs as his heroes and was searching for a career to better the world. "There is a Jewish tradition of the utopian, and the ethical," he explained, "and I was pretty definitely looking for the improvement of mankind. I became impatient with philosophy, at all the talking that didn't get any place."[22] Watson, it appeared, offered more than talk.

In behaviorism's promise to control human behavior, Maslow saw the "possibility of *a science* of psychology, a program of work which promised real progress, real advance, real solutions of real problems."[23] He was already sold on the efficacy of science. Now behaviorism's stimulus and response methods appeared to produce results, and he trusted Watson's claim that he could take a "dozen healthy infants" and "train them to become any type of specialist." Furthermore, he saluted Watson's contempt for racism and corporal punishment.[24]

Watson built his case partly on William Graham Sumner's ideas. This pleased Maslow, who had been dazzled by Sumner's book *Folkways*.[25] In this 1906 publication, the great evangelist of social Darwinism pitted science against religion. He offered a chronicle of human savagery and blamed it on superstition, ethnocentrism, and prejudice. But Sumner declared that all was not despair, for he believed that religion was fading and science—the preeminent voice of reason—ascending. Scientists, whom Sumner deemed superior—akin to Plato's "philosopher-kings"—would free society of its "dead weight of ignorance, poverty, crime, and disease" and steer the masses who lived "by routine and tradition" and who were "shallow, narrow-minded, and prejudiced."[26]

Maslow gave the masses more credit, but as one who withstood anti-Semitic taunting, pictured his own mother as "shallow, narrow-minded, and prejudiced," detested racism, scoffed at institutional religion, and embraced science, his attraction to Sumner and Watson fed his utopian longings and messianic views. Attracted to the notion that every age harbored a few superior individuals, he began to see himself as one of the elite, one who could lead people out of superstition and into the light. He pledged to use his mind to make the world a better place, seeing his commitment as "something like the religious ceremonies of vowing and of offering oneself on the altar of science.... This was a total dedication."[27] Though he bowed before science's altar all his life, he eventually challenged behaviorism. At twenty, however, this approach appealed. Looking back years later, Maslow admitted, "My goals were very definitely utopian and messianic and world-improving and people-improving...here it looked to me as if I'd got the secret by the tail."[28]

Shortly after reading Watson, he transferred to the University of Wisconsin in Madison to study psychology. Armed with a new sense of his mission in life, he declared: "That was it. I was off to Wisconsin to change the world."[29] He chose Madison to flee his family and because of the university's liberal reputation and faculty. The department's emphasis—like most at the time—was experimentalist-behaviorist, and from 1928 to the completion of his doctorate in 1934, his work largely followed this model. While the country suffered through the Great Depression, he studied physiology and anatomy, conducted laboratory experiments on animals, and ran statistics. He also became fascinated with Freud and Adler's dispute over motivation, eventually testing their theories in his dissertation on dominance and social hierarchy in the sexual behavior of monkeys. Weighing Freud's theory that the unconscious and sexual impulses drive behavior against Adler's emphasis on humanity's will to power, Maslow sided with Adler.[30]

At Madison, he continued to read socialist writings and found the socialist spirit attractive. In New York, he had attended lectures on socialism. Now, he and Bertha frequented Socialist Party meetings and joined a housing cooperative. But they were not activists. Maslow never did much politically beyond signing an occasional petition; when his cousin Will campaigned for Socialist Norman Thomas, he hung back. To a large extent, Maslow's socialism corresponded with his understanding of Judaism. Though unsympathetic toward institutional religion, a target of anti-Semitism, and a committed atheist, he never renounced his Jewish heritage. Jewish teachings shaped his humanism and social consciousness, and the anti-Semitism he encountered evoked in him empathy for others. Anti-Semitism also heightened his Jewish identity. To help him gain employment after obtaining his doctorate, some professors encouraged a name change to hide his roots. No, he wrote belligerently in his diary, "If I'm a Jew, I'm a Jew, and I'll stuff it down your throat if you don't like it." He also refused to join the university's alumni association because of the anti-Semitism he felt existed there. Later, he provided financial support to Brooklyn College's Jewish students, helped establish the Jewish University, Brandeis, and declared his allegiance to the State of Israel, especially during the Six Days' War.[31]

Without a job, he enrolled in medical studies at Wisconsin. Barely a semester later, he dropped out. Certainly his impatience with rote anatomical learning played a role in his withdrawal, but more than that, he found the profession callous. Speaking to an audience of premed majors at Brandeis in 1965, Maslow lambasted what he perceived to be a "taboo of tenderness" in medicine. A sense of amazement for the human body and the desire to help one's fellow should permeate medical work, but instead he claimed medicine was too atomistic, reductionistic, and thick-skinned. Instructors desacralized the patient and taught future doctors "to confront death and pain and disease in a cool, objective, unemotional manner." He described the first operation he witnessed as an attempt to "remove the sense of awe, of privacy, of fear, of shyness before the sacred." Excising a cancerous breast, the casual-talking physician appeared cavalier. With an electrical scalpel, he cut off the breast, "tossing this object through the air onto the counter where it landed with a plop." Maslow said, "It had changed from a sacred object into a lump of fat." In Maslow's own dissection of the surgery, he contrasted the physician's attitude with "preliterate societies" where he imagined the procedure would have been performed with respect. Instead in his society, which valued technological skill, the expert was "emotionless, cool, calm," and "no prayers, rituals or ceremonies of any kind" could be heard.[32]

Critiquing the medical profession as dehumanizing has a history. In the nineteenth century, as the medical community professionalized and bureaucratized its growing scientific knowledge, it became more reductionistic and specialized. Scientific experts, relying on laboratory tools, objective analysis, and technical terms, learned to diagnose the cause of illness, but this often came at the expense of a more holistic, humanistic patient approach. Resistance to this "specificity revolution," historian Charles Rosenberg explained, existed from at least the first years of the twentieth century.[33] Furthermore, Maslow's humanistic assertions echoed a strong personalist cultural critique articulated in the 1940s and 1950s by Martin Luther King, Paul Goodman, A. J. Muste, David Dellinger, Beat poets like Kenneth Rexroth, Esalen founders Michael Murphy and Richard Price, and others who found society impersonal in business, education, politics, and science. To break the objectivistic, inhumane approach of his scientific society, essayist Dwight Macdonald called for "the primacy of the individual human being." Lewis Mumford joined the critique of science, especially finding fault with what Mumford called the "detached and depersonalized scientific intelligence" of the Manhattan Project and America's acquiescence to militarism.[34]

Public railings against dehumanization in medicine grew in the 1960s and 1970s, and Maslow contributed to this sentiment. So did popular culture. Coldhearted Nurse Ratched in Ken Kesey's *One Flew Over the Cuckoos Nest* (1962 novel; 1975 film) personified abusive patient care and bureaucratic efficiency. Actor Alan Alda, who played a doctor on the hit television series *Mash*, echoed Maslow's views in a 1979 address to medical students with his characteristic humor: "Will you be the kind of doctor who cares more about the case than the person? ('Nurse, call the gastric ulcer and have him come in at three.') You'll know you're in trouble if you find yourself wishing they would mail in their liver in a plain brown envelope." Alda ended with a medical lesson: "The head bone is connected to the heart bone. Don't let them come apart."[35] Maslow's, Kesey's, and Alda's humanism became central to the burgeoning holistic health care movement in the latter decades of the century.[36]

During his short stint in medical classes, Maslow affirmed the dignity of those he studied. Before conducting his first dissection, he learned the man's name, profession, and cause of death. Finding he was working on a lumberman killed in a fight seemed to help him wield the scalpel with reverence.[37] Still, he concluded medicine was heartless and quit. His zeal for behaviorism waned for similar reasons. Watson said scientists should put "no dividing line between man and brute"; the psychologist "must describe the behavior of a man in no other terms than those you would use in describing the behavior of the ox you slaughter."[38] Maslow disagreed.

In 1935, Maslow returned to New York to work with Columbia University's Edward L. Thorndike, but he found the esteemed psychologist's project "silly" and neglected his assignment. Instead, without permission, he began to study human sexuality, theorizing "that working on sex was the easiest way to help mankind. If I could discover a way to improve the sexual life of even one per cent, then I could improve the whole species."[39] When he used Thorndike's office to interview women about their self-esteem and sexuality, he reported that "everybody was scandalized."[40] Especially Thorndike. Surprisingly, he kept his job. An expert in measuring intelligence, Thorndike had tested Maslow and was awed by his exceptionally high IQ score of 195. He granted his young rebel carte blanche to study anything. He also disclosed the IQ results to Maslow, who in turn shared them with his friends. The news bolstered the young psychologist's feelings of superiority: "Thereafter, if I retreated in the face of [intellectual] oppositions, I'd [sometimes] wake up in the middle of the night and say, 'But dammit, I'm smarter than he is. Why should I feel that he's right and I wrong?'"[41]

Studying human beings rather than monkeys signaled Maslow's growing frustration with objectivism and his willingness to voice unorthodox views. He quit laboratory experiments that most psychologist-researchers endorsed and undertook a more subjective methodology. He chose the unconventional field of human sexuality to demonstrate his readiness to explore new territory, and some, including sexologist Alfred Kinsey, took notice.[42] Eventually, he parted ways with behaviorism. Fatherhood, he claimed, was the "thunderclap that settled things." Mice running through mazes could not compare with the mysterious human baby; stimulus and response studies could not explain creativity and individuality. "It made the behaviorism I had been so enthusiastic about look so foolish that I couldn't stomach it anymore."[43] Instead, he surmised, something like instincts must influence personality. Though this called forth Freudian understandings, Maslow rejected America's craze for psychoanalysis as a tool for social adjustment. Unlike the pessimistic Austrian master, he refused to squelch his enthusiastic endorsement of humanity.

When Maslow moved back to New York in 1935, he began attending lectures at both the New School for Social Research and Columbia University. These lectures and ensuing discussions, particularly with holistic thinkers Max Wertheimer and Ruth Benedict, proved instrumental to the development of his holistic sensibility. Hence, it is worth exploring both. First, at the New School, a gathering place bordering Greenwich Village for New York's European refugees, Maslow met Wertheimer and other renowned thinkers such as Alfred Adler, Erich Fromm, and Karen Horney. Wertheimer impressed Maslow most, eventually becoming a primary model for Maslow's "self-actualized" person.[44] He admired the émigré's intellectual curiosity, compassion, and calm, good-humored nature. Wertheimer, a founder of Gestalt psychology, introduced his protégé to one of the most important early twentieth-century expressions of holism. While it would be misleading to think of Gestalt psychologists as only holistic, holism was nonetheless an important component. As Michael Wertheimer, a historian of psychology and Max's son, explained, the Gestalt system was "the radical view that *the whole is psychologically, logically, epistemologically, and ontologically prior to its parts. A whole is not only more than the sum of its parts, it is entirely different from a sum of its parts: thinking in terms of a sum does violence to the very nature of the dynamics of genuine wholes* [emphasis in original]."[45] This holistic psychology played a fundamental role in Maslow's thinking. It also had an enormous effect on the work of academic and clinical psychologists after World War II, including various offshoots such as the Gestalt therapy developed by Frederick Perls, Paul Goodman, and Ralph Hefferline.[46] Culturally, as the Esalen experience demonstrates, Gestalt ideas made their mark on the counterculture, the human potential movement, and changing religious practices.

Gestalt psychology took its name from the German word *Gestalt*—meaning "pattern," "configuration," or "unified whole"—Wertheimer and other psychologists claimed that the mind perceives reality in terms of *Gestalten*, or wholes. People do not understand experience in piecemeal fashion. Instead, they interpret reality based on organizational patterns and meaningful wholes. Wertheimer's teacher Christian von Ehrenfels (1859–1932), who was trained in Austrian and German philosophy, coined the term "gestalt" and laid the groundwork for Gestalt psychology when he said musical melodies have "gestalt qualities." A melody is composed of musical notes, yet it is more than just a collection of notes. It follows a distinct form. If the notes are rearranged, the melody is lost. Hence, a melody is a whole that is more than the sum of its parts.[47] Wertheimer extended these ideas to studies on the perception of movement and established the Gestalt school. He argued, contra reductionism, that perception could not be understood bit by bit. One must look at the whole.[48] Later, he explained cognition as

holistic, too. He called this the "aha" experience. When we perceive a pattern, solve a problem, or answer a riddle, we exclaim, "Aha!" We understand. After seeing the whole, we discern the nature, positioning, and
functioning of the parts.[49]

Eastern religion gave Wertheimer's psychology an even stronger holistic
stance. His "Being and Doing" lecture introduced Maslow to "Taoism, Lao-
tze, and Buddhism," and his questions about human cognition, motivation,
and personality opened Maslow to investigate the role of play, aesthetics,
awe, and mysticism in the human experience. Similarly, Wertheimer's ethics spurred Maslow to ask, as he did when he confronted the parade in 1941,
what motivated people.[50] It was in 1941 that he regularly attended Wertheimer's lectures and conversed with him informally.

While Gestalt psychology and other early twentieth-century expressions
of holism were important precursors to the post-1945 holistic moment highlighted in this book, influencing many disciplines, providing important
alternatives to reductionistic science, and contributing to the intellectual
development of Carson, Maslow, and others, none of these earlier models
were successful in capturing the imagination of the public in the same way
that 1960s holists did. Nor did these predecessors feed social reform in the
ways that postwar holism did. World War II concentration camps, nuclear
weaponry, the Cold War, McCarthyism, suburbanization, decolonization,
the rights revolution, and economic prosperity helped create the conditions
that allowed for the flowering of holism in the long 1960s. In that environment, holists delivered an important and applicable message.

Maslow appropriated ideas from Wertheimer and at least three other
important Gestalt psychologists: Kurt Goldstein, Kurt Koffka, and Wolfgang
Köhler. Praising Goldstein, who worked on brain-damaged soldiers in
World War I and developed an organismic theory, Maslow wrote: "I agree
with his work and system in practically everything."[51] He also lauded Koffka's
broad approach and concurred with Köhler's attacks on Pavlovian reflex
studies and Watsonian stimulus-response theories.[52] Simultaneously, he,
like the Gestaltists, upheld science's epistemological value. Critiquing scientific methods did not mean a dismissal of science. As one historian noted,
Gestalt psychologists attempted to "advance holistic thought *within* natural
science."[53] They worked to reinvent science, modify methodologies, shift
assumptions, and adjust metaphors to fit holistic theories. Like their colleagues in physics, Albert Einstein and Max Planck, they carved out a worldview that they hoped accommodated a more dynamic understanding of
reality.[54] Maslow approved.

In sum, Gestalt psychology offered a vision of the world as whole.
Historian Michael Wertheimer called his father a "prophet," declaring
Gestalt psychology not simply a theory but "a *Weltanschauung*, an all-

encompassing religion. The core of this religion is the hope that the world is a sensible, coherent whole, that reality is organized into meaningful paths."[55] Though many psychologists rejected this religio-scientific view, Maslow's dedication to science and naturalism mirrored Wertheimer's pursuit for a "sensible, coherent whole." Later Maslow professed, "Science at its highest level is ultimately the organization of, the systematic pursuit of, and the enjoyment of wonder, awe, and mystery." Science, he thought, was "the religion of the nonreligious, the poetry of the nonpoet, the art of the man who cannot paint, the humor of the serious man, and the lovemaking of the inhibited and shy man. Not only does science begin in wonder; it also ends in wonder."[56]

While revering science, he, like his Gestalt teachers, critiqued it in its "analytic-dissecting-atomistic-Newtonian" form.[57] Köhler said methodologies appropriate to some scientific inquiries might not be applicable to studies of human beings.[58] Maslow agreed: the "classical science model" was insufficient for answering "questions about the higher reaches of human nature." It was an "impersonal model" that focused on "things, objects, animals, and part-processes" and worked well for some inquiries but "failed with the personal, the unique, the holistic" and "inadequate when we attempt to know and to understand whole and individual persons and cultures." Its "fatal weakness," he declared, was "its inability to deal impersonally with the personal, with the problems of value, of individuality, of consciousness, of beauty, of transcendence, of ethics."[59] Ultimately, as he had already determined in medical school, "slice and dice" science was dehumanizing.

Though he never abandoned his "love and admiration for objectivistic research," Maslow, like many in the counterculture who came to admire him, felt "its limitation, its partial quality, its failure as a general and comprehensive philosophy of all psychology, its futility when certain questions are put to it, its total failure to generate a true and usable image of man." He decided it was "just one kind of tool, usable for certain purposes and not for others, *part* of the armamentarium of the psychologist but not the whole of it."[60] Striving for a synthetic epistemology, he wanted a more comprehensive approach. Focusing on minutiae was necessary, at times, but to use only mechanistic-reductionistic ("mechanomorphic") models was, to him, like one who has only a hammer for a tool and treats everything as if it were a nail.[61]

To signal his intellectual debts and convey that his psychology was new, different, and superior, he invented a unique lexicon and positioned his work within history. He concocted words such as "aggridants," "being-cognition," "deficiency-needs," "eupsychia," "hierarchy of prepotency," "holistic-dynamic model,""metapathology,""metamotivation,""mechanomorphic,""specieshood," and "Taoistic receptivity." He called his approach "epi-Freudian" and "epi-behavioristic," employing the prefix "epi" to communicate that he was building upon and going beyond others.[62] He called humanistic psychology the "Third Force," insinuating its historical importance. Behaviorism and psychoanalysis, he postulated, were dated first and second forces.

Maslow's intellectual debts extended beyond psychology to anthropology. While they were in Wisconsin, his wife studied anthropology, and he read with her. He appreciated the field's global outlook. Psychology, he thought, was "ethnocentric. I decided for myself to be a part-time anthropologist because that was *sine qua non* for being a good psychologist. Otherwise, you were simply a naïve local."[63] During his time at Columbia and the same time he listened to Wertheimer's lectures at the New School, he attended Columbia's anthropology department's weekly colloquia and marveled at the ideas of Ralph Linton, Margaret Mead, and Ruth Benedict. He became close friends with Benedict, admiring her as he did Wertheimer. He found her work a "holistic rather than an atomistic effort to describe societies as unitary organisms of wholes."[64]

Patterns of Culture, Benedict's widely acclaimed treatise from 1934, drew on the understandings of her teacher Franz Boaz and Gestalt psychology. She condemned reductionism and argued that each culture was a work of art, a configuration dominated by a particular idea. It should, she thought, be read as a whole. "The whole, as modern science is insisting in many fields, is not merely the sum of all its parts," Benedict argued, "but the result of a unique arrangement and interrelation of the parts that has brought about a new entity." To illustrate, she wrote, "Gunpowder is not merely the sum of sulphur and charcoal and saltpeter, and no amount of knowledge even of all three of its elements in all the forms they take in the natural world will demonstrate the nature of gunpowder.... Cultures, likewise, are more than the sum of their traits." She called on colleagues to focus on "the whole configuration as over against the continued analysis of its parts."[65] Benedict was not the only anthropologist to express holistic conceptions in the 1930s. Margaret Mead linked Benedict's thoughts with her own, as well as with the ideas of Gregory Bateson, Clifford Geertz, and Geoffrey Gorer, when she said, "It was a time when all of us were struggling with the question of how to present whole cultures in their full uniqueness and beauty."[66] Bateson, like Maslow, later became an adviser to Esalen leaders, and his holistic ideals, as we shall see, helped mark its development.

From 1937 to 1951, Maslow taught psychology at Brooklyn College and then moved to chair Brandeis University's psychology department. At Brooklyn, he began to study motivation and carve out his holistic position. He wondered how individuals achieved excellence. How did people mature healthily, transcend sorrow, develop talents, and live full, meaningful lives? Describing the Pearl Harbor parade as he did captured his conundrum. So did two pictures on the cover of his 1941 book on abnormal psychology. One photo showed a row of happy babies, the next a crowded group of weary, gaunt-faced subway riders. The caption read, "What happened?"[67] To answer this, Maslow increasingly rejected current preoccupations with neuroses and psychoses, psychoanalytical couches, and Freudian analysis. Instead, he focused on healthy persons. "Human life," he contended, "will never be understood unless its highest aspirations are taken into account." Psychologists must examine human "growth, self-actualization, the striving toward health, the quest for identity and autonomy, the yearning for excellence."[68]

Escaping his childhood misery and achieving greatness remained personal goals and explain some of Maslow's engagement with these questions. If he could determine how others attained excellence, perhaps he could do the same. This focus helped him establish a new psychology. In 1943, he produced a pathbreaking article that presented a new model of human nature. "A Theory of Motivation" hypothesized that human needs are organized hierarchically, beginning with needs for food and shelter and culminating in needs for self-actualization. He credited Kurt Goldstein for the term "self-actualization" but made it his own by weaving it into his theory of human development.[69] Maslow moved onto the national scene in 1954, with the publication of his book *Motivation and Personality*. In it he castigated his peers for following a "low-ceiling psychology" that focused on human ills. In 1970, he reaffirmed his position and called for more studies on imagination, creativity, mysticism, peak experiences, and dreams that would "enlarge our conception of the human personality by reaching into the 'higher' levels of human nature."[70]

Maslow began studying self-actualization by scrutinizing Wertheimer and Benedict. Both seemed to be reaching their potential. He then looked for other "self-actualizers" and charted common characteristics and achievements. His list included contemporary and historical figures: Jane Addams, Martin Buber, George Washington Carver, Pablo Casals, Eugene Debs, Albert Einstein, Ralph Waldo Emerson, Benjamin Franklin, Aldous Huxley, William James, Camille Pissarro, Eleanor Roosevelt, Albert Schweitzer, Adlai Stevenson, and Harriet Tubman.[71] He also included himself, assuring himself that he belonged: "I talk over the heads of the people in front of me to my own private audience. I talk to people I love and respect. To Socrates and Aristotle and Spinoza and Thomas Jefferson and Abraham Lincoln. And when I write, I write for them."[72] In this confession, he conveyed his quest for self-worth and his less-than-democratic and rather arrogant side. Hence, while each person had potential, all did not make the grade.

He concluded that exceptional individuals exhibited qualities of self-acceptance, awareness, autonomy, freedom, honesty, spontaneity, and trust. They were well integrated emotionally, mentally, and physically. Each felt a special mission in life and confidently pursued it. Self-actualization, he explained, "refers to man's desire for self-fulfillment, namely, to the tendency for him to become actualized in what he is potentially. This tendency might be phrased as the desire to become more and more what one is, to become everything that one is capable of becoming." A person who is not doing "what he is fitted for" will become discontented. "A musician must make music, an artist must paint, a poet must write, if he is to be ultimately at peace with himself. What a man *can* be, he *must* be."[73]

Logically, one could read this statement as an expression of extreme individualism, and herein lies the tension within Maslow's holism and the holism of this era. His self-actualizers sounded like "self-made men," filled with Emersonian "self-reliance" and Turnerian "rugged individualism." This individualist bias conflicted, however, with his desire for community. To some extent, he (and other holists) never got beyond this individualistic position. Conceptually, the self-actualized person was the focal point of his psychology and central to his holism. In his personal life, too, he preferred a solitary trail and struggled continually with individual significance. Still, the psychologist never claimed that becoming a whole person was an end in itself, and he realized the contradiction in his work. He criticized Thoreau for retreating to Walden.[74] The end was not self-gain. Eupsychia was. Self-actualizers, who made up society's healthiest individuals, were also Maslow's candidates to make community work. This was possible, he contended, because self-actualizers are not narcissistic; they are outer-directed, mission-minded, and intent on using their gifts to benefit others. He saw these qualities in the people he put on his self-actualizer list, and he hoped it described himself. Though never able to resolve the contradictions between individual and communal interests fully (or successful at keeping some of his followers from a solipsistic path), he tried to keep social betterment the focus. First, however, he explained how a person became self-actualized.

Maslow asserted that all human beings were born with potential talents, and each could reach these potentials. It is in this ideal of self-actualization especially where many in the human potential movement and counterculture found the psychologist and humanistic psychology so attractive. Both the push for individual wholeness and Maslow's following assertion that self-actualized individuals created better communities found favor. In all people, he claimed, "there is an active will toward health, an impulse toward growth, or toward the actualization of human potentialities."[75] He called this inner drive an "instinctoid," because he thought it akin to an instinct though not as strong or determinative. Like the acorn "'pressing toward' being an oak tree," nature gave human beings "potentialities and capacities...in inchoate or embryonic form."[76] Contrary to his existentialist friends, he denied that existence precedes essence. He also separated himself from Enlightenment ontology. "To talk of self-actualization," he stated, "implies that there is a self to be actualized. A human being is not a *tabula rasa*, not a lump of clay."[77] In the nature versus nurture argument, he came down somewhere in the middle. Environment, education, and culture mattered: "Culture doesn't create a human...doesn't implant with him the ability to love, or to be curious, or to philosophize....Culture is not the seed," but it is "sun and food and water."[78] Additionally, this time agreeing with existentialists, he declared human volition pivotal. The self was "a creation of the person himself....Every person is, in part, 'his own project' and makes himself."[79]

With these assumptions, the psychologist constructed his hierarchy of needs growth chart in 1943.[80] He arranged five basic drives or needs, which he thought determined growth, into a pyramid. The most important physical needs made up the base of the pyramid. In ascending order, he put safety; belonging and love; esteem; and self-actualization. He then divided his pyramid in two. At the bottom sat basic motivation D-needs (D for deficiency) and on top metamotivation B-needs (B for Being). D-needs referred to drives that must be satisfied in order to reduce deficit states. Someone who is hungry is in a deficit state, which eating satiates. Once appeased, the person is free to think of other things. Likewise, a person who feels safe may pursue other activities. Self-actualization becomes possible when basic needs are met. Satisfaction levels varied, and meant different things to different people, but he contended that when primary requirements ceased to distract, one could pursue truth, beauty, and spiritual ideals, develop talents and gifts, and realize one's potential. He thought people were "motivated primarily by trends to self-actualization (defined as ongoing actualization of potentials, capacities and talents, as fulfillment of mission (or call, fate, destiny, or vocation), as a fuller knowledge of, and acceptance of the person's own intrinsic nature, as an unceasing trend toward unity, integration or synergy within the person)."[81]

Perhaps Maslow had himself in mind when he created this pyramid. It represented basic needs that had not been satisfied in his childhood, and it explained his constant search for meaning, his pursuit of meaningful research topics, and his independent, superior attitude. Crafting this chart helped him explain his past and his own quest for wholeness. Regardless of his motivation, the pyramid has been used by many to explain human motivation and quest for meaning.

The hierarchical order he drew was not rigid. Deficiency and being needs were "interrelated rather than sharply separated," he noted, "synergic rather than antagonistic."[82] There were overlaps, reversals, exceptions, and individual idiosyncrasies. In effect, there was no mind-body split. Ontologically, the person was united physically, mentally, and emotionally, which implied "a repudiation of any dichotomizing of the mind and the body or of flesh and spirit or of higher nature and lower nature."[83] Thus, an "individual is an integrated, organized whole."[84] Maslow defined "wholeness" as "unity; integration; tendency to one-ness; interconnectedness; simplicity; organization; structure; dichotomy-transcendence; order."[85] In this, too, holistic health advocates in the late 1960s found his work helpful.

Complementing his understanding of the whole person, the psychologist developed a corresponding worldview that was, as he put it, "holistic rather than atomistic, functional rather than taxonomic, dynamic rather than static, dynamic rather than causal, purposive rather than simple-mechanical."[86] Methodologically, this required looking at the whole person in context. "If I want to learn something more about you as an individual person," he surmised, "then I must approach you as a unit, as a one, as a whole."[87] The "various atomistic dissections and reductions" render knowledge incomplete. Hence, he argued, "Not only must I perceive you holistically, but I must also analyze you holistically rather than reductively."[88] Rather than isolating a giggle, a sneeze, an aggressive act, or a fearful response, a psychologist should examine the behavior in context. What did the person do, believe, think? What relationships did the person have with family, friends, and the community? Before delving into specific research questions, he sought "to understand each subject as a whole, functioning, adjusting individual."[89]

All of this implied a subjective, intuitive approach, far removed from the ideals of objective, value-free science, which he thought impossible to achieve.[90] Since his days in Thorndike's lab, he frequently gained information through interviews: "I tried to get to know one single person after another as profoundly and deeply and as fully as I could (as unique, individual persons) to the point where I felt I understood them as a whole person."[91] He admitted his approach was unconventional and potentially erroneous, but he relished that his "style of investigation" freed him from the "classical scientific (atomistic) method," and he believed that he was able to "invent holistic interviewing techniques" that offered a fuller picture of the person than would otherwise be possible. He felt he was "getting very full case-histories of whole lives and whole people *without* having particular problems or questions in mind, that is, without abstracting one aspect of the person rather than another."[92]

Contextualizing, listening, and focusing on relationships and interpersonal dynamics were the building blocks of Maslow's epistemological model. This approach wove together the intuitive, mystical, and transcendent. As he listened to his subjects, he gained respect for people who trusted their feelings, emotions, mystical experiences, and intuition. He found their creativity, intensity, and idiosyncratic wisdom attractive. Steadily, he felt that science could learn from these intuitive, mystical types, and that scientific methods stood to gain by practicing "the idiographic, the experiential, the Taoistic, the comprehensive, the holistic, the personal, the transcendent."[93] Relying on his and his subject's intuition did not mean he discarded reason. His approach was synthetic, rather than an affirmation of one over another.

Placing himself at even greater distance from positivism, the unorthodox psychologist developed an intuitive methodology he called "Taoistic receptivity." He defined this as a path to knowledge that demanded keeping "your hands off and your mouth shut, to be patient, to suspend action and be receptive and passive. It stresses careful observation of a noninterfering sort."[94] Passivity did not mean dispassion. It meant reserving judgment and allowing subjects free expression. It meant loving the subject and cultivating an "interpersonal (I-Thou) knowledge." Moving further from objective methods, he encouraged psychologists to fully empathize, love, care for, and experience the other "through *becoming* the other." Hence, "Taoistic receptivity" sought a "mystical fusion in which the two people become one in a phenomenological way that has been best described by mystics, Zen Buddhists, peak experiencers, lovers, estheticians, etc." Doing this, Maslow said, ensured greater insight.[95]

Defying standard scientific methods made him think that many would dismiss him. Some did. Maslow faced opposition from psychoanalysts and behaviorists who found his work iconoclastic. Especially later, as he started writing on transcendent experiences, mystical states, and Buddhism, he found it difficult to publish in prominent journals.[96] But things began to change in 1954 when he published *Motivation and Personality*. His ardent endorsement of humanity impressed lay and academic audiences alike. The book sold more than 15,000 copies in hard cover and more than 100,000 in paperback.[97] Multiple speaking engagements, consulting positions, and awards followed. Maslow's name became linked with pioneering psychologists Erich Fromm, Rollo May, and Carl Rogers, who were also interested in personality, freedom, self-actualization, and client-centered therapy. Together they emphasized human value and enunciated what became known as humanistic ("Third Force") psychology. In the 1950s and 1960s, humanistic psychology gained a large audience, though it still was not without contestation, as the famous debates between Carl Rogers and behaviorist B. F. Skinner indicated. These debates began in the 1950s, but the controversy spilled into the 1960s, including at Esalen in 1965 when Rogers and Skinner conducted seminars.[98] Maslow's stature throughout the 1960s increased. In

1961, colleagues in the American Psychological Association (APA) voted him one of the nation's most creative psychologists. In 1967, the American Humanist Association gave him their Humanist of the Year Award.[99]

As a humanistic psychologist, Maslow worked from a holistic perspective. We have already seen in both his hierarchical chart and his methodology that the psychologist interpreted the person as an integrated being in pursuit of wholeness. As the person self-actualized, he or she could become "more integrated and less split," become more "fully functioning, more creative, more humorous, more ego-transcending, more independent of his lower needs,...more perfectly actualizing his potentialities, closer to the core of his being, more fully human."[100] This appealed to many, especially those who felt caught in the modern condition, divided from nature and dehumanized by the corporate world, and for counterculturalists who critiqued Cartesian rationality, industrial capitalism, and suburban culture that isolated people from traditional forms of community.[101]

To be self-actualized was to become whole, but again, this was not the end. His holism did not stop with the individual. Maslow's ultimate goal was communal wholeness, both in terms of a practical social oneness with others and in terms of a vague, transcendent cosmic oneness with the universe. In his studies on creativity, he noted that self-actualizers moved beyond themselves to experience a "fusion" with the world. The act of creating, he wrote, "tends to be the act of a whole man (ordinarily); he is then *most* integrated, unified, all of a piece, one-pointed, totally organized in the service of the fascinating matter-in-hand." The artist becomes intricately connected with the subject. "Creativeness is therefore systemic; i.e., a whole—or Gestalt—quality of the whole person; it is not added-to the organism like a coat of paint, or like an invasion of bacteria. It is the opposite of dissociation. Here-now-allness is less dissociated and more one." The creative process was, to Maslow, a "spider web of interrelationships"; there is an "isomorphism, a molding of each to each other, a better and better fitting together or complementarity, a melting into one." Discerning this helped him "understand what Hokusai [Japanese painter and wood engraver (1760–1849)] meant when he said, 'If you want to draw a bird, you must become a bird.'"[102]

Studies on peak experiences reinforced his conclusions that self-actualization encouraged altruism. Ecstatic and mystical experiences—those joyous, serene, wondrous moments—occurred, Maslow explained, during ordinary and extraordinary moments, from the profound contentment one woman felt sitting with her child and husband at the breakfast table to intellectual achievements, sexual encounters, musical performances, and mountain hikes. Interpreting these stories as a nineteenth-century romantic might describe a "sublime" moment, he concluded that peak experiences provoked great exhilaration and a loss of time and space. They transformed and strengthened while bringing a kind of satisfaction that "the universe is all of a piece and that one has a place in it—one is part of it, and one belongs to it."[103] He saw peaks as natural, not supernatural, phenomena and respected his subjects' abilities to rise above self: "I would call peakers transcenders.... They are transcendent in the sense of transcending the ego, the selfish, or the skin-enclosed person." Maslow interpreted a loss of self-consciousness as an opening to the world. Forgetting oneself, he wrote, "is a nice feeling."[104]

Transcendental experiences were, ironically, as much about self-pursuit as self-abnegation and merging. Peaks gave people a sense of power, identity, and meaning at the same time they moved the person beyond self. This had been the central paradox of nineteenth-century transcendentalism, and it remained the source of tension in expressions of holism. Sublime moments in nature, mystical reveries, or drug-induced altered states could prompt self-knowledge and individual godlike status as much as they could facilitate communal oneness. Maslow preferred to see peak experiences as both, though for some it was a precarious balancing act. As the 1960s wore on, the psychologist grew agitated with what he thought were solipsistic tendencies in youthful protesters and the human potential movement.[105]

When Maslow began developing his motivational theories, he started with the individual, and his self-actualizers became his model for wholeness, a teaching tool to convey his holistic philosophy and practical prescription for health. As he grew intrigued with social wholeness in the 1950s and 1960s, he wondered how self-actualizers might influence business, politics, and religion. Conversely, he pondered how society might promote self-fulfillment among its citizens. *Towards a Psychology of Being* reflected these interests and appealed to college students, counterculture members, and mainstream audiences. It sold 200,000 copies even before it was reissued in 1968.[106] *Religions, Values, and Peak-Experiences* (1964) continued these themes. One year later, *Eupsychian Management* detailed his consulting work at the California engineering company Non-Linear Systems and argued that businesses could prosper if they adopted management styles that fostered worker creativity and well-being. Hoping to "rehumanize" science as well as business, he asked scientists in *The Psychology of Science* (1966) to generate "eupsychian or utopian social psychology, of religion, of work, play, and leisure, of esthetics, of economics, and politics."[107] By 1969, when he and Bertha moved to Menlo Park, California, for a fellowship at Saga Administrative Corporation, he was applying his ideas to politics, education, and experimental communities and was in high demand as a speaker and consultant.

At the end of his life, Maslow began to see "Third Force" psychology as a transitional step to a "still 'higher' Fourth Psychology," which he described as "transpersonal, transhuman, centered in the cosmos rather than in human needs and interests, going beyond humanness, identity, and self-actualization."[108] Building on the work of William James and Carl Jung, psychologists developed transpersonal therapy to address myths, religions, archetypes, dreams, and mystical events. *Farther Reaches of Human Nature* (1971) examined such experiences, though Maslow never saw the final copy. At the age of sixty-two, a massive heart attack ended his life.

Throughout his life, this holist articulated a vision of a better, healthier society. From early attachments to socialism to hatred of prejudice to studies of self-actualization, he indicated social concern. This did not translate into political action, however, in part because he fell away from Marxism, judging its view of humanity too negative.[109] McCarthyism may have squelched action, too. After the Senate censured McCarthy and the Supreme Court ruled on *Brown v. Board of Education* in 1954, Maslow began working with Harvard sociologist Pitirim Sorokin and other scholars on altruism and the advancement of world peace.[110] Within a circle of scholars and professional associations, Maslow felt most comfortable voicing calls for social reform. As a founder of the Society for the Psychological Study of Social Issues, Maslow implored scientists to tackle projects that would abet "human and social emancipation."[111] In 1968, as APA president, he pushed colleagues to support civil rights and recruitment of African American psychologists. He also promoted group therapy to address racial prejudice.[112] Antipathy for racism and encouragement by his activist daughter Ellen prompted such actions.

To Maslow, the relationship between the individual and the community was symbiotic; "improving individual health is one approach to creating a better world."[113] Like Martin Luther King Jr., he quoted the poet John Donne: "No man is an island." He explained, "Ultimately the world is one and interconnected; everything is everything else as well in the very empirical sense that we are part of each other."[114] Personal health depended on communal cooperation: "Sick people are made by a sick culture; healthy people are made possible by a healthy culture."[115] On another occasion he elaborated: "There is a kind of feedback between the Good Society and the Good Person. They need each other, they are *sine qua non* to each other."[116] These "'synergic' conditions," he explained, promote "personal fulfillment" and "the health and prosperity of the organization (factory, hospital, college, etc.)."[117]

To describe his ideal balance between individual and community, he relied on the concept of "synergy," which describes a relationship of cooperation in which two or more organisms, organs, or substances act together to attain something that could not be achieved by any one individually.

Buckminster Fuller applied the term to his geodesics to explain how the parts worked together for the tensile strength of the whole.[118] In her cross-cultural assessments, Benedict mapped cultures by their synergy level. Low-synergy societies were marked, she thought, by individual and institutional "acts which are mutually opposed and counteractive." In under-achieving societies, the "advantage of one individual becomes a victory over another, and the majority who are not victorious must shift as they can." Conversely, high-synergy societies displayed generosity, cooperation, and mutualism. Maslow expanded Benedict's thesis to describe healthy individuals, relationships, and societies.[119] Self-actualizers, unlike unhealthy people, functioned in a "collaborative and synergic" way to "coalesce into an organismic unity."[120] Between individuals, "synergy" depicted mutually beneficial relations. "High-synergy love" resulted when "two people have arranged their relationship in such a fashion that one person's advantage is the other person's advantage."[121] For an example of synergetic societies, he pointed to his observation of the Blackfeet Indian's yearly redistribution of wealth. At the encouragement of Ruth Benedict, Maslow had traveled to Alberta, Canada, in 1938 to study the Blackfeet.[122] There he observed a man who gave his "pile of wealth" to widows, orphans, and the infirm. This, Maslow interpreted, was a "synergetic" act because the poor had their needs met, and the rich person, though stripped of everything, raised his communal standing.[123]

Following this line of reasoning, the psychologist promoted building a "high-synergy" or "holistic" society—the terms were synonymous to him.[124] "One can set up social institutions which will guarantee that individuals will be at each other's throats," he explained, "or one can set up social institutions which will encourage individuals to be synergic with each other."[125] "Jungle" societies—those marked by animalistic struggle and selfish interests, that is, "low-synergy"—did not need to be the norm.[126] With this, he challenged Freudian assumptions that alienation necessarily characterized the human experience.

Just as Fuller created synergetic geometry to explain the success of his geodesic, so Maslow fashioned synergistic relationships to forward a successful community: "I would say no Utopia can be constructed henceforth by the knowledgeable person without making peace with the concept of synergy. It looks to me at this time as if any Utopia, or Eupsychia (which I think is a better name), must have as one of its foundations a set of high-synergy institutions."[127] Synergy between individuals and the community was thus a fundamental axiom to his construction of the good society.

Brandeis colleague and friend Frank Manuel said Maslow liked being called a utopian, for he "dreamed of a grand, heroic world where all men would be strong, fulfilled, and self-actualized; where peak emotional experiences breaking the calm felicity of life would give tonus to the whole of existence."[128] In *Motivation and Personality*, Maslow introduced the possibilities of his "psychological Utopia" by wondering what kind of culture 1,000 healthy families on a deserted island would invent: "What kind of education would they choose? Economic system? Sexuality? Religion?"[129] Using "eupsychia" instead of "utopia" advertised his humanistic leanings. In exchange for the Greek root *topo*, meaning place, he adopted *psyche*, the Greek word for soul, spirit, or animating breath. In doing so, he made explicit his focus on the human dimension. Eupsychia literally meant "good soul" or "well-being."

His vision of utopia was not as coherent as Thomas More's elaboration of 1516. And he never rivaled contemporary B. F. Skinner's specificity in *Walden II*. Still, the broad outline was clear: eupsychia described a place where self-actualizers achieved greater wholeness individually and worked together synergistically to form a harmonic society. Imagining this eupsychian ideal, Maslow pushed his audiences "toward holism in each of our professions (e.g., away from adversary law, politics, economics, and so forth) in each of our atomistic, separate fields of knowledge. The holistic movement must occur also for each of our social institutions, religion, work and management, education, and administration of justice."[130]

This eupsychian ideal rested on a humanistic ethos that Maslow described as "the brotherhood of man, the holistic philosophy that a man is of society."[131] In ways, the psychologist, like the other holists in this study, voiced a global holism. Teilhard's "Omega Point" spanned the planet. Carson's ecosystems paid no respect to human fences. Fuller's maps reoriented global conceptions. King's beloved community included the impoverished in Africa, America, and Asia. Maslow's globalism may have been more provincial, more nationalistic. He never traveled the world like Fuller, King, or Teilhard. Nor did he map the planet. Unlike King, he supported the Vietnam War. Still, he expressed universal ties that bound one individual to another. His universalism, he thought, began when reading Sumner: "My ethnocentrism dropped away like old clothes, and...I became a citizen of the world."[132] Probably his globalism came more from anthropological and religious studies; nonetheless, his conceptualization of eupsychia approximated the idea of a global village: "By Good Society I mean ultimately one species, one world."[133] Hence, unlike the imagined communities conceived for nation-building that scholars have highlighted, mid-twentieth-century holists dreamed of global, not national, projects that stretched the dimensions and even the meaning of geographic borders.[134] In this, holism contributed not to the formation of the nation-state but to globalism. Holism even became a venue for questioning national identities and boundaries and for the dismantling of nationalism.

Maslow doubted whether eupsychia could ever be a reality, but that did not stop his dreams or hopes of linking with like-minded individuals. He was, in his estimation, an "optimistic realist."[135] In the 1950s, he began creating a "holistic movement" list that he called the "Eupsychian Network." It comprised "groups, organizations and journals" that he thought were "interested in helping the individual grow toward fuller humanness, the society grow toward synergy and health, and all societies and all peoples move toward becoming one world and one species." This eventually included psychologists, alternative healing groups, educators, and ecologists. He listed Rachel Carson, though it is doubtful the two ever met or exchanged correspondence. He also added organizations (the Association for Humanistic Psychology [AHP], the American Humanist Association, the Sierra Club, and the Audubon Society); institutions (Harvard Business School and Massachusetts Institute of Technology); and loosely affiliated groups (organic farmers and Esalen experimenters).[136]

A subsection of people on this list came together to express their holistic views in the form of humanistic psychology. In the late 1950s, Maslow and Clark Moustakas convened meetings with Rogers, May, and other psychologists that led to the establishment of the AHP and the *Journal of Humanistic Psychology*.[137] AHP's holistic orientation was clear from the start. In 1963, the association's first president, James Bugental, published "Humanistic Psychology: A New Breakthrough," and the new organization adopted much of his text as a statement of aims. It outlined five assumptions: (1) a person supersedes the sum of his or her parts; (2) we are affected by our relationships with others; (3) a person is aware; (4) a person has choice and responsibility, and (5) a person is intentional and meaning-seeking. In a membership drive, the *Newsletter* reiterated this holistic position: "If you are dissatisfied with a psychology that views man as a composite of part functions, a psychology whose model of science is taken over from physics, and whose model of a practitioner is taken over from medicine—and you want to do something to change this state of affairs, fill out this application."[138] One early proponent of humanistic psychology and a prominent therapist at Esalen in the 1960s was Charlotte Buhler, who wrote: "*Man in his wholeness* is generally seen as the humanistic psychologist's concern."[139]

This holistic message struck a chord. Prominent psychologists such as Gordon Allport, Henry Murray, Gardner Murphy, and Virginia Satir aligned themselves with the AHP and brought holistic assumptions to their writings, practices, and institutions. The association drew 75 individuals to its first meeting in 1963 and more than 200 to the second; by 1966, the group boasted 500 members.[140] The older, more established APA took notice and organized the Division of Humanistic Psychology in 1971.[141]

Among lay audiences, too, humanistic psychology made a significant mark, and Maslow was one of the most popular exponents. So too were Kurt Lewin, a Gestalt psychologist, and Carl Rogers, famous for his client-centered therapy. In the 1940s, independent of one another, they started developing small-group psychological techniques to facilitate personal and social growth. Each contributed to what became a popular therapeutic practice in the 1960s known alternately as encounter sessions, T-groups ("T" for "training group"), or sensitivity groups. Rogers called small-group therapy "the most rapidly spreading social invention of the century, and probably the most potent."[142] Esalen practiced and spread the invention. Confidence in psychology was not new. America's enthusiasm for Freud and the "talking cure" in the first half of the twentieth century indicated a widespread belief that psychology could provide insights in a scientific age. "Third Force" psychologists built on this assumption, though they established their own cures in the form of group therapies, encounter sessions, and retreat centers.

To nurture the movement, Maslow traveled between psychotherapy hot spots such as the National Training Laboratory on the East Coast and the Western Behavioral Sciences Institute in California. He also frequented "personal growth centers," including Esalen, and Synanon, a drug-rehabilitation program. Groups drew his ire, however, when he felt they became too self-indulgent and introspective. He wanted people to develop themselves not for narcissistic gain but as "Utopian Do-Gooders" or what he also called "Bodhisattvas," borrowing from a story of Buddha's return to earth from heaven in order to help the unenlightened.[143]

While humanistic psychology influenced the work of clinical therapists, psychological researchers, and personal growth seekers, it also became a tool for such diverse groups as corporate managers and social reformers. Following Maslow's assertion that self-actualizers help construct healthy communities and that caring communities foster personal growth, some advocated changing social institutions and customs that hindered wholeness. Business and government agencies sought Maslow's help in creating more caring, personal, holistic work environments.[144] Feminists, too, applied his ideas to their call for women's equality. Betty Friedan conversed with the psychologist and employed his hierarchy of needs and sexuality studies to make her case in her best-selling work, *The Feminine Mystique* (1963). She argued that cultural constructions of femininity and limited opportunities hampered a woman's psychological development and self-actualization. She advocated instead the development of the full human identity of women as well as men.[145] Student Nonviolent Coordinating Committee activists Casey Hayden and Mary King wrote a much publicized memo in 1965 articulating similar concerns about "women's problems in trying to live in our personal lives and in our work as independent and creative people." Based on what they learned in fighting racism, they challenged institutional, political, and personal sexism by asking others to "think radically about the personal worth and abilities of people" and to "shape the institutions to meet human needs rather than shaping people to meet the needs of those with power." As James Farrell wrote, they wanted to be treated as whole persons.[146] Abbie Hoffman, one of Maslow's students in the 1950s, also embraced his teacher's views. He applauded Maslow's assertions that nonconformity could be healthy, that societal rebellion did not mean mental illness, and that self-actualizers had a responsibility to change society. Humanistic psychology, to Hoffman, legitimated social protests designed to revolutionize institutions and cultural codes and spurred him on as a civil rights reformer, Vietnam War protester, Yippie cofounder, and one of the Chicago Seven prosecuted for intending to incite a riot at the Democratic National Convention in 1968. His actions, however, did not always please Maslow.[147] Hoffman may have agreed with Maslow's altruism, but Maslow did not view Hoffman as a "Bodhisattva." Regardless of his approval or disapproval, the psychologist's notions of the whole person and society reverberated in various corners throughout American life.

Beginning with his ecstatic dance outside New York's Forty-second Street library in 1927 while high on Watson's words, and bolstered later by associations with Wertheimer and other socially minded intellectuals, Maslow became convinced that psychology could ameliorate social ills. In 1957, he reaffirmed his "calling" to end "sorrow, greed, exploitation, prejudice, contempt, cowardice, stupidity, jealousy, selfishness." He argued that a psychologist "ought to feel the weight of duty upon his shoulders as no other scientist." The psychologist's task was to help people understand themselves. He saw this not only in terms of the individual, but in terms of society, as he explained: "If we die in another war or if we continue being tense and neurotic and anxious in an extended cold war, then this is due to the fact that we don't understand ourselves and we don't understand each other. Improve human nature and you improve all."[148] Psychology for him held the keys to the sustainability of human life: "I believe that the world will either be saved by the psychologists or it won't be saved at all.... the fate of the human species rests more upon their shoulders than upon any group of people.... All the important problems of war and peace, exploitation and brotherhood, hatred and love, sickness and health, misunderstanding and understanding, of the happiness and unhappiness of mankind will yield only to a better understanding of human nature."[149]

Still, his holistic philosophy was not generic. It spoke to his personal quest for affirmation. In revolt against the insignificance he felt as a child, in defiance of his mother who belittled him, and in rebellion against his anti-Semitic neighbors, he crafted a holism that gave him importance and made him feel like "a somebody." Just a few months before he died, he wrote that "every man can be a king and must therefore be *treated* like a king.... Such a point of view makes it then possible for me to love myself, respect myself, to treat myself with the greatest respect, and even to sacralize myself."[150]

Motivated by his personal desires for significance and purpose as well as by his messianic desire to set the table for world peace, he devised a holism that was both individual and communal. Certainly he wanted both and believed there was no inherent strain between the individual and the collective. He held—contrary to Freud's assessment that human beings needed to be freed *from* their sick society—that psychology could free the human *and* make society better. Thus, he denied an either-or relationship between the individual and society. This was a both-and relationship, a non-zero-sum game in which, he believed, everyone could win. Living in a prosperous era encouraged such notions.

By 1968, Maslow boldly claimed that this new "humanist trend in psychology" was part of a revolution along the likes of "Galileo, Darwin, Einstein, Freud, and Marx." It offered "new ways of perceiving and thinking, new images of man and of society, new conceptions of ethics and of values, new directions in which to move."[151] The "new conception" trumpeted human significance. This was the project of humanistic and transpersonal psychology. As Bugental explained, humanistic psychologists "find we are ill content to be psychologists if psychology is a 'nothing-but' process for reducing us—and all men—to a larger white rat or a slower computer."[152] Specifically, Maslow saw his move to resacralize the human as revolutionary, as a retort to the "debunkers." This was the aim of his holistic outlook. Freud, Marx and others had expressed "skepticism, cynicism, and despair," born out of attitudes of "debunking, down-leveling, or devaluing human nature and humankind."[153] In contrast, he believed his holistic movement was ushering in a new "Zeitgeist," a "counter philosophy," of "considerable revolt against the mechanistic, dehumanized view of man and the world."[154]

In large part, Maslow was correct. Humanistic psychology offered an alternative to prevailing dualistic views, signaled changed understandings of human personality and development, and suggested ways to improve society. His work resonated with psychologists and their patients. It fit alongside Rogers's constructivist view of the person as an organizing, gestalt entity, continually in process of forming and re-forming the self. It complemented May's work on self-actualization and society's pressure to conform.[155] It substantiated Carl Jung's interest in the human as more than a mechanical frame. All these psychologists captured the public imagination. For example, Jung's attention to archetypes, the spiritual, and the collective unconscious captured the imagination of increasing numbers in the 1960s.[156]

In his revolt against a mechanistic perspective, Maslow expressed a salient aspect not only of humanistic psychology but also of postwar holistic thought generally. Science was valuable, but a science that disavowed the specialness of the human was a science that he and other holists rejected. This complaint reverberated among counterculturalists in the 1960s and alternative health practitioners in the 1970s. Openness to his humanistic ideals and a transcendental epistemology testified to a renewed openness in American culture to mystical and religious ideas, and it signaled a cultural discomfort with a depersonalized, inequitable approach to the person, to science, management, and social relations. Taken together, this was a time ripe for expressions of an alternative world, a more perfect union. Holism, it appears, provided the intellectual underpinnings for many of those alternatives.

Holistic expressions flourished in 1962 and 1963, introducing a plethora of Americans to its application in a variety of arenas. Rachel Carson published *Silent Spring*; Buckminster Fuller erected his "Geoscope" and published *Operating Manual for Spaceship Earth*; Martin Luther King pushed the non-violent campaign for integration to the March on Washington; and scientists and theologians formed the American Teilhard Association. Abraham Maslow released *Towards a Psychology of Being*, and he and other psychologists started the Association for Humanistic Psychology. Social reformers lit the fires of change all around, and holistic ideas helped stoke the flames. The times, as musician Bob Dylan made clear, were "A-Changin'."

Maslow rode the winds of change, but ultimately his eupsychian ideal, like other holistic projects of this era, fell short as the communal ideals of the 1960s became stuck in the labyrinth of individualism. Few places revealed this tension between individualism and communitarianism in American society more than the Esalen Institute. This experiment on the rim of the Pacific Ocean, influenced by Maslow and other humanistic psychologists, created a place that fostered self-actualization and eupsychia. It had social aims, but Maslow felt the undertaking slipped too frequently into individualistic excesses in the late 1960s. At the same time, Esalen's deeply spiritual culture pointed to some of the ways that Americans used holistic ideas to forge connections between the scientific and the religious. Focusing on Esalen's story in the next chapter points, then, to both the triumph and the demise of holism in late twentieth-century America.

T'ai chi at Esalen, Big Sur, California. *Image courtesy of Daniel Bianchetta, Esalen Institute*

6

The Esalen Institute
A Center for Holistic Pursuits

At the same time the holistic visions of Rachel Carson, Buckminster Fuller, Martin Luther King Jr., Pierre Teilhard de Chardin, Abraham Maslow, and other like-minded individuals stirred Americans to think about their connections to the earth and one another, to march for civil rights, humanize technology, create bridges between science and religion, and plot paths to human growth and global accord, a holistic project was beginning on the western edge of the continental United States that brought these multiple expressions together and illuminated some of the ways that this holistic sensibility radiated into the culture. In its vision, practices, and mission, the Esalen Institute, launched in 1962, produced a tangible version of this particular holistic moment.

Stanford graduates Michael Murphy and Richard Price started Esalen to explore "the human potential." They located their retreat on the rugged California coast near Big Sur, about 150 miles south of San Francisco, and began inviting philosophers, psychologists, religious leaders, and scientists to speak. Aldous Huxley, Abraham Maslow, and Alan Watts were among the first. As *Look* journalist and Esalen enthusiast George Leonard explained, Murphy and Price "didn't know exactly how it would turn out, but they dreamed of a sort of forum for lectures and seminars on the marriage of Eastern and Western thought, the latest trends in psychology, the anatomy of personal and social transformation."[1] Murphy recalled that he felt "all human beings were on the threshold of a whole new era of self-discovery about our potential on this planet. We had no clear plan for Esalen, but we envisioned it as a refuge for people with new ideas, as a center where those ideas could be expressed and tested."[2] Thousands of young, well-off, educated adults responded, anxious to discuss new ideas, glean mystical insights, revel in the natural beauty, and soak in hot tubs filled by nearby mineral springs.[3]

Though unsure about their goals, the two thirty-year-old men knew they did not want to follow a conventional American path. They belonged to an emerging counterculture that rejected established practices and mainstream values. Society, they thought, esteemed the material too much. It built "larger, more complex, and better organized" institutions, Murphy said, but it failed people in that "many of us feel our individual importance and sense of worth diminishing." Despite more leisure and education, Americans did not appear to be developing deep personal relationships or increasing their happiness; "most of us, I think, have a lurking suspicion that in the midst of plenty we are not living well."⁴ And so, during one of the most prosperous times in American history, Esalen was born to help facilitate personal growth and development.

The center's fame grew throughout the 1960s, especially as it took on a more experiential flavor, hosted rock concerts, and attracted public intellectuals, Hollywood personalities, and the media. Indeed, this human potential center became known for its individualistic excesses and Dionysian explorations of self through yoga, massage, t'ai chi, meditation, and psychedelic drugs. Yet, while Esalen drew those in search of what one attendee called the "very honey pot of eroticism," the place was always more than hot springs and narcissistic exploits.⁵ Workshops promoted a fusion of science and faith, cross-cultural exchanges, environmental responsibility, and an end to racism, sexism, and the Cold War. Speakers and participants, many of whom were disgruntled with Western rationalism and dualistic separations of mind and body, human beings and nature, religion and science, investigated new developments in psychology and physics and experimented with a variety of holistic rituals. They combined Eastern and Western thought and embraced an eclectic spirituality that welcomed the exploration—mind, body, and soul—of a variety of paths to make sense of self and the world. As a result, Esalen participants reflected and contributed to shifting understandings of personal health (psychological, physical, social, and spiritual) and religion in American society.⁶

Culturally, Esalen stood on the fringe of society, just as it stood geographically on the edge of the Pacific Rim; yet, in its embodiment of holism, it exposed twentieth-century holism's temperament and paradoxes. Like many of the cultural producers of this post–World War II version of holism, participants spoke in a vague way about their dreams and endeavors. Simultaneously, they represented intellectual and cultural moments that had very similar antecedents. Dissatisfied with contemporary practices, they saw themselves struggling against individualistic, competitive value systems and hegemonic pursuits. They strove for individual wholeness, fulfilling relationships, and a more harmonious world. They believed their projects could provide a map to negotiate the fragmentation they felt in their own lives and in the world around them. Here, this communal and often utopian perspective fed dreams that helped drive social reform, changed the ways individuals understood themselves and their environment, guided plans for building a harmonious global community, and altered conceptions of science and religion. Ironically, at the same time they sought communal accord, many holists acted in solitary ways and upheld personal development at the expense of community.

This final chapter tells Esalen's story. Profiling how and why Michael Murphy and Richard Price started the center and charting Esalen's history demonstrate some of the ways holistic thinking filtered into American life and contributed to discussions about the individual, nature, and community. Moreover, it signals one of the ways that a holistic synthesis of Eastern and Western thought influenced the transformation of spiritual belief and practice in this era and contributes to my argument that holism was one avenue for religion's continuing presence in a scientific age.

By highlighting the exchange and cross-fertilization of ideas and rituals at Esalen, this chapter adds to our understanding of religion as a dynamic cultural process. It points to some of the ways that religion is formed, re-formed, and rejuvenated by mingling and modifying beliefs and customs. In this, it exemplifies Catherine Albanese's contention that American religion has been an ongoing process of additions and combinations. Through encounter and exchange, "religious mixing," she finds, "was surely the name of the spiritual game in the United States."[7] Taking my cue from Albanese and others who have written on the role that contacts among groups have played in the evolution of cultural and religious understandings and practices, I suggest that Esalen operated as a spiritual borderland that encouraged this type of commingling. As such, the institute became an experimental hothouse for germinating a variety of religious hybrids and contributed to the changing nature of spirituality in late twentieth-century America. Like other experiments before it, Esalen provided a forum for revitalizing religion.

As we saw in our discussion of Teilhard, the story of American religion after World War II has been dynamic. Certainly one of the most noted developments of the late twentieth century has been the rise of conservative evangelical Protestants and Mormons and the decline of mainline Protestants. Yet, as might be expected given America's pluralistic tradition, even while the Evangelical Right gained political and cultural power, America's religious constellation became more expansive. Catholicism boasted the largest membership of any single faith in the United States, while Buddhism, Hinduism, Islam, and Judaism gained ground and contributed more to the tenor of American life.[8] At the same time, scholars estimate up to 20 percent of today's population includes individuals who defy traditional religious classification, who see themselves as "spiritual" rather than "religious," and who have chosen to craft a very personalized faith. These believers—often identified with, though certainly not the sole province of, New Age spiritualities—borrowed ideas from a variety of belief systems and scientific findings for inspiration. In the process, distinctions between faiths blurred. Historian Tamar Frankiel explained: "A religious person in the 1980s could sit in Buddhist meditation, eat a Japanese macrobiotic diet, practice t'ai chi, attend Alcoholics Anonymous meetings, and elicit no reaction at all from neighbors in the pews of her suburban Methodist church."[9]

Fascination with the mystical and trust in one's "inner light"—markers of late twentieth-century spirituality—were not new, nor were they exceptional in their attempts to merge science and faith. They harkened back to Puritan reliance on the Holy Spirit and internal experiences. This spirituality, grounded as it often was in holistic paradigms, not surprisingly had roots in nineteenth-century romanticism, transcendentalism, mesmerism, spiritualism, New Thought, and theosophy. Twentieth-century contributions can be traced to Pentecostalism, psychology, and physics. At the same time, late twentieth-century spirituality also reflected its time. New developments in science, changes in immigration patterns and globalization, critiques of Western thought, challenges to Christianity, and an increased affinity for and practice of Asian religion in America also shaped this loose association of individuals. Some still retained ties to Christianity, but for many the term "spirituality" became associated with a loosening of Protestant doctrine and indicated a freedom to explore.[10]

Esalen reflected and contributed to this eclectic spirituality.[11] Noting it helps us understand key points in the tale of twentieth-century holism. Its founders opened the doors to a wide variety of religious and scientific thought, and the institute became a cornucopia of spiritual possibilities. Speakers and participants, often disgruntled with Western rationalism, militarism, and materialism, explored religion, science, and mixtures of the two; they practiced meditation, prayer, martial arts, and psychological techniques. Many were enamored with the literature and ideas of the romantics. Certainly, Michael Murphy read Ralph Waldo Emerson and Henry David Thoreau.[12] No one theory, ritual, or person dominated, although some individuals certainly tried. This was, in part, facilitated by Esalen's setup. Most people came for weekend sessions, and the participants were in constant flux. Workshops encouraged experimentation and development of the individual's potential through any number of transformative practices designed to harmonize body, mind, and spirit. Esalen's marketplace of opportunities and blend of beliefs were sometimes informed by liberal Christian theologians such as Paul Tillich, John Cobb, and Harvey Cox, but they differed from the denominational practices of Protestant America. As such, the institute did not suit everyone. Some Christians condemned it as hedonistic, questioned its humanistic base, or castigated it as cultish.[13] Still, the story of Esalen has much to tell about holism and late twentieth-century spiritual culture.

The center's setting is suggestive of its function as an East-West borderland. Bounded by the Pacific Ocean on the west and the Santa Lucia Mountains on the east, the institute is located in a remote area, accessed only by a private road off two-lane Highway 1, a few miles south of the village of Big Sur. The grounds boast mountain streams, exotic and indigenous plants, and organic vegetable and herb gardens. Simple redwood buildings provide lodging for staff and guests and house workshops, seminar rooms, and dining hall facilities. Massage tables and hot tubs sit precariously along cliffs reinforced with rebar. A few round buildings dot the landscape, signaling an Eastern presence, as do the occasional Buddha and the yin-yang symbol inlaid within a pool of water outside the meditation hut.

Locating Esalen at Big Sur made sense materially and spiritually. It sits on land that had been in Murphy's family since 1910. Richard Price, an equal partner from the start, leveraged $17,000 in stock he and his father owned to secure a $10,000 loan for operations.[14] Moreover, California has long attracted metaphysical religions and alternative faiths.[15] Big Sur's rugged landscape especially fostered an appreciation for nature and religious fervor. Novelist Henry Miller, who lived in the region in the 1940s, centuries after the first known inhabitants of the region, the Esselen Indians (from whom Murphy and Price drew their name) roamed the area, exclaimed, "If the soul were to choose an arena in which to stage its agonies, this would be the place for it. One feels exposed—not only to the elements, but to the sight of God." The rural spot also offered freedom to experiment. As Murphy stated, "I don't think it would have worked as well if we started Esalen in, say, New Jersey. The sheer magnitude of the land and the power of the elements are what shape lives in Big Sur."[16]

All was not idyllic, however, when Murphy and Price gained permission from the family to settle on the property. They stepped into an inhabited spot, and it took some time to make it their own. Murphy's grandmother had turned the family property into Slate's Hot Springs, a rustic motel, bar, and restaurant. A few old bathtubs sufficed for soaking in waters that poured over the cliffs. At the end of the 1950s, an unusual mix gathered there. Pentecostals managed the motel, and several semipermanent residents, including the not-yet-famous folk singer Joan Baez, lived in log cabins. Locals with a wild reputation and criminal past frequented the bar, and homosexual men from San Francisco and Los Angeles visited the baths. Twenty-two-year-old Hunter Thompson, later lauded for his self-conscious, subjective style of "Gonzo" journalism, served as guard. In April 1961, Thompson, unaware that Murphy and Price had come to stay, woke Murphy up the first night with a gun and a shout, "Who the hell are you, and what are ya' doing here?"[17] Though pacified, Thompson soon moved on. So did the Pentecostals, but it took signs establishing a hot tub curfew, steel fences, and aggressive dogs to scare away the bathers. After one group refused to heed verbal warnings, Murphy, Price, Baez, and others marched Doberman pinchers down the lane to the tubs. Loud barking and snarling worked; the party left; and the baths belonged to Esalen.

After claiming the area for their own alternative educational experiment, Murphy and Price forbade spontaneous visits. Lecturers and participants came initially by invitation only. Then, catalogs advertised workshops and people registered, but throughout its history, Esalen was selective. This control kept cult leaders and those unsympathetic with the mission from the gates. Fees also kept people out. In the 1960s, when Bay Area students could live on less than $100 per month, sessions at Esalen cost between $40 and $300. "Hippies" who camped out in communes in the surrounding foothills referred to Esalen as the "country club."[18] That did not stop some trespassers, but generally participants came from higher economic standing, held stable jobs, or worked at Esalen to afford the experience. Many tended to be young professionals. Most were searching for an alternative to the status quo, something different from conventional academic programs, mainstream churches, the corporate world, and Cold War culture.

Seminars ordinarily lasted for a weekend or a week and catered to twelve to fifty participants. Guest lecturers generally stayed only for their session, although some intellectuals, writers, and artists resided on the premises. Attendees slept in dormitory-like settings and cottages. At times, some camped on the grounds or stayed at local hotels. Meals were shared in a common space.

Talk of evolution, consciousness-raising, and the human potential animated the founders and those they invited to participate. The first formal seminar series was titled "Human Potentiality." Appropriately, one of the assigned books was Maslow's *Toward a Psychology of Being.*[19] The psychologist's writings on "self-actualization," or as Maslow defined it, "man's desire for self-fulfillment...to become actualized in what he is potentially," found great appeal.[20] After stumbling across the place in the summer of 1964, he became an adviser. Although started, as Murphy was fond of saying, "to create a space for everything that was excluded from the academy," the center resembled a sort of open university, and Maslow fit right in.[21] It was a cerebral start.

By the mid-1960s Esalen's course catalogs expanded to include Gestalt, reflexology, Rolfing, transactional analysis, yoga, and other practices. This

"inflection into the experiential," as Murphy described it, opened the institute to all kinds of individuals who were selling any number of techniques
designed to explore body, soul, and mind.[22] Big Sur also attracted musical
celebrities such as Joan Baez, Bob Dylan, George Harrison, Ringo Starr,
David Crosby, Stephen Stills, Graham Nash, Ravi Shankar, Paul Simon,
and Art Garfunkel. Some of Baez's folk festivals drew up to 2,000 people.
Along with music, Esalen promised mineral waters, massage, and—unoffi-
cially—drugs and sex. The place had, after all, a very antinomian flavor. At
some concerts, Murphy surmised, comparing them to the Woodstock
Festival, half the participants were stoned on drugs and the other half on the
beauty of the place.[23] While the institute officially forbade the use of illegal
drugs, no bags were searched, and workshops, including those led by former Harvard LSD researchers Timothy Leary and Richard Alpert, explored
psychedelics and hallucinogens. Some exploration reflected the center's and
era's serious investigation of altered states of consciousness; some was
purely recreational and the reason for many to cast a leery glance at this far-
out place in California.

One prominent resident healer in the 1960s was Frederick "Fritz" Perls,
author of the popular book *In and Out of the Garbage Pail*. A short, bearded
Jewish man of German birth, Perls practiced a dramatic form of group therapy. Though trained as a Freudian psychoanalyst, he modified his approach.
Between 1926 and his emigration to the United States in 1946, he dabbled
in various schools of psychology, as well as Marxism, existentialism, and
Buddhism. In Frankfurt, he worked with Gestalt psychologist Kurt Goldstein,
whose organismic views influenced Perls's holistic understanding of the
person. Perls also borrowed from Freudian and Marxist revisionist Wilhelm
Reich's therapeutic techniques of touch and attention to patient actions and
expressions. When Adolf Hitler rose to power, Perls fled to South Africa,
where he practiced psychoanalysis and wrote about his view of the person in
Ego, Hunger, and Aggression. He moved to New York after the war and published, with writer Paul Goodman and psychology professor Ralph
Hefferline, *Gestalt Therapy: Excitement and Growth in the Human Personality*
(1951). The book asserted that human beings can only be understood as a
whole—body, mind, and spirit—and that neurosis stems from being cut off
from one's emotions and senses. Therapy aimed to reintegrate the self and
construct individual meaning.[24]

By the time Perls made his way to Esalen in 1964, he had merged his
particular blend of Freudian and Reichian psychoanalysis and Gestalt psychology with "psychodrama," a group therapy developed by psychiatrist
Jacob Moreno. In a group setting, Perls alternately put volunteers in the
"hot seat." With a participant—and himself—center stage, he prodded, ridiculed, coaxed, and tantalized individuals to confront themselves. Only when

one faced what Perls contended was the divided self could one begin to synchronize body and mind: "The previously robotized corpses begin to return to life, gaining substance and beginning the dance of abandonment and self-fulfillment; the paper people are turning into real people."[25]

Murphy claimed that Gestalt therapy was designed to counter the "dehumanization that now threaten[s] our society," yet some of Perls's techniques and words belittled the person and contradicted the very humanizing process he set out to accomplish.[26] Probably his love for histrionics (he had studied theater in Germany) and the fact that playing to emotions pulled in larger audiences swayed his therapeutic approach. "Those evenings were high drama," exclaimed a journalist. Murphy concurred: Perls "would run dream workshops which were fantastic!...It was certainly show biz."[27] The Gestalt therapist set up shop at Esalen from 1964 to 1969 and was one of its biggest draws, but others contributed in like fashion.

The therapeutic parade remade Esalen and stamped it with an anything-goes spirit, but it also created a place of religious and psychological exchange. In the midst of experimentation, the quest for personal wholeness and a better society persisted. This was reinforced by a steady influx of speakers who pushed for personal transformation and either actively promoted or expressed openness to a religio-scientific synthesis. On any one weekend, one might hear lectures by photographer Ansel Adams; anthropologist Gregory Bateson; politician Jerry Brown; English professor S. I. Hayakawa; novelist Ken Kesey; social critic Herbert Marcuse; psychologists B. F. Skinner, Carl Rogers, Rollo May, and Virginia Satir; scientist Linus Pauling; social critic Susan Sontag; or Episcopalian bishop James Pike. The eclectic list provided avenues to explore multiple angles of body, mind, and spirit. In these forums, dialogue promoted alternative understandings of the self and the world. Together, it was, as Albanese argues of other religious exchanges, "a vast bazaar of the spirit" where any number of religions and religious combinations were bought and sold.[28]

In this market of experience, most attendees came only for a weekend, although some returned again and again. Some preferred specific speakers; others sought a particular exercise, training, or issue. In the words of staff member Stuart Miller, the center offered an education "of the soul, of the heart, of the veins and arteries and the subtle messages and meanings of the blood."[29] What this meant in practice was as varied as the attendees, but Murphy claimed the aim was "self-actualization" and "peak experiences." Drawing on Maslow's psychology, Murphy explained that, within "these dynamic moments, personal conflicts seem to be integrated; the world is seen as a unity; perception is relatively ego-transcending and self-forgetting, egoless." Workshop leaders planned, he added, "to evoke and support such experiences."[30]

While workshops promised help for those negotiating the fragmentation they felt in their personal lives and the world around them, participant reactions were mixed, ranging from life-altering experiences that led to new careers, new relationships, and new understandings to grave disappointments, denunciations, and even suicides. Still, for many spiritual seekers, Esalen provided a temporary interlude in life's journey and a chance to explore such things as humanistic psychology, Buddhist mindfulness, deep breathing techniques, chanting, and relationships with humans and nature.

Esalen, as Murphy admitted, "was filled with excesses" in the 1960s, but the organization matured and became more stable in the ensuing decades.[31] Psychology, always a staple at Esalen, became more focused on the "we" than the "me." Even from its beginning, it had a social mission. Conferences and social programs, first initiated in 1963 with calls for ecological responsibility, racial awareness, changes in education, and peaceful relations between countries, expanded to include women's studies programs, a confluent education program that trained elementary and secondary teachers in affective modes of teaching and learning, and partnerships with the National Institute of Mental Health, the National Council of Churches, and the Ford Foundation. The Esalen Soviet-American Exchange Program engaged in "citizen-diplomacy" by gathering Soviets and Americans together to discuss common interests. In 1989, this program sponsored Boris Yeltsin's trip to the United States.[32]

An influential and socially concerned member of Esalen's leadership team was George Leonard, a white southern integrationist and journalist for *Look* magazine who had covered the civil rights movement and was committed to ending racism and advancing revolutionary changes in education. He marched with Martin Luther King Jr., discussed race and education with Robert Kennedy, and eventually led encounter groups at Esalen to ameliorate racial divisions. He also wrote sympathetic articles on the Beat generation and the human potential movement. When he met Murphy at a dinner in 1965, the two hit it off, talking about their dreams of individual and social change into the wee hours of the morning. Both rejoiced in the changes wrought by the civil rights movement and felt their society was on the cusp of something radically new. They discussed ways for people to "start liberating [themselves] from the unacknowledged, unseen oppression that keeps us from achieving our potential." Both saw Esalen as facilitating such liberation.[33]

Esalen tried to interweave personal and social change. In spite of some narcissistic behavior at their center, the leaders scorned changes in self for solely egotistical reasons.[34] Murphy argued that self-fulfillment could not be a solitary aim; rather, he, like Maslow, thought planetary evolution depended on individual evolution. If enough people actualized their potential, then "a new kind of life" could be generated that "would involve new types of social interaction, new styles of energy consumption, greater care for the physical environment, more wisdom in dealing with human aggressiveness, new rituals of work and play."[35] What was meant by "new" was vague, but it certainly echoed a political agenda that promoted democracy and individual freedom; condemned materialism, racism, and sexism; valued human worth and dignity (body, soul, and mind); and honored the environment. Specifics on how to change society were few. Esalen resisted organized protests, despite Baez's urging, and recoiled from becoming a policy center or political machine.[36] Unlike Tom Hayden, who forged Students for a Democratic Society (SDS) in the same year Esalen began, Murphy and Price never drafted a political manifesto. Though they likely agreed with SDS's Port Huron Statement about humanity's "unrealized potential for self-cultivation, self-direction, self-understanding, and creativity" and need for "fraternity," Esalen creators found hope in religion and humanistic psychology, not politics.[37] It operated more as a think tank, a forum for cross-cultural dialogue, and a greenhouse for individual spiritual growth.

None of this happened in a vacuum. Situated on the Pacific Rim of the United States, Esalen grew out of what was already happening on the West Coast in the 1940s and 1950s. Placing Esalen within its larger geographic and historical context helps explain the individuals who started it, the many who flocked there, the influence it enjoyed in promoting a holistic mind-set, and the spiritual exchange that occurred there. Like other geographic arenas, the Pacific world has served competing agendas, alternately providing a theater for war and peace. During World War II and the Cold War, national animosities elicited anxiety and devastation, but they also opened communication channels. Some soldiers, business figures, artists, and religious people (many within San Francisco's religious studies programs, beatnik circles, and immigrant communities) used the Pacific as a bridge to facilitate cultural exchange.[38] Understanding Esalen as part of this Pacific borderland—this mixing ground of East and West—helps explain how fertile the soil was for cultivating spiritual combinations, especially those with a particular holistic sensibility. The lives of Murphy and Price help illuminate this.

When the two men opened the doors of Esalen, they had known each other for only two years. While both obtained psychology degrees from Stanford University in 1952, they did not meet until 1960. At that point each man lived at San Francisco's Cultural Integration Fellowship (CIF) house, a meditation center opposite Golden Gate Park. Started in 1951, CIF was run by Haridas Chaudhuri, a religious teacher from India who was deeply committed to bridging Eastern and Western cultures.[39] Murphy and Price came from well-to-do families. Both were athletic, had served in the military, and had tried and abandoned graduate school. Most important, both had grown disillusioned with materialism, were intrigued with psychology, and found much to like in Eastern religions.[40] These were significant factors in their individual lives and symbolic of patterns within the larger culture that welcomed holistic thought and practices and changing spiritual beliefs. Examining their individual journeys and the world they inhabited places the work of Esalen on a continuum with other East-West projects on the West Coast and sets the stage for understanding how Esalen became a Western ashram and mixing ground for contemporary spirituality that had a decidedly holistic cast.

Murphy's transformation occurred in college whereas Price's came after, but both came through Frederic Spiegelberg (1896–1994). One of two sons born to a successful Salinas, California, lawyer, Murphy contemplated becoming an Episcopal priest, but he discarded Christianity when introduced to Darwinian ideas: "I became an instant atheist at Stanford. The first year I thought, 'My gosh!' after sitting in the evolution course.... All these Salinas Episcopalian versions of the Christian myths just crumbled."[41] A gregarious individual, Murphy enrolled in a premed curriculum when he entered college, joined a fraternity, played intramural sports, and participated in student government. He gave all that up the next year when, through a scheduling fluke, he landed in Spiegelberg's comparative religions class.

Spiegelberg was a popular professor of Indian religion and culture in Stanford's Department of Asiatic Studies. Through his tutelage of Murphy and Price, he played a role in Esalen's development. A 1937 émigré from Nazi Germany, he had studied with Martin Heidegger, Paul Tillich, and Carl Jung. En route to the United States, he stopped in London. There he met Deisetsu Teitaro Suzuki, a Zen scholar and popularizer, and Alan Watts, a young Englishman who later joined Spiegelberg in San Francisco. Spiegelberg's theology was syncretic. He considered himself a "refugee" from Christianity and claimed he felt at home in all religions, even while he insisted that no religion cornered the truth.[42] Contending that the "highest form of religion was to transcend religion," he called his system "the religion of nonreligion."[43]

In 1949, Spiegelberg traveled to Asia on a Rockefeller grant to meet mystics, including Sri Aurobindo Ghose, who had a profound effect on him and later Murphy. Born to a wealthy Calcutta family, Aurobindo was educated at Cambridge University. Like the younger Mahatma Gandhi, he longed for individual and social change, and like Teilhard he fused religion and science. In 1910, after serving prison time for revolutionary activities against British colonial rule, he took refuge in the French colony of Pondicherry and formed an ashram. Aurobindo developed an evolutionary theory mixed with Hindu spirituality. He argued that evolution moved forward with spiritual purpose. Humans, he surmised, were not the culminating act in the evolutionary process. Instead, he believed that humanity was progressing individually and collectively into a fully conscious "Supermind." In *The Future Evolution of Man*, he described the evolution of consciousness as an "unconquerable impulse of man towards God, Light, Bliss, Freedom, Immortality." Spiegelberg proclaimed Aurobindo "the Great Sage of India" and urged his students to read *The Life Divine*. Murphy did and said it was the seminal text that made everything fit together.[44]

Aurobindo's synthesis of Hinduism and evolutionary thought bore a striking resemblance to Teilhard's coupling of Catholicism and evolution. Each embraced a teleological design and utopian spirit. Teilhard's suggestion that everything—matter and spirit—was evolving toward greater unity, advancing toward one final, complete, harmonious whole, the "Omega Point," paralleled Aurobindo's "Supermind." This was not lost on Spiegelberg, who urged students to read Teilhard's *Phenomenon of Man* just as he urged them to read Aurobindo.[45] Though more Christian than Murphy might have liked, some of the priest's ideas resonated with the Esalen founder, too. He read Teilhard in 1961 and occasionally echoed Teilhard's belief that "evolution is becoming conscious of itself in man."[46] Both mystics eventually nurtured Esalen's utopian leanings and helped mark the place as open to religion and science.

In 1951 Spiegelberg partnered with businessman Louis Gainsborough and established the American Academy of Asian Studies (AAAS) in San Francisco. Gainsborough ran a large trading company called Login Corporation. Returning from one of his many business trips, he conceived the idea of starting the school in what he later described as "a spiritual experience that changed the direction of my life." Engaged with Asia financially and philosophically, he wanted to create international bridges of cultural understanding. He first imagined starting an aid program, then settled on a school. Believing that "Western religions all originated in the East" and that Westerners had forgotten these common roots, he lamented what he believed was a lack of cultural tolerance. "Most Western impressions of Eastern teachings," he thought, "were colored by visions of Swamis, naked men contemplating their navels, Buddhists in sack-cloth whirling prayer wheels, wild-eyed Moslems waving bloody swords in jihad religious wars." Finding few universities teaching Asian studies, he asked Spiegelberg to help him start the AAAS.[47]

The AAAS was not the equivalent of the academic program in "Oriental Studies" at the University of California, Berkeley, nor did it seek to be. Instead, it offered students an applied education, exposing them to Zen meditation, prayer, Tantric yoga, calligraphy, hypnosis, and lectures by Hindu swamis, Zen masters, and Christian theologians. CIF leader Chaudhuri, an expert on Aurobindo's teachings, frequently lectured at the AAAS. The school fed the "San Francisco Renaissance," which Watts, an AAAS instructor and administrator, described as a "huge tide of spiritual energy in the form of poetry, music, philosophy, painting, religion, communications techniques in radio, television, and cinema, dancing, theater, and general life-style [that] swept out of this city and its environs to affect America and the whole world" between about "1958 and 1970."[48]

Beginning with Speigelberg's class, Murphy radically altered his lifestyle and worldview. He forswore student politics and parties, moved out of the fraternity, and read Buddhist, Hindu, Christian, and transcendental texts. He quit premed studies and enrolled in psychology. Eventually, he meditated eight hours a day, joined an East-West philosophy study group, and attended AAAS classes. Later he explained his actions as "exhaustion with being popular" and frustration with university "authoritarianism." As he phrased it, he "jump[ed] out of the culture" and into "the outlaw territory."[49] He remained in the culture long enough, however, to obtain his bachelor's degree, serve two years in the army, and try graduate school. In 1956, he abandoned the customary for a sixteen-month stint at Aurobindo's ashram.

On his way to India, he toured European cathedrals and played golf on Scotland's legendary greens. This itinerary made it clear that he had financial means and that physical joys would not be sidelined by spiritual commitments. Avid about sports—a love he gained from his father, who had boxed professionally—he was determined all his life to link sport and spirituality. In the 1970s, he fictionalized his Scottish experience in his mystical novel, *Golf in the Kingdom*.[50] Later at Esalen, he encouraged contemplative habits without "belittling" the body and initiated several projects that integrated mind, body, heart, and soul.[51]

Murphy pursued physical and metaphysical disciplines in India. Aurobindo's ashram, unlike other Indian spiritual communes, encouraged competitive sports, and so while Murphy lived and enjoyed the contemplative life of a monk, he also coached basketball and softball. Because Aurobindo had died in 1950, Murphy never met him, but the ashram continued under the leadership of the "Mother" of Auroville, Mira Richard, a French woman. Murphy disliked what he saw as blind devotion to her.[52] When he established Esalen, he promoted the ashram's dedication to contemplation, meditation, and Aurobindian thought. But, with Price's agreement, he refused to give any person sole authority. "No one," they liked to say, "captures the flag." Thus, Esalen became a retreat center with an Eastern cast and a democratic thrust. This commitment to individualism and egalitarianism made Esalen, as Jeffrey Kripal has observed, "a quintessentially American phenomenon, immeasurably enriched but never finally defined or limited by its Indian influences."[53]

Participant autonomy and freedom to choose one's own spiritual practice or combination of beliefs corresponded to the Americanization of Eastern religion in the larger culture. As religious historian Amanda Porterfield noted, the Americanization process of Buddhism involved "min[ing] Buddhist philosophy for its salutary and pragmatic benefits" and "recast[ing] Buddhist ideas in the context of social frameworks that are more democratic and egalitarian than those associated with more traditional forms of Asian Buddhism."[54] At the same time, Murphy's respect for individual autonomy stemmed from a communitarian ethic deeply indebted to individual dignity. In this, he was similar to King and Teilhard.

Price, like Murphy, also testified to the transformative power of Spiegelberg's lectures. He grew up in a wealthy, segregated Chicago suburb. To buy property in the subdivision, his parents hid their Jewish identity and had their children baptized in the Episcopalian Church. Price felt little affinity for Christianity and did not think about religion until he signed up for Spiegelberg's class in 1955. By this time he had withdrawn from Harvard University's graduate program in psychology and joined the air force. He was serving at Parks Air Force Base, a mere half hour from Stanford University, and so he enrolled in classes. Spiegelberg's course on the Bhagavad Gita captivated him. "For the first time," he explained, "I began thinking there was something in religion; it was more than a system of deceit and enforcement of social rules."[55] He read Buddhist texts and immersed himself in life at the AAAS.

While Murphy's enthusiasm for the East led him to India, Price's step out of the culture was of a tragic nature. The excitement of these new ideas, his recent marriage to a woman he had known only a few months, his air force job, and lack of sleep (two hours per night was not uncommon) eventually consumed him, resulting in hallucinations and a mental breakdown. His parents, distraught over his turn to Buddhism and unconventional lifestyle, wanted him out of California. In a series of duplicitous actions, without either Price's knowledge or permission, they moved him to Chicago, had his marriage annulled, and directed his medical care. Eventually they committed him, against his wishes, to the Institute for Living, a Connecticut psychiatric hospital, with a diagnosis of paranoid schizophrenia.

The Institute for Living became a place of torture to Price. Over a period of a year, he endured fifty-nine insulin treatments, ten electroshock treatments, and multiple doses of Thorazine, a powerful drug that dulls the senses. The treatment experience, which he likened to that of a boxer being knocked out cold, took him in and out of consciousness and stultified his will. Kept in a locked ward, he had no access to the exercise room. The once-champion athlete gained weight, shooting from 145 to 175 pounds within a few months. Initially, he passively accepted his fate, but as the year wore on and his weight increased to 240 pounds, he felt he must escape or die. He began "cheeking" his Thorazine doses and walking the halls. In August 1957 he straggled over the tall exterior wall and shuffled down Hartford's streets. His escape was short-lived, for he soon realized his health had been so diminished that he could not make it on his own. He bummed a dime to call his father, begging him to force the doctors to stop the shock treatments. His father relented, and Price reentered the hospital and managed to get well enough for a Thanksgiving Day release. Still weak, he returned to Chicago and worked at his uncle's business, but he was not happy. In 1960 he departed again for California.[56] It was at this point that he moved into the CIF house and met Murphy.[57] The two attended lectures by Chaudhuri, Watts, and Spiegelberg and shared their enthusiasm for meditation and psychology.

Turning to humanistic psychology and Eastern religion partly reflected Murphy's and Price's reaction to their Cold War culture. Instead of conforming to parental dreams of a career in medicine or business or settling into suburban life, they chose a path more in keeping with the quixotic characters in J. D. Salinger's novels that Murphy admired in those who scorned traditionalism and searched for insights among world religions.[58] Alienated from mainstream society, they joined Watts, novelist Aldous Huxley, and Beat poets in questioning the status quo. They criticized American consumerism and exercises of military might. Beat writer Michael McClure summarized his group's *mentalité* when describing the 1950s decade as a "bitter, gray one," with no way "to escape the pressures of the war culture." He described a feeling of being "locked in the Cold War and the first Asian debacle—the Korean War." He added, "We hated the war and the inhumanity and the coldness."[59] Instead, they wanted a way out from the military-industrial complex, or, as Watts put it, the "martial, mechanically marching, tick-tock, and saw-toothed jagged life-rhythm which has been rattling the world."[60] Murphy, Price, Watts, and others found a way out in Eastern religion. It gave them a means to critique their own culture. In this way, Eastern religion served as a foil, an "other" to expose what they disliked in Western society.

Watts was the person at the AAAS who most impressed Price. Watts turned to Zen Buddhism at fifteen and published the first of many books, *The Spirit of Zen*, at twenty. In London, he attended lectures and absorbed the teachings of D. T. Suzuki. In 1939, Watts moved to New York City and studied with Zen master Sokei-an Shigetsu Sasaki. He also became an Episcopal priest, even though he never practiced Christianity with much seriousness. The poet Gary Snyder contended Watts became a priest to gain credibility and financial means; as Northwestern University's chaplain, Watts "basically taught a Buddhist version of Episcopalianism."[61] By the time Spiegelberg invited him to join the AAAS, Watts had left Northwestern to preach a universalistic faith. In 1958, Stephen Mahoney, writing in the *Nation*, dubbed Watts "the brains and Buddha of American Zen."[62] His following included Beat poets Allen Ginsberg, Jack Kerouac, and Snyder. Watts also found an appreciative community through his program *Way beyond the West* on Berkeley's Pacifica Radio station KPFA. Started by pacifists at the end of the 1940s, KPFA became the Bay Area's dominant voice against the Cold War.[63] In the 1960s, Watts became a celebrity at Esalen, blessing buildings and bathtubs, performing marriages, celebrating Episcopalian mass, invoking Buddhist prayers, delivering sermons on Eastern thought and Western psychology, and sharing his "infectious, outrageous laughter" and "sense of play."[64]

While the Cold War ignited animosity, it also stirred curiosity in Eastern culture. Watts explained, "What we were doing in San Francisco in the 1950s must, of course, be seen in the context of America's military involvements in Japan, Korea, and then Vietnam, for these exploits were bound to bring the cultures of those areas back home."[65] Returning soldiers brought art, customs, stories, and sometimes wives and children and sparked intrigue. Through individual voyages and accounts, civilians furthered cross-cultural dialogue. Spiegelberg and Murphy exemplified this in their treks to India, as did Ginsberg, Watts, Snyder, and Beat poet Joanne Kyger in trips to Japan. Snyder's decade-long stay in Japan made him feel "very at home in Buddhism." His poetry often focused on Buddhist themes.[66] Watts promoted Zen on his radio broadcasts. He also led Asian tours. San Francisco's East-West House, Kyger recalled, "was started essentially as a place where people could study with Alan Watts and study Japanese in preparation for going to Japan." In the 1950s, Kyger explained, people were fascinated with Japanese "gardening, tea ceremonies, beautiful fold craft, music, sense of nature.... What we think of Japan is its competition with the car industry, transistor radios, the computer chip, etc. Back then, Japanese culture was seen to be a way of being with nature."[67] As she suggested, the postwar turn to the East offered ways to reinvest nature with the sacred.

Spiegelberg, Watts, and the Beats were not the only ones fascinated by Asia, nor was it the first time Americans encountered Eastern ideas. Trade, travel, immigration, and religious leaders, particularly before various exclusion acts barred Asians from citizenship, had brought Asia to American shores. Transcendentalists wrote about Eastern ideas in their poetry and essays. The Hindu Vedanta Society found a small American following after the World's Parliament of Religions met at the Chicago World's Fair in 1893. The first Vedanta temple in San Francisco opened in 1906, followed by a monastery and convent. In the 1920s, Vedanta centers opened elsewhere, including Hollywood, where English émigrés Huxley, Gerald Heard, and Christopher Isherwood contributed to the spread of Eastern religious ideas (many of which espoused holism) through their writings and projects.[68] By the middle of the twentieth century, a sprinkling of communities practiced Hinduism and Buddhism at a handful of temples, monasteries, and convents. In 1959, Zen master Shunryu Suzuki-roshi moved from Japan to San Francisco and established the Zen Center. Chinese immigrant Gia-Fu Feng (who joined Esalen in the 1960s) helped initiate San Francisco's East-West House.[69]

Murphy and Price immersed themselves in this vibrant religious and cultural mix. When the two began to dream about a center, they looked to Chaudhuri, Heard, Huxley, Spiegelberg, and Watts for direction. This group voiced optimism about humanity's future. Though distraught about genocide, nuclear blasts, superpower tensions, and racial segregation, they did not despair. Instead, they asserted, as George Leonard would later frequently say, "*It doesn't have to be this way. We could do it better.*"[70] Each believed that society could be more just, more harmonious, that human beings could live more fulfilled lives. Huxley voiced these hopes in a speech about "the human potential." Working within an evolutionary framework, he argued that human beings had "actualized an immense number of things," but "there are still a great many potentialities—for rationality, for affection and kindliness, for creativity—still lying latent in man; ... perhaps ... we might be able to produce extraordinary things out of this strange piece of work that a man is."[71]

Pursuing this potential—via mystical experiences, psychology, drugs, or other means—was certainly one of the goals of this group. Murphy preferred meditation, telling Leonard that contemplative practices gave him "direct experience" with "an Essential Ground of All Being."[72] Huxley experimented with pharmacology. Inducing trances and mind-altering states through drugs, he believed, could liberate people and advance human evolution. He pointed to the power of hallucinogenic drugs such as LSD, first synthesized in 1943, and peyote cactus, long used by indigenous peoples to induce mystical states. Borrowing a line from William Blake's "Marriage of Heaven and Hell," Huxley surmised that drugs could open the "doors of perception." An intellectual and mystic, he experimented with mescaline (the psychotropic alkaloid in dried peyote flowers) in 1953 at the age of fifty-eight, wrote the *Doors of Perception* in 1954, and took LSD in 1955. Heard similarly thought drugs could be a path to higher consciousness, and both he and Huxley supported scientific studies of LSD. Huxley urged scientists to experiment on themselves to see the value of these drugs. As LSD moved beyond labs and onto the streets, tales of drug abuse tempered enthusiasm for this mode of perceptual change. Still, one cannot ignore the seriousness of the search for altered states of consciousness that prompted the initial reception for LSD. For Huxley and others, harnessing drugs for spiritual enlightenment was a real possibility.[73]

The Bay Area provided the seeds and fertile ground for Esalen's emergence. Here, Americans and immigrants made contact, shared interests, and taught others through their art, broadcasts, schools, and monasteries. Multicultural exchanges fed American interest in the East, captivated Murphy and Price, and helped catapult Esalen to prominence. Well-known people such as Huxley and Watts, in turn, gave the center a head start. Coming out of the East-West San Francisco scene marked Esalen as open to both holistic practices and spiritual thought, helping it to become a vehicle for the spread of Eastern religions. Although influenced by the East, Esalen did not become a Hindu monastery, Zen center, or Buddhist temple. Some Christian, Jewish, and indigenous beliefs were also welcome at this pluralist camp. As Asian beliefs combined with Western notions, they were modified, and the institute became a crossing point for cultural interchange, adaptation, and another reinvention of American holism.

Just as the story of Esalen as a center for postwar holism and late twentieth-century spirituality cannot be fully told without attention to its geographic context, it cannot be fully told without acknowledging the scientific culture in which it sat and the connections its attendees made between spiritual cosmologies and scientific theories. Borrowing concepts from the sciences and looking to overall syntheses such as Aurobindo's and Teilhard's evolutionary mysticism, Esalen directors, workshop leaders, and participants reinjected religious notions into their technological society. Highlighting a few discussions in evolution, physics, ecology, psychology, and medicine illustrates some of the permutations of this mix.

First, as noted, evolutionary ideas contributed to Esalen's founding. Spiegelberg, Murphy, Price, Heard, and Huxley—grandson of "Darwin's bulldog" Thomas Huxley—employed evolution to chart future possibilities. In 1966 the transformationalist spirit still resounded at Grace Cathedral in San Francisco when Leonard extolled Esalen's purpose in Teilhardian fashion: "The atom's soul is nothing but energy. Spirit blazes in the dullest clay. The life of every man—the heart of it—is pure and holy joy." To celebrate that joy, venerate each person's possibilities, and promote its actualization, Leonard claimed, was Esalen's task.[74] Though both Aurobindo and Teilhard died before they could speak at the institute, some of their followers did, including Chaudhuri and American Teilhard Association members Brian Swimme and Thomas Berry.[75]

Words like "evolution," "potentialities," and "transformation" peppered multiple conversations. Leaders and participants also talked of "awakenings," a familiar cultural pattern to Americans who had long participated in revivals. Yet the religious awakenings Esalen summoned and the evolutionary schema it favored garnered enemies, too. The institute's marriage of science and religion found little appeal among fundamentalists, who tended to view evolution as a threat and who found conflict, not harmony, between science and religion. Indeed, understanding this attitude helps explain why some Americans responded so angrily to Esalen. For traditionalists who shunned Darwinian conceptualizations, celebrated the outcome of the Scopes trial, and still pushed for creation science or intelligent design in school curricula, talk of evolutionary change threatened core beliefs.[76]

Fundamentalist Christians were not the only ones Esalen alienated. Positivists and scientific materialists, who considered religion irrational and irrelevant, dismissed them. Watts noted the animosity: "We were concerned with the practical transformation of human consciousness, with the actual living out of the Hindu, Buddhist, and Taoist ways of life at the level of high mysticism: a concern repugnant to academics and contemptible to businessmen, threatening to Jews and Christians, and irrational to most scientists."[77]

Murphy and Price did not set out to please fundamentalists or positivists. They actively sought philosophers, artists, and scientists who coupled the natural and supernatural, spirit and matter, religion and science. They invited speakers who borrowed concepts from biology, physics, and psychology and fused the mystical into their theories. Workshop participants followed suit, resisting absolutist dogmas of either science or religion that denied the legitimacy of the other. They wanted a middle way. The result, as Murphy put it, was a "neo-Aurobindian marriage of science and metaphysics."[78]

Aurobindo's and Teilhard's evolutionary teleology offered one mix of spirit and matter, but there were other opportunities to bridge physical and metaphysical at Esalen. Many found quantum physics particularly intriguing, not the least of whom was Murphy, whose metaphysical novel *Jacob Atabet* wove quantum theory into his main character's exploration of mind, matter, and transformative experiences.[79] The science of quantum mechanics relied, in part, on Heisenberg's uncertainty principle and Bell's theorem that matter both transcended and sat within space and time, and seemed to prove the limitations of mechanistic science and dualistic separations of matter and spirit. Between 1976 and 1988, Esalen's interest in quantum physics was evident, with the institute sponsoring eleven conferences on the subject. The conferences sprang from conversations among a group of physicists at the University of California, Berkeley, who were interested in connections between consciousness and energy. Gary Zukav's book *The Dancing WuLi Masters: An Overview of the New Physics* was based in part on the Esalen discussions.[80] These Berkeley scientists, though not always thrilled with the ways their science became coupled with Asian religion, argued that mind and matter are both different and the same, that reality includes both mental and physical.[81] For Esalen members, this appeared to confirm holistic ontologies. Although physicist Fritjof Capra, author of *The Tao of Physics* and *The Web of Life*, did not join this set of conferences, he frequently spoke at Esalen. He posited that the earth was a living organism intertwined and interdependent, fluid and dynamic. His work represented a paradigmatic shift in physics, a change in focus from the part to the whole, from structure to process, from "objective" to "epistemic" science, from the use of building-block metaphors to metaphors of networks, from "truth" statements to statements of approximate description.[82]

Capra's holism came from many sources. In addition to physics, he drew from general systems theory, the Gaia hypothesis, ecofeminism, deep ecology, and Eastern mysticism. Two teachers linked with Esalen had a particular influence. One was Watts, who had earlier connected physics and Eastern mysticism in his book *The Joyous Cosmology* (1962). The other was Gregory Bateson, who laid out his thoughts of an interconnected world in *Mind and Nature*. Leaning on the words of one of his most admired poets, William Blake, who wrote that "man has no body distinct from his soul," Bateson shunned dualistic separations of mind and body, human and energy, God and human beings. He applied his holistic approach to anthropological projects, including schizophrenia studies, and carried it into environmental and antinuclear campaigns. Involved with Esalen since its inception, he served as an adviser and conducted workshops.[83]

Zukav, Capra, Bateson, and others translated their holistic science into popular books. In many ways, their writings, as Jeffrey Kripal points out, were more "modern mystical literature" than science books, and as such their goal was to "remythologize and rehumanize a cosmos that the dualisms of science had previously demythologized and rendered inhuman, objective, and cold."[84] Humanistic physics echoed Abraham Maslow's resacralization of the human. Just as he had scorned the surgeon who removed a patient's cancerous breast and cavalierly tossed it like "a lump of fat, garbage, to be tossed into a pail," so, to many of these physicists, mechanistic ways of doing science seemed "emotionless, cool, calm."[85] Holism's emphasis on the whole person and the whole person's connections with the environment demanded more.

Resacralizing nature had consequences at Esalen. Environmentalism shaped the way people thought about the earth and the way they lived. Residents and guests tended organic vegetable and herb gardens. Capra,

Bateson, and others such as George Leonard endorsed Carson's world of ecological wholeness and contributed to philosophical discussions and practical actions concerning the environment. Leonard especially made environmentalism a fundamental part of the Esalen agenda. Like others around the country, his environmental concerns began in 1962 and increased when he saw the first pictures of earth. In the NASA photographs, he said he saw a "shining globe floating in the loneliness of space," an "emblem of human unity," and a cry for peace and sustainability. For him, it was "brotherhood and sisterhood or death." He suggested that "the environmental movement and our work with human potential" were "traveling essentially in the same direction." Both took a stand against "aggression and exploitation" even while the larger society "stifled the realization of human capabilities" and "threatened the survival of the planet. The mechanization of relationships, the deadening of the emotions, the general depersonalization of life," Leonard contended, "would ultimately make possible the ruin of the biosphere as well as the murder of human potential."[86]

Esalen hosted workshops to address environmental concerns. After Earth Day in 1970, the center sponsored a workshop titled "The Ecological Psyche." Historian Lynn White, the Sierra Club's David Brower, and Watts used "experiential techniques such as fantasy and sensory awareness" to focus on the "ecological crisis and social and behavioral challenges."[87] The workshop description in the Esalen catalog echoed Carson's assertion that human beings were part and parcel of the natural world: feelings of "alienation may come as much from our disconnection from the living fabric of nature as from our difficulties with each other." Given the assumption that "we are ultimately not simply man or woman, but man and woman and fish, glacier, mountain and shorebird," we must look at the ecological crisis as a time to "question our whole way of experiencing ourselves, one another, cities, trees, the heavens." Since "our life history is the life history of the planet," new lifestyles are in order. Esalen took such admonitions seriously and responded by planting organic gardens and embarking on ventures with the environmental group Friends of the Earth to promote a "psycho-ecological approach to man and his problems."[88] At this same seminar, members played Fuller's World Game to discuss sustainability issues and practical solutions. Occasionally, Fuller appeared at Esalen to give one of his whirlwind talks on saving planet earth and argue for a more equitable distribution of natural resources. Murphy billed one of the architect's seminars, "Designing Environments for Expanding Awareness," as an endeavor to integrate the built environment with the consciousness revolution. By the late 1990s, Esalen's built environment seemed to complement the center's emphasis on harmony. No geodesics stood, but yurts—similar to domes— hinted at Fuller's countercultural message.

Esalen activities continued to emphasize ecological themes in the coming years. Leaders of one workshop conducted an "ecodrama" that was meant to create an "experiential intensification of the encounter of man, technology and natural resources" in order "to develop awareness of the impact of ecological factors on the nature and evolution of human and social relationships." Participants explored "possibilities for the development of human societies."[89] In the 1990s, Theodore Roszak held a conference on ecopsychology, a synthesis of ecology, physics, psychology, and spirituality. One of the invited speakers was Charlene Spretnak, author of *The Spiritual Dimension of Green Politics.*[90] A little later, the institute sponsored symposiums titled "Sustainability Consciousness" and "The Business of Restoration."[91]

As these workshops indicated, no matter the topic, psychology found a place, reaffirming that Esalen was "a deeply psychological culture."[92] Particularly open to pioneering new scientific studies, religious experiences, and a holistic development of mind, body, and spirit, Esalen made common cause with Maslow and Perls, Rollo May, Virginia Satir, and other practitioners of humanistic psychology in the 1960s, followed by a line of transpersonal psychologists, including Stanislav Grof, in the 1970s and 1980s. Price especially advocated bringing new psychological practices to the institute. As Murphy stated, Esalen was Price's revenge against medical hospitals.[93] Price envisioned Esalen as a place that offered alternatives to the "quite brutalizing" treatments he had endured in psychiatric care.[94] He was particularly interested in medical treatments for schizophrenia and psychosis, welcoming to Esalen those who challenged conventional understandings of mental illness. This included, among others, psychologists Joe Adams, Gregory Bateson, R. D. Laing, and Thomas Szasz. In 1967, Price met Julian Silverman, the head of perceptual and cognitive studies in the Adult Psychiatry Branch at the National Institutes of Health. Together they conducted a three-year, double-blind research study that involved Esalen, the National Institute of Mental Health, and two groups of schizophrenic patients at nearby Agnews Hospital.[95] Price's interest in medical studies was supplemented by his training with Perls in Gestalt therapy and his interest in Eastern spirituality. He led workshops titled "Gestalt and Taoism."[96] He also incorporated Buddhist mindfulness and meditation, making his Gestalt practice gentler than his teacher's. Indicative of this, Price's patients sat in the "open seat" not Perls's "hot seat."[97]

Price's approach highlights one of the ways that Esalen fostered an eclectic mix of science, spirituality, and somatic practices. As Americans encountered Buddhism through religious texts, rituals, Zen masters, and popular culture (Jack Kerouac's *Dharma Bums*, the cartoon character Yogi Bear, Bruce Lee's martial arts, *Star Wars*, for example), Buddhism became increasingly visible and accepted within American life. As it filtered into psychological literature and self-help manuals, American ideals of individualism, democracy, and pragmatism mixed with Buddhist notions of suffering and enlightenment. This in turn shaped psychological understanding and treatment, initiating more focus on intuition, mind-body-spirit connections, and contemplative practices.[98] Esalen, like Colorado's Naropa Institute, provided opportunities for learning about this psychospiritual exchange. Conferences and studies relied on the humanistic revolution in psychology and holistic treatments that offered either an alternative to pharmacology or a combination of drug treatments with other practices such as psychotherapy, biofeedback, diet, meditation, breathing exercises, yoga, reflexology, and religious rituals. Perls's synthesis of Gestalt and Buddhism fit within this mix.

In addition to these various psychological practices, Esalen promoted care of the body through organic agriculture, preventative care, and alternative medical treatments. Dietary habits—akin to nineteenth-century Grahamism—catered to a naturalistic fare of pure water, whole grains, and vegetables.[99] Somatic therapies included yoga, t'ai chi, sensory awareness work, and the Alexander Technique. Australian actor F. Matthias Alexander developed the technique based on the belief that greater awareness of how one moved results in a greater understanding of self. A 1974 Esalen catalog described Alexander Technique as "a method of re-educating the body that can have dramatic effects on the whole person. By applying sensory awareness, inhibition and conscious choice to such everyday activities as sitting, standing, walking and bending, under conditions of continuous feedback from an instructor, we can experience the specific ways in which we interfere with the natural flow of our total pattern and learn to permit and encourage a response that will strengthen our innate tendency towards an integrated use of ourselves—allowing new alternatives of movement and being. Guided by the direct touch of the instructor's hands, the process involves a gentle reorganization of the body in movement and at rest."[100]

Even the first seminar paid some attention to health care with the assignment of physician Franz Winkler's book *Man: The Bridge between Two Worlds*. Winkler, like Rachel Carson's friend Marjorie Spock, was a follower of Rudolf Steiner's anthroposophy, which advocated addressing the "whole child" and following a holistic health approach that combined traditional knowledge of anatomy, biochemistry, and physiology with homeopathy and naturopathy.[101] Neither Spock nor Carson visited Esalen, but anthroposophy's holistic assumptions were just the sort that made the center popular.

In the 1970s, Esalen became more instrumental in making holistic medicine a part of mainstream culture. Mind-body-spirit connections and doctor-patient relations infused discussions. Complementary health care professionals Kenneth Pelletier and Andrew Weil sounded out their ideas at Esalen before their books could be purchased in every bookstore chain across America.[102] Workshop topics included acupuncture, altered states, organic gardening, herbology, martial arts, homeopathy, and shamanism. In 1972, Stuart and Sukie Miller started Esalen's Program in Humanistic Medicine to humanize the profession. They invited health professionals to learn how to treat the patient as a whole and to introduce alternative techniques commonly practiced at Esalen. Two years later the Department of Health, Education, and Welfare granted the program $1.2 million, and it became an independent organization at San Francisco's Mount Zion Hospital.[103]

The Esalen Sports Center, created in 1973, added to Esalen's merging of body, mind, and spirit. Murphy, in Esalen catalogs, denounced the "mind-body split" in America's value system and promoted athletics as "one vehicle for the comprehensive development of the whole person."[104] He connected sport with altered states of consciousness in his mystical novel, *Golf in the Kingdom*, and in his academic study of extraordinary human capacities, *The Future of the Body*. With Leonard, he wrote books about "transformative practices," such as martial arts and meditation. The two advocated long-term exercises, not quick, short-term fixes, to promote integration of body, heart, mind, and soul and to transform relationships and society. They started Integral Transformative Practice (ITP) to promote their holistic message through workshops and books. In all, they continued to stress as they did at Esalen that the individual was the final authority on what practice was chosen and how it was practiced.[105]

The push for holistic health care at Esalen developed alongside America's increasing interest in personal health care, natural healing systems, physical exercise, and general attention to the body. Though earlier advocates such as Adele Davis, Linus Pauling, and Rudolf Steiner, as well as organizations such as the Rodale Institute, stressed the importance of health in relation to the environment, the holistic health movement did not explode until the 1970s and 1980s. A general interest in holistic ideas within the fields explored in this book along with new immigrants from Asia and an attention to the body by many in the women's movement helped foster this interest. Humanistic psychology's attention to the linkages of body and mind and the human potential movement's focus on growth of the whole person did, too.[106] Public fascination with holistic medicine was evident in the large numbers who turned out for public symposiums on the topic. In 1971 one of the first seminars, "Varieties of Healing," was held at De Anza College in California and drew more people than the 2,700-seat auditorium could accommodate. Stanford University held a widely attended symposium in 1972 on acupuncture. Book publications on this topic and others escalated during these same years.[107] Esalen reflected these interests and helped disseminate the ideas through its own workshops and practices.

Holistic health practices varied in the last half of the twentieth century, but, mirroring Esalen's message, practitioners generally rejected reductionistic views of the body, specialization without concern for other parts of the system, and a solitary focus on disease. Instead, they explained health in terms of "wholeness." As one historian of the movement stated, this position rests on the belief that "health is that state of being in which a person's body, mind, and spirit are in balance, functioning with utmost capacity or potential (high-level wellness), and in tune with the natural and social environments, as well as with the cosmos (the spiritual environment)."[108] They objected to instrumentalist approaches toward a patient as an assemblage of disparate organs and functions, decried metaphors of the body-as-machine, condemned hierarchical relations between patient and healer, and denounced what they perceived to be an emphasis on the disease rather than the patient in traditional medicine. Instead, they proposed a person-centered approach that stressed connections of body, soul, and mind and relied on the patient to play an integral part in the healing process. Holistic medicine presumed "that there is some way to cure, to make whole, without disrupting the entire ecology of the body/mind."[109] Maslow made comparable critiques against a biomechanical medical model, while others at Esalen, particularly Price, offered a similar reproof.

Health was thought of broadly. Biological, mental, relational, and environmental health were all part of the package. Maslow contributed to this holistic model. Bodily health was related, he thought, to the satisfaction of emotional and relational needs. Physical health formed the base of his self-actualization charts. In 1968, when asked by Jonas Salk, the developer of the polio vaccine and director of the Salk Institute of Biological Studies in California, to comment on the relationship between his psychology and biology, Maslow said, "My whole psychology is fundamentally biological." He added that "to make the Good Person and to make the Good Society," biological knowledge was essential. He pointed to promising developments in biofeedback techniques and stressed the importance of environment to individual health.[110] The workshops Maslow conducted at Esalen communicated such mental-physical connections.

Healthy relationships also included interpersonal dynamics, and there was no shortage of workshops for couples, families, and groups. Attendees could learn better communication techniques and participate in family therapy programs. As the nation wrestled with changing racial and gender relations, Esalen did too. According to Esalen leader Julian Silverman, the center in the early 1970s had its share of "male chauvinism."[111] Egalitarian ideals forwarded by the civil rights and women's movements and accepted by many at Esalen led to significant changes. Women gained more leadership roles and decision-making power. While most participants were and still are white, the institute also addressed race relations. Here, too, the center has made strides in treating all as equal, but this has not been easy.

Leonard, a white southerner, interpreted the race problem as "a touchstone. If racial attitudes could be transformed, a society could perhaps be transformed."[112] He used his position to confront racial attitudes. In 1967, he asked the African American psychiatrist Price Cobbs to help him conduct an interracial encounter group. Cobbs declined. He was busy writing a book about black anger and contemplating involvement in the growing Black Power movement. He doubted reconciliation meetings could solve much. But Leonard persisted, Cobbs relented, and the workshop called "Racial Confrontation as Transcendental Experience" went forward.[113]

The first session was difficult. Confrontations and accusations—characteristic of encounter groups—seemed particularly harsh and bitter. Still, the nervous leaders pushed the racially mixed group of thirty-five, and after an all-night marathon session, weeping and hugging replaced rantings and clashes. Participants testified that they felt they had broken through some of their culture's racial barriers. Giddy with delight, Cobbs and Leonard drove back to San Francisco together. Cobbs said, "George, we've got to take this to the world."[114]

Esalen sponsored other interracial encounter groups, but the project ended about a year after Martin Luther King Jr. was assassinated, with an uncomfortable and bitter argument between one of the group leaders, Ron Brown, and manager Bill Smith. The quarrel erupted over remuneration for leading encounter sessions and turned especially sour when Smith, a white, threatened to call the police. Brown, an African American, interpreted the threat as racist. He claimed Smith never would have conceived of calling authorities if Brown had been white. When Smith denied the accusation and refused to apologize, Cobbs and Leonard tried to resolve the crisis through the process they knew best: they called an encounter session. The meeting failed. Racial encounters ended at Esalen, and Leonard and Cobbs dissolved their formal ties with the center.[115] The quest for a more beloved community proved difficult in practice. Part of this can be tied to America's long practice of racial inequality. The center also appeared to be caught in America's paradoxical embrace of individualism and community. It was easier to take the route of individual transformation than the group encounter.

Esalen was and is undeniably American. It reflects the culture's pluralistic tradition, democratic understandings, and individualistic sentiments. As a spiritual and communal expression, it followed a long line of religious, millennial, and utopian experiments. Its history, though at odds with many of the tenets of Christianity, recalls the emotional fervor of past religious revivals and tent-meeting pledges. Contrite hearts, altered convictions, new commitments, and changed paths: these were the testimonials of Esalen graduates, just as they had been the testimonials of "enthusiasts" converted by New Light ministers in the eighteenth century or Cane Ridge campgoers in the nineteenth century or "born-again" believers at a Billy Graham crusade in the twentieth century. The reverential tone, zealous devotion, and high emotion, though expressive of very different theologies, would have been recognizable in all these awakenings. Esalen participants might have sat in Perls's "hot seat," not the "anxious bench" of Charles Grandison Finney, but the sorts of anguish that Perls inflicted induced similar tensions, shame, and eye-opening revelations that Finney had encouraged in those who occupied his chair of penance. The histrionic Perls put on a theatrical show analogous to the best of religious revivalists, too. He could have competed with George Whitefield, Billy Sunday, or Aimee Semple McPherson. Likewise, disciples who commingled body therapy and spirituality in the human potential movement probably would not have scandalized at least some converts of the Second Great Awakening either. In the nineteenth century, John Humphrey Noyes's Oneida Community advocated "complex marriages," and healing therapies, such as mesmerism, homeopathy, and Swedenborgianism emphasized the spiritual in the healing process.[116]

While similar in emotional fervor to elements of past American awakenings, Esalen's strong individualistic bent, Eastern inclinations, and pluralistic mission cannot be seen as one with American Christianity. As Murphy has noted, there are "clear differences" between the passions and breakthroughs of Esalen attendees and the zeal of Christian fundamentalists.[117] Instead, Esalen is more closely associated with nineteenth-century romantics and transcendentalists, especially the writings of Blake, Emerson, and Thoreau. In this, the heart of Esalen follows a more mystical spiritualism that prioritizes individual truth and shuns unquestioning devotion to any one dogma. It falls within America's "metaphysical religion," as Albanese has termed this esoteric, individualistic, mystical tradition in American society.[118]

Yet, with all its similarities to things past, Esalen spoke most forcefully to the anomie of its day, answering it not with angst and frustration but with expressions of joy, hope, and faith. The profound disappointment the founders and those around them felt with Western culture and their frustration with Cold War militarism and its debacles in Korea and Vietnam prompted a search for different worldviews and lifestyles. They were not willing to give up on science, but they demanded of science new priorities and more openness to the mystical. They also demanded of religion more openness to a postmodern pastiche of spiritual perspectives rather than obedience to the dictates of one. Asian cosmologies, though not new to the West, appealed to some because of their power to re-enchant a technological, highly industrialized world that separated human beings from nature. For those alienated from society, for those searching for new potentials, or for those merely curious, Esalen and its holistic sensibility provided a panoply of possibilities.

In the first decade of the twenty-first century, about 10,000 guests visit Esalen every year. Of these, Murphy reported, one-quarter come from outside the United States.[119] Most still come for workshops, paying between $400 and $1,700, depending on the prestige of the speaker, the length of stay, and the accommodations. Much is as it has always been. Catalog offerings for 2006 included Tibetan Buddhist meditation, Ericksonian hypnosis, and Gestalt, yoga, massage, and reflexology. Teachers, including Muslim imam Faheem Shuaibe and biologist Rupert Sheldrake, continue to emphasize spiritual matters and connections between science and faith. Murphy, still chairperson of the board of trustees, has written in a recent mission statement that the "institute exists to promote the harmonious development of the whole person. It is a learning organization dedicated to continual exploration of the human potential, and resists religious, scientific and other dogmas. It fosters theory, practice, research, and institution-building to facilitate personal and social transformation."[120]

Though active, Esalen does not attract the same media attention it did in the 1960s. Nor is it as controversial. This is due, in part, to the fact that much of what goes on at the center is practiced elsewhere and therefore not so unusual. Leonard reported that as early as the mid-1970s, programs that were once the province of places like Esalen alone could be found at community colleges, church groups, and self-help gatherings. His aikido training workshops alone extended beyond Esalen to the East Coast and into America's heartland, from Minnesota to Texas.[121] By the beginning of the twenty-first century, local gyms and businesses regularly advertised yoga and martial arts classes. Esalen massage could be found worldwide. Spiritual programs blending religion with science in health care, psychotherapy, and sport were commonplace. Thus, despite the fact that Esalen did not enjoy political influence comparable to that of the Christian Right, practices pioneered and celebrated at Esalen had filtered into mainstream culture.

While Esalen was not alone in spreading holistic practices, its role was key. A simple reading of Esalen catalogs offered a tutorial in the latest experiments in religion, philosophy, psychology, and spirituality. Word of these offerings spread first to the California world in which it was born; then, thanks to media interest and participant revelations, Esalen's windows flew open to others. Journalists for popular magazines *Life*, *Look*, *New Yorker*, and *Time* covered the sensational behavior and daring personalities, as well as Zen mindfulness and t'ai chi. The fact that Esalen was not a commune contributed to its power. People came, experimented, and returned home. Some witnessed to others through conversation. Others wrote books. Some transplanted practices to family, work, and church life. Esalen's remote location only added to its influence. Dislodged from daily routines, removed from employment and common surroundings, attendees relinquished inhibitions and tried new perspectives. Especially in such liminal spots where exploration and experimentation are celebrated, religious experiences can become heightened. Workshops and encounter groups promoted these ecstatic experiences through all-night sessions, intense dialogue, and demanding self-evaluation activities. What does it mean to be human? Why are we here? How can we live to our fullest potential? What can we do to help shape a better future? All these questions were central to this spiritual-scientific enterprise.

All religious forms throughout American history have, in Albanese's words, "tales to tell about contact, encounter, and exchange."[122] The story of holistic ideas and a personalized spirituality, especially as seen through the Esalen project, demonstrates this. Throughout the institute's history, it has operated as a crossroads for East and West, feeding conversations about the body, spirit, and mind, and the relationship between science and religion. Like the spirituality it represents, Esalen remains hopeful, even utopian, eager to harness science and faith to bring about a progressive agenda. Its history signals that the story of late twentieth-century American religion is more than a tale of conflict between evolution and intelligent design and more than an account of conservative evangelicals jockeying for political power. In understanding America's persistent religious character, one must look not only at fundamentalists who have opposed science but also at those who incorporate scientific assumptions and conclusions into their worldviews and daily lives. By attending to the center's mix of faiths and coupling of faith and science, it is apparent that Esalen served as a middle ground, providing a path for a subsection of Americans to hold both spirituality and science in close embrace.

Still, in the tension to achieve balance between the community and the individual, Esalen's "whole" broke down largely into individual parts. In this way, it stood as a microcosm of what happened to holism as a twentieth-century cultural moment: ideals of a community-oriented and globally based holism metamorphosed into concentrations upon the individual. Central programs for holism—new religious movements, humanistic psychology, and alternative medicine—became more focused on the self, talks of diversity triumphed over unity, and the holistic projects of integration and ecological responsibility lost power.

Thus, Esalen exposes both holism's triumph and its demise. The center captured some of the spirit of this holistic moment, served as an important forum for sundry holistic messages, generated enthusiasm for multiple holistic projects, and provided a springboard for sending holistic ideas and practices into the larger culture. It fed religious pluralism and new conceptions of science and spirituality, and represented one of the high points in the cycling of this intellectual current. At the same time, Esalen's failure to gain a stronger hold in mainstream society signaled some of the cycle's denouement. During the 1970s, the postwar version of holism, with its communal vision and grand projects, diminished in power. But it did not fade completely. As America entered the twenty-first century, holistic language and ideas continued to float in the culture in a variety of ways.

Epilogue

"*How* do we think in terms of *wholes?*" Buckminster Fuller wondered. To solve problems and operate "spaceship earth," this architectural holist thought, we must eschew specialization and reductionistic approaches. We must think about general systems rather than isolated parts. We must "explore ways to make it possible for anybody and everybody in the human family to enjoy the total Earth without...gaining advantage at the expense of another."[1] Psychologist Abraham Maslow agreed, going so far as to say that he was "inclined to think that the atomistic way of thinking is a form of mild psychopathology."[2] Fuller and Maslow were not unique. Each person in this study embraced a holistic sensibility with a particularly strong communitarian impulse. They looked to whole systems instead of parts and focused on connections, interdependencies, and integration. Each relied on a constellation of ideas that elevated harmony, balance, and completeness among people and between humanity and nature.

Some of these holistic visions were utopian and intangible. Central metaphors—"web of life," "spaceship earth," the "beloved community," the "Omega Point," or "eupsychia"—were colorful, yet vague and indeterminate; and neologisms such as "noosphere," "cosmogenesis," "tensegrity," and "Guinea Pig B" tended to obscure rather than illuminate.

Yet in other ways, these holists advocated projects that had specific, material results, contributing to social reform, the counterculture, and changing views of religion and health care. Each manipulated holistic concepts to provide an ethical framework and practical solutions for handling the crises of the twentieth century, from nuclear holocaust to environmental devastation to racism and poverty. Rachel Carson crafted an ecological web to challenge the chemical industry. Buckminster Fuller designed buildings to meet housing needs and created maps and charts to redistribute resources. Martin Luther King Jr. invoked visions of "somebodiness" and communal oneness to fight racism, poverty, and war. Pierre Teilhard de Chardin configured a religious cosmology to reconcile Catholicism and evolution. And Maslow fashioned a humanistic psychology to counter scientific reductionism. Within each sphere, these individuals questioned materialism, critiqued dualism, and aimed to break down internal and external divisions. Then they promoted environmental action, social equality, integration, and treatment of the person as inherently valuable, an agent, and not a mere cog in the system.

Scores of Americans discussed *Silent Spring* and joined environmental groups. Officials revised pesticide policies, and Congress created environmental regulatory commissions. Academics and laypersons flocked to hear Fuller's marathon speeches, read *Operating Manual for Spaceship Earth*, and play the World Game to create a more sustainable future. The government showcased geodesics at world expositions, and members of the counterculture opted to live in Fuller's round spaces rather than Levittown's rectilinear ramblers. Civil rights activists banded together to demand, demonstrate, march, petition, and vote for an end to racial discrimination, and government, businesses, organizations, and private individuals responded. Together, the civil rights movement created the groundwork for new economic, political, and social relationships. Simultaneously, Catholics, scientists, students, and people in new religious movements read *The Phenomenon of Man* and harmonized scientific ideas with religious faith. Young and old circulated Maslow's *Towards a Psychology of Being* and pursued self-actualization and peak experiences. Humanistic psychology, the human potential movement, personalized spirituality, and the inchoate holistic health movement gained power first at places like Esalen, then more broadly within mainstream culture.

While both elusive and practical, these creative intellectuals and multiple counterparts conveyed a particularly optimistic tone that reverberated throughout significant segments of the culture. For those who felt the fragmentation of war, the trepidation of environmental devastation, and the alienation of modernity, holism, in multiple ways and through many avenues, offered a message of hope about human significance and social cooperation. As more sophisticated communication, transportation, and economic systems connected people around the world with greater ease and frequency, holistic ideas about interlocking webs of association provided an appealing worldview. In the postindustrial age of global capitalism, in a world where actions—even the flapping of a butterfly's wing—in one corner affected actions in another, where the possibilities of atomic weaponry could have deadly consequences for the entire earth, holistic worldviews offered a mazeway to make sense of it all.

Depicting the world both as it was and as it could be did not mean consensus among these holists. Communal prescriptions about the relationships between human beings, nature, and technology illustrated this. For Carson and King, technology held the potential to destroy their ideal communities. The zoologist signaled the end of spring if humans did not protect the organic interdependencies between themselves and the rest of the planet. King feared that any gains in civil rights would be for naught in a world of nuclear proliferation and war. Fuller despised weaponry too, but ever the sanguine soul he expressed optimism about humanity's tool-making abilities. Technology, he thought, offered greater liberty and joy and a higher standard of living. His operating manual ensured the planet's sustainability. Additionally, Fuller suggested that the built and natural environments enjoyed an organic relationship. Not only was humanity part and parcel of nature, as Carson asserted, but so were human inventions. In his mind, geodesics became one with the garden. Conversely, the globe was one vast machine.

While neither Carson nor King paralleled Fuller's enthusiastic endorsement of technology, neither was a Luddite. At the same time they agitated for a moratorium on nuclear weaponry, regulation of pesticides, and more disciplined, morally responsible uses of technology for environmental and social harmony, they welcomed scientific contributions. Indeed, in this scientific age, all of the holists in this study and many of their counterparts hailed and often contributed to scientific knowledge.

At the same time, religion as well as science fired these holists' imaginations. Neither was dismissed. King was explicit: "Science keeps religion from sinking into the valley of crippling irrationalism and paralyzing obscurantism. Religion prevents science from falling into the marsh of obsolete materialism and moral nihilism."[3] Consequently, in multiple ways, these intellectuals successfully revived, strengthened, and reinvigorated spirituality in a scientific age. Whether it came through the romantic, transcendentalist faith of Carson and Fuller, the African American church and personalist theology of King, the Catholic and paleontological writings of Teilhard, the Jewish-Buddhist-personalist assumptions of Maslow, or the marriage of East and West at Esalen, holists endorsed physical and metaphysical understandings. So did their followers. Noting, for example, the attention that the press gave Teilhard when he spoke at Villanova—pegging him as the priest who believed man descended from apes—and Teilhard's popularity in the 1960s highlights American intrigue with science and religion and the cultural attachments that Americans placed on both. Indeed, holistic thinking fed the spiritual renewal that marked much of American life in the 1960s and 1970s.

Observing how a diverse set of Americans found Teilhard's and other combinations of religion and science attractive contributes to our understanding of holism's appeal. It helps us understand how Americans wrestled with each to address their modern world, and it speaks to the persistence of religion in the United States. Since the Enlightenment, many have sounded the death knell of religious faith. Science, secularists assumed, would pave the road to modernity, and in the process render religion obsolete. Perhaps the nineteenth-century positivist Auguste Comte summed this attitude up best in his evolutionary schema of history where he predicted the rise of a scientific age, free of the trappings of religion. Modernization theories in the twentieth century continued to prophesy religion's demise. But Americans as a whole have yet to shed the frock of faith, and science has yet to gain full sway. Instead of casting off religious traditions, Americans have rejuvenated faith through revival, reconfigured beliefs to accommodate new knowledge, or readjusted faith as different peoples of various faiths encountered one another and exchanged ideas. The story of American religion has been a dynamic story of revival, combination, and hybridization, and not a story of shrinking relevance.[4]

Scholars of American culture have charted a variety of reasons to explain America's enduring religious character. Some have found that this resiliency resides in the willingness of religious people to adapt to changing times. They have pointed to historical shifts in theological tenets and accommodations in rituals, or they have demonstrated how the faithful have participated in the marketplace of ideas and political movements. Others have focused on the lack of an established state church, and the democratic and pluralistic character of the American Republic, noting especially how this has fostered myriad Christian denominations and other faiths. Some have highlighted aggressive Americanization programs and missionary projects. Still others have recognized counterhegemonic activities of immigrants and subaltern classes; despite pressure to relinquish traditional beliefs, these groups often maintained trust in the supernatural. Yet other scholars have drawn attention to the link between pulpit and entertainment, showing how religious leaders have creatively employed the stage and technological innovations to assist their appeal. All of these have explanatory power. So do American cultural attitudes and understandings of science and religion.[5]

Even during science's heyday after World War II, religion continued to provide convincing stories about the nature of the universe to people. Demonstrating the viability of religion in his book on the interface between religion and science in American culture from the 1930s to the 1960s, historian James Gilbert has shown that in this often-contentious relationship, people of faith refused to take a backseat in conversations about science. Instead, religious figures explained, used, and commingled science and religion in their cultural productions (1960s holistic paradigms offer perfect examples of this). Religious leaders both started and engaged popular and academic institutions to further their interpretations and values. By the

1960s, "Religion as a cultural element had prized open a large place for itself, despite the brilliant accomplishments of science and technology. It maintained a central place; it had grown, reshaped itself, and above all persisted as a vital element of culture."[6]

A turn to holistic cosmologies after World War II within a variety of fields was one of the ways that religious notions maintained a place in the front seat. In the fields of biology, chemistry, cosmology, ecology, physics, and psychology, to name a few, reductionistic and mechanistic paradigms were overshadowed by holistic systems models, many of which welcomed spiritual ideals and contributed to shifts in the culture from traditional religious affiliations to a new personalized spirituality. Deep ecology, Gaia science, the physics of Fritjof Capra and David Bohm, and various mixes of humanistic and transpersonal psychology serve as examples of various incorporations of science and religion, physical and metaphysical beliefs and practices. The ecumenical movement, new Asian immigrants, more openness to Eastern religion, and greater democratization and pluralistic notions fed these new sciences and forms of spirituality in the 1960s. So did the human potential movement and holistic practices that emphasized mind-body integration. Though many have rightly noted the growth of the evangelical movement and the conservative Right during these years, holism in its various permutations contributed in different but consequential ways to the changing shape of religion in American society.[7]

Addressing questions about humanity's relationship to the earth and one another and about the interconnections between science and religion, holists spoke to lay and academic audiences alike. The synchronicity of this medley of holistic voices entering American culture at virtually the same time but within separate domains reinforced each articulation and contributed to holism's resonance at this particular moment. However diverse in tone and approach, each sounded themes of community and expressed loyalty to both science and religion. Bringing these individuals together and illuminating the intellectual synergy of their works deepens our comprehension of the 1960s. Each becomes a fundamental part of a whole—a geodesic dome of thought. Together they point to others with a similar mind-set, and as a whole they add to our understanding of one way that Americans negotiated these Cold War years.

By 1970, many valued holistic thinking. Those who came of age during Kennedy's New Frontier, delighted in the first pictures of the earth taken from outer space, embraced Johnson's ideas of the Great Society, and pursued the integrated self at Esalen thought that "seeing, thinking, feeling wholes" made common sense.[8] During the 1970s, individuals in the burgeoning field of alternative medicine found holistic ideas especially meaningful. They began hosting symposiums on healing therapies and techniques that communicated holistic understandings of the person and health care and drew large audiences. In 1983, science writer Mark Davidson embraced the holistic outlook. Sounding very much like the post-1945 holists he admired, he attacked "piecemeal approaches" to understanding the world and called for a "holistic, gestalt, global, molar, integrative, organismic, synergistic, synergetical, synholistic, and systems" perspective. "The unprecedented interconnectedness of civilization compels us to face the fact that the world is greater than the sum of its parts," he argued. Continuing, he stated: "We therefore must begin paying attention to the fate of the whole earth rather than just the sum of its nations, . . . to consider the whole society rather than just its separate groups, and the whole person rather than just the person's separate roles."[9] For Davidson, the language of wholes promulgated by earlier twentieth-century thinkers, proved to be a usable concept.

By the dawn of the twenty-first century, the word "holism" seemed to be everywhere. Education specialists designed "holistic curricula"; farmers implemented "holistic agricultural" methods and sold organic foods; artists experimented with ways of integrating body and mind; physicists spoke of the "Tao of physics" and wholeness as "the implicate order of the universe"; Gaia scientists, deep ecologists, and ecofeminists assumed the earth was an organic whole and based their conclusions on a web of relations between people and the planet; academics adopted interdisciplinary methodologies; financial experts encouraged clients to approach their finances holistically; and alternative religious devotees commingled psychology, physics, and biological theories with sacred scriptures and a medley of rituals. In the health field especially, holistic practices including reflexology and Rolfing gained influence. Health clinics housing both conventional medical doctors and alternative practitioners opened their doors to an increasing number of patients. Duke University Medical School established the Center for Integrative Medicine that promoted mind-body-spirit health methods in addition to conventional techniques in cardiology, internal medicine, obstetrics, and gynecology. Georgetown University Medical School added nonmainstream treatments to its required curriculum in 2001. The University of Arizona started the Arizona Center for Integrative Medicine, under the leadership of Harvard-trained Dr. Andrew Weil in the 1990s, then developed the first residency program in integrative medicine. Consistent with other centers, the Arizona Center explains integrative medicine as "healing-oriented medicine that takes account of the whole person (body, mind, and spirit), including all aspects of lifestyle."[10] Perhaps most telling, some insurance companies, albeit on a limited basis, began to cover acupuncture and biofeedback treatments.[11] Marketing professionals also recognized the power of holism in the popular vernacular. "Whole," "holism," and "holistic" became advertising slogans, used to entice customers to any number of businesses, schools, Web sites, and nonprofit organizations. The grocery chain Whole Foods, started in Austin, Texas, in 1982, captured this in its slogan, "Whole foods, whole people, whole planet."[12]

Even while holism drifted into the culture in deep and surprising ways, capturing imaginations and motivating action, holistic projects did not remain constant. In many ways the 1960s version was an episodic moment in the long history of holistic thought, a period of high interest in one of the cycles of an old impulse that had very real consequences. It was marked by the prosperity of the time, global cultural exchanges, new scientific and technological knowledge, new immigration patterns, and a medley of religious views. Holists dreamed of achieving equality through social and political reform. Their communal ideals matched the exuberance of others who plotted to send a man to the moon, create a modern-day Camelot, or rechart global relations through the United Nations, the World Federation of Churches, the international community of scientists, and the Peace Corps. For many, creating the Great Society seemed entirely possible. But this moment did not last, and the 1960s version of holism did not either.

As the 1960s wore into the 1970s, the sensibility shifted to reflect a much more individualistic era. Holists again manipulated and remade holistic projects to meet new times and circumstances. Consequently, this anthology of ideas lost much of its communitarian drive, optimistic impulse, and utopian thrust in exchange for more personal, local articulations.

The catalysts for this change from a more communal to a more individualistic holistic perspective are legion. Economically, politically, and socially, communal ideals and projects faced challenges. Conservative voices contested liberal visions. Grand hopes deflated under the weight of the Vietnam War. President Lyndon Johnson's Great Society programs lost resources. King confessed his dream began to turn into a nightmare when four girls were murdered in a Birmingham church. Hopes of integration fragmented more with the rise of the Black Power movement and political and cultural dissension over the passage of the Civil Rights Act and Voting Rights Act. In 1968, though King still yearned for beloved community, he became more and more convinced that he would not make it to the mountaintop. In his last sermons, he said, "The world is all messed up. The nation is sick. Trouble is in the land. Confusion is all around."[13] His and Robert F. Kennedy's assassinations coupled with urban riots and political dissension only added to the chaos. So did sharp divisions over busing children to achieve integration and racial quotas in education and employment.

Disillusionment within the civil rights movement, the counterculture, and mainstream society increased with Watergate, the economic downturn, stagflation, and the energy crisis of 1973. Controversies over women's liberation, the equal rights amendment, and gay rights further divided Americans. Cultural fragmentation in some places and the celebration of cultural differences in others led to an increased emphasis on pluralism, multiculturalism, and diversity programs. Among intellectuals, postmodern skepticism in metanarratives reflected and contributed to significant changes in the ways that Americans thought about the world and acted in it.

Some fields reflected these changes in notable ways. Scientists turned to other models to explain phenomena, either abandoning holistic assumptions outright or adjusting holistic understandings substantially. For example, even while environmentalists such as the Sierra Club's David Brower and students at Earth Day concurred that Carson "removed a veil" and showed the interconnections between the parts and the whole, taking them as a matter of fact, biologists in the 1970s began working from another paradigm.[14] These ecologists studied small, isolated patches of land and spoke of nature altogether differently than Carson had. Disturbance not harmony, individualism not community, heterogeneity not homogeneity were the norms. Instead of viewing nature as Carson contended—an ordered and harmonic system, an earth that over eons reached a state of balance—this new generation of ecologists told a story of nature as fragmented, chaotic, random, out of balance, and in disequilibrium. Notions of stability, order, and predictability and assumptions of community and interdependence gave way to fluidity, impermanence, and scattered, undirected processes. While this was not a new frame, during the middle years of the twentieth century, the individualistic, competitive, noncooperative vision took a backseat. By the 1990s it revived, and the assumption that nature operated as a smoothly operating ecosystem lost its explanatory power for numerous scientists. This loss of faith could be seen in the ecology textbooks of the early 1990s, which, in sharp contrast with those of the 1950s, 1960s, and 1970s, scarcely mentioned the word "ecosystem" or used the phrase "balance of nature."[15]

The tale of Rachel Carson and the popularity of her naturalistic writings serve as one of the best examples of how powerful the 1960s holistic vision was for a great variety of people. Its demise within the scientific community is also telling. The point, I think, that is significant here is that the communalistic sentiment met fundamental challenges. An ecologist could still see the world as holistic insofar as the parts of an ecosystem were interdependent, but much of Carson's whole was lost. Gone was the picture of equilibrium and harmony. The notion of an ordered, dependent, predictable world gave way in science just as it did within the larger social and political world. This disjuncture between ecological frames is of great interest to the student of holism, for it indicates a shift in allegiance within the scientific community from holistic assumptions to a far more individualistic and fragmented order. It narrows the focus from large global views to small, segregated, patch dynamics. And the shift had consequences in the ways individuals lived and in political decisions made.

It is not that Carson's holistic vision faded completely. Certainly, the popularity of the *Whole Earth Catalog* and the push for alternative technologies, green architecture, and sustainability indicated broad environmental concerns into the twenty-first century. But for those who kept a holistic framework, assumptions and projects changed in the 1970s. Holists scaled back and retreated to more personal expressions. The age of great dreams gave way to personalized spirituality; small, alternative, local energy sources; and do-it-yourself technologies, kits, and programs. The back-to-nature movement—supported by the *Whole Earth Catalog*, books like *Diet for a Small Planet*, and organic farming—grew in popularity. Global visions gave way to more localized projects, not always because people became self-centered and narcissistic, as some have characterized the 1970s; rather, many came to see local actions as a more practical way to impact global challenges. Changing the individual first, rather than the entire society, seemed more doable and more promising.

This individualistic turn proved to be especially sharp in the human potential and holistic health movements. Spurred by a holistic mind-set and developments in the 1960s, these movements grew in scope and size in the 1970s and 1980s and became a multibillion-dollar industry by the turn of the century. As noted in some of the examples mentioned earlier, holistic health in alternative and complementary medicine became more accepted in medical programs and within the insurance business. Abraham Maslow, with his affirmation of the human potential through his self-actualization charts and eupsychian hopes, was one of many in humanistic psychology who contributed to this growth. Workshops and seminars at places such as Esalen helped spread the word. At the same time, new conceptions of gender and the body within the women's movement and scholarly studies influenced American attitudes and fed the holistic health movement. So did increasing awareness of Asian cultures. The Korean War, the Vietnam War, and a relaxation of immigration laws in 1965 exposed Americans to different cultural systems, religious practices, foods, and understandings of health. A more personalized and eclectic spirituality reinforced and reflected these changes.

Holistic practitioners and patients focused on individual human health. Most within these circles upheld a view of the person as an integrated whole of mind-body-spirit, and they saw the person as influenced by the environment. Many adopted a skeptical attitude toward Western science, specialization, and the doctor as expert. This did not translate for most into a complete

dismissal of science, but it did mean that science was but one epistemological frame. Instead of privileging the doctor in the doctor-patient relationship,
holistic medicine accorded more value and wisdom to the patient and called
on the patient to be active in healing, wellness, and growth. This included
preventive care in diet, exercise, and lifestyle choices as well as health care
in times of illness. Intuition, spirituality, and other ways of knowing also
informed physical and psychological health. Significant numbers gravitated
to Eastern religious understandings of the body and medical treatments,
many of which came with holistic assumptions.

Concentration on self-care and self-responsibility spoke to and revived a
deep individualistic strain within American society. In some ways it facilitated less social responsibility, government action, and social reform. But
not always. Positioning the person within a wider universe, holistic health
advocates called for healthy relationships, social and environmental obligations, and political responsibility. Some holistic health spokespersons
argued that the focus on the self was not narcissistic but rather the basis for
a strong community. Like Maslow, these individuals claimed that developing the individual provided a path to social transformation. Charles Reich,
in his book *The Greening of America*, announced a new consciousness in
thought, a revolution that "will originate with the individual" but lead to
social and environmental gain.[16] Transcendental Meditation leaders asserted
that personal meditation had a spillover effect on society. Exploring inner
dimensions could have real social consequences. Certainly this was at the
heart of what Abraham Maslow, Michael Murphy, and Richard Price envisioned. Still, this was a new era and a much diminished appropriation of
holistic thought. The contrast between the two frames helps to periodize
and highlight one of the times that holistic metaphors guided cultural
understandings in significant ways.

While holism, like other episodic ideas, has ebbed and flowed throughout American history, ebbed and flowed in its attention toward the individual and community, it has never completely disappeared. To demonstrate,
the case of former vice president Albert Gore is instructive. As a world
spokesman for environmental issues, he was profoundly influenced by
holistic ideas in the 1960s and carried his understandings to his political,
social, and environmental activities. In his personal life, Gore testified that
he came "to believe in the value of a kind of inner ecology that relies on the
same principles of balance and holism that characterizes a healthy environment." In his campaign for the earth, Gore often employed holistic language and logic to fight for political, corporate, and personal change. After
his election to Congress in 1976, he held the first congressional hearings on
the greenhouse effect. In 1992 he published *Earth in the Balance*, which suggested that humans had grown addicted to resource consumption. This

dependency, he claimed, stemmed from modern humanity's alienation from nature and the deep pain that separation inflicted on the human psyche. As a result, societies were dysfunctional, and the earth teetered on the brink of disaster.[17]

Gore's commitment to the environment reflected his upbringing in the 1960s. His father, Senator Albert Gore Sr., communicated concern for the natural world in his political stances and at his farm in Tennessee. He opposed nuclear testing, for instance, because of its harmful environmental effects, and after a trip to India, he supported population control measures.[18] Spending summers on the farm, Gore Jr. said he "exulted in being able to walk across the farm and swim in the river and walk through the woods." He, along with his mother, read *Silent Spring* and learned about ecosystems.[19] Though later informed by others—especially his college professor Roger Revelle, the first to measure carbon dioxide levels in the atmosphere—Gore credited Carson for influencing his views. Reiterating her prose in his introduction to a later edition of *Silent Spring*, he reminded readers: "Poisoning the food chain anywhere ultimately poisons the food chain everywhere."[20] In *Earth in the Balance*, he followed in the Carsonian tradition by arguing, "The world's ecological balance depends on more than just our ability to restore a balance between civilization's ravenous appetite for resources and the fragile equilibrium of the earth's environment." Sustainability hung on the smooth functioning of each part of the whole system. It demanded a change of priorities and action to right the balance of nature and humanity. All "must take a greater personal responsibility for this deteriorating global environment; each of us must take a hard look at the habits of mind and action that reflect—and have led to—this grave crisis."[21]

Another holist helped Gore find spiritual hope in the earth's future. As a student at Vanderbilt University's School of Religion, he read Pierre Teilhard de Chardin, eventually calling him "one of the greatest theologians of the twentieth century." Gore, raised in the Baptist denomination, understood humanity's frailness and potential for sin. The Catholic priest reminded him that not all was bleak. Teilhard's optimistic outlook inspired faith in the future. "Armed with such faith," Gore declared, "we might find it possible to resanctify the earth, identify it as God's creation, and accept our responsibility to protect and defend it." In doing so, Gore believed that we could "restore the balance now missing in our relationship to the earth."[22]

Described as the "ozone man" by President George Herbert Walker Bush in 1992, Gore appeared at the helm of a revolutionary change in attitude about the environment in the first decade of the twenty-first century. In February 2007, the film of Gore's work on global warming, *An Inconvenient Truth* (2006), won two Oscars for best documentary and best original song.

In that same month, the film boasted a gross of $45 million in worldwide box office sales, the third-highest documentary sales in history. By that same month, his book by the same name had sold close to a million copies and translation rights in twenty-four languages. In July 2007, he organized "Live Earth," a benefit concert held around the world to address global warming. And in October, he won the Nobel Peace Prize for his work on climate change. In between, Gore moved like a rock star from one gig to another talking about the fate of the earth to sold-out crowds. The *Washington Post* reported that his popularity—far greater in 2007 than it ever was while he was in political office—could be seen around the world as he carried his one-man slide show from the United Nations to Tokyo, Berlin, Sydney, Helsinki, Hong Kong, and places in between. Three minutes after the University of Toronto opened its online ticket site for Gore's show, 23,000 people logged on to gain a seat and crashed the system. Ten thousand tickets to see Gore in Boise, Idaho, sold "faster than Elton John."[23]

Gore's story indicates one way holistic understandings continue to float in American society. The former vice president's message carries great political and cultural capital today. Widespread attention is now paid to the consequences of human action upon the environment. Discussions about the shrinking of Greenland and polar ice caps, carbon footprints, energy-saving lightbulbs, climate control, and resource depletion top newscasts. Carson's call to see the world whole and Aldo Leopold's land ethic have maintained currency. Many take it as common sense that we are all part of the web of life and bear responsibility for the planet's health.

Still, the report is mixed. Though Gore's holistic environmentalism resonates, it is nonetheless different from its 1960s counterpart, and it is far from universally held or practiced. He ends his talks on an up note with an encouraging word that we can reverse directions, but much of his message is a jeremiad. It is couched in a record of dismal actions and cataclysmic forecasts of what will happen should the present course be maintained. Environmental concerns continue to be limited by corporate and individual economic considerations, personal convenience, and political disagreements. During George W. Bush's presidency, wars in Afghanistan and Iraq, oil industries, and immigration fears overshadowed environmental concerns. Vice President Richard Cheney intervened personally in numerous environmental issues, including policy choices to ease air pollution regulations, make Yucca Mountain in Nevada the national dumping ground for nuclear waste, and allow snowmobiles into Yellowstone National Park. In autumn 2007, Homeland Security secretary Michael Chertoff prioritized border defense over protection of southeastern Arizona's San Pedro Riparian National Conservation Area. His decision to build a fence through the area found favor in federal court. The Bush administration refused to sign the

United Nations Kyoto Protocol for Climate Change. European nations sur-
passed the United States in their efforts to limit greenhouse gases and rein
in industrial wastes.[24] The presidency of Barack Obama is poised to change
course, but how much the global economic downturn of 2008 will allow it is
yet to be seen.

As the example of Gore indicates, the constellation of ideas that helped
define and shape the long 1960s has percolated into the society in a variety
of ways, but its power is uneven and its message changed. A more individualistic attitude reigned in the latter decades of the twentieth century and well
into the twenty-first. Earlier optimism and calls for social reform and utopian endeavors to build a more beloved community seemed somewhat
strange, even naive, in the post-9/11 period of fear, fundamentalism, and
nativism. Nevertheless, the holistic ideas of the long 1960s continue to be
refracted and reframed to the present day.

Recharting the 1960s in terms of a holistic worldview opens a new window onto significant shifts and experiences in American culture that characterized these years: the expansion of democracy within U.S. society;
increased understandings about the environment and humanity's role in it;
greater global awareness; increased cultural encounters with the Asian
world; changing religious views and practices; rising social hopes and
dreams. It also exposes some of the ways this worldview filtered into society
even while it shrank and narrowed to a more individualistic perspective.
Attending to the ways holism has been bent, shaped, and used to mold reality and noting the changes in this holistic mind-set within the 1960s and
after illuminates the power of the 1960s version.

The individuals profiled in this book confronted difficult challenges and
applied holistic understandings to improve their world. They drew from and
contributed to an intellectual tradition that emphasized optimism, cooperation, and interconnectedness. They wielded the intellectual tool of holism to
forge social order, to promote greater peace and harmony, to articulate a
hopeful future. Holism, in their hands, was the yin to alternative and equally
prevalent yang sensibilities that saw the world as filled with competition,
disorder, corruption, violence, and selfishness. Both of these yin and yang
notions describe the world we live in, and both perhaps also inhere deeply
in all of us.

Notes

INTRODUCTION

1. Olga Owens Huckins, "Letter to the Editor," *Boston Herald*, January 29, 1958. Carson explained that Huckins's letter brought her "sharply back to a problem with which I had long been concerned" in the acknowledgments to *Silent Spring* (Boston: Houghton Mifflin, 1962). Linda Lear puts Huckins's letter in context in her thoroughly researched biography, *Rachel Carson: Witness for Nature* (New York: Holt, 1997), 314, 545–46n10.

2. Carson repeatedly used the phrase "balance of nature"; see, for example, *Silent Spring*, 246.

3. Rachel Carson to Olga Owens Huckins, October 3, 1962, as quoted in Paul Brooks, *The House of Life: Rachel Carson at Work* (Boston: Houghton Mifflin, 1972), 233. By 1945 Carson was in contact with biologists at Patuxent Research Refuge in Laurel, Maryland, who were studying the new synthetic pesticide dichloro-diphenyl-trichloroethane (DDT). The results alarmed her and the biologists. For more on Carson's decision to write a book on pesticides, see Brooks, *House of Life*; and Mary Kersey Harvey, "Using a Plague to Fight a Plague," *Saturday Review*, September 29, 1962, 18. For Carson's early engagement with naturally occurring poisons in the environment, as well as the detrimental effects of human actions on the ecosystem, see Lear, *Rachel Carson*, 118–20.

4. Carson, *Silent Spring*, 189.

5. For studies of Carson, see especially Linda Lear's biography, *Rachel Carson*; see also Brooks, *House of Life*; Carol B. Gartner, *Rachel Carson* (New York: Ungar, 1983); Maril Hazlett, " 'Woman vs. Man vs. Bugs': Gender and Popular Ecology in Early Reactions to *Silent Spring*," *Environmental History* 9 (Oct. 2004), 701–29; H. Patricia Hynes, *The Recurring Silent Spring* (New York: Pergamon Press, 1989); and Hynes, "Ellen Swallow, Lois Gibbs and Rachel Carson: Catalysts of the American Environmental Movement," *Women's Studies International Forum* 8 (1985): 291–98; Ralph H. Lutts, "Chemical Fallout: Rachel Carson's *Silent Spring*, Radioactive Fallout, and the Environmental Movement," *Environmental History Review* 9 (Fall 1985): 210–25; reprinted in *And No Birds Sing: Rhetorical Analyses of Rachel Carson's Silent Spring*, ed. Craig Waddell (Carbondale, Ill.: Southern Illinois University Press, 2000), 17–41; Mark Hamilton Lytle, *Gentle Subversive: Rachel Carson, Silent Spring, and the*

Rise of the American Environmental Movement (New York: Oxford University Press, 2007); Mary A. McCay, *Rachel Carson* (New York: Twayne, 1993); Vera Norwood, "Heroines of Nature: Four Women Respond to the American Landscape," *Environmental Review* 8 (1984): 34–56; and Philip Sterling, *Sea and Earth: The Life of Rachel Carson* (New York: Crowell, 1970).

6. Just months before Carson published *Silent Spring*, Lewis Herber (Murray Bookchin), released similar findings in *Our Synthetic Environment* (New York: Knopf, 1962). For the chemical society's perspective, see Gino J. Marco, Robert M. Hollingworth, and William Durham, et al., eds., *Silent Spring Revisited* (Washington, D.C.: American Chemical Society, 1987). For the battle over pesticides in the 1960s, see Frank Graham Jr., *Since Silent Spring* (Boston: Houghton Mifflin, 1970); see also John Tierney, "Fateful Voice of a Generation Still Drowns Out Real Science," *New York Times*, June 5, 2007, Health and Fitness, 1; Rudy Baum, "Rachel Carson," *Chemical and Engineering News* 85, no. 23 (2007): 5; Brian Bethune, "Was Rachel Carson Wrong?" *Maclean's* 120, no. 21 (2007): 42–43. Priscilla Coit Murphy demonstrates how national debates fed the popularity of *Silent Spring* in *What a Book Can Do: The Publication and Reception of Silent Spring* (Amherst: University of Massachusetts Press, 2005). Concerns over science, including the thalidomide controversy, also fed interest in Carson's book. See Helen B. Taussig, "The Thalidomide Syndrome," *Scientific American* 207 (August 1962): 29–35. Postwar affluence, social changes, suburban development, and more time in the outdoors also helped precondition Americans for Carson's message. See Samuel P. Hays, *Beauty, Health, and Permanence: Environmental Politics in the United States, 1955–1985* (New York: Cambridge University Press, 1987); and Adam Rome, *Bulldozer in the Countryside: Suburban Sprawl and the Rise of American Environmentalism* (New York: Cambridge University Press, 2001). For an overview of the various theories for Carson's success, see Craig Waddell, "The Reception of *Silent Spring*," in Waddell, *And No Birds Sing*, 1–16, especially 9–12.

7. Carson, *Silent Spring*, 64.

8. Rachel Carson, "The Pollution of Our Environment," in *Lost Woods: The Discovered Writing of Rachel Carson*, ed. Linda Lear (Boston: Beacon Press, 1998), quote on 231.

9. Carson, *Silent Spring*, 39, 51, 75, 78.

10. Henry A. Gleason, "The Individualistic Concept of the Plant Association," *Bulletin of the Torrey Botanical Club* 53 (1926): 26, and as quoted in Donald Worster, "The Ecology of Order and Chaos," *Environmental History Review* 14 (Spring/ Summer 1990): 9. See also Donald Worster, *Nature's Economy: A History of Ecological Ideas*, 2nd ed. (New York: Cambridge University Press, 1994), 237–40; Robert P. McIntosh, "H. A. Gleason's 'Individualistic Concept' and Theory of Animal Communities: A Continuing Controversy," *Biological Reviews* 70 (1995): 317–57.

11. Holists generally argue that reality can only be understood as a whole. This whole, be it a living organism, society, system, planet, or entire universe, cannot be explained by any individual part or simple aggregation. Instead, holists focus on the relationships between parts and what is produced when these parts are brought together. For general definitions and holism's place in philosophy, see *The Cambridge Dictionary of Philosophy* (Cambridge: Cambridge University Press, 1995). Within disciplines there are many definitions of holism. For the initial use of the word, see

Jan C. Smuts, *Holism and Evolution* (New York: Macmillan, 1926). For a historical and Catholic treatment of Smuts's work, see Frederick C. Kolbe, *A Catholic View of Holism: A Criticism of the Theory Put Forward by General Smuts in His Book, Holism and Evolution* (New York: Macmillan, 1928). For historical and philosophical accounts of the holistic worldview, see Stephen G. Brush, "The Chimerical Cat: Philosophy of Quantum Mechanics in Historical Perspective," *Social Studies of Science* 10 (1980): 393–447; Stephen C. Pepper, *World Hypotheses: A Study in Evidence* (Berkeley: University of California Press, 1942); and Harry Settanni, *Holism—A Philosophy for Today: Anticipating the Twenty-first Century* (New York: Peter Lang, 1990).

12. Worster, *Nature's Economy*, 330–33; Anna Bramwell, *Ecology in the Twentieth Century: A History* (New Haven, Conn.: Yale University Press, 1989); Joel B. Hagen, *An Entangled Bank: The Origins of Ecosystem Ecology* (New Brunswick, N.J.: Rutgers University Press, 1992); and Frank Benjamin Golley, *A History of the Ecosystem Concept in Ecology: More Than the Sum of the Parts* (New Haven, Conn.: Yale University Press, 1993). Golley ties the story of the "ecosystem" to a holistic trend in post–World War II America.

13. For an insightful understanding of the cultural historians' use of "sensibility," see Daniel Wickberg, "What Is the History of Sensibilities? On Cultural Histories, New and Old," *American Historical Review* 112 (June 2007): 660–84.

14. For a sampling of other holists at this time, see Daniel Belgrad, *The Culture of Spontaneity: Improvisation and the Arts in Postwar America* (Chicago: University of Chicago Press, 1998), especially 109–15. For holistic notions in physics, see David Bohm, *Wholeness and the Implicate Order* (London: Routledge, 1980); Fritjof Capra, *The Tao of Physics: An Exploration of the Parallels between Modern Physics and Eastern Mysticism* (New York: Random House, 1975); and Gary Zukav, *The Dancing Wu Li Masters: An Overview of the New Physics* (New York: Morrow, 1979).

15. Viewing the era as the long 1960s has become common. See, for example, Maurice Isserman and Michael Kazin, *America Divided: The Civil War of the 1960s* (New York: Oxford University Press, 2000). For other studies of the sixties, see Terry H. Anderson, *The Movement and the Sixties* (New York: Oxford University Press, 1996); David Farber, *The Age of Great Dreams: America in the 1960s* (New York: Hill and Wang, 1994); Todd Gitlin, *The Sixties: Years of Hope, Days of Rage* (New York, Bantam Books, 1987); and Stephen J. Whitfield, *The Culture of the Cold War* (Baltimore: Johns Hopkins University Press, 1991).

16. All these movements and ideologies are complex, multifaceted, and difficult to place under one label. The "counterculture" especially defies definition because it varied over time and between groups. Most commonly it refers to young people who rebelled against authority, capitalism, and the military-industrial complex and embraced the individual person, communitarian anarchism, freedom of expression, and popular music. For the derivation, definitions, and historicization of the term, see Howard Brick, *Age of Contradiction: American Thought and Culture in the 1960s* (Ithaca, N.Y.: Cornell University Press, 2000), 113–19; and Peter Braunstein and Michael William Doyle, eds., *Imagine Nation: The American Counterculture of the 1960s and 1970s* (New York: Routledge, 2002), especially Braunstein's and Doyle's essay, "Historicizing the American Counterculture of the 1960s and 1970s," 5–14. They indicate that J. Milton Yinger first brought the term to light in 1960. Yinger borrowed the term "contraculture" from sociologist Talcott Parsons and used it to

discuss moral opposition to the status quo and dominant society. Braunstein and Doyle have rightly raised a red flag at using the term "as an exclusive signifier for the Sixties version of cultural radicalism." Nonetheless, "counterculture" has largely been used to refer to the Beat generation and 1960s nonconformists. See Theodore Roszak's use of the term to refer to a generation of youth disaffected by the status quo in *The Making of a Counter Culture: Reflections on the Technocratic Society and Its Youthful Opposition* (Garden City, N.Y.: Doubleday, 1969).

17. This book helps us "place environmentalism in the context of the times," as Adam Rome encouraged scholars to do in "Give Earth a Chance: The Environmental Movement and the Sixties," *Journal of American History* 90 (September 2003): 525–54.

18. Lippmann, as quoted in James T. Patterson, *Grand Expectations: The United States, 1945–1974* (New York: Oxford University Press, 1996), 7–8.

19. Henry R. Luce, "The American Century," *Life*, February 17, 1941, 61–65.

20. Brick, *Age of Contradiction*.

21. Abraham H. Maslow, *Motivation and Personality*, 2nd ed. (New York: Harper and Row, 1970), xi.

22. This was a common refrain for King. See, for example, Martin Luther King Jr., "The Ethical Demands for Integration," *Religion and Labor* 6 (May 1963): 1, 3–4, 7–8, reprinted in *A Testament of Hope: The Essential Writings and Speeches of Martin Luther King, Jr.*, ed. James Melvin Washington (San Francisco: HarperSanFrancisco, 1986), 122.

23. Charlotte Buhler, "Human Life as a Whole as a Central Subject of Humanistic Psychology," in *Challenges of Humanistic Psychology*, ed. James F. T. Bugental (New York: McGraw-Hill, 1967), 83–91, quote on 84. Buhler summarizes and uses the work of Floyd Matson, *The Broken Image: Man, Science, and Society* (New York: Braziller, 1964), to illustrate humanistic psychology's primary concern of viewing the patient as a whole person.

24. Andrew Kirk, *Counterculture Green: The Whole Earth Catalog and American Environmentalism* (Lawrence: University Press of Kansas, 2007), 41–42; Neil Maher, "Neil Maher on Shooting the Moon," *Environmental History* 9 (July 2004): 526–31.

25. Phil Nelson, "Environment and Establishment: A Student Letter," *National Parks and Conservation Magazine* 44 (1970): 11–12, quote on 11. Also quoted in Roderick Nash, *Wilderness and the American Mind*, rev. ed. (New Haven, Conn.: Yale University Press, 1973), 252 and reprinted in *E: The Environmental Magazine* 6 (March/April, 1995): 32.

26. D. Brett King and Michael Wertheimer, *Max Wertheimer and Gestalt Theory* (New Brunswick, N.J.: Transaction, 2005), 41.

27. Ehrenfels published his remarks in "On Gestalt Qualities," in Richard Avenarius's *Quarterly for Scientific Philosophy*; for the English translation, see *Foundations of Gestalt Theory*, trans. and ed. Barry Smith (Munich: Philosophia Verlag, 1988), 82–117.

28. The quote is from "Phaedrus" of *The Dialogues of Plato*, trans. Benjamin Jowett, The Classical Library online http://www.classicallibrary.org/plato/ dialogues/7_phaedrus.htm (accessed December 24, 2009). See Richard H. Svihus, "On Healing the Whole Person: A Perspective," *Western Journal of Medicine* 131 (1979): 479, for a discussion of Plato and Hippocrates. For another helpful discussion

on Plato's ideas and how his thought has influenced the modern environmental movement and conceptions of the earth as a living organism, most notably in the "Gaia hypothesis," see J. Donald Hughes, *Pan's Travail: Environmental Problems of the Ancient Greeks and Romans* (Baltimore: Johns Hopkins University Press, 1994). In these and other instances, Plato voiced a holistic view, but in his division of the world into ideas and matter, he expressed a mind-body dualism.

29. Hildegard of Bingen, as quoted in Carol MacCormack, "Hildegard of Bingen: A 12th Century Holistic World View," in Carol MacCormack and Jack Monger, *The Blossoming of a Holistic World View* (Landenberg, Pa.: Quaker Universalist Fellowship, 1992), 9.

30. Postmodernist understandings, illuminate the frail nature of metanarratives and the plasticity of ideas. See, for example, Jean-François Lyotard, *The Postmodern Condition: A Report on Modernity* (Minneapolis: University of Minnesota Press, 1984).

31. For histories of alternative, complementary, and holistic health in American history, see Robert H. Abzug, *Cosmos Crumbling: American Reform and the Religious Imagination* (New York: Oxford University Press, 1994), especially 163–82; Kristine Alster, *The Holistic Health Movement* (Tuscaloosa: University of Alabama Press, 1989); Norman Cousins, *Anatomy of an Illness as Perceived by the Patient* (New York: Norton, 1979); Cousins, "The Holistic Health Explosion," *Saturday Review*, March 31, 1979, 17–20; Christopher Lawrence and George Weisz, eds. *Greater Than the Parts: Holism in Biomedicine, 1920–1950* (New York: Oxford University Press, 1998); June Lowenberg, *Caring and Responsibility: The Crossroads between Holistic Practice and Traditional Medicine* (Philadelphia: University of Pennsylvania Press, 1989); Phyllis H. Mattson, *Holistic Health in Perspective* (Palo Alto, Calif.: Mayfield, 1982); J. Warren Salmon, "The Holistic Alternative to Scientific Medicine: History and Analysis," *International Journal of Health Services* 10 (1980): 133–47; James C. Whorton, *Crusaders for Fitness: The History of American Health Reformers* (Princeton, N.J.: Princeton University Press, 1982); and Whorton, *Nature Cures: The History of Alternative Medicine in America* (New York: Oxford University Press, 2002), especially chaps. 11 and 12.

32. For semantic holism, see Jerry Fodor and Ernest Lepore, *Holism: A Shopper's Guide* (Cambridge, Mass.: Basil Blackwell, 1992); and Jerry Fodor and Ernest Lepore, eds., *Holism: A Consumer Update* (Amsterdam: Rodopi, 1993).

33. For general systems theory, see Donald Polkinghorne, "Systems and Structures," in his *Methodology for the Human Sciences: Systems of Inquiry* (Albany: State University of New York Press, 1983), chap. 4; Charles West Churchman, *The Systems Approach* (New York: Delacorte Press, 1968); Peter B. Checkland, "Science and the Systems Paradigm," *International Journal of General Systems* 3 (1976): 127–34; John P. Van Gigch, *Applied General Systems Theory*, 2nd ed. (New York: Harper and Row, 1978); and Lars Skyttner, *General Systems Theory: Ideas and Applications* (River Edge, N.J.: World Scientific, 2001). For the development of general systems theory in the 1930s and 1940s, turn especially to the writings of Ludwig von Bertalanffy, *General Systems Theory: Foundations, Development, Applications* (New York: Braziller, 1968). For an explanation of his life and views, as well as interpretations by two of his followers, Buckminster Fuller and the economist Kenneth Boulding, see Mark Davidson, *Uncommon Sense: The Life and*

Thought of Ludwig von Bertalanffy (1901–1972), Father of General Systems Theory, foreword by R. Buckminster Fuller, introduction by Kenneth E. Boulding (Los Angeles: Tarcher, 1983).

34. Norbert Wiener, *The Human Use of Human Beings: Cybernetics and Society* (Boston: Houghton Mifflin, 1954).

35. Vladimir I. Lenin, "Philosophical NotebooksSummary of Dialectics," in *The Collected Works of Vladimir Lenin*, 2nd English ed. (Moscow: Progress Publishers and Foreign Languages Press, 1965), 38:221–22; http://www.marxists.org/archive/lenin/works/1914/cons-logic/summary.htm (accessed October 22, 2007); and Stefan T. Possony, ed., *Lenin Reader* (Chicago: Henry Regnery, 1966), 9–10.

36. John Muir, *My First Summer in the Sierra* (Boston: Houghton Mifflin, 1911), chap. 6; and Sierra Club, http://www.sierraclub.org/john_muir_exhibit/ (accessed October 22, 2007).

37. Joseph Wood Krutch, *The Measure of Man: On Freedom, Human Values, Survival and the Modern Temper* (London: Redman, 1956); and Krutch, *The Best Nature Writing of Joseph Wood Krutch* (Salt Lake City: University of Utah Press, 1995).

38. Aldo Leopold, *A Sand County Almanac, and Sketches Here and There* (New York: Oxford University Press, 1968), 224–25.

39. James Gilbert, *A Cycle of Outrage: America's Reaction to the Juvenile Delinquent in the 1950s* (New York: Oxford University Press, 1986), 4; Gilbert, *Redeeming Culture: American Religion in an Age of Science* (Chicago: University of Chicago Press, 1997). For further examples on decoding a cultural moment, see Robert Darnton, *The Great Cat Massacre and Other Episodes in French Cultural History* (New York: Oxford University Press, 1986); Clifford Geertz, *The Interpretation of Cultures: Selected Essays* (New York: Basic Books, 1973).

40. Culture has been defined in various ways and connotes many more. It is at once the beliefs of a society (or subsection of society) and the set of rituals and acts they practice. Culture is found in signs, symbols, language, actions, and expressions, and it is concretized in institutions and material artifacts. All these components contribute to behavior and the narratives that give meaning to daily life. As the anthropologist Clifford Geertz aptly phrased it, culture is the collection of stories we tell ourselves about ourselves; see "Deep Play: Notes on the Balinese Cockfight," in Geertz, *Interpretation of Cultures*, 448. See also William J. Cronon, "A Place for Stories: Nature, History, and Narrative," *Journal of American History* 78 (March 1992): 1347–76; Warren I. Susman, *Culture as History: The Transformation of American Society in the Twentieth Century* (New York: Pantheon, 1984).

41. Martin Luther King Jr., "Facing the Challenge of a New Age," *Phylon* 28 (April 1957): 24–34, reprinted in *Testament of Hope*, 135–44, quote on 140.

42. See Ralph Abraham, Frank Jas, and Willard Russell, *The Web Empowerment Book: An Introduction and Connection Guide to the Internet and the World-Wide Web* (Santa Clara, Calif.: TELOS, 1995), 12, note 29; Ralph Abraham, *Chaos, Gaia, Eros: A Chaos Pioneer Uncovers the Three Great Streams of History* (San Francisco: HarperSanFrancisco, 1994); and Jennifer Cobb Kreisberg, "A Globe, Clothing Itself with a Brain," *Wired* (June 1995), http://www.wired.com/wired/archive/3.06/teilhard.html (accessed January 21, 2010).

43. Herbert Marcuse, *One-Dimensional Man: Studies in the Ideology of Advanced Industrial Society* (Boston: Beacon Press, 1964).

44. William H. Whyte, *The Organization Man* (New York: Simon and Schuster, 1956).

45. John Cheever, *The Enormous Radio and Other Stories* (New York: Funk and Wagnalls, 1953); David Riesman, *The Lonely Crowd: A Study of the Changing American Character* (New Haven, Conn.: Yale University Press, 1950); and Sloan Wilson, *The Man in the Gray Flannel Suit* (New York: Simon and Schuster, 1955). For discussions of the individualist critique of America, see John Patrick Diggins, *Proud Decades: America in War and Peace, 1941–1960* (New York: Norton, 1988), 207–11, 220–72; David Halberstam, *The Fifties* (New York: Villard, 1993); William O'Neill, *American High: The Years of Confidence, 1945–1960* (New York: Free Press, 1986); Patterson, *Grand Expectations*, 337–42; and Richard H. Pells, *The Liberal Mind in a Conservative Age: American Intellectuals in the 1940s and 1950s* (New York: Harper and Row, 1985).

46. For this seminal thesis, see Frederick Jackson Turner, *The Frontier in American History* (New York: Holt, 1920).

47. John Winthrop, "A Model of Christian Charity," in *The Journal of John Winthrop, 1630–1649*, ed. Richard S. Dunn, James Savage, and Laetitia Yeandle (Cambridge, Mass.: Harvard University Press, 1996), 1–11, quote on 9–10. One could find examples of communal values among other groups as well, including indigenous peoples and Africans. These, too, shaped the fabric of American society.

48. There is a vast literature on the communitarian impulse in American life. For an encyclopedic account of utopian and communal projects in the twentieth century, see Yaakov Oved, *Two Hundred Years of American Communes* (New Brunswick, N.J.: Transaction, 1988); and Timothy Miller, *The Quest for Utopia in Twentieth-Century America* (Syracuse, N.Y.: Syracuse University Press, 1998). For utopian projects in architecture, see Dolores Hayden, *Seven American Utopias: The Architecture of Communitarian Socialism, 1790–1975* (Cambridge, Mass.: MIT Press, 1976).

49. Christine Stansell, *American Moderns: Bohemian New York and the Creation of a New Century* (New York: Holt, 2001); and Ross Wetzteon, *Republic of Dreams: Greenwich Village: The American Bohemia, 1910–1960* (New York: Simon and Schuster, 2003).

50. For shifts in American perceptions of science in post–World War II culture, see Paul Boyer, *By the Bomb's Early Light: American Thought and Culture at the Dawn of the Atomic Age*, rev. ed. (Chapel Hill: University of North Carolina Press, 1994); Gilbert, *Redeeming Culture*; and Jessica Wang, *American Science in an Age of Anxiety: Scientists, Anticommunism, and the Cold War* (Chapel Hill: University of North Carolina Press, 1999).

51. Louis Ridenour and Raymond Fosdick, as quoted in Boyer, *By the Bomb's Early Light*, 269.

52. For Eisenhower's views, see James Gilbert, *Another Chance: Postwar America, 1945–1968* (Philadelphia: Temple University Press, 1981), 158–59; and Patterson, *Grand Expectations*, 440–41.

53. Richard M. Fagley and Lewis Mumford, as quoted in Boyer, *By the Bomb's Early Light*, 273.

54. Frankfurt school Marxian critics Theodor Adorno and Max Horkheimer delivered their famous critique of the Western Enlightenment project in *The Dialectic of Enlightenment* (New York: Herder, 1972). See Carolyn Merchant, *The Death of Nature: Women, Ecology, and the Scientific Revolution* (San Francisco: Harper and Row, 1980), for an extension of this argument.

55. For the prediction of science's triumph over religion, see, for example, Auguste Comte, *Auguste Comte and Positivism: The Essential Writings*, ed. Gertrud Lenzer (New Brunswick, N.J.: Transaction, 1998); Émile Durkheim, *The Elementary Forms of the Religious Life* (New York: Free Press, 1965); and Max Weber, *From Max Weber*, ed. H. H. Gerth and C. W. Mills (New York: Oxford University Press, 1946). For secularization theories and debates, see Peter Berger, *The Sacred Canopy* (Garden City, N.Y.: Doubleday, 1967); José Casanova, *Public Religions in the Modern World* (Chicago: University of Chicago Press, 1994); Karel Dobbelaere, *Secularisation: A Multi-dimensional Concept* (Beverly Hills, Calif.: Sage, 1981); L. Giorgi, "Religious Involvement in a Secularised Society: An Empirical Confirmation of Martin's General Theory of Secularisation," *British Journal of Sociology* 43 (1992): 639–56; Andrew Greeley, *Unsecular Man: The Persistence of Religion* (New York: Schocken Books, 1972); Malcolm B. Hamilton, *The Sociology of Religion: Theoretical and Comparative Perspectives* (New York: Routledge, 1995), 163–82; Thomas Luckmann, *Invisible Religion* (New York: Macmillan, 1967); David Martin, *A General Theory of Secularization* (New York: Harper and Row, 1978); Martin, *The Religious and the Secular* (New York: Schocken Books, 1969); Rodney Stark and William Sims Bainbridge, *The Future of Religion* (Berkeley: University of California Press, 1985); Immanuel Wallerstein, "Modernization: Requiescat in Pace," in *The Capitalist World Economy* (Cambridge: Cambridge University Press, 1979), 132–37; and Bryan Wilson, *Religion in a Secular Society* (London: C. A. Watts, 1966). For American innovation and changes in American religion after World War II, see Catherine Albanese's *Nature Religion in America: From Algonquin Indians to the New Age* (Chicago: University of Chicago Press, 1990); William Clebsch, *American Religious Thought: A History* (Chicago: University of Chicago Press, 1973); Robert Fuller, *Spiritual but Not Religious: Understanding Unchurched America* (New York: Oxford University Press, 2001); Edwin S. Gaustad and Leigh E. Schmidt, *A Religious History of America: The Heart of the American Story from Colonial Times to Today* (San Francisco: HarperSanFrancisco, 2004); Gilbert, *Redeeming Culture*; Amanda Porterfield, *The Transformation of American Religion: The Story of a Late-Twentieth-Century Awakening* (New York: Oxford University Press, 2001); Leigh E. Schmidt, *Restless Souls: The Making of American Spirituality* (San Francisco: HarperSanFrancisco, 2005); Thomas A. Tweed, ed., *Retelling U.S. Religious History* (Berkeley: University of California Press, 1997); and Robert Wuthnow, *After Heaven: Spirituality in America since the 1950s* (Berkeley: University of California Press, 1998).

56. Jacques Barzun, in *Classic, Romantic, and Modern* (New York: Anchor Books, 1961), contends that the questions people ask are the significant markers for discerning and defining a particular mood or period. Peter Gay marks the Enlightenment by economic, cultural, and philosophical factors; *The Enlightenment: An Interpretation*, 2 vols. (New York: Norton, 1969). For a discussion of modernism and its competing definitions, see James Gilbert, "Many Modernisms," *Reviews in American History* 29 (2001): 264–70. See also Daniel Joseph Singal, "Towards a

Definition of American Modernism," *American Quarterly* 39 (1987): 7–26, for further explication of the lack of consensus on modernism and yet the importance of capturing the shape of an age. Naming an era has come under attack recently. Ann Douglass reviews some of the problems in "Periodizing the American Century: Modernism, Postmodernism, and Postcolonialism in the Cold War Context," *Modernism* 5 (1998): 71–98. Discussions on postmodernism, though perhaps expressing more trouble with naming than any other period, also reflect a need to explain through naming. See, for example, Fredric Jameson, *Postmodernism, or, the Culture of Late Capitalism* (Durham, N.C.: Duke University Press, 1991).

57. Samuel P. Hays, *A History of Environmental Politics since 1945* (Pittsburgh: University of Pittsburgh Press, 2000); Patterson, *Grand Expectations*; Elaine Tyler May, *Homeward Bound: American Families in the Cold War Era* (New York: Basic Books, 1988).

58. Donald Critchlow, *The Conservative Ascendancy: How the GOP Right Made Political History* (Cambridge, Mass.: Harvard University Press, 2007); Damon Linker, *The Theocons: Secular America under Siege* (New York: Doubleday, 2006); Martin E. Marty and R. Scott Appleby, eds., *Fundamentalisms Observed* (Chicago: University of Chicago Press, 1994); George Nash, *The Conservative Intellectual Movement in America since 1945*, 2nd ed. (1976; Wilmington, Del.: Intercollegiate Studies Institute, 2006); and Clyde Wilcox and Carin Larson, *Onward Christian Soldiers: The Christian Right in American Politics* (Boulder, Colo.: Westview Press, 2006).

59. Others have recognized the saliency of holistic ideas in twentieth-century American culture, and some reflect this holistic moment. British social psychologist and holistic proponent William Bloom connects holism and New Age religion in *Holistic Revolution: The Essential New Age Reader* (London: Penguin, 2000). Comparative literature scholar Betty Jean Craige and philosopher Harry Settanni both see Western culture, as Craige phrases it, moving from a "dualistic, atomistic, hierarchical model of reality to a holistic model"; Betty Jean Craige, *Laying the Ladder Down: The Emergence of Cultural Holism* (Amherst: University of Massachusetts Press, 1992), ix. Craige is especially interested in applying holistic models to literary studies and politics. See Craige, *Reconnection: Dualism to Holism in Literary Study* (Athens: University of Georgia Press, 1988): "In *Reconnection* I shall investigate the discipline of literary study in relation to Cartesian dualism, which provided for the objectification of knowledge and, consequently, academic specialization in a body of knowledge. Although my major interest is the discipline's present function in American society, I shall trace its development from the time of the Scientific Revolution, with the hypothesis that literature and the discipline of literary study obtained definition in opposition to science and, later, in opposition to other apparently utilitarian endeavors. I wish to show how the emergence of the holistic paradigm means an increase in interdisciplinary, or nondisciplinary, research and teaching in the humanities and a shift in focus from canonized texts to methods of contextual interpretation, a shift that is occurring now" (1). For her juxtaposition of political dualism and political holism and her advocacy of the holistic model in international affairs, see Craige, *American Patriotism in a Global Society*, SUNY Series in Global Politics (Albany: State University of New York Press, 1996); and her speech, "Political Holism and the Pursuit of Peace," at the Veterans for Peace convention, Arlington, Virginia, August 16, 1997, http://www.cha.uga.edu/bjc/vfp.htm (accessed November 2, 2002). Some

of Craige's fascination with holism is due to her interest in ecosystems and her intellectual appreciation of Eugene Odum. She dedicated *Laying the Ladder Down* to him and wrote a book on him, *Eugene Odum: Ecosystem Ecologist and Environmentalist* (Athens: University of Georgia Press, 2001). Settanni, in *Holism*, offers a history of the philosophical uses of holism, including romanticism and the works of Smuts, and argues for a holistic approach to solving social problems.

60. Martin E. Marty, *Modern American Religion: The Noise of Conflict, 1919–1941*, vol. 2 (Chicago: University of Chicago Press, 1991), 391; and Marty, *Modern American Religion: Under God, Indivisible, 1941–1960*, vol. 3. (Chicago: University of Chicago Press, 1996).

CHAPTER 1

1. Rachel Carson, *The Edge of the Sea* (New York: Signet, 1955); Carson, *The Sea around Us*, rev. ed. (1951; New York: Oxford University Press, 1961); Carson, *Under the Sea Wind* (New York: Simon and Schuster, 1941).

2. "Supplementary Extracts from Reviews," 4, from the *Columbus Dispatch*, April 13, 1952, Box 3, Folder 37 in Rachel Carson Papers, MSS 46, Beinecke Library, Yale University, New Haven, Connecticut (hereafter cited as Carson MSS).

3. Rachel Carson, as quoted in Mary A. McCay, *Rachel Carson* (New York: Twayne, 1993), 6.

4. "Red, in tooth and claw," is a line from Alfred Lord Tennyson's *In Memoriam A. H. H.*, 1850. There are many excellent studies of Carson. Start with Linda Lear's biography, *Rachel Carson: Witness for Nature* (New York: Henry Holt, 1997). See also Paul Brooks, *The House of Life: Rachel Carson at Work* (Boston: Houghton Mifflin, 1972); Carol B. Gartner, *Rachel Carson* (New York: Ungar, 1983); Maril Hazlett, "'Woman vs. Man vs. Bugs': Gender and Popular Ecology in Early Reactions to *Silent Spring*," *Environmental History* 9 (October 2004): 701–29; Hazlett, "Voices from the Spring: *Silent Spring* and the Ecological Turn in American Health," in *Seeing Nature through Gender*, ed. Virginia Scharff (Lawrence: University Press of Kansas, 2003), 103–28; H. Patricia Hynes, *The Recurring Silent Spring* (New York: Pergamon Press, 1989); Hynes, "Ellen Swallow, Lois Gibbs and Rachel Carson: Catalysts of the American Environmental Movement," *Women's Studies International Forum* 8 (1985): 291–98; Ralph H. Lutts, "Chemical Fallout: Rachel Carson's *Silent Spring*, Radioactive Fallout, and the Environmental Movement," *Environmental History Review* 9 (Fall 1985): 210–25; Mark Hamilton Lytle, *Gentle Subversive: Rachel Carson, Silent Spring, and the Rise of the American Environmental Movement* (New York: Oxford University Press, 2007); McCay, *Rachel Carson*; Priscilla Coit Murphy, *What a Book Can Do: The Publication and Reception of Silent Spring* (Amherst: University of Massachusetts Press, 2005); Vera Norwood, "Heroines of Nature: Four Women Respond to the American Landscape," *Environmental Review* 8 (1984): 34–56; Philip Sterling, *Sea and Earth: The Life of Rachel Carson* (New York: Crowell, 1970); and Craig Waddell, ed., *And No Birds Sing: Rhetorical Analyses of Rachel Carson's Silent Spring* (Carbondale: Southern Illinois University Press, 2000).

5. Letter from Rachel Carson to Dorothy Freeman, February 1, 1958 in *Always Rachel: The Letters of Rachel Carson and Dorothy Freeman, 1952–1964*, ed. Martha Freeman (Boston: Beacon Press, 1995), 248–49.

6. Rachel Carson, "Undersea," in *Lost Woods: The Discovered Writing of Rachel Carson*, ed. Linda Lear (Boston: Beacon Press, 1998), 5, 7. "Undersea" was first published in the *Atlantic Monthly*, September 1937, 322–25.

7. Letter from Carson to Dorothy Freeman, November 7, 1957, in *Always Rachel*, 233.

8. Carson, "The Pollution of Our Environment," speech given to the Kaiser Foundation Hospitals and Permanente Medical Group, San Francisco, California, October 18, 1963, in *Lost Woods*, 228.

9. Donald Worster, *A Passion for Nature: The Life of John Muir* (New York: Oxford University Press, 2008). For the conservation movement, see Samuel P. Hays, *Conservation and the Gospel of Efficiency: The Progressive Conservation Movement, 1890–1920* (Cambridge, Mass.: Harvard University Press, 1959); for antimodernist strains within environmental thinking, see Andrew Kirk, *Counterculture Green: The Whole Earth Catalog and American Environmentalism* (Lawrence: University Press of Kansas, 2007); Stephen Fox, *The American Conservation Movement: John Muir and His Legacy* (Madison: University of Wisconsin Press, 1981); and Max Oelschlaeger, *The Idea of Wilderness: From Prehistory to the Age of Ecology* (New Haven, Conn.: Yale University Press, 1991).

10. Carson, "Pollution of Our Environment," in *Lost Woods*, 235.

11. Letter from Carson to Lois Crisler, February 8, 1962, Box 102, Folder 1939 "Silent Spring," Carson MSS. Carson explained her motivation for writing *Silent Spring* to her friend Crisler: "No, I myself never thought the ugly facts would dominate, and I hope they don't. The beauty of the living world I was trying to save has always been uppermost in my mind—that, and anger at the senseless, brutish things that were being done. I have felt bound by solemn obligation to do what I could—if I didn't at least try I could never be happy in nature. But now I can believe I have at least helped a little. It would be unrealistic to believe one book could bring a complete change."

12. Others have placed Carson within the jeremiad tradition; see Norwood, "Heroines of Nature," 47 and n. 33; and John Opie and Norbert Elliot, "Tracking the Elusive Jeremiad: The Rhetorical Character of American Discourse," in *The Symbolic Earth: Discourse and Our Creation of the Environment*, ed. James C. Cantrill and Christine L. Oravec (Lexington: University Press of Kentucky, 1996), 9–35. For the literature of the jeremiad in American culture, see Sacvan Bercovitch, *The American Jeremiad* (Madison: University of Wisconsin Press, 1978); and David Minter, "The Puritan Jeremiad as a Literary Form," in *The American Puritan Imagination: Essays in Revaluation*, ed. Sacvan Bercovitch (New York: Cambridge University Press, 1974), 45–55. For links between Protestant Christianity and environmentalism, see J. Baird Callicott, "That Good Old-Time Wilderness Religion," in *The Great New Wilderness Debate*, ed. J. Baird Callicott and Michael P. Nelson (Athens: University of Georgia Press, 1998), 387–94.

13. Carson was certainly not the first to voice concern over pesticides. James Whorton puts *Silent Spring* in historical perspective in *Before Silent Spring: Pesticides and Public Health in Pre-DDT America* (Princeton, N.J.: Princeton University Press, 1974).

14. Throughout her book, Carson calls on democratic notions to argue her point, echoing the democratic voice of John Muir; Worster, *Passion for Nature*.

15. Rachel Carson, *Silent Spring* (Boston: Houghton Mifflin, 1962), 64.

16. Ibid., 69.

17. Carson, "The Pollution of Our Environment," 231.

18. Carson, *Silent Spring*, quotes on 39, 189, 187.

19. For more recent conversations on the environment and cancer, see Robert N. Proctor, *Cancer Wars: How Politics Shapes What We Know and Don't Know about Cancer* (New York: Basic Books, 1995). See also Linda Nash, *Inescapable Ecologies: A History of Environment, Disease, and Knowledge* (Berkeley: University of California Press, 2006).

20. Carson, *Silent Spring*, quotes on 50, 27, 239.

21. Hazlett, "Voices from the Spring," 104; Hazlett, " 'Woman vs. Man vs. Bugs,' " 701.

22. Liberty Hyde Bailey, *The Holy Earth* (New York: Scribner's, 1915), 15.

23. Carson as quoted in Lear, *Rachel Carson*, 16.

24. Rachel Carson, *The Sense of Wonder* (New York: Harper and Row, 1965), quotes on 43, 52, 55. The text was first published as "Helping Your Child to Wonder," in *Woman's Home Companion*, July 1956, 25–27, 46–48.

25. Rachel Carson, *Guarding Our Wildlife Resources. Conservation in Action Series*, no. 5, (Washington, D.C.: U.S. Fish and Wildlife Service, Government Printing Office, 1948), as quoted in Brooks, *House of Life*, 101.

26. Lear, *Rachel Carson*, 179; Hazlett, " 'Woman vs. Man vs. Bugs,' " 701–19.

27. Bailey, *Holy Earth*, 15.

28. Brooks, *House of Life*, 9.

29. Carson to James E. Bennet, November 1, 1952, as quoted in Brooks, *House of Life*, 9, 331. See also Lear, *Rachel Carson*, 227–28.

30. Rachel Carson to Dorothy Freeman, December 31, 1957, in *Always Rachel*, 241.

31. Catherine L. Albanese, *Nature Religion in America: From the Algonkian Indians to the New Age* (Chicago: University of Chicago Press, 1990).

32. Rachel Carson, speech given after the publication of her book *The Sea around Us* to Theta Sigma Phi Matrix Table Dinner, April 21, 1954, Columbus, Ohio, in *Lost Woods*, 147–63; quote on 163; see also Brooks, *House of Life*, 324–26.

33. Carson offered these words in a speech to women journalists in 1954, "The Real World around Us," in *Lost Woods*, 163.

34. Carson's hopes for her funeral went largely unfulfilled. Her brother circumvented her plans to have Unitarian pastor Duncan Howlett conduct the services by arranging a state funeral at the Washington National Cathedral. Quaker Friends honored Carson more in line with her wishes on the following Sunday with Howlett officiating. See Lear, *Rachel Carson*, 480–83.

35. She read "a few pages [of Thoreau's *Journal*] before turning out the light"; Brooks, *House of Life*, 5. For a discussion of Thoreau's philosophy, see Nash, *Wilderness and the American Mind*, 84–95; and Donald Worster, *Nature's Economy: A History of Ecological Ideas*, 2nd ed. (New York: Cambridge University Press, 1994), 58–111.

36. Comparisons in style and theme set her firmly within the nature-writing tradition. See McCay, *Rachel Carson*, 109. See Donald Fleming for an early account of Carson's transcendentalism in his seminal article, "Roots of the New Conservation Movement," *Perspectives in American History* 6 (1972): 7–91, quote on 9. See also Roderick Nash, *Wilderness and the American Mind*, rev. ed. (New Haven, Conn.: Yale

University Press, 1973); Worster, *Nature's Economy*; and Hans Huth, *Nature and the American: Three Centuries of Changing Attitudes* (Berkeley: University of California Press, 1957).

37. Nature writer Henry Williamson's *Tarka the Otter* and *Salar the Salmon* influenced her book *Under the Sea-Wind*. Carson confessed that she "read and reread [Williamson's and Beston's] books more than I can count; they are among the books that I have loved best and that have influenced me the most"; Brooks, *House of Life*, 6. H. M. Tomlinson's *Sea and the Jungle*, Joseph Conrad's *Mirror of the Sea*, and Thor Heyerdahl's *Kon Tiki* also topped her list of favorites. She wrote Heyerdahl and told him he had succeeded in writing "one of the truly great books of the sea. You have somehow managed to get into it the elemental quality such a book must have, and the feeling of the timeless, cosmic forces that rule the sea"; Carson letter to Heyerdahl, as quoted in Brooks, *House of Life*, 130.

38. For the transcendentalist ethos, see Fleming, "Roots of the New Conservation Movement," 8–9.

39. "Walking," in *The Major Essays of Henry David Thoreau*, ed. Richard Dillman (Albany, N.Y.: Whitston, 2001), 161.

40. Rachel Carson, "Biological Sciences," in *Lost Woods*, 167. This selection is taken from an essay Carson wrote for a National Council of the Teachers of English reference book, *Good Reading* (New York: New American Library, 1956).

41. Bailey, *Holy Earth*, 14, 30–31. See, for example, Liberty Hyde Bailey, *The Nature-Study Idea* (New York: Doubleday, 1903); and Anna Botsford Comstock, *Handbook of Nature Study* (Ithaca, N.Y.: Cornell University Press, 1911). For an introduction to the nature-study movement, see Lear, *Rachel Carson*, 14–15. The quotes in Lear, page 15, are from Anna Comstock's *Handbook of Nature Study*. See also Marcia Myers Bonta, "Anna Botsford Comstock," in her *Women in the Field: America's Pioneering Women Naturalists* (College Station: Texas A&M University Press, 1991); Ralph H. Lutts, *The Nature Fakers: Wildlife, Science, and Sentiment* (Golden, Colo.: Fulcrum, 1990), especially 25–31; and Tyree Goodwin Minton, "The History of the Nature-Study Movement and Its Role in the Development of Environmental Education" (Ph.D. diss., University of Massachusetts, 1980), 84–92, 106–10. Comstock and Bailey were representative of others who promoted nature study. Before they published their work, nature study was widely taught. Scientist and educator Louis Agassis conducted his own natural history school for teachers in 1873. Writer John Burroughs and President Theodore Roosevelt helped popularize a love for the out-of-doors at the same time.

42. Linda Lear demonstrates on many occasions that family matters intruded upon Carson's work and happiness. See *Rachel Carson*, 214, 236–37, for examples.

43. Ibid., 84.

44. Brooks, *House of Life*, 242. From Maria's perspective, Rachel provided a companionship that eluded her in marriage; in her daughter's success, she experienced the joy and fulfillment denied to her when she gave up her own teaching career. Except for Rachel's days at college, the two lived together, with both moving to Maryland at the same time. After Rachel took her job in Washington, D.C., her mother relocated with her. When Rachel traveled to the Maine Coast in the summer, her mother accompanied her. Even death did not keep them far apart for long, for Maria died only six years before her daughter.

45. When a reporter inquired why she never married, Carson quipped, "No time"; Lear, *Rachel Carson*, 429.

46. Carson, as quoted in Brooks, *House of Life*, 270.

47. See Lear, *Rachel Carson*, for Carson's poor health. See especially 367–68 for an account of Carson's cancer and the dishonesty she encountered from her doctors.

48. Rachel Carson, "Memo for Mrs. Eales," in *Lost Woods*, 52.

49. Brooks, *House of Life*, 9.

50. Carson, *Sea around Us*, 19, 22–23, 28, 196; Carson, *Edge of the Sea*, 215–16.

51. For Carson's friendship with Skinker and her friend in later years, Dorothy Freeman, see Lear, *Rachel Carson*; and *Always Rachel*. Skinker left Pennsylvania College to attend Johns Hopkins University, earning her doctorate in 1933. She worked as a zoologist in the U.S. Bureau of Animal Industry and helped Carson gain employment at the Fish and Wildlife Service; Lear, *Rachel Carson*, especially 43–53, 78, 150. The relationship between the older female scientist and student was characteristic of other nineteenth- and twentieth-century teachers and their protégées. See Hynes, *Recurring Silent Spring*, 60–61; Margaret Rossiter, *Women Scientists in America*, vol. 1, *Struggles and Strategies to 1940* (Baltimore: Johns Hopkins University Press, 1982), 18–20. Carson's correspondence with Freeman testifies to their mutual affection. In many ways, her friendship with Freeman resembled the deep personal relationships of women in the nineteenth century that Carol Smith-Rosenberg has uncovered in "The Female World of Love and Ritual," in *Disorderly Conduct: Visions of Gender in Victorian America* (New York: Oxford University Press, 1985), 53–76. See also Nancy Sahli, "Smashing: Women's Relationships before the Fall," *Chrysalis* 8 (Summer 1979): 17–27. For a study of Carson's female community, see Vera Norwood, *Made from This Earth: American Women and Nature* (Chapel Hill: University of North Carolina Press, 1993): 143–71.

52. For an overview of Western civilization's gendered conceptions of nature, see Carolyn Merchant, *The Death of Nature: Women, Ecology, and the Scientific Revolution* (San Francisco: Harper and Row, 1980), especially xv–41.

53. Carson, *Sea around Us*, ix.

54. Carson challenged some of the tenets of science that more self-conscious feminists later attacked. For a start, see Sandra Harding and Merrill Hintikka, eds., *Discovering Reality: Feminist Perspectives on Epistemology, Metaphysics, Methodology, and Philosophy of Science* (Dordrecht: Reidel, 1983); Harding, *The Science Question in Feminism* (Ithaca, N.Y.: Cornell University Press, 1986); Harding, *Whose Science? Whose Knowledge?: Thinking from Women's Lives* (Ithaca, N.Y.: Cornell University Press, 1991); Evelyn Fox Keller, *Reflections on Gender and Science* (New Haven, Conn.: Yale University Press, 1986); Keller, "The Gender/Science System: Or, Is Sex to Gender as Nature Is to Science?," *Hypatia* 2, no. 3 (Fall 1987): 37–49; Evelyn Fox Keller and Helen E. Longino, eds., *Feminism and Science* (New York: Oxford University Press, 1996); Donna Haraway, *Simians, Cyborgs, and Women: The Reinvention of Nature* (New York: Routledge, 1991); and Londo L. Schiebinger, *The Mind Has No Sex? Women in the Origins of Modern Science* (Cambridge, Mass.: Harvard University Press, 1989). Carson's hope to establish a feeling for her scientific subjects was not unlike that of Barbara McClintock, the subject of Evelyn Fox Keller's seminal study on the scientist in *A Feeling for the Organism: The Life and Work of*

Barbara McClintock (New York: Freeman, 1983). The linking of the feminist and environmental movements has been made by many. See, for an introduction, Merchant, *Death of Nature*; and Carolyn Merchant, *Earthcare: Women and the Environment* (New York: Routledge, 1995).

55. For a history of the role of women in science, see Rossiter, *Women Scientists in America: Struggles and Strategies to 1940*, and Margaret Rossiter, *Women Scientists in America*, vol. 2, *Before Affirmative Action, 1940–1972* (Baltimore: Johns Hopkins University Press, 1995).

56. See Philip Sterling, *Sea and Earth: The Life of Rachel Carson* (New York: Crowell, 1970), 47–49, for a retelling of the story. Mary McCay suggests that Carson may have had her mother in mind. Maria sacrificed a career for marriage, and Carson may have feared repeating her mother's life of dependence on a husband whom she felt was less talented and intelligent; *Rachel Carson*, 5.

57. Carson, speech given at the *New York Herald-Tribune* Book and Author Luncheon, October 16, 1951, New York City, New York, in *Lost Woods*, 77. See also Lear's discussion of the public response to Carson's scientific writings and her reply; *Rachel Carson*, 206–8.

58. Carson, "Real World around Us," 151.

59. Carson, *Edge of the Sea*, vii-viii.

60. Haeckel as quoted in Anna Bramwell, *Ecology in the 20ᵗʰ Century: A History* (New Haven, Conn.: Yale University Press, 1989), 40; see also Worster, *Nature's Economy*; and Robert McIntosh, *The Background of Ecology* (Cambridge: Cambridge University Press, 1995). Rexford F. Daubenmire, in *Plants and Environment: A Textbook of Plant Autecology*, 2nd ed. (New York: Wiley, 1959), claims that the "term ecology was proposed in 1885 by the zoologist Reiter....A year later [1886] Haeckel, another zoologist, formulated a simple definition" (1), but most credit Haeckel for the coinage.

61. Charles Darwin, *The Origin of Species* (1859; reprint, New York: Oxford University Press, 1996), quote on 59. Thomas Malthus was one of the key shapers of Darwin's thought. Malthus's competitive views tied population growth to natural resources and food supply.

62. Carson, *Silent Spring*, 65.

63. Darwin, *Origin of Species*, 373.

64. Carson, *Silent Spring*, 64, 66.

65. Though Darwin primarily saw a world of conflict, he at times expressed a world of equilibrium and balance. As historian Donald Worster explained, Darwin read naturalist von Humboldt's *Personal Narrative* (1744–1804) and surely did not miss his predecessor's holistic views of nature. Humboldt's ecological harmony emerged occasionally in Darwin's writings but was trumped largely by Darwin's theme of competition; Worster, *Nature's Economy*, 137–39.

66. Carson, *Silent Spring*, 64.

67. Darwin, *Origin of Species*, 373–74.

68. Carson, *Silent Spring*, 53–56.

69. Carson's notes and references indicated that she was familiar with the ecological literature. She also was not shy about contacting ecologists, and ecologists contacted her. For example, the Harvard entomologist Edward O. Wilson, during the Long Island trial on pesticides, directed Carson to field research on gypsy moth spraying and encouraged her to consult Charles Elton's *Ecology of Invasions by Animals*

and Plants (London: Methuen, 1958) for insects' life cycles. See Lear, *Rachel Carson*, for a complete record of Carson's influences, specifically 332 for Wilson's letter.

70. See Worster's discussion of the Arcadian vision of nature for one example of prior conceptualizations of holistic thought in *Nature's Economy*, 3–25. In this chapter, Worster spells out some of the differences between the holistic mind-set and the industrialized machine age, see especially 20–22.

71. One of the chief contributors to this communal view of nature was the plant ecologist Frederic Clements. Other scientists, especially Henry Gleason, challenged his ideas, but Clements's paradigm held sway well into the middle of the century. For a sample of their arguments, see Frederic E. Clements, *Plant Succession* (Washington, D.C.: Carnegie Institution, 1916); and Henry A. Gleason, "The Individualistic Concept of the Plant Association," *Bulletin of the Torrey Botanical Club* 53 (1926): 1–20. A later version of the article appeared in *American Naturalist* 111 (November–December 1977): 1119–44. See Worster's discussion on the dispute between Gleason and Clements in *Nature's Economy*, 237–40. In "The Ecology of Order and Chaos," *Environmental History Review* 14 (Spring/Summer 1990): 1–18, Worster records the rebirth of the individualistic ethos in the mid-1970s, leading to a significant paradigm shift away from organicism and order.

72. For the history of ecological studies, including the transition from a guiding paradigm of holistic order to one of disturbance and fragmentation, see Worster, "Ecology of Order and Chaos." See also Bramwell, *Ecology in the Twentieth Century*; and Andrew Brennan, *Thinking about Nature* (Athens: University of Georgia Press, 1988). Michael G. Barbour describes a paradigm shift from holistic to reductionistic thinking among ecologists in the 1950s in his "Ecological Fragmentation in the Fifties," in *Uncommon Ground: Toward Reinventing Nature*, ed. William Cronon (New York: Norton, 1995), 233–55. Robert P. McIntosh documents an increasing number of citations of Gleason's articles, especially by animal ecologists supporting the individualistic concept from 1965 to 1990 in "H. A. Gleason's 'Individualistic Concept' and Theory of Animal Communities: A Continuing Controversy," *Biological Reviews* 70 (1995): 317–57, especially 327. The important point is that the science of ecology has not remained constant, and the philosophy that has guided its practitioners has shifted with the culture. For evidence of the scientific shift to disturbance in the 1970s, see Seth R. Reice, "Nonequilibrium Determinants of Biological Community Structure," *American Scientist* 82 (September–October 1994): 424–35. Reice explains that the equilibrium theory of Charles Elton did not last; instead the "normal state" switched to suggest that chaos, not equilibrium, was the norm.

73. At one point Carson was explicit about choosing to interpret the shore as a community; see Lear, *Rachel Carson*, 242–43. Ecologist John Arthur Thomson, earlier employed Carson's favored web metaphor. He described the environment as a "web of life" linked by "long nutritive chains" to create a "balanced correlated system." "All flesh is grass," he said, "and all fish is diatom," as quoted in Fleming, "Roots of the New Conservation Movement" and taken from Thomson's *System of Animate Nature: Gifford Lectures delivered in the University of St. Andrews in the years 1915 and 1916*, 2 vols. (New York: Holt, 1920), 1:58–59.

74. For Eugene Odum's ecology, start with his textbook *Fundamentals of Ecology* (Philadelphia: Saunders, 1953), and Odum, "Introductory Review: Perspective of Ecosystem Theory and Application," *Ecosystem Theory and Application*, ed. Nicholas

Polunin, (New York: Wiley, 1986), 1–11. For more on the ecosystem, see Frank Benjamin Golley, *A History of the Ecosystem Concept in Ecology: More Than the Sum of the Parts* (New Haven, Conn.: Yale University Press, 1993); and Worster, "Ecology of Order and Chaos," 4–5. Golley ties the story of the ecosystem to American culture, and he acknowledges and shows how it is part of the holistic trend in post–World War II America. Ironically, as Joel Hagen notes, Arthur Tansley introduced his idea about the ecosystem in opposition to holism; *An Entangled Bank: The Origins of Ecosystem Ecology* (New Brunswick, N.J.: Rutgers University Press, 1992), 136. See also Worster, *Nature's Economy*, 312–13, for a discussion of the ecosystem.

75. Carson was certainly not alone in her nuclear fears. See Paul Boyer, *Fallout: A Historian Reflects on America's Half-Century Encounter with Nuclear Weapons* (Columbus: Ohio State University Press, 1998); see also Boyer, *By the Bomb's Early Light: American Thought and Culture at the Dawn of the Atomic Age* (Chapel Hill: University of North Carolina Press, 1994), for an account of American reactions to atomic warfare in the immediate five years after Nagasaki and Hiroshima.

76. Strontium 90, a long-lasting radioactive isotope and a dangerous part of nuclear fallout, was found in milk products in the United States in 1953. It is not found in nature, and when it lodges in the bone, it gives off radiation that can cause cancer. Within a few years, studies to determine the extent of strontium 90 in milk and in the teeth of children alarmed the public. Strontium 90 was potentially very dangerous and widespread. The "Baby Tooth Study," begun in 1959, was particularly effective in educating the public about the dangers. It initiated a public campaign to ask for baby teeth and then quickly disseminated information on the dangers of contaminated milk. Fledgling environmental groups broadcast the results, and soon the public realized that fallout was a real danger to them, not just those within close range of a nuclear test site. See Lutts, "Chemical Fallout," 215–16; and "Baby Tooth Survey Launched in Search of Data on Strontium-90," *Nuclear Information* 24 (December 1958): 1–5. Carson was one of those who paid attention to the strontium scare. She also was attentive to the cranberry scare in 1959. Cranberries were pulled off the shelves because of fears that pesticide use threatened the safety of consumers.

77. Carson, *Sea around Us*, x.

78. Ibid., xi–xii.

79. See Brooks, *House of Life*, 227–46, for a synopsis of her growing interest in pesticides, including some correspondence between Carson and Huckins; see also Lear, *Rachel Carson*; and Frank Graham Jr., *Since Silent Spring* (Boston: Houghton Mifflin, 1970). For her letter to *Reader's Digest* editor Harold Lynch, July 15, 1945, Box 44, Folder 821, Carson MSS.

80. Carson wrote Huckins "that it was not just the copy of your letter to the newspaper but your personal letter to me that started it all"; Brooks, *House of Life*, 233.

81. Carson as quoted in Ibid. She made the statement in an article for the *Saturday Review Syndicate*, September 29, 1962.

82. Carson, *Silent Spring*, 246.

83. See especially McCay, *Rachel Carson*, 108.

84. Rachel Carson to the Women's National Book Association, as quoted in Graham, *Since Silent Spring*, 53.

85. Carson, "Remarks made on acceptance of the John Burroughs Medal for Excellence in Nature Writing," April 7, 1952, New York, New York, as quoted in *Lost Woods*, 94; also see Lear, *Rachel Carson*, 221.

86. Carson, *Edge of the Sea*, 215.

87. Carson, *Sea around Us*, 93–94.

88. Ibid., 93–95, quotes on 93.

89. George Perkins Marsh, *Man and Nature* (New York: Scribner, 1864), 36.

90. Carson, *Silent Spring*, 85.

91. Ibid., 7.

92. Ibid., 5–7.

93. Ibid., 13.

94. Ibid., 127.

95. Carson appealed to the U.S. Constitution and the Bill of Rights to argue that citizens should have some say in pesticide policy decisions; *Silent Spring*, 12–13.

96. Concerned about animal protection and rights, Carson was an honorary board member for the Animal Welfare Institute, wrote parts of the institute's publications, lobbied congressmen with letters and phone calls, and developed friendships with animal rights activists. The Animal Welfare Institute recognized her belief in animal rights by awarding her its Schweitzer Medal in 1963. In her acceptance speech, she said, "What is important is the relation of man to *all life*"; Carson, "Albert Schweitzer Award Speech," January 1963, Box 101, Folder 1900, Carson MSS). See also Lear, *Rachel Carson*, 438–40. And note Carson's preface in Ruth Harrison, *Animal Machines: The New Factory Farming Industry* (London: Vincent Stuart, 1964), for her concern about humanity's moral obligation to animals. During the time that she was writing *Silent Spring* and in the heat of the controversy that ensued, Carson and her publicists strove to keep quiet her concern for animal rights for fear that she might be labeled an extremist and discredited; see Lear, *Rachel Carson*, 371.

97. Carson, "The Real World around Us," 154–61.

98. Carson, *Silent Spring*, 297.

99. Ibid., 187. Her publicist, biographer, and friend Paul Brooks said the larger message of *Silent Spring* was a questioning of "the basic irresponsibility of an industrialized, technological society toward the natural world"; *House of Life*, 293.

100. Carson, *Silent Spring*, 1–3.

101. The Japanese seamen of the *Lucky Dragon* saw the light of the bomb but did not recognize it as a nuclear test. The fish they brought back were also contaminated, but they were sold before the contamination was detected. A panic set in and, as a result, the Japanese fishing industry suffered huge losses. The world press covered the story for months. See Ralph E. Lapp, *The Voyage of the Lucky Dragon* (New York: Harper, 1958), for a chronicle of the events; and Lutts, "Chemical Fallout," 213–14, for an analysis of the events in relation to Carson. Lutts's article is especially helpful in linking Carson's concern about nuclear fallout and pesticides. Later in her book, she explicitly compared the death of the fisherman on the *Lucky Dragon* to a Swedish farmer who died after dusting a field with DDT and benzene hexachloride. "For each man a poison drifting out of the sky carried a death sentence. For one, it was radiation-poisoned ash; for the other, chemical dust"; Carson, *Silent Spring*, 229–30. See also Martin V. Melosi, *Coping with Abundance: Energy and Environment in Industrial America* (Philadelphia: Temple University Press, 1985), 234–35.

102. Carson, *Silent Spring*, 6.

103. Ibid., 1.

104. Ibid., 10.

105. Carson never said that chemical insecticides must never be used; she did, however, condemn what she saw as a "crusade to create a chemically sterile, insect-free world," which seemed to her to have come from "a fanatic zeal on the part of many specialists and most of the so-called control agencies"; *Silent Spring*, 12. Citing with approval a Canadian entomologist, she argued, "We must change our philosophy, abandon our attitude of human superiority and admit that in many cases in natural environments we find ways and means of limiting populations of organisms in a more economical way than we can do it ourselves"; *Silent Spring*, 261. For her advocacy of other methods, see *Silent Spring*, 11–12, 184; see especially her last chapter, where she promoted biotic solutions.

106. I am indebted to historian James Gilbert for this term.

107. For a discussion of an "earth manager's" employment of the ecosystem concept for maximum agricultural production and human gain, see Worster, *Nature's Economy*, 313–14.

108. The growth of environmental ethics as a discipline from the 1970s to the 1990s testifies to these shifting attitudes. For an introduction to the subject and seminal essays in the field, see Joseph R. Desjardins, *Environmental Ethics: An Introduction to Environmental Philosophy* (Belmont, Calif.: Wadsworth, 1993); Robert Elliot, ed., *Environmental Ethics* (New York: Oxford University Press, 1995); Max Oelschlaeger, ed., *Postmodern Environmental Ethics* (Albany: State University of New York Press, 1995); and Clare Palmer, *Environmental Ethics* (Santa Barbara, Calif.: ABC-CLIO, 1997). For some of the connections with environmental ethics and holistic philosophy through the contribution of process philosophy, see Clare Palmer, *Environmental Ethics and Process Thinking* (Oxford: Clarendon Press, 1998).

109. I refer here to Aldo Leopold's land ethic that ties human actions to the entire biotic community, *A Sand County Almanac, and Sketches Here and There* (New York: Oxford University Press, 1949), 262.

110. Brooks, *House of Life*, 318.

111. Rachel Carson, "Man against Himself," speech to the Kaiser-Permanente Symposium, San Francisco, California, October 18, 1963, in *Lost Woods*, 228.

112. Harrison, *Animal Machines*.

113. Lear, *Rachel Carson*, 364.

114. For Carson's medical ailments and treatment, including the prevarication of doctors, see Lear, *Rachel Carson*, especially 367–68.

115. For her correspondence with Dr. Morton Biskind of Connecticut, Box 42, Folder 762, Carson MSS. For Biskind's findings linking pesticide sprays to human illness, see Morton S. Biskind, "Public Health Aspects of the New Insecticides," *American Journal of Digestive Diseases* 20 (November 1953): 331–41. For his recommendation of bioflavonoids, see Morton S. Biskind and William Coda Martin, "The Use of Citrus Flavonoids in Infections II.," *American Journal of Digestive Diseases* 22 (February 1955): 41–45.

116. Stewart C. Easton, *Rudolf Steiner: Herald of a New Epoch* (Hudson, N.Y.: Anthroposophic Press, 1980).

117. See Rachel Carson's correspondence with Marjorie Spock, Box 105, Folder 2007, and her correspondence with Dr. Morton Biskind of Connecticut, Box 42, Folder 762, in Carson MSS.

118. See from Carson to Knecht [1959?], Box 103, Folder 1957, Carson MSS. Also see Graham, *Since Silent Spring*, 32; Lear, *Rachel Carson*, 367–68.

119. Linus Pauling, *Vitamin C and the Common Cold* (San Francisco: Freeman, 1970).

120. Hazlett, "'Woman vs. Man vs. Bugs,'" 701, 703.

121. See Carson's summation of the public reception in her "National Women's Press Club Speech," 203. For a particularly insightful article on the gendered critique voiced against Carson, see Hazlett, "'Woman vs. Man vs. Bugs.'" See also Hazlett, "Voices from the Spring."

122. Michigan State University horticulturalist, as quoted in Brooks, *House of Life*, 296.

123. Birmingham, *Alabama Journal*, October 21, 1962, Carson MSS; for comparisons to Harriet Beecher Stowe's *Uncle Tom's Cabin*, see Walter Sullivan, "Books of the Times," *New York Times*, September 27, 1962, 35; and Robert Kirsch, "Cleaning Air in Pollution Controversy," *Los Angeles Times*, February 8, 1970, Q38; for William Douglas's quote, see William O. Douglas, "Silent Spring by Rachel Carson: A Report," *Book-of-the-Month-Club News*, September 1962, 2–4. For both the scorn and embrace Carson garnered by writing *Silent Spring*, see Lear, *Rachel Carson*, especially chaps. 17 and 18; Brooks, *House of Life*, chaps. 20 and 21; Graham, *Since Silent Spring*; and Hazlett, "'Woman vs. Man vs. Bugs.'"

124. C. J. Briejèr to Carson, as quoted in Graham, *Since Silent Spring*, quote on 87.

125. Graham, *Since Silent Spring*, 83–85.

126. For Sierra Club membership statistics, see "Sierra Club History," Sierra Club, February 26, 2003, http://www.sierraclub.org/history/timeline.asp (accessed August 20, 2004). Carson contributed to the growth of the Sierra Club financially, too. She left more than $300,000 to the club in her will, according to David Brower in *For Earth's Sake: The Life and Times of David Brower* (Salt Lake City, Utah: Gibbs Smith, 1990), 215. Some estimate more than 20 million in attendance at the Earth Day events of April 22, 1970; see "Earth Day," *E: The Environmental Magazine* 6 (March/April 1995): 32; and Melosi, *Coping with Abundance*, 297. For the growth of the environmental movement, see Robert Gottlieb, *Forcing the Spring: The Transformation of the American Environmental Movement* (Washington, D.C.: Island Press, 1993).

127. See Schultz cartoons in Brooks, *House of Life*.

128. M. H. Herrick to Editor, Richmond, *Virginia News-Leader*, January 23, 1963, Carson MSS.

129. Brower, *For Earth's Sake*, 214.

130. "Who Was David Brower," David Brower Center, http://www.browercenter.org/node/17 (accessed July 14, 2008).

131. For Gaia science, see James Lovelock, *The Age of Gaia: A Biography of Our Living Earth* (New York: Norton, 1988); and James Lovelock, *Gaia: A New Look at Life on Earth* (Oxford: Oxford University Press, 1979); for deep ecology, see the Norwegian philosopher Arne Naess's seminal article, "The Shallow and the Deep, Long-Range Ecology Movement: A Summary," *Inquiry* 16 (1973): 95–100; Arne Naess, *Ecology, Community and Lifestyle: Outline of an Ecosophy*, trans. and ed. David Rothenberg

(Cambridge: Cambridge University Press, 1989); Bill Devall and George Sessions, *Deep Ecology: Living as If Nature Mattered* (Salt Lake City, Utah: Peregrine Smith, 1985). For ecofeminism, see Rachel L. Bagby, "Building the Green Movement," *Women of Power* 9 (Spring 1988): 14; Irene Diamond and Gloria Feman Ornstein, eds., *Reweaving the World: The Emergence of Ecofeminism* (San Francisco: Sierra Club Books, 1990); Ynestra King, *What Is Ecofeminism?* (New York: Ecofeminist Resources, 1990); Mary Mellor, *Feminism and Ecology* (New York: Polity Press, 1997); Rosemary Radford Reuther, *Ecology and Feminism* (Poughkeepsie, N.Y.: Vassar College, 1989); and Reuther, *Gaia and God: An Ecofeminist Theology of Earth Healing* (San Francisco: HarperSanFrancisco, 1994).

132. Barry Commoner, *The Closing Circle: Nature, Man and Technology* (New York: Knopf, 1971); Commoner, "The Closing Circle: Nature, Man, and Technology," in *Thinking about the Environment: Readings on Politics, Property, and the Physical World*, eds. Matthew Alan Cahn and Rory O'Brien (New York: M.E. Sharpe), 165.

133. Albanese, *Nature Religion in America*; and Thomas R. Dunlap, *Faith in Nature: Environmentalism as Religious Quest* (Seattle: University of Washington Press, 2004); see William Cronon's foreword to Dunlap's book for the quote, p. xv.

CHAPTER 2

1. The Moscow exhibit and a parallel Soviet exhibit in New York City arose out of a 1955 Geneva summit between the superpowers. The summit promoted cultural exchanges and raised hopes that the two nations might attempt to "persuade rather than bludgeon each other," in the words of Cold War historian Warren Cohen. See Cohen, *America in the Age of Soviet Power, 1945–1991* (New York: Cambridge University Press, 1993), 91; and Elaine Tyler May, *Homeward Bound: American Families in the Cold War Era* (New York: Basic Books, 1988), 18–20. See also "What the Russians Will See," *Look*, July 21, 1959, 52–54; "Main Street Goes to Moscow," *Newsweek*, July 20, 1959, 31–38; "The Two Worlds: A Day-Long Debate," *New York Times*, July 25, 1959, 1, 3; Stephen E. Ambrose, *Nixon: The Education of a Politician, 1913–1962* (New York: Simon and Schuster, 1987), 521–26; and John Gaddis, *Russia, the Soviet Union, and the United States: An Interpretive History*, 2nd ed. (New York: McGraw-Hill, 1990), chap. 8.

2. "The U.S. in Moscow: Russia Comes to the Fair," *Time*, August 3, 1959, quote on 14. Fuller's earlier geodesics resembled a galvanized steel grain bin. The round grain bin was a source of inspiration for Fuller, who first saw the storage unit on a trip to the Midwest in 1940. J. Baldwin dubbed them "Corrugated Cottages" in *Bucky Works: Buckminster Fuller's Ideas for Today* (New York: Wiley, 1996), 35.

3. "The Dymaxion American," *Time*, January 10, 1964, 46, 48, 50. In 1962, Fuller counted more than 2,000 of his structures in forty countries; Buckminster Fuller, *Ideas and Integrities: A Spontaneous Autobiographical Disclosure*, ed. Robert W. Marks (Englewood Cliffs, N.J.: Prentice-Hall, 1963), 278. Higgot reported 300,000 in 1985, as noted in Dennis Sharp, "Buckminster Fuller: A Tribute," *Architectural Journal* 23 (December 14, 1995), 21. For an insightful discussion of organic art and architecture after World War II, see Brooke Kamin Rapaport and Kevin L. Stayton, *Vital Forms: American Art and Design in the Atomic Age, 1940–1960* (Brooklyn: Brooklyn Museum of Art, 2001).

4. Theodore Roszak, *From Satori to Silicon Valley: San Francisco and the American Counterculture* (San Francisco: Don't Call It Frisco, 1986), 17–22, quote on 22. See also Andrew G. Kirk, *Counterculture Green: The Whole Earth Catalog and American Environmentalism* (Lawrence: University Press of Kansas, 2007), 60–61.

5. As Roszak's comments suggest, not all in the counterculture liked Fuller. For the term "counterculture," see Peter Braunstein and Michael William Doyle, "Historicizing the American Counterculture of the 1960s and 1970s," in *Imagine Nation: The American Counterculture of the 1960s and 1970s*, ed. Peter Braunstein and Michael William Doyle (New York: Routledge, 2002), 5–14. Stewart Brand wrote: "Back in 1967 the insights of Buckminster Fuller initiated the *Whole Earth Catalog*. The artists I hung out with in those days had all been electrified by Fuller's earlier, most radical book—*Nine Chains to the Moon*"; Stewart Brand, ed., *The Next Whole Earth Catalog: Access to Tools*, 2nd ed. (New York: Random House, 1981), 32. See also Stewart Brand, ed., *The Whole Earth Catalog: Access to Tools* (New York: Portola Institute and Random House, 1968), 2; and view Catalogs online at The Whole Earth, http://www.wholeearth.com/index.php (accessed January 23, 2010). For a history of Brand and the *Whole Earth Catalog*, see Kirk, *Counterculture Green*; and Fred Turner, *From the Counterculture to the Cyberculture: Stewart Brand, the Whole Earth Network, and the Rise of Digital Utopianism* (Chicago: University of Chicago Press, 2006). Kirk notes (*Counterculture Green*, 1) that Brand conceived the idea of his catalog while reading Barbara Ward's book *Spaceship Earth: The Impact of Science on Society* (New York: Columbia University Press, 1966). Ward, a British economist, pioneer in sustainability, and devout Catholic, believed care for the environment and equitable distribution of resources were a moral obligation. A colorful introduction to Brand and his days as a Merry Prankster can be found in Tom Wolfe's *Electric Kool-Aid Acid Test* (New York: Bantam, 1969).

6. M. W. Newman, "Bucky," *Inland Architect* 27 (September/October, 1983): 4. Edward Stone, an architect, exclaimed: "He's a great visionary, a prophet of the twentieth century," as quoted in Calvin Tomkins, "Architecture: Umbrella Man," *Newsweek*, July 13, 1959, 84. Donald Robertson, Fuller's patent lawyer, cataloged the reception of Fuller's inventions in *Mind's Eye of Richard Buckminster Fuller* (New York: Vantage Press, 1974).

7. For a full list of Fuller's accomplishments and awards, see his "Basic Biography," March 1, 1983, in R. Buckminster Fuller Papers. I accessed Fuller's papers at the Buckminster Fuller Institute, Sebastopol, California, but the papers have since moved to Stanford University; see R. Buckminster Fuller Papers, M1090, Department of Special Collections, Stanford University Green Library, Stanford, California. See the Stanford University Libraries and Academic Information Resources online for access to the R. Buckminster Fuller Archive at http://www-sul.stanford.edu/depts/spc/fuller/index.html. Stanford's website has a timeline of Fuller's life, as does the Buckminster Fuller Archive Web site, http://www.bfi.org/our_programs/who_is_buckminster_fuller/basic_biography; see also Joachim Krausse and Claude Lichtenstein, eds., *Your Private Sky: R. Buckminster Fuller, The Art of Design Science* (Baden, Germany: L. Müller, 1999), 26–41.

8. Scientists Harry Kroto, Robert Curl, and Richard Smalley recognized the molecule's soccer ball-like pattern and compared it to the geodesic; Baldwin, *Bucky Works*, 74–75; and E. J. Applewhite, "The Naming of Buckminsterfullerine," in

Buckminster Fuller: Anthology for the New Millennium, ed. Thomas T. K. Zung (New York: St. Martin's Press, 2001), 332–36.

9. Henry Nash Smith, *Virgin Land: The American West as Symbol and Myth* (Cambridge, Mass.: Harvard University Press, 1950). See also Roderick Nash, *Wilderness and the American Mind*, rev. ed. (New Haven, Conn.: Yale University Press, 1974). While Smith's work has been improved upon, his understanding of the power of mythology in cultural understandings remains convincing. For a discussion of his work fifty years later, see Roger E. Chapman, "Review of Henry Nash Smith, *Virgin Land: The American West as Symbol and Myth*," H-Ideas, H-Net Reviews, July 2000, http://www.h-net.msu.edu/reviews/showrev.cgi?path=7216964552182 (accessed June 10, 2008). Turn also to David Wrobel, *The End of American Exceptionalism: Frontier Anxiety from the Old West to the New Deal* (Lawrence: University Press of Kansas, 1993), 3–12, for a concise overview of the development of conceptions of America as "Eden Unmarred" and the relationship between the myth of the garden, a narrative of American exceptionalism, and perceptions of the closing of the American frontier in the 1880s and 1890s.

10. Leo Marx, *The Machine in the Garden: Technology and the Pastoral Ideal in America* (London: Oxford University Press, 1964). See also Thomas P. Hughes, *American Genesis: A Century of Invention and Technological Enthusiasm, 1870–1970* (New York: Penguin, 1989); Smith, *Virgin Land*; Perry Miller, *The Life of the Mind in America* (New York: Harvest, 1965), David Nye, *American Technological Sublime* (Cambridge, Mass.: MIT Press, 1996), Jennifer Price, *Flight Maps: Adventures with Nature in Modern America* (New York: Basic Books, 2000); Alan Trachtenberg, *The Incorporation of America: Culture and Society in the Gilded Age* (New York: Hill and Wang, 1982); and Trachtenberg, *Brooklyn Bridge: Fact and Symbol* (Chicago: University of Chicago Press, 1965).

11. Leo Marx explains Emerson's views of technology and the coming industrial age in *Machine in the Garden*, 236–42. James W. Carey and John J. Quirk compared Fuller to these futurist thinkers in "The Mythos of the Electronic Revolution," *American Scholar* 39 (Spring 1970): 219–41; 39 (Summer 1970): 395–424.

12. For Fuller's ideas on weaponry, evolution, and progress, see R. Buckminster Fuller, *Operating Manual for Spaceship Earth* (New York: Dutton, 1963); and Fuller, *Ideas and Integrities*, especially chaps 15–19.

13. Fuller, *Operating Manual for Spaceship Earth*, 52.

14. There is some controversy over who first employed the metaphor of the earth as spaceship. The nineteenth-century economist Henry George wrote, "It is a well-provisioned ship, this on which we sail through space," *Progress and Poverty* (1879; reprint, New York: Cosimo, 2005), 173. In the 1960s, Kenneth E. Boulding used the term to explain his economics. Martin Melosi claims that Boulding conceived the phrase in Martin V. Melosi, *Coping with Abundance: Energy and Environment in Industrial America* (Philadelphia: Temple University Press, 1985), 315. Boulding criticized unrestrained growth, arguing that a spaceship economy is finite. He advocated an "ecological economy" (in contrast with what he called a "cowboy economy") that de-emphasized growth and focused on wise usage. See Kenneth E. Boulding, "The Economics of the Coming Spaceship Earth" (1966), in *Collected Papers*, ed. Fred R. Glahe and Larry D. Singell, 6 vols. (Boulder: Colorado Associated University Press, 1971–85), 1:383–94. Barbara Ward used the phrase in *Spaceship*

Earth (1966). Senator Adlai Stevenson said, "We travel together, passengers on a little spaceship, dependent on its vulnerable reserves of air and soil; all committed for our safety to its security and peace; preserved from annihilation only by the care, the work and, I will say, the love we give our fragile craft"; quoted in George Schindler Jr., "It Didn't Begin with Earth Day: The Green Momentum Was Building Long before 1970," *E: The Environmental Magazine* 6 (March/April 1995): 32. For a discussion of "spaceship earth," see John Woodcock, "The Garden in the Machine: Variations on Spaceship Earth," *Michigan Quarterly Review* 18 (Spring 1979): 308–17.

15. Fuller kept records of his genealogy, writings, correspondence, activities, sketches, receipts, and even tiny scraps of paper in his "Chronofile," which is now housed at Stanford University's Special Collections, M1090. Records of his family history may be found in Series 1, "Family History." For biographies, see Lloyd Steven Sieden, *Buckminster Fuller's Universe: An Appreciation* (New York: Plenum Press, 1989); E. J. Applewhite, *Cosmic Fishing* (New York: Macmillan, 1985); Baldwin, *Bucky Works*; Alden Hatch, *Buckminster Fuller: At Home in the Universe* (New York: Dell, 1974); Hugh Kenner, *Bucky: A Guided Tour of Buckminster Fuller* (New York: Morrow, 1973); Robert W. Marks, *The Dymaxion World of Buckminster Fuller* (New York: Reinhold, 1960); John McHale, *R. Buckminster Fuller* (New York: Braziller, 1962); Robert Snyder, ed., *R. Buckminster Fuller: An Autobiographical Monologue/Scenario* (New York: St. Martin's Press, 1980); Calvin Tomkins, "Profiles: In the Outlaw Area," *New Yorker*, January 8, 1966, 35; Tomkins, "Architecture: Umbrella Man."

16. Fuller, *Ideas and Integrities*, 9–10, 17.

17. Fuller fought to keep the island in its "natural state"; Sieden, *Buckminster Fuller's Universe*, 349.

18. Harvard dismissed him for "lack of ambition"; ibid., 22. Fuller referred to being "fired" from Harvard in his book *Ideas and Integrities*, 41.

19. Fuller watched navy pilots-in-training die because they missed the pontoon landing and crashed their planes into the sea. Because rescuers found it difficult to free pilots from their seat belts before they drowned, Fuller hooked a winch onto rescue boats so the plane could be pulled above water, giving rescuers time to free the pilot; Sieden, *Buckminster Fuller's Universe*, 50–52.

20. Fuller felt lucky that he "was ejected so frequently from the Establishment that I was finally forced either to perish or to employ some of those faculties with which we are all endowed"; quoted in Harold Taylor, "Inside Buckminster Fuller's Universe," *Saturday Review*, May 2, 1970, 56–57. For his daughter's sickness and their housing, see Fuller, *Ideas and Integrities*, 23, 42–43.

21. Fuller, *Ideas and Integrities*, 9.

22. Ibid., 46.

23. Buckminster Fuller, "Turning Points: You Do Not Belong to You. You Belong to the Universe," *Quest*, November/December 1979, 104.

24. Ibid. Fuller's exasperation with the inefficiency of the housing industry can be found in numerous sources. A good place to start is in his *Ideas and Integrities*, chaps. 1 and 2, especially 23–25.

25. R. Buckminster Fuller, *No More Secondhand God and Other Writings* (Carbondale: Southern Illinois University Press, 1963), 35.

26. William E. Akin, *Technocracy and the American Dream: The Technocrat Movement, 1900–1941* (Berkeley: University of California Press, 1977). Thorstein

Veblen inspired technocracy leaders; see, for example, "Prophets of Technocracy Tell How Industry Might Be Ruled," *Science Newsletter* 23 (January 28, 1933): 52, 62. See the utopian influence of Saint-Simon on the technocracy movement in Robert B. Carlisle, "The Birth of Technocracy: Science, Society, and Saint-Simonians," *Journal of the History of Ideas* 35 (July–September 1974): 445–64.

27. Ludwig von Bertalanffy, *General Systems Theory: Foundations, Development, Applications* (New York: Braziller, 1968). For Bertalanffy's life and views, as well as interpretations by two of his followers, Buckminster Fuller and the economist Kenneth Boulding, see Mark Davidson, *Uncommon Sense: The Life and Thought of Ludwig von Bertalanffy (1901–1972), Father of General Systems Theory*, foreword by R. Buckminster Fuller, introduction by Kenneth E. Boulding (Los Angeles: Tarcher, 1983). See also Lars Skyttner, *General Systems Theory: Ideas and Applications* (River Edge, N.J.: World Scientific, 2001).

28. Soleri's work can be seen at his ongoing project of Arcosanti, Arizona; Paolo Soleri, *Arcology: The City in the Image of Man* (Cambridge, Mass.: MIT Press, 1969); Peter Blake, "Paolo Soleri's Visionary City," *Architectural Forum* 114 (March 1961): 111–18; Walter Karp, "Soleri: Designer in the Desert," *Horizon* 12 (1970): 30–39; Tevere J. McFayden, "The Abbot of Arcosanti: Praised and Damned, Architect Paolo Soleri Carves Out His Dream in the Desert," *Horizon* 23 (1980): 54–61; and Georgi Stanishev, "Soleri's Laboratory," *World Architecture* 21 (1993): 58–63.

29. R. Buckminster Fuller, *The Artifacts of R. Buckminster Fuller*, ed. James Ward, 4 vols. (New York: Garland, 1985), 1: xxviii.

30. Fuller, "Turning Points," 104.

31. Fuller, as quoted in Snyder, *R. Buckminster Fuller*, 19. Fuller first became interested in his great-aunt upon reading Frederick Augustus Braun, *Margaret Fuller and Goethe: The Development of a Remarkable Personality, Her Religion and Philosophy, and Her Relation to Emerson, J. F. Clarke, and Transcendentalism* (New York: Holt, 1910), when he was exploring conceptions of time in 1927, according to Fred Kutchins, "The Elite Feature Interview: 'Inquiring for Buckminster Fuller,'" *Chicago's Elite* 2 (November/December 1977): 1–2. See Fuller, *Ideas and Integrities*, 67–71.

32. Fuller, "Turning Points," 104.

33. "The Dymaxion American," 46. See also Fuller, *Ideas and Integrities*, 45.

34. By "nature's coordinate system," Fuller meant the underlying laws of nature. This coordinate system was a "comprehensive mathematical scheme of patterning," and his "geometry exploration" was his attempt to uncover this scheme. He believed he found it: the "discovered synergetic system is probably nature's spontaneously employed coordinate system"; Fuller, *Ideas and Integrities*, 21.

35. Buckminster Fuller, *Grunch of Giants* (New York: St. Martin's Press, 1983), 10.

36. Though he made numerous references to politicians as pirates, the work that most clearly reveals his thoughts is *Operating Manual for Spaceship Earth*, chaps. 2 and 3.

37. Fuller, *Ideas and Integrities*, 173.

38. Fuller self-published *4D Timelock* in Chicago in 1928 to explain his house and 4D ideas. It was reprinted by the Lama Foundation in Corrales, New Mexico, in 1970. The self-congratulatory, visionary work presages much of his later thought. For McHale's quote, see *R. Buckminster Fuller*, 43n5.

39. McHale gives a complete description of the house in *R. Buckminster Fuller*, 16–18.

40. See a glossary of terms in Amy C. Edmondson, *A Fuller Explanation: The Synergetic Geometry of R. Buckminster Fuller* (Boston: Birkhauser, 1987). McHale also discusses Fuller's use of the word "Dymaxion" in terms of efficiency, quoting Fuller as saying that it is a "maximum gain of advantage from minimal energy input"; *R. Buckminster Fuller*, 17.

41. Fuller, as quoted in John McHale, "Richard Buckminster Fuller," *Architectural Design* 31 (July 1961): 297.

42. Hugh Aldersey-Williams, "The Rise and Fall of Dymaxion Man," *World Architecture* 39 (1995): 138.

43. Le Corbusier, *Towards a New Architecture*, trans. Frederick Etchells (New York: Praeger, 1946), 10–13, quote on 10. See also "Le Corbusier Citrohan House," *Digital Arts*, October 23, 2007, http://www.digitalarts.dk/2007/10/citrohan/ (accessed June 13, 2008). See also Villa Savoye, for one of the best examples of Le Corbusier's functional modernist architecture; "Fine Art on the Web," Fine Arts Department, Boston College, Boston, Massachusetts, http://www.bc.edu/bc_org/avp/cas/fnart/Corbu.html (accessed March 16, 2009).

44. Sieden, *Buckminster Fuller's Universe*, 126–27.

45. Robert Malthus held that as human beings moved from agricultural to industrial societies, the earth would be stripped of its resources, resulting in periods of starvation; *An Essay on the Principle of Population as It Affects the Future Improvement of Society* (1798; New York: A. M. Kelley, 1965). For a helpful overview of Malthusian ideas and anxieties in the 1920s, see Wrobel, *End of American Exceptionalism*, 112–21. Fuller's concern over housing and resources began within this cultural milieu. For the 1960s and 1970s conversation and Paul R. Ehrlich's views, turn to his prolific writings, including *The Population Bomb* (New York: Ballantine, 1968), and Paul R. Ehrlich and Anne H. Ehrlich, *Population, Resources, Environment: Issues in Human Ecology* (San Francisco: Freeman, 1970). For a discussion of Ehrlich's work, see Kirk, *Counterculture Green*, 33–35. For environmentalist interest in Malthus's ideas, see Bob Pepperman Taylor, *Our Limits Transgressed: Environmental Political Thought in America* (Lawrence: University Press of Kansas, 1992), 27–50.

46. Fuller, *Operating Manual for Spaceship Earth*, especially chap. 8, quotes on 131 and 79–80. For Fuller's critique of Malthus, see Sieden, *Buckminster Fuller's Universe*, 373. See also Eric Burgess, "Fuller Insists World Can End Poverty within 25 Years," *Christian Science Monitor*, August 13, 1969, 15–16.

47. Fuller also reported that the car could reach 120 miles per hour. No official tests measured the car's efficiency; Aldersey-Williams, "The Rise and Fall of Dymaxion Man," 139.

48. The AIA rejected Fuller's patents in 1929: "Be it resolved that the AIA establish itself on record as inherently opposed to any peas-in-a-pod-like, reproducible designs." A month before the Sokolniki Exhibit opened, the AIA awarded Fuller an honorary membership. For his rejection by the AIA, see Kutchins, "'Inquiring for Buckminster Fuller," 2–3; Cedric Price, "Buckminster Fuller, 1895–1983," *Architectural Review* 174 (August 1983), quote on 4; Newman, "Bucky," 4–5; and Sieden, *Buckminster Fuller's Universe*, 130.

49. Sieden, *Buckminster Fuller's Universe*, chap. 12, especially p. 282; Hatch, *Buckminster Fuller*, 172–81; and Baldwin, *Bucky Works*, 37–61. For the housing boom and rise of suburban tract housing, see Adam Rome, *The Bulldozer in the Countryside:*

Suburban Sprawl and the Rise of Modern Environmentalism (New York: Cambridge University Press, 2001), chap. 1; Kenneth Jackson, *Crabgrass Frontier: The Suburbanization of the United States* (New York: Oxford University Press, 1985); Willem Van Vliet, *Encyclopedia of Housing* (Thousand Oaks, Calif.: Sage, 1998), 329. Peter Blake, *God's Own Junkyard: The Planned Deterioration of America's Landscape* (New York: Holt, Rinehart and Winston, 1964); Dolores Hayden, *Building Suburbia: Green Fields and Urban Growth, 1820–2000* (New York: Vintage, 2003); and Barbara M. Kelly, *Expanding the American Dream: Building and Rebuilding Levittown* (Albany: State University of New York Press, 1993).

50. For information on Fuller's mathematical system, see Fuller, *Synergetics: Explorations in the Geometry of Thinking*, in collaboration with E. J. Applewhite (New York: Macmillan, 1975); and *Synergetics 2: Further Explorations in the Geometry of Thinking*, in collaboration with E. J. Applewhite (New York: Macmillan, 1979). For an introduction to synergetics and Fuller's obtuse language, see Edmondson, *A Fuller Explanation*.

51. Fuller, *Ideas and Integrities*, 21; in the same work he defines synergy as "the integrated interbehaviors of all systems unpredicted by behaviors or characteristics of any of the systems' parts when considered separately" (64). See also Fuller, *Operating Manual for Spaceship Earth*, 71–99; and John McHale, "Buckminster Fuller," *Architectural Review* 120 (July 1956): 19.

52. Sherrington's quote is a paraphrase by Lindy Roy in "Geometry as a Nervous System," *ANY* 17 (1997): 24–27, quotes on 25 and taken from Sherrington's classic book *The Integrative Action of the Nervous System* (New York: Charles Scribner, 1906), 178–79. Roy explains the holistic paradigm shift in neurology in this essay. For "synergy," and its uses, see *Oxford English Dictionary*, 2nd ed. (Oxford: Clarendon Press, 1991), 17: 479–80.

53. Fuller, *Ideas and Integrities*, 199–204, quotes on 203. See also *Operating Manual for Spaceship Earth*, 49–52.

54. One of Fuller's discussions on Einstein can be found in his book *Nine Chains to the Moon* (New York: Lippincott, 1938). Roy discusses Fuller's employment of Einstein's theories in "Geometry as a Nervous System," 27.

55. Fuller, *Ideas and Integrities*, chap. 6. Hatch reports the map's popularity in *Buckminster Fuller*, 167. Robertson traces the story of the map's creation and patent in *Mind's Eye*, chapter 2.

56. To view the Dymaxion Map as flat and as a globe, see Chris Rywalt's animation on the Buckminster Fuller Institute's Web page, http://www.bfi.org/map_animation. html (accessed June 9, 2009).

57. Hatch, *Buckminster Fuller*, quote on 186–87; and Fuller, *Ideas and Integrities*, 213. For the link between map and dome, see Fuller, *Ideas and Integrities*, chap. 6; Baldwin, *Bucky Works*, 117–18; and Kenner, *Bucky*, 234–35. For the geodesic patent, see Robertson, *Mind's Eye*, chap 4; and R. Buckminster Fuller, *Inventions: The Patented Works of R. Buckminster Fuller* (New York: St. Martin's Press, 1983), 127–44.

58. See Martin Duberman, *Black Mountain: An Exploration in Community* (Garden City, N.Y.: Anchor Books, 1973), 293–303, quote on 297–98; Baldwin, *Bucky Works*, 131.

59. Fuller, *Ideas and Integrities*, 213.

60. Reyner Banham, *Age of the Masters: A Personal View of Modern Architecture* (New York: Harper and Row, 1975), 89.

61. In 1954, before the U.S. government used Fuller's domes to sell the American enterprise, Fuller won prizes for two domes that the magazine *Interiors* commissioned for the Trienniale, "How to Print a House, and Why," *Interiors* 113 (May 1954): 18–19; Fuller, *Ideas and Integrities*, 278–81; and David Cort, "Darkness under the Dome," *Nation*, March 1, 1958, 187–88.

62. Clyde Wilson, "Brave Old World," *Inland Architect* 35 (July/August 1991): 72.

63. Baldwin, *Bucky Works*, 119–27.

64. Joseph A. Wilkes, ed., *AIA Encyclopedia of Architecture: Design, Engineering, and Construction*, 5 vols. (New York: Wiley, 1988), 1:547–72. See also Baldwin E. Smith, *The Dome: A Study in the History of Ideas* (Princeton, N.J.: Princeton University Press, 1978).

65. Sharp, "Buckminster Fuller," quote on 20.

66. McHale, "Richard Buckminster Fuller," 313.

67. Bélanger (1744–1818) created the Halle aux Blé, the first iron and glass structure in Western architecture in 1813. It anticipated more famous designs such as Joseph Paxton's Glass Palace. Paxton's work, in turn, inspired other glass projects, many of them domed. See Dora Wiebenson, "The Two Domes of the Halle au Blé in Paris," *Art Bulletin* 54 (June 1973): 262–79; and John Hix, *The Glass House* (Cambridge, Mass.: MIT Press, 1974), chap. 9.

68. Joachim Krausse, "The Miracle of Jena," *World Architecture* 20 (November 1992): 46–53. See also Walter Bauersfeld, *Projection Planetariums and Shell Construction* (London: Institute of Mechanical Engineers, 1957); and Baldwin, *Bucky Works*, 118.

69. For architectural overviews of the dome, see Edward Popko, *Geodesics* (Detroit, Mich.: School of Architecture, University of Detroit, 1968); Shoji Sadao, "Geodesic Domes," in *AIA Encyclopedia of Architecture: Design*, 12:577–85; and Fuller, *Ideas and Integrities*, 216–23.

70. Sieden, *Buckminster Fuller's Universe*, 328–31; Hatch, *Buckminster Fuller*, 204; and F. Robert Naka and William W. Ward, "Distant Early Warning Line Radars: The Quest for Automatic Signal Detection," *Lincoln Laboratory Journal* 12 (2000): 181–204, online at Lincoln Laboratory, Massachusetts Institute of Technology, http://www.ll.mit.edu/news/journal/pdf/vol12_no2/12_2distantearly.pdf (accessed July 13, 2007).

71. McHale, "Richard Buckminster Fuller," 308.

72. Ibid., 315.

73. "Fuller's Initial Concept for the U. S. Pavilion at Expo '67," *Domus* 464 (July 1968): quote on 3; "R. Buckminster Fuller Talks about Transparency," *House Beautiful*, September 1968, 92–94; "Bucky's Biggest Bubble," *Architectural Forum* 124 (June 1966): 74–79; special issue of *Architectural Design* 37 (February 1967); Hix, *Glass House*, 188; and "The Dymaxion American," 50–51.

74. Baldwin, *Bucky Works*, 182–89; Sieden, *Buckminster Fuller's Universe*, 405–13.

75. Hix, *Glass House*, 188.

76. Hans Meyer, "Interview with R. Buckminster Fuller," in Lloyd Kahn, and others, *Domebook 2* (Los Gatos, Calif.: Pacific Domes, 1971), 90–91, quote on 91. For

his Montreal dome, see Sieden, *Buckminster Fuller's Universe*, 360–62; and Baldwin, *Bucky Works*, 166–67.

77. Fuller, *Ideas and Integrities*, quotes on 216, 219. Atomic explosions were on Fuller's mind. He compared the Bikini Island explosion and the flow of energy in nature and suggested the geodesic could withstand nearby atomic bombing; *Ideas and Integrities*, 221–23. Fuller may have also considered Einstein's use of the term "geodesic"; McHale, *R. Buckminster Fuller*, 44n14.

78. Reinhold Martin, "Crystal Balls," *ANY* 17 (1997): 36.

79. Sieden, *Buckminster Fuller's Universe*, 409; and Baldwin, *Bucky Works*, 109.

80. Fuller, *Ideas and Integrities*, quote on 220; R. Buckminster Fuller, "U.S. Patent No. 2–682–235," Box 2, Folder 4, Subseries 1 (U.S. Patents), Series 5 (Fuller Patents), in R. Buckminster Fuller Papers, M1090, Department of Special Collections, Stanford University Green Library, Stanford, California; and Popko, *Geodesics*, 6. See also Fuller, *Inventions*, 127–44.

81. Fuller, *Ideas and Integrities*, quotes on 219, 170.

82. Lester Walker, *American Shelter: An Illustrated Encyclopedia of the American Home* (Woodstock, N.Y.: Overlook Press, 1981), 272.

83. Steve Baer, *Dome Cookbook* (Corrales, N.M.: Lama Foundation, 1968); Lloyd Kahn, and others, *Domebook 1* (Los Gatos, Calif.: Pacific Domes, 1970); and Kahn, *Domebook 2*.

84. Sieden, *Buckminster Fuller's Universe*, 259–63, quote on 259. For Fuller's thinking on the geoscope and his various versions, see R. Buckminster Fuller, *Critical Path* (New York: St. Martin's Press, 1981), chap. 5.

85. For maps as models, see Benedict Anderson, *Imagined Communities: Reflections on the Origin and Spread of Nationalism*, rev. ed. (London: Verso, 1991), 173–74; Sieden, *Buckminster Fuller's Universe*, quote on 127.

86. Quotes from Fuller, *Ideas and Integrities*, 125; R. Buckminster Fuller and Anwar S. Dil, *Humans in Universe* (New York: De Gruyter, 1983), 209; and *Operating Manual for Spaceship Earth*, 52. Fuller's references to "east" and "west" followed older constructions of these spatial paradigms. For the usage of "orient" and the "occident" in geography, see Martin W. Lewis and Karen E. Wigen, *The Myth of Continents: A Critique of Metageography* (Berkeley: University of California Press, 1997), chaps. 2 and 3.

87. Stewart Brand created lapel buttons reading, "Why haven't we seen a photograph of the whole Earth yet?" and mailed them to political and cultural leaders, including Buckminster Fuller. In 1968, *Apollo 8* crews snapped the famous "Earthrise" photos, but these were not complete views of the earth. Stewart Brand, "Why Haven't We Seen the Whole Earth Yet?" in *The Sixties: The Decade Remembered Now, by the People Who Lived It Then*, ed. Lynda Rosen Obst (New York: Random House/Rolling Stone Press, 1977), 168; Neil Maher, "Neil Maher on Shooting the Moon," *Environmental History* 9 (July 2004): 526–31; and Kirk, *Counterculture Green*, 40–41.

88. Fuller, *Critical Path*, 188–92. For Cousins's memories, see his foreword to Sieden, *Buckminster Fuller's Universe*, vii–ix; and "More Talks with the Russians— Part I," *Saturday Review*, September 26, 1964, 30. For the Dartmouth Conference, see James Voorhees, *Dialogue Sustained: The Multi-level Peace Process and the Dartmouth Conference* (Washington, D.C.: United States Institute of Peace, 2002).

89. Sieden, *Buckminster Fuller's Universe*, 344–45; Hatch, *Buckminster Fuller*, 214; and R. Buckminster Fuller and Anwar S. Dil, *Humans in Universe* (New York: De Gruyter, 1983).

90. Fuller, quoted in Tomkins, "Architecture: Umbrella Man," 87.

91. Fuller discusses his World Game in multiple places. See, for example, Buckminster Fuller, *Education Automation: Freeing the Scholar to Return to His Studies* (Carbondale: Southern Illinois University Press, 1962); Fuller, *Critical Path*, chap. 6; and Buckminster Fuller, "World Game Series: Document 1," in Fuller, *The World Game: Integrative Resource Utilization Planning Tool* (Carbondale: Southern Illinois University Press, 1971). See also Baldwin, *Bucky Works*, 192–203, motto quoted on v; and Sieden, *Buckminster Fuller's Universe*, 367–89.

92. Medard Gabel, ed., *Energy, Earth and Everyone: A Global Strategy for Spaceship Earth* (San Francisco: Straight Arrow Books, 1975). Youngblood's series appeared December 19, 1969, through June 19, 1970, in the *Los Angeles Free Press*; reprinted in a special issue of *Earth Times* (June 1970). See also Gene Youngblood, "World Game: The Artist as Ecologist," *Arts/Canada* 27 (August 1970): 42–49.

93. Baldwin, *Bucky Works*, 199.

94. For green architecture, see Gordon Alastair, "True Green: Lessons from 1960s'–70s' Counterculture Architecture," *Architectural Record* 196 (April 2008): 42. Kirk writes a salient explanation of the development of the appropriate technology movement in *Counterculture Green*, especially 26–31 and chap. 3. See also Andrew Kirk, "Appropriating Technology: The Whole Earth Catalog and Counterculture Environmental Politics," *Environmental History* 6 (July 2001): 374–94; and James J. Farrell, *The Spirit of the Sixties: The Making of Postwar Radicalism* (New York: Routledge, 1997), 242–44. For Baldwin, see Kirk, *Counterculture Green*, 61–73, quote on 61.

95. Brand's motto may be found on the first pages of any *Whole Earth Catalog*. "Whole-systems thinking shaped the form and content of the first catalogs," Kirk rightly explained in *Counterculture Green*, "and provided the foundation of all of the *Whole Earth* publications and activities that followed"; Kirk, *Counterculture Green*, 56–57. See also Stewart Brand, "Understanding Whole Systems," *The Last Whole Earth Catalog* (New York: Random House, 1971), 3.

96. Kirk, *Counterculture Green*, quote on 16. Historian Godfrey Hodgson dubbed this the "suburban-industrial complex," noting its influence, even more than Eisenhower's "military-industrial complex," was "the driving force behind the postwar boom," *America in Our Time: From World War II to Nixon—What Happened and Why* (Garden City, N.Y.: Doubleday, 1976), 51, and noted in Rome, *Bulldozer in the Countryside*, 43; Lizabeth Cohen, *A Consumers' Republic: The Politics of Mass Consumption in Postwar America* (New York: Vintage, 2003).

97. Kirk, *Counterculture Green*, 16–17, quote on 17.

98. E. F. Schumacher, *Small Is Beautiful: Economics as If People Mattered* (New York: Harper and Row, 1973).

99. The quote is taken from Timothy Miller, "Roots of Communal Revival 1962–1966," The Farm Web site, http://www.thefarm.org/lifestyle/root2.html (accessed July 17, 2007). See also Timothy Miller, *The 60s Communes: Hippies and Beyond* (Syracuse, N.Y.: Syracuse University Press, 1999); Miller, "Drop City: Historical Notes on the Pioneer Hippie Commune," *Syzygy: Journal of Alternative Religion and Culture* 1 (Winter 1992): 22–23; John Curl, *Memories of Drop City: The First 1960s Hippie*

Commune and the Summer of Love (Lincoln, Neb.: iUniverse Books, 2007), http://www. red-coral.net/DC_Chapter_1.html (accessed June 12, 2008); Simon Sadler, "Drop City Revisited," *Journal of Architectural Education* 59 (February 2006): 5–14; Clark Secrest, "No Right to Be Poor': Colorado's Drop City," *Colorado Heritage*, Winter 1998, 14–21; Felicity D. Scott, "Acid Visions," *Grey Room* 23 (Spring 2006): 22–39, http://magazines. documenta.de/frontend/article.php?IdLanguage=1&NrArticle=1739 (accessed July 31, 2008). For an intriguing part fictional/part nonfictional account, see Drop City resident Peter Rabbit's *Drop City* (New York: Olympia Press, 1971); and Charlotte Trego, "Drop City: New Life for Old Cars," *Architectural Forum* 127 (September 1967): 74. For photos of Drop City domes and the Fuller award, see Clark Richert's Web site, http://www.clarkrichert.com/dropcity (accessed June 10, 2008). For connections between Fuller and Drop City, see "Drop City Revisited," in *Shelter*, ed. Lloyd Kahn (Bolinas, Calif.: Shelter Publications, 1973), 118. For zomes, see Baer, *Dome Cookbook*; and Baer, *Zome Primer* (Albuquerque, N.M.: Zomeworks Corporation, 1970).

100. Clark Richert, as quoted in Christine Macy and Sarah Bonnemaison, eds., *Architecture and Nature: Creating the American Landscape* (New York: Routledge, 2003), 324–25; see 293–46 for the dome, ecological consciousness, and Fuller's "whole world thinking."

101. Doug Dahlin, "Intentional Community"(unpublished paper, Department of Architecture, University of California, Berkeley, n.d. [1971?]), as quoted in Dolores Hayden, *Seven American Utopias: The Architecture of Communitarian Socialism, 1790–1975* (Cambridge, Mass.: MIT Press, 1976), 338; Bill Voyd, "Funk Architecture," in *Shelter and Society*, ed. Paul Oliver (New York: Praeger, 1969), 156–64. See also Hayden, *Seven American Utopias*, 335–36; Banham, *Age of the Masters*, 130. John Curl recalls one of the City's founders explaining the dome to him in *Memories of Drop City*, http://www.red-coral.net/DC_Chapter_1.html (accessed June 12, 2008); Farrell, *Spirit of the Sixties*, 153.

102. Orson Fowler, *The Octagon House: A Home for All* (1853; reprint, New York: Dover, 1973). See also Walter Creese, "Fowler and the Domestic Octagon," *Art Bulletin* 28 (June 1946): 89–102; John H. Martin, "Saints, Sinners and Reformers: The Burned-over District Re-visited," *Crooked Lake Review* 137 (Fall 2005), http://www.crookedlakereview.com/books/saints_sinners/martin12.html (accessed July 10, 2008); Carl F. Schmidt, *The Octagon Fad* (New York: Schmidt, 1958); Mary Mix Foley, *The American House* (New York: Harper and Row, 1980), 159–60; and Hayden, *Seven American Utopias*, 38, 335.

103. Architectural historian Dolores Hayden quotes the Oneida and Hog Farm songs and notes the connection between Fowler, Oneida, Fuller, and counter-culturalists in *Seven American Utopias*, 320–41, quotes on 320 and 340. See also Hugh Romney, "The Hog Farm," *Realist* 86 (November–December 1969): 18. *The Hog Farm Movie* (1970) captured the Yippie presidential candidate's forty-bus caravan road trip to Chicago in 1968.

104. Herbert Muschamp, "Critic's Notebook: When Design Huffed and Puffed, Then Went Pop," *New York Times*, June 18, 1998; Jung Yun Chi and Ruy Marcelo de Oliveira Pauletti, "An Outline of the Evolution of Pneumatic Structures," Faculty of Architecture and Urban Planning and the Polytechnic School of the University of São Paulo, http://www.lmc.ep.usp.br/people/pauletti/Publicacoes_arquivos/ Chi-and-Pauletti.pdf (accessed July 11, 2008).

105. "Earthonauts, USA," *L.A. Architect*, September 1993, 1. See "Domes House LA's Homeless," *Architecture* 83 (January 1994): 95; and also Frances Anderton, "Dome Sweet Dome," *Architecture Review* 193 (November 1993): 66. See the Justiceville Web site at http://www.domevillage.org/JHUSA.html (accessed July 26, 2007) and Dome Village Web site at http://www.domevillage.org/index.html (accessed April 12, 2009).

106. For a description of the dome and an account of the experiment to live within it, see Jane Poynter, *The Human Experiment: Two Years and Twenty Minutes inside Biosphere 2* (New York: Thunder's Mouth Press, 2006). For Fuller's influence on Pearce, see Peter Pearce, *Structure in Nature Is a Strategy for Design* (Cambridge, Mass.: MIT Press, 1978).

107. Buckminster Fuller Institute, http://www.bfi.org/ (accessed July 6, 2007).

108. Henry Adams understood the power of the machine as the initiator of a fatal chain of events. See his essay "The Dynamo and the Virgin," in *The Education of Henry Adams*, ed. Ernest Samuels (Boston: Houghton Mifflin, 1973), 379–90. Mark Twain voiced a similar view in his novel *A Connecticut Yankee in King Arthur's Court* (New York: Charles L. Webster, 1889).

109. Buckminster Fuller, quoted in Aldersey-Williams, "Rise and Fall of Dymaxion Man," 138.

CHAPTER 3

1. Martin Luther King Jr., "An Address before the National Press Club," July 19, 1962, Washington, D.C., reprinted in *A Testament of Hope: The Essential Writings and Speeches of Martin Luther King, Jr.*, ed. James Melvin Washington (San Francisco: HarperSanFrancisco, 1986), 99–105, quote on 105. See also "I have a Dream," Lincoln Memorial, March on Washington, D.C., for Civil Rights, August 28, 1963, reprinted in *Testament of Hope*, 217–20.

2. W. E. B. Du Bois, *The Souls of Black Folks* (1903; reprint, New York: Bantam Books, 1989), xxxi; Martin Luther King Jr., *Where Do We Go from Here: Chaos or Community?* (New York: Harper and Row, 1967), 173.

3. Martin Luther King Jr., "Our Struggle," *Liberation* 1 (April 1956): 3–6, reprinted in *Testament of Hope*, 75–81, quote on 81.

4. Martin Luther King Jr., "Facing the Challenge of a New Age," *Phylon* 28 (April 1957): 24–34, quote on 30, reprinted in *Testament of Hope*, 135–44, quote on 140. King delivered this address in December 1956 at the First Annual Institute on Non-violence and Social Change in Montgomery, Alabama. Though not generally associated with the communitarian movement of the 1980s and 1990s in America, King's vision parallels some aspects of later theorists' emphasis on communal values; see Amitai Etzioni, *The Spirit of Community: The Reinvention of American Society* (New York: Touchstone, 1993); and Etzioni, ed., *New Communitarian Thinking: Persons, Virtues, Institutions and Communities* (Charlottesville: University of Virginia Press, 1995).

5. King repeatedly used and refined phrases and examples; for this holistic "single garment," which I point to at various points in this chapter, see, for example, Martin Luther King Jr., "The American Dream," commencement address at Lincoln University, June 6, 1961, Pennsylvania, reprinted in *The Negro History Bulletin* 31

(May 1968): 10–15, quote on 12; and Martin Luther King Jr., "The Ethical Demands for Integration," *Religion and Labor* (May 1963): 1, 3–4, 7–8, reprinted in *Testament of Hope*, 117–25, quote on 122.

6. Taylor Branch, *Parting the Waters: America in the King Years, 1954–63* (New York: Simon and Schuster, 1988); Branch, *Pillar of Fire: America in the King Years, 1963–65* (New York: Simon and Schuster, 1998); Branch, *At Canaan's Edge: America in the King Years, 1965–68* (New York: Simon and Schuster, 2006); David Garrow, *Bearing the Cross: Martin Luther King, Jr. and the Southern Christian Leadership Conference* (New York: Morrow, 1986); Coretta Scott King, *My Life with Martin Luther King, Jr.* (New York: Holt, Rinehart and Winston, 1969); Stephen B. Oates, *Let the Trumpet Sound: The Life of Martin Luther King, Jr.* (New York: Harper and Row, 1982). For an overview of studies on King, see Washington's introduction to *Testament of Hope*, xx–xxii.

7. Certainly, Martin Luther King Jr. was not the sole catalyst for the civil rights movement. He was one figure, flawed yet mighty, who played a significant role in civil rights events during the 1950s and 1960s. This was a movement that cannot be explained with a single focus or on a single group of people; for the historiography, see Steven F. Lawson, "Freedom Then, Freedom Now: The Historiography of the Civil Rights Movement," *American Historical Review* 96 (April 1991): 456–71.

8. Keith D. Miller, *Voice of Deliverance: The Language of Martin Luther King, Jr. and Its Sources* (New York: Free Press, 1992). Branch, in his biographical trilogy of King, especially tells the tales of the inner workings of King's circle, including the help that others gave in writing speeches. I see none of King's borrowings and collaborations as detracting anything from King's worldview; rather, this suggests further evidence that King's holistic vision and understandings resonated among many.

9. Martin Luther King Jr., "An Autobiography of Religious Development," November 22, 1950, in *The Papers of Martin Luther King, Jr.*, vol. 1, *Called to Serve: January 1929–June 1951*, ed. Clayborne Carson, Ralph E. Luker, and Penny A. Russell (Berkeley: University of California Press, 1992), 360–61; and *The Autobiography of Martin Luther King, Jr.*, ed. Clayborne Carson (New York: Intellectual Properties Management in Association with Warner Books, 1998), 1–5.

10. The separatist voice of Black Panther Emory Douglas, a visual artist for propaganda for the Panthers, serves as a contrast. Born in Michigan, Douglas moved to San Francisco with his mother in 1951. Burglary convictions placed him in juvenile homes and detention centers. Eventually, he expressed his anger through his art and by joining the Panther Party. For his story, see Erika Doss, "Imaging the Panthers: Representing Black Power and Masculinity, 1960s–1990s," *Prospects: An Annual of American Culture* 23 (1998): 483–516.

11. Benjamin E. Mays, *The Negro's God as Reflected in His Literature* (New York: Russell and Russell, 1938), 23–24. Clayborne Carson uses Mays's quote and then categorizes King in *The Papers of Martin Luther King, Jr.*, vol. 2, *Rediscovering Precious Values, July 1951–November 1955*, ed. Clayborne Carson, Ralph E. Luker, Penny A. Russell, and Peter Holloran (Berkeley: University of California Press, 1994), 2.

12. Carson, "Introduction," *Papers of Martin Luther King*, 1:1–3, quotes on 1.

13. Ibid., 1:4–18.

14. Martin Luther King Sr., "Moderator's Annual Address, Atlanta Missionary Baptist Association," October 17, 1940, Christine King Farris Collection ([CKFC], in private hands), as quoted in *Papers of Martin Luther King*, 2:2.

15. Carson, "Introduction," *Papers of Martin Luther King*, 1:29–30. For the crucial involvement of women in the creation and sustenance of the black church as a powerful political institution, see Evelyn Brooks Higginbotham, *Righteous Discontent: The Women's Movement in the Black Baptist Church, 1880–1920* (Cambridge, Mass.: Harvard University Press, 1993).

16. For some of Coretta Scott's political involvement, see Clayborne Carson, "Introduction," in *The Papers of Martin Luther King, Jr.*, vol. 3, *Birth of a New Age: December 1955–December 1956*, ed. Clayborne Carson, Stewart Burns, Susan Carson, Dana Powell, and Peter Holloran (Berkeley: University of California Press, 1997), 13.

17. For the importance of King's academic education, see Kenneth L. Smith and Ira G. Zepp Jr., *Search for the Beloved Community: The Thinking of Martin Luther King, Jr.* (Valley Forge, Pa.: Judson Press, 1974); John J. Ansbro, *Martin Luther King, Jr.: The Making of a Mind* (Maryknoll, N.Y.: Orbis Books, 1982); Ira G. Zepp Jr., *The Social Vision of Martin Luther King, Jr.* (Brooklyn: Carlson, 1989); Carson, "Introduction," *Papers of Martin Luther King*, quote on 2:1; James H. Cone, "Martin Luther King, Jr., Black Theology-Black Church," *Theology Today* 15 (January 1984): 409–20, quotes on 410, 412. Many works, King scholar Lewis V. Baldwin complained, take an elitist approach, "which assumes that the black church and the larger black community are not healthy and vital contexts for the origin of intellectual ideas regarding theology and social change." These accounts have erred by separating King's intellectual development from his social and black religious roots. See Baldwin's quote in Jimmie Lewis Franklin's "Review Essay: Autobiography, the Burden of Friendship, and Truth," in *Georgia Historical Quarterly* 74 (Spring 1990): 84–98, quote on 94. For Baldwin's analysis of the influence of the black church on King's development, see Lewis V. Baldwin, *There Is a Balm in Gilead: The Cultural Roots of Martin Luther King, Jr.* (Minneapolis, Minn.: Fortress Press, 1991); and Baldwin *To Make the Wounded Whole: The Cultural Legacy of Martin Luther King, Jr.* (Minneapolis, Minn.: Fortress Press, 1992). Miller, in his careful analysis of King's sources in *Voice of Deliverance*, demonstrates King's debt to black folk Christianity and popular white preachers whose sermons could be heard across the country on radio and read in multiple publications.

18. King, "Autobiography of Religious Development," 361–63. King skipped the ninth and twelfth grades. Morehouse College, at low enrollment in 1944 because of the war draft, accepted promising juniors at this time; Carson, "Introduction," *Papers of Martin Luther King*, 1:35–36.

19. For some of King's interpretation of the Bible, God, and Christ at this point, see his college papers, "What Experiences of Christians Living in the Early Christian Century Led to the Christian Doctrines of the Divine Sonship of Jesus, the Virgin Birth, and the Bodily Resurrection"; "The Sources of Fundamentalism and Liberalism Considered Historically and Psychologically"; "Six Talks in Outline"; "How to Use the Bible in Modern Theological Construction," and "The Humanity and Divinity of Jesus," in *Papers of Martin Luther King*, 1:225–62.

20. Cornel West, "Prophetic Christian as Organic Intellectual: Martin Luther King, Jr.," in Cornel West, *The Cornel West Reader* (New York: Basic Civitas Books,

1999), 429. Lewis Baldwin points out that while King differed somewhat from his father theologically, they were harmonious in their ethical beliefs in "The Minister as Preacher, Pastor, and Prophet: The Thinking of Martin Luther King, Jr.," *American Baptist Quarterly* 7 (1988): 79–97. For more on King's views of science, see Martin Luther King Jr., *The Strength to Love* (New York: Harper and Row, 1963), 493.

21. Ansbro, *Making of a Mind*; Stephen B. Oates, "The Intellectual Odyssey of Martin Luther King," *Massachusetts Review* 22 (1981): 301–20; John W. Rathbun, "Martin Luther King: The Theology of Social Action," *American Quarterly* 20 (1968): 38–53; Smith and Zepp, *Search for the Beloved Community*; Warren E. Steinkraus, "Martin Luther King's Personalism and Non-violence," *Journal of the History of Ideas* 34 (1973): 97–111; and Zepp, *Social Vision of Martin Luther King, Jr.*

22. Martin Luther King Jr., *Stride toward Freedom: The Montgomery Story* (New York: Harper, 1958), 91.

23. Walter Rauschenbusch, *Christianity and the Social Crisis* (New York: Macmillan, 1907); for the Social Gospel, see Susan Curtis, *A Consuming Faith: The Social Gospel and Modern American Culture* (Baltimore: Johns Hopkins University Press, 1991); and Donald K. Gorrell, *The Age of Social Responsibility: The Social Gospel in the Progressive Era, 1900–1920* (Macon, Ga.: Mercer University Press, 1988).

24. King, *Autobiography*, 18. See also King, *Stride toward Freedom*, 91; and Martin Luther King Jr., "Pilgrimage to Nonviolence," *Christian Century* 77 (April 13, 1960): 440.

25. For King's views on Marxism, see King, *Autobiography*, 19–22; King, *Stride toward Freedom*, 92–95; and King, "Examination Answers, History of Recent Philosophy," in *Papers of Martin Luther King*, 2:153–54. For King's condemnation of the white church for not living up to his social gospel, see "Playboy Interview: Martin Luther King, Jr.," *Playboy*, January 1965, 117 ff., reprinted in *Testament of Hope*, 340–77, quotes on 345.

26. King, *Stride toward Freedom*, 19–20; King, *Autobiography*, 8, 12; King, "Pilgrimage to Nonviolence," 440; and Carson, "Introduction," *Papers of Martin Luther King*, 1:33.

27. For the beginnings of this paradox of slavery and freedom, see Edmund S. Morgan, *American Slavery, American Freedom: The Ordeal of Colonial Virginia* (New York: Norton, 1975).

28. Gunnar Myrdal, *An American Dilemma: The Negro Problem and Modern Democracy* (New York: Harper and Row, 1944).

29. Martin Luther King Jr., "Nonviolence: The Only Road to Freedom," *Ebony*, October 1966, 27–30; and King Jr., "A Gift of Love," *McCall's*, December 1966, 146–47, reprinted in *Testament of Hope*, quotes on 57 and 62.

30. King, "Ethical Demands for Integration," 121.

31. King, *Stride toward Freedom*, 97–99, quote on 99.

32. Martin Luther King Jr., "How Modern Christians Should Think of Man," a paper written in 1949 for one of George Davis's classes, *Papers of Martin Luther King* 2:273–79, quotes on 274–75. See also Carson, "Introduction," *Papers of Martin Luther King*, 1:52.

33. King, *Stride toward Freedom*, 100; King, *Autobiography*, 31–32. See Ansbro, *Making of a Mind*, chap. 3, for a discussion of King's personalism.

34. King, *Stride toward Freedom*, 100. Walt Whitman used the term first in "Personalism," *Galaxy* (May 1868). For a discussion of Whitman's link with personalism, see William A. Huggard, "Whitman's Poem of Personalism," *Personalist* 28 (Summer 1947): 273–78. See Ralph Tyler Flewelling, "Studies in American Personalism," *Personalist* 31 (Summer 1950): 229. For an overview of personalism, see also Ralph Tyler Flewelling, "This Thing Called Personalism," *Personalist* 28 (Summer 1947), 229–36.

35. For an excellent discussion of personalism in the 1960s, see James J. Farrell, *The Spirit of the Sixties: The Making of Postwar Radicalism* (New York: Routledge, 1997).

36. King, *Where Do We Go from Here*, 186. See also King, *Stride toward Freedom*, 93; and King, "Facing the Challenge of a New Age," 26, for his assertions that men must not be treated as ends or depersonalized cogs in a system.

37. For the Boston personalists, see especially Edgar S. Brightman, "Personalism," in *A History of Philosophical Systems*, ed. Vergilius Ferm (New York: Philosophical Library, 1950), 340–52; Borden Parker Bowne, *Personalism* (1908; reprint, Norwood, Mass.: Plimpton Press, 1936); L. Harold DeWolf, "Personalism in the History of Western Philosophy," *Philosophical Forum* 12 (1954): 29–51; Paul Deats and Carol Robb, eds., *The Boston Personalist Tradition in Philosophy, Social Ethics, and Theology* (Macon, Ga.: Mercer University Press, 1986); and Albert C. Knudson, *The Philosophy of Personalism: A Study in the Metaphysics of Religion* (1927; reprint, New York: Abingdon Press, 1969).

38. Borden Parker Bowne, "The Failure of Impersonalism," in *The Development of American Philosophy*, ed. Walter G. Muelder and Lawrence Sears (Boston: Houghton Mifflin, 1940), 278–90. See also Borden Parker Bowne, *Personalism* (1908; reprint, Norwood, Mass.: Plimpton Press, 1936); and Donald H. Smith, "An Exegesis of Martin Luther King, Jr.'s Social Philosophy," *Phylon* 31 (1970): 96–97.

39. Edgar S. Brightman, "A Personalistic Philosophy of History," *Journal of Bible and Religion* 18 (January 1950): 3.

40. Albert Knudson, *The Doctrine of God* (New York: Abingdon Press, 1930), 305–6.

41. Martin Luther King Jr., "A Comparison of the Conceptions of God in the Thinking of Paul Tillich and Henry Nelson Wieman" (Ph.D. diss., Boston University, 1955), in *Papers of Martin Luther King* 2:512–13. King used the Knudson passage freely in his dissertation, and Carson footnotes the passage in *Papers of Martin Luther King*, 2:512n14. In the same footnote, Carson points to a similar passage in King, *Strength to Love*, 141–42, where King summarizes his steady belief in a "living" God but thought that the idea was no longer merely a metaphysical category. Rather, it "has been validated in the experiences of everyday life." On King's plagiarism, see Carson, "Introduction," *Papers of Martin Luther King*, 2:6; Martin Luther King, Jr., Papers Project, "The Student Papers of Martin Luther King, Jr.: A Summary Statement on Research," *Journal of American History* 78 (June 1991): 23–31; and Clayborne Carson, Peter Holloran, Ralph E. Luker, and Penny A. Russell, "Martin Luther King, Jr., as Scholar: A Reexamination of His Theological Writings," *Journal of American History* 78 (June 1991): 93–105. Theodore Pappas was one of the first to expose King's plagiarism in *Plagiarism and the Culture War: The Writings of Martin Luther King, Jr., and Other Prominent Americans* (Tampa, Fla.: Hallberg, 1998). It should be noted that

while King plagiarized significant sections of his dissertation, his subsequent writings and actions confirm that he held firmly to the views that God was personal; he was, as Miller asserts, "sincere." Miller also notes that King's borrowing of sermons from black and white pastors was not limited to him; it was common practice, frequently justified by the "assumption that Christian truth is repeated and repeatable"; *Voice of Deliverance*, especially 125–28, quotes on 9 and 126.

42. Martin Luther King Jr., "Examination Answers, Christian Theology for Today," in *Papers of Martin Luther King*, 1:290.

43. Henry Nelson Wieman, "Theocentric Religion," in *Contemporary American Theology: Theological Biographies*, ed. Vergilius Ferm (New York: Round Table Press, 1932), 346, as quoted in *Papers of Martin Luther King*, 2:24.

44. King, "Comparison of the Conceptions of God in the Thinking of Tillich and Wieman," in *Papers of Martin Luther King*, 2:511.

45. King, "Examination Answers, Christian Theology for Today," in *Papers of Martin Luther King* 1:290–94.

46. For King's evaluation of Tillich's and Wieman's views on a personal God, see "Comparisons of the Conceptions of God in the Thinking of Tillich and Wieman," in *Papers of Martin Luther King*, 2:507–14, quotes on 2: 511–12. For King's summation of Tillich's and Wieman's dispute with the idea of a personal God, see *Papers of Martin Luther King*, 2:445–47, 492–95. See also Ansbro, *Making of a Mind*, 60–63.

47. Carson argues this as well in his "Introduction," *Papers of Martin Luther King*, 2:25–26. For a comparison of the theological views of King to Tillich, Barth, and James Cone, see Noel Leo Erskine, *King among the Theologians* (Cleveland, Ohio: Pilgrim Press, 1994). Others have affirmed that personalism was akin to African American faith; Ansbro, *Making of a Mind*, 76–77; and Farrell, *Spirit of the Sixties*, 84–86. Miller, while acknowledging personalism's influence, argues that the balancing effect of black religion's "struggle against oppression" was King's basic stance; *Voice of Deliverance*, 62–63.

48. West, "Prophetic Christian as Organic Intellectual," 427.

49. King, *My Life with Martin Luther King, Jr.*, 92.

50. King, *Strength to Love*, 172.

51. This story was told by King on numerous occasions; see King, *Autobiography*, 77–78; King, *Stride toward Freedom*, 134–35; and King, *Strength to Love*, 106–7. For David J. Garrow's and James Cone's discussions of this pivotal moment in King's life, see Garrow, "Martin Luther King, Jr., and the Spirit of Leadership," *Journal of American History* 74 (September 1987): 441–42; Garrow, "Martin Luther King, Jr.: Bearing the Cross of Leadership," *Peace and Change* 12 (Spring 1987): 1–12; and Cone, "Martin Luther King: The Source for His Courage to Face Death," *Concilium* 183 (March 1983): 74–79.

52. King, "Pilgrimage to Nonviolence," 441; and King, *Stride toward Freedom*, 106.

53. Keith Miller notes King's use of the kitchen experience in King's sermons; *Voice of Deliverance*, 137–39.

54. For DeWolf's notions of human nature and the connection between King and DeWolf and other personalists, see Ansbro, *Making of a Mind*, 18–22.

55. L. Harold DeWolf, *A Theology of the Living Church*, rev. ed. (New York: Harper and Row, 1960), 201–3, as quoted in Ansbro, *Making of a Mind*, 20. Biblical texts cited are Genesis 1:27, 31; Psalm 82:6; 1 Corinthians 11:7; and James 3:9.

56. King, "Ethical Demands for Integration," 119.

57. Orlando Patterson, *Slavery and Social Death: A Comparative Study* (Cambridge, Mass.: Harvard University Press, 1982).

58. See West, "Prophetic Christian as Organic Intellectual," 428; and James H. Cone, "Black Theology in American Religion," *Journal of the American Academy of Religion* 53 (Dec. 1985): 755–71.

59. For Brightman's quote and definition of personalism, see Brightman, "A Personalistic Philosophy of History," 3; Bowne, "The Failure of Impersonalism," quote on 222.

60. Warren Steinkraus shows that, prior to King, personalism had not been a social force. Bowne's personalism leaned toward the socially conservative and individualistic. King united personalism with nonviolent action and gave it social impetus; see "Martin Luther King's Personalism and Non-Violence." Still, that does not mean his teachers did not hope for an ideal community. Davis claimed that "God intends human life to achieve solidarity," and he called for agape love and self-sacrifice to usher in a "new world of cooperation and brotherhood" (King borrowed these words later). Brightman and DeWolf, at Boston University, held the same high ambition. Ansbro writes that the personalists believed that the "purpose of altruism is to create a brotherhood in which all individuals may preserve their dignity, realize their rational potential, and fulfill their destiny"; *Making of a Mind,* 17, 24–25.

61. King, "Ethical Demands for Integration," 122.

62. Ibid., 119; Ansbro, *Making of a Mind,* 22.

63. King, "Nonviolence: The Only Road to Freedom," 61; and Martin Luther King Jr., "Love, Law, and Civil Disobedience," *New South,* 16 December 12, 1961, 3–11, reprinted in *Testament of Hope,* 43–53, quote on 51.

64. Martin Luther King Jr., "A Christmas Sermon on Peace," in Martin Luther King, Jr., *The Trumpet of Conscience* (New York: Harper and Row, 1967), reprinted in *Testament of Hope,* 253–58, quote on 255.

65. Friend Sybil Haydel Morial recalled sermons in which King praised women for their nurturing side; see her statement in *Papers of Martin Luther King,* 2:11.

66. This message is ongoing in his writings. See, for example, "Our Struggle," 75–76.

67. See Erskine, *King among the Theologians,* for an overview of womanist theology and the hopes of building a beloved community. See also Jacqueline Grant, ed., *Perspectives on Womanist Theology* (Atlanta, Ga.: ITC Press, 1995); and Katie G. Cannon, *Black Womanist Ethics* (Atlanta, Ga.: Scholars Press, 1988).

68. For King's blending of black and white traditions, see especially Miller, *Voice of Deliverance,* especially chap. 6; Juanita Abernathy, as quoted in Miller, *Voice of Deliverance,* 11; Ella Baker, quoted in Garrow, *Bearing the Cross,* 625.

69. Claudette Colvin quote in Stewart Burns, ed., *Daybreak of Freedom: The Montgomery Bus Boycott* (Chapel Hill: University of North Carolina Press, 1997), 5. For the bus boycott, also see King, *Stride toward Freedom*; Branch, *Parting the Waters,* 128–96; and *Papers of Martin Luther King,* vols. 2 and 3.

70. King, *Autobiography,* 23; and King, *Stride toward Freedom,* 96.

71. See a short summary of Rustin's pacifist actions in Farrell, *Spirit of the Sixties,* 90–91.

72. Burns, *Daybreak of Freedom*, 20–31; see also Farrell, *Spirit of the Sixties*, 88–92. Clare Wofford and Harris Wofford, *India Afire* (New York: J. Day, 1951). Wofford worked on civil rights in the Kennedy administration and with Sargent Shriver on the Peace Corps. He and Shriver admired the works of Teilhard de Chardin; see Woodstock Forum with James Salmon, S.J., Nicole Schmitz-Moormann, Philip Hefner, and Harris Wofford (April 11, 2005), "Teilhard de Chardin and His Relevance for Today," *Woodstock Report* 82 (June 2005), and at Georgetown University, http://woodstock.georgetown.edu/resources/articles/Teilhard-de-Chardin-His-Relevance-for-Today.html (accessed June 2, 2008).

73. King, as quoted in Burns, *Daybreak of Freedom*, 15.

74. Burns, *Daybreak of Freedom*, 4.

75. Craig Werner, *A Change Is Gonna Come: Music, Race, and the Soul of America* (New York: Plume, 1999), 106–7.

76. In a plea bargain, segregationist James Earl Ray confessed to the murder and was convicted and sentenced to ninety-nine years in prison. He recanted and maintained his innocence until his death in 1998. For his account, see James Earl Ray, *Who Killed Martin Luther King, Jr.? The True Story by the Alleged Assassin*, 2nd ed. (New York: Marlowe, 1997). See also Gerald L. Posner, *Killing the Dream: James Earl Ray and the Assassination of Martin Luther King, Jr.* (New York: Random House, 1998).

77. King, "I See the Promised Land," Mason Temple Sermon, Memphis, Tennessee, April 3, 1968, reprinted in *Testament of Hope*, 279–86, quote on 286.

78. King, "Facing the Challenge of a New Age," 27. King believed that many twentieth-century events were sparking new hope and a new sense of "somebodiness" in blacks. Personalism, to him, was the grounding for the self-respect. He addressed the First Annual Institute on Non-Violence and Social Change in Montgomery in December 1956, then printed these words in *Phylon* 28 (April 1957): 24–34, reprinted in *Testament of Hope*, 135–44 and *Papers of Martin Luther King, Jr.* 4: 73–89; for "somebodiness," see 77.

79. King, "Facing the Challenge of a New Age," 27.

80. King, "Ethical Demands for Integration," 119; see also *Where Do We Go from Here*, 43.

81. Martin Luther King Jr., "Remaining Awake through a Great Revolution," sermon delivered on March 31, 1968, at the National Cathedral, Washington, D.C., and reprinted in *Testament of Hope*, 268–78, quote on 270.

82. King, "Ethical Demands for Integration," 119.

83. King, *Stride toward Freedom*, 106; see also King, "An Experiment in Love," *Jubilee* (September 1958): 13–16, reprinted in *Testament of Hope*, 16–20.

84. King, "Ethical Demands for Integration," 122.

85. Martin Luther King Jr., "Letter from Birmingham City Jail," April 16, 1963, Birmingham, Alabama, reprinted in *Testament of Hope*, 289–302, quote on 290.

86. King, "Remaining Awake through a Great Revolution," 269; King, "Facing the Challenge of a New Age," 28; and King, "American Dream," 12.

87. King, *Where Do We Go from Here*, 52–53.

88. King, "An Experiment in Love," 20.

89. Lerone Bennett claimed, "King's genius was not in the application of Gandhism to the Negro struggle but in the transmuting of Gandhism by grafting it onto the only thing that could give it relevance and force in the Negro community,

the Negro religious community." American pacifists drew on Gandhi's work and appropriated it to their own situations; see Farrell, *Spirit of the Sixties*, 89–90, quote on 89. Miller shows King's reliance on other Americans' uses of Gandhi's philosophy, such as Harry Wofford, Harry Fosdick, and William Stuart Nelson; *Voice of Deliverance*, 50–55, 88–98.

90. King, "An Experiment in Love," 19–20. King relied on Swedish theologian Anders Nygren for his understanding of agape love. This love, Nygren contended, was the most creative power of all; see *Testament of Hope*, 16.

91. Martin Luther King Jr., "Nobel Peace Prize Acceptance Speech 1964," *Les Prix Nobel.* Ed. Göran Liljestrand, [Nobel Foundation], Stockholm, 1965, Nobelprize.org, http://nobelprize.org/nobel_prizes/peace/laureates/1964/king-acceptance.html (accessed December 29, 2009).

92. King, *Autobiography*, 249.

93. King, "Remaining Awake through a Great Revolution," 272–73.

94. King, "An Address before the National Press Club," 105.

95. King, "Nonviolence: The Only Road to Freedom," 58.

96. King, "I Have a Dream," 217.

97. See, for example, King's explanation of the problems in Los Angeles and other cities in a television interview, *Face to Face*, July 28, 1967, in *Testament of Hope*, 396–97.

98. Falwell quote in *Testament of Hope*, xiv–xv. The full text may be found in "Ministers and Marches," in Perry Deane Young, *God's Bullies: Native Reflections on Preachers and Politics* (New York: Holt, Rinehart and Winston, 1982), 310.

99. For a summation of King's response to Vietnam, see "The Vietnam War (1961–1975)," Martin Luther King Papers Project, http://www.stanford.edu/group/King/about_king/encyclopedia/vietnam.htm (accessed November 12, 2007); and Henry E. Darby and Margaret N. Rowley, "King on Vietnam and Beyond," *Phylon* 47 (1986): 43–50.

100. King, "Pilgrimage to Nonviolence," 441.

101. Farrell, *Spirit of the Sixties*, 95.

102. Amanda Porterfield, *The Transformation of American Religion: The Story of a Late-Twentieth-Century Awakening* (New York: Oxford University Press, 2001), 125–26.

103. King, *Trumpet of Conscience*, 21. King repeats his opposition to the war in numerous public speeches and books; see another, Martin Luther King Jr., "The Drum Major Instinct," reprinted in *Testament of Hope*, 259–67, quote on 265.

104. King, "A Christmas Sermon on Peace," 254.

105. King frequently talked about the destiny of the United States being tied to the destiny of India; see, for example, "Remaining Awake through a Great Revolution," 272; and "A Christmas Sermon on Peace," 254. For his trip to India, see King, *Autobiography*, chap. 13; and Branch, *Parting the Waters*, 250–55.

106. King, "A Christmas Sermon on Peace," 255.

107. King, *Trumpet of Conscience*, 62, 64.

108. King, Jr., "Facing the Challenge of a New Age," 28.

109. Martin Luther King, Jr., "A Time to Break Silence," *Freedomways* 7 (Spring 1967): 103–17, reprinted in *Testament of Hope*, 231–44, quote on 234.

110. King, *Where Do We Go from Here,* 167–74, quote on 169. Jamaican historian C. L. R. James connected events in Montgomery to Ghana's independence movement

as early as March 1957 in a letter to Martin and Jessie Glaberman, as noted in Burns, *Daybreak of Freedom*, 3, 33n4.

111. King, "Facing the Challenge of a New Age," 26.

112. King, "Remaining Awake through a Great Revolution," 269.

113. King, "Nobel Peace Prize Acceptance Speech."

114. King, *Where Do We Go from Here*, 169.

115. King, *Strength to Love*, 493.

116. King, "An Address before the National Press Club," 103.

117. March on Washington leaders planned the event to evoke a sense of *communitas* and political commitment; see Scott A. Sandage, "A Marble House Divided: The Lincoln Memorial, the Civil Rights Movement, and the Politics of Memory, 1939–1963," *Journal of American History* 80 (June 1993): 153–67, quote on 157. For music in the civil rights movement, see Werner, *A Change Is Gonna Come*, especially xi–64.

118. Kenneth Rexroth, "The Dragon and the Unicorn," in Kenneth Rexroth, *The Collected Longer Poems* (New York: New Directions, 1968), 241. Farrell discusses the personalistic impulse within the Beats in *Spirit of the Sixties*, chap. 3; for his discussion of these lines from Rexroth, see p. 58.

119. Barbara Deming, *Prisons That Could Not Hold* (San Francisco: Spinsters Ink, 1985); Farrell, *Spirit of the Sixties*, 127–28.

120. John F. Kennedy, "Inaugural Address," Washington, D.C., January 20, 1961, Papers of John F. Kennedy: President's Office Files, January 20, 1961–November 22, 1963, John F. Kennedy Library; National Archives and Records Administration, John F. Kennedy Presidential Library and Museum Historical Resources, http://www.jfklibrary.org/Historical+Resources/Archives/Reference+Desk/Speeches/JFK/003POF03Inaugural01201961.htm (accessed January 22, 2009).

121. King, *Stride toward Freedom*, 107.

CHAPTER 4

1. For Teilhard's visit to America in 1937, see Ursula King, *Spirit of Fire: The Life and Vision of Teilhard de Chardin* (New York: Orbis, 1996), 163–64; Mary Lukas and Ellen Lukas, *Teilhard* (Garden City, N.Y.: Doubleday, 1977), 145–46; Robert Speaight, *The Life of Teilhard de Chardin* (New York: Harper and Row, 1967), 230; and Claude Cuénot, *Teilhard de Chardin: A Biographical Study*, trans. Vincent Colimore, ed. René Hague (Baltimore: Helicon Press, 1965), 164–65. Teilhard's papers have been archived in Paris at the Foundation of Teilhard de Chardin; they have been collected and published in *Oeuvres de Teilhard de Chardin*, ed. Nicole Schmitz-Moormann and Karl Schmitz-Moormann (Paris: Editions du Seuil, 1955–76); and *Pierre Teilhard de Chardin, L'Oeuvre Scientifique*, ed. Nicole Schmitz-Moormann and Karl Schmitz-Moormann (Freiburg im Breisgau: Walter-Verlag Olten, 1971). Most of Teilhard's essays, twenty-plus personal journals, and correspondence (including more than 8,000 letters) have been translated into English and published. Georgetown University has a vast collection of books by and on Teilhard, and the Lauinger Library Special Collections contains the papers of many who corresponded with the priest, as well as some papers, tapes, and conference videos of the American Teilhard Association.

2. For a timeline of Teilhard's life, see the American Teilhard Association, http://www.teilharddechardin.org/timeline.html (accessed December 3, 2008), and the British Teilhard Association, http://www.teilhard.org.uk/frameset.asp (accessed December 3, 2008). For a sample of his writings, see Pierre Teilhard de Chardin, *Building the Earth*, trans. Noel Lindsay and Norman Denny (London: Chaplin, 1965); *Christianity and Evolution*, trans. René Hague (New York: Harcourt Brace Jovanovich, 1971); *Divine Milieu*, trans. Bernard Wall (New York: Harper and Row, 1965); *The Future of Man*, trans. Norman Denny (New York: Harper and Row, 1964); *Heart of Matter*, trans. René Hague (New York: Harcourt Brace Jovanovich), 1978; *Hymn of the Universe*, trans. Gerald Vann (New York: Harper and Row, 1969); *The Phenomenon of Man*, trans. Bernard Wall (New York: Harper and Row, 1959); *Science and Christ*, trans. René Hague (New York: Harper and Row, 1968); and *Toward the Future*, trans. René Hague (New York: Harcourt Brace Jovanovich, 1975). For a later translation of *Phenomenon of Man*, see *The Human Phenomenon*, trans. Sarah Appleton-Weber (Portland, Ore.: Sussex Academic Press, 1999). For the difference in translation between the titles and in the understanding of the book, see Appleton-Weber's introduction, xviii. I refer in the text to the more common title, *The Phenomenon of Man*, but because the translation in *The Human Phenomenon* is often clearer, I more often use it for quoting.

3. Winifred McCulloch reports the number in *A Short History of the American Teilhard Association* (Chambersburg, Pa.: American Teilhard Association, 1979), 3, American Teilhard Association, http://www.teilharddechardin.org/history.html (accessed September 3, 2008).

4. "Orthogenesis" is the paleontological term for direction or cause in the evolutionary process. For a discussion of the differences between Simpson and Teilhard—differences between the neo-Darwinian modern synthesis and Teilhardian theories—see Lodovico Galleni, "Relationships between Scientific Analysis and the World View of Pierre Teilhard de Chardin," *Zygon* 27 (June 1992): 153–66, especially 160–62. See also Philip Hefner, *The Promise of Teilhard: The Meaning of the Twentieth Century in Christian Perspective* (Philadelphia: Lippincott, 1970), 47–49.

5. Julian Huxley, "Introduction," to Pierre Teilhard de Chardin, in *Phenomenon of Man*, 11, 27–28. See also Huxley, *Evolution: The Modern Synthesis* (London: Allen and Unwin, 1942). Huxley met Teilhard in 1946. He saw the paleontologist not only as a friend and partner in UNESCO but as "a partner in the intellectual and spiritual adventure." Though Huxley "approached the problem of human destiny...from that of an agnostic and zoologist," he found the two "had come to astonishingly similar conclusions." They looked at "human destiny (that is to say, man, his cosmic background and home, and the relation between them) as a phenomenon, not as a metaphysical, an ethical, or theological problem. In such an approach, man is seen not as a creation alien or separate from nature, but as a part (and a very essential part) of the phenomenon of evolution. And mind and spirit appear not as an irrelevant epiphenomenon nor as a supernatural injection, but as highly important natural phenomena"; Huxley as quoted in Cuénot, *Teilhard de Chardin*, 303.

6. See, for example, Theodosius Dobzhansky, "Teilhard de Chardin and the Orientation of Evolution: A Critical Essay," *Zygon* 3 (September 1976): 242–58. See also the afterword to Pierre Teilhard de Chardin, *Letters to Two Friends: 1926–1952* (New York: New American Library, 1967), 221–27; Wernher von Braun, as quoted by

James Gilbert in *Redeeming Culture: American Religion in an Age of Science* (Chicago: University of Chicago Press, 1997), 250. For an overview of von Braun's strange career, see pp. 240–50.

7. As quoted in McCulloch, *Short History of the American Teilhard Association*, 18.

8. A review of the Society of Jesus archives in 1969 revealed that "never in the history of the Society has so much been written about one of its sons." Between 1963 and 1970, a total of 1,188 indexed articles and books appeared on Teilhard (out of 4,591 on Jesuits total during the same period); Hefner, *Promise of Teilhard*, 14. For a more recent example of work that shows the influence of Teilhard's synthesis, see Karl Schmitz-Moormann, *Theology of Creation in an Evolutionary World* (Cleveland, Ohio: Pilgrim Press, 1997).

9. Teilhard, *Heart of Matter*, 96–97. He wrote this autobiographical work in 1950.

10. Ibid., 18.

11. National and local laws mandated the separation of church and state in France at the turn of the century. Some of these laws forbade the commingling of church and state activities in education, prompting the Jesuit move to the Isle of Jersey; Lukas and Lukas, *Teilhard*, 26–27.

12. Ursula King writes that Teilhard's *Sur la Structure de l'Ile de Jersey* (1920) remains academically valid, and that Jersey island residents commemorated Teilhard in 1982 by issuing a set of postage stamps and short biography; King, *Spirit of Fire*, 21.

13. Teilhard, "Cosmic Life," in *Writings in Time of War*, trans. René Hague (New York: Harper and Row, 1968), 60–61.

14. Teilhard, "Hymn to Matter," in *Heart of Matter*, 75. He included "Hymn to Matter," written in 1919, in his autobiography, thinking it most representative of his early thought; see his explanation on p. 61.

15. Teilhard, "Cosmic Life," 60; and Teilhard, *Heart of Matter*, 22–24.

16. Teilhard, *Heart of Matter*, 24.

17. Teilhard, as quoted in Henri de Lubac, *Teilhard de Chardin: The Man and His Meaning*, trans. René Hague (New York: Hawthorn Books, 1965), 22. See also Pierre Teilhard de Chardin, *Human Energy*, trans. J. M. Cohen (New York: Harcourt Brace Jovanovich, 1969), for his thoughts on a personal universe.

18. See, for example, Teilhard, *Heart of Matter*, 53. Lucile Swan was convinced that he wanted to start a new religion, writing Teilhard in October 1939: "You are really wanting to establish a religion—I mean the existence and the kind of God—and trying to prove that He does really exist—and you use modern scientific methods to prove what the old boys more or less took on Faith"; Swan to Teilhard in Pierre Teilhard de Chardin, *The Letters of Teilhard de Chardin and Lucile Swan*, ed. Thomas M. King, S.J., and Mary Wood Gilbert (Washington, D.C.: Georgetown University Press, 1993), 139.

19. Teilhard, *Heart of Matter*, 23; Ursula King, "Teilhard's Reflections on Eastern Religions Revisited," *Zygon* 30 (March 1995): 50, 71n4.

20. Teilhard, *Heart of Matter*, 23.

21. Porterfield, *Transformation of American Religion*, 66–72.

22. For an overview of scholasticism, see the entry in the *New Catholic Encyclopedia*, vol. 13 (New York: McGraw-Hill, 1967), 1165–70. At the heart of the

debate over Scholasticism was the science of evolution. The church denied evolutionary theory at least until the late 1940s and early 1950s. See Pope John Paul II's thoughts in brief on "Evolution and the Living God," in *Science and Theology: The New Consonance*, ed. Ted Peters (Boulder, Colo.: Westview Press, 1998), 149–52. John Paul points out that Pius XII in *Humani Generis* (1950) stated that there was no opposition between evolution and Christianity as long as certain qualifications were agreed to, primarily that the human was considered ontologically unique and that each soul, if not the body, was individually created by God. See also George V. Coyne's overview of the late twentieth-century church's view on evolution, "Evolution and the Human Person: The Pope in Dialogue," 153–61, in *Science and Theology*.

23. King, *Spirit of Fire*, 36.

24. Teilhard, *Heart of Matter*, 25–26.

25. See Henri Bergson, *Creative Evolution*, trans. Arthur Mitchell (1911; reprint, London: Macmillan, 1960).

26. Teilhard, *Heart of Matter*, 25.

27. Others have also noted that Teilhard failed to give Bergson enough credit. See, for example, H. James Birx, *Interpreting Evolution: Darwin and Teilhard de Chardin* (Buffalo, N.Y.: Prometheus Books, 1991), especially chaps. 4 and 5; Birx, *Pierre Teilhard de Chardin's Philosophy of Evolution* (Springfield, Ill.: Thomas, 1972); and Hefner, *Promise of Teilhard*, 23.

28. Teilhard, "Cosmic Life," 61; and "Creative Union, in *Writings in Time of War*," 159. In a later work, *The Two Sources of Morality and Religion*, trans. R. Ashley Audra and Cloudesley Brereton with the assistance of W. Horsfall Carter (1935; reprint, Notre Dame, Ind.: University of Notre Dame Press, 1977), Bergson modified his vitalism and gave a more theistic explanation of evolution.

29. Teilhard, *Heart of Matter*, 44; Teilhard, "The Mystical Milieu," in *Writings in Time of War*, 128. This piece was written in 1917; subsequent writings echoed the theme. Ursula King points to the importance of fire in Teilhard's rhetoric in *Spirit of Fire*, 58.

30. Teilhard, "Mystical Milieu," 130.

31. Teilhard talks about convergence in his early and later essays. See, for example, "Creative Union," 157 and multiple essays in *Christianity and Evolution*.

32. Hefner, *Promise of Teilhard*, 36. Karl Schmitz-Moormann, in "Teilhard de Chardin's View on Evolution," in *Evolution and Creation*, ed. Svend Anderson and Arthur Peacocke (Aarhus, Denmark: Aarhus University Press, 1987), 162–69.

33. Teilhard, *Heart of Matter*, 27–28.

34. Ibid., 17–24.

35. Ibid., 26.

36. Ibid., 20.

37. David L. Hull, *The Metaphysics of Evolution* (Albany: State University of New York Press, 1989), 36.

38. Boule praised Teilhard's powers of observation and rare combination of "keenness for minute analysis and a gift of wide synthesis"; Marcellin Boule as quoted in King, *Spirit of Fire*, 42.

39. For many of these essays, see Teilhard, *Writings in Time of War*.

40. Teilhard letter, May 28, 1915, as quoted in King, *Spirit of Fire*, 51. For a revealing glimpse of Teilhard during the war, see his letters to his cousin and friend

Marguerite Teilhard-Chambon in Pierre Teilhard de Chardin, *The Making of a Mind: Letters from a Soldier-Priest, 1914–1919*, trans. René Hague (New York: Harper and Row, 1965).

41. Teilhard, "Cosmic Life," 70.

42. See "The Universal Element," in *Writings in Time of War*, 290–302, quote on 297. Teilhard's view of Christ permeated his essays and letters, e.g., "The Christic," in *Heart of Matter*, 80–102. For other discussions on Teilhard's "Cosmic Christ," see Lubac, *Teilhard de Chardin*, chap 5. See Christopher Mooney, S.J., *Teilhard de Chardin and the Mystery of Christ* (New York: Harper and Row, 1966), for a study of Teilhard's theology.

43. See Colossians 1:17, 2:10, 3:11. Teilhard wrote about his "Universal Christ," referring to John, Ephesians, and Colossians; Teilhard to Lucile Swan, August 2, 1935, reprinted in *Letters of Teilhard de Chardin and Lucile Swan*, 43. Speaight sees these as significant in the formation of Teilhard's theology; *Life of Teilhard de Chardin*, 38.

44. Teilhard, "Cosmic Life," 58.

45. Ibid., 48.

46. Teilhard, "Cosmic Life," 45; see also 31. For more on individual personhood in a collective, see Teilhard, *Phenomenon of Man*, 260–64.

47. Teilhard to Lucile Swan, June 4, 1935, in *Letters of Teilhard de Chardin and Lucile Swan*, 36, emphasis in original.

48. Teilhard, "Cosmic Life," 48–49.

49. Letter from Teilhard to Teilhard-Chambon in Teilhard, *Making of a Mind*, 125.

50. Teilhard, "Cosmic Life," 41. His optimism was a deliberate decision. He was not naive. He knew personal suffering, having lost an older brother and sister by the time he was ordained. Two brothers were killed in battle, and a third died later due to poison gas. In addition, a younger sister lived life as an invalid.

51. Teilhard declared, "Thanks to the atom bomb it is war, not mankind, that is destined to be eliminated.... The shock which threatened to destroy us will have the effect of re-orienting us, of instilling a new dynamic and finally (within certain limits) of making us one whole. The atomic age is not the age of destruction but of union in research. For all their military trappings, the recent explosions at Bikini herald the birth into the world of a Mankind both inwardly and outwardly pacified. They proclaim the coming of the *Spirit of the Earth*"; see "The Spiritual Repercussions of the Atom Bomb," first written for *Etudes* in 1946 and reprinted in Teilhard, *The Future of Man*, trans. Norman Denny (New York: Harper and Row, 1964), 146–47.

52. Teilhard, "Cosmic Life," 14.

53. For Teilhard's relationships with women and gendered understandings, see King, *Spirit of Fire*, especially 72–82, quote on 80.

54. See Ibid., 80–82. Also see Pierre Teilhard de Chardin, *Letters to Léontine Zanta*, trans. Bernard Wall with introductions by Robert Garric and Henri de Lubac (London: Collins, 1969).

55. See *Letters of Teilhard de Chardin and Lucile Swan* for a glimpse of this very close relationship. Swan repeatedly confessed her love and pressed many times for its consummation, but Teilhard chose chastity. Asked by her niece later if there ever

was anything physical between them, Swan replied "Never." See Mary Wood Gilbert's prologue to *Letters of Teilhard de Chardin and Lucile Swan*, xvii. Teilhard did not deny the strong attraction but wanted to redirect the sexual energy to their own fulfillment as persons and as a force to bring them closer to God. He explained his views many times to a hurt Swan, some of which is captured in their correspondence. He also wrote several essays on chastity and human love and built his views of love into his understanding of holism. For him, the love between a man and a woman was beautiful, but it pointed to higher things, to a spiritualization of the earth and a convergence of all. See "The Evolution of Chastity," in Pierre Teilhard de Chardin, *Toward the Future*, trans. René Hague (New York: Harcourt Brace Jovanovich, 1975), 60–87; and his section on sexuality in "Sketch of a Personalistic Universe," in *Human Energy*, 72–84. He wrote in "The Evolution of Chastity" that "convergence at a higher level" is achieved when there is "no physical contact." He ended the essay with the following: "Someday when men have conquered the winds, the waves, the tides, and gravity, they will harness for God the energies of love, and then, for the second time in the history of the world, man will have discovered fire." When Teilhard wrote his "Chastity" paper in 1934, he sent a copy to his Jesuit friend Père Valensin in Lyon, who warned him that such essays would certainly get him in great trouble, Lukas and Lukas, *Teilhard*, 135.

56. Teilhard, *Heart of Matter*, 59.

57. Ibid., 59–61.

58. Teilhard, "The Eternal Feminine," in *Writings in Time of War*, 191–202. He dedicated the work to Béatrix for the Beatrice of Dante's *Divine Comedy* and he called on images of the Virgin Mary. In all, however, the feminine was equated with love as the attractive force that had unitive power in nature. For a collection of some of Teilhard's writings on love, see Pierre Teilhard de Chardin, *On Love and Happiness*, trans. René Hague (San Francisco: Harper and Row, 1984). For a discussion of his view of the feminine, see Henri de Lubac, *The Eternal Feminine: A Study on the Poem by Teilhard de Chardin*, trans. René Hague (New York: Harper and Row, 1971).

59. In addition to biographies on Teilhard for his days in China, see George B. Barbour, *In the Field with Teilhard de Chardin* (New York: Herder and Herder, 1965); and Pierre Teilhard de Chardin, *Letters from a Traveller*, trans. René Hague (New York: Harper and Row, 1962).

60. Letter from Teilhard to Breuil, July 16, 1923, in *Letters from a Traveller*, 81.

61. Letter from Teilhard to Breuil, September 30, 1923, in *Letters from a Traveller*, 90–91.

62. Joseph Needham, as quoted in Speaight, *The Life of Teilhard*, 273.

63. Teilhard, *Letters from a Traveller*, 103.

64. Teilhard, *Human Phenomenon*, 168.

65. Teilhard, as quoted in Speaight, *The Life of Teilhard*, 234.

66. Pierre Leroy, "The Man," in *Letters from a Traveller*, 31.

67. Teilhard, as quoted in Max Begouen's foreword to *Building the Earth and the Psychological Conditions of Human Unification*, introduction by John Kobler (New York: Avon Books, 1969), 17.

68. Lukas and Lukas, *Teilhard*, 110–14; Cuénot, *Teilhard de Chardin*, 76–77.

69. Teilhard to Ida Treat, October 1926, as quoted in King, *Spirit of Fire*, 112.

70. Teilhard, *Heart of Matter*, 47.

71. Teilhard, "Mass on the World," in Pierre Teilhard de Chardin, *Hymn of the Universe*, trans. Gerald Vann (New York: Harper and Row, 1969), 19.

72. Letter from Teilhard to an anonymous friend, October 12, 1926, in Teilhard, *Letters to Two Friends*, 44, and quoted in part in King, *Spirit of Fire*, 105.

73. Pierre Teilhard de Chardin, "Note on Some Possible Historical Representations of Original Sin," in *Christianity and Evolution*, trans. René Hague (New York: Harcourt Brace Jovanovich, 1971), 45–46. See also in the same volume his return to the problem of the story of the Fall, written in 1947: "Reflections on Original Sin," 187–98.

74. Mary Lukas and Ellen Lukas wrote: "If anything saved Teilhard's essays from being dubbed clearly heretical, it was the simple fact that they were so bizarrely phrased"; *Teilhard*, 55.

75. Troubled by the papal order, Teilhard wrote to his friend the Jesuit Auguste Valensin: "I feel I should, in conscience, reserve for myself (1) the right to carry on research with professional men...; (2) the right to bring help to the disturbed and troubled"; quoted in King, *Spirit of Fire*, 107.

76. Leroy, "Introduction," *Letters from a Traveller*, 44.

77. The quote is taken from a letter from Teilhard to Ida Treat; King, *Spirit of Fire*, 111.

78. Teilhard, *The Divine Milieu*, 127.

79. For his dedication to the church and his frustrations, see Leroy, "Introduction," *Letters from a Traveller*, 16–17, 35; and Lubac, *Teilhard de Chardin*, 71–75. Lubac said Teilhard never wavered in his loyalty. After one imposition of silence, Teilhard wrote a superior: "You know that these administrative frictions do not weaken my ever more profound attachment to a Church without which I can see no way of 'valorizing,' or 'amorizing' a 'hominization' to the forwarding and advancing of which I have definitely dedicated my life" (73).

80. Teilhard, "The Sense of Man," in *Toward the Future*, 38.

81. Letter from Teilhard to Swan, Calcutta, December 16, 1935, in *Letters of Teilhard de Chardin and Lucile Swan*, 55. Teilhard began to think when he converted to evolutionary thinking that a new Christianity needed to be crafted. Furthermore, after World War I, he believed that his fellows sought new avenues of worship. Christianity, he believed, did not meet their understandings of nature and the world, and so they turned to other, more pantheistic, world-loving religions. That explained for him the "the present proliferation of neo-Buddhisms, of theosophies, of spiritualist doctrines"; Teilhard, "Pantheism and Christianity," in *Christianity and Evolution*, 64. This fed his desire to make Christianity more accommodating to the new sciences and create what he called a Christianity "re-born." See also his essay, "Christianity and Evolution: Suggestions for a New Theology," in the same volume, 173–86.

82. Teilhard, *Heart of Matter*, 57–58.

83. Geologist George Barbour discussed the scientific milieu of China in the 1920s and 1930s in *In the Field with Teilhard de Chardin*; see especially 21–22 for the "New Thought Movement." Lodovico Galleni notes the cultural shift Teilhard experienced in China, where scientists, largely persuaded by Darwinian assumptions, were playing with neo-Darwinism or "the modern synthesis" that took genetics into account; Galleni, "Relationships between Scientific Analysis and the World View of Pierre Teilhard de Chardin," 155.

84. For Teilhard's scientific works, see *L'oeuvre scientifique*. See Teilhard's summation of his work in *Heart of Matter*, 157–64.

85. Teilhard discussed his hope of a more holistic science with others. In a letter to Lucile Swan, March 25, 1937, Teilhard enthusiastically recounted meeting Edmund Walsh, S.J., a priest who worked at the School of Foreign Service in Georgetown University: "I have met here, in Washington, a really intelligent and influential colleague of mine (F. Walsh), who told me that he had just had a long talk with Dr. Carrel [Alexis Carrell, French surgeon and Nobelist]: he thinks of starting a kind of 'Institute of Man,' in order to study Man 'as a whole,' and is searching for specialists who could attack the problem from different and wide angles. Exactly what de Terra [and I] were dreaming." Helmut de Terra of Yale University accompanied him on geological expeditions in Asia, *The Letters of Teilhard de Chardin and Lucile Swan*, 74.

86. For historical perspective and definitions, including Teilhard's influence on the field of biospheric studies, see R. J. Huggett, "Ecosphere, Biosphere, or Gaia? What to Call the Global Ecosystem," *Global Ecology and Biogeography* 8 (November 1999): 425–31. For Teilhard's relationship with Le Roy, see King, *Spirit of Fire*, 84–89.

87. Letter from Teilhard, January 14, 1924, as quoted in Cuénot, *Teilhard de Chardin*, 52.

88. Jia Lanpo and Huang Weiman, *The Story of Peking Man: From Archaeology to Mystery* (Beijing: Foreign Languages Press; Hong Kong: Oxford University Press, 1990); Pierre Teilhard de Chardin, *The Appearance of Man* (London: Collins, 1965); Davidson Black, Pierre Teilhard de Chardin, C. C. Young, and W. C. Pei, "Fossil Man in China: The Choukoutien Cave Deposits with a Synopsis of Our Present Knowledge of the Late Cenozoic in China," *Memoirs, Geological Survey in China* 11 (1933): 1–166.

89. Galleni, "Relationships between Scientific Analysis and the World View of Pierre Teilhard de Chardin," 157.

90. Teilhard, "Introduction" to the September 1943 edition of *Geobiologia*, as quoted in Cuénot, *Teilhard de Chardin*, 228–29, emphasis in original.

91. The journal produced only two issues. Begun in 1943, it did not survive the war.

92. Plato, as quoted in J. Donald Hughes, *Pan's Travail: Environmental Problems of the Ancient Greeks and Romans* (Baltimore: Johns Hopkins University Press, 1994), 55.

93. Donald Worster points to Alexander von Humboldt as a source of holistic ideas in environmentalism; *Nature's Economy: A History of Ecological Ideas*, 2nd ed. (New York: Cambridge University Press, 1994), 132–38.

94. For Gaia science, Deep Ecology, and Ecofemism, see the Carson chapter in this book, n. 131.

95. Teilhard, *Letters of Teilhard de Chardin and Lucile Swan*, 140.

96. Teilhard, Peking, June 18, 1940, in *Letters to Two Friends*, 145.

97. Teilhard, *Human Phenomenon*, quote on 182. For his view of the personal and his dislike of pantheism, see Ibid., 186. For an explanation of Teilhard's view of the individual and the community, see Hefner, *Promise of Teilhard*, 39–40. See also Karl Schmitz-Moormann, "Teilhard de Chardin, Theologian of an Evolutionary

Creation," *Insights: The Magazine of the Chicago Center for Religion and Science* 8 (October 1996): 5–12, where Schmitz-Moormann situates Teilhard with Martin Buber in his view of a personalistic universe.

98. Teilhard, *Human Phenomenon*, 186.

99. Teilhard, *Future of Man*, 82.

100. Teilhard letter, Peking, November 20, 1939, and January 10, 1940, in *Letters to Two Friends*, 136, 140.

101. Teilhard, "Cosmic Life," 35.

102. Teilhard discussed consciousness and its importance within his system in multiple passages. Quote in "The Human Rebound of Evolution," in *Future of Man*, 206.

103. Teilhard, *Human Phenomenon*, 183. A few pages earlier, he made this even more specific, stating, "Evolution = Rise of Consciousness," 172.

104. Teilhard, *Human Phenomenon*, 163; Teilhard, *Phenomenon of Man*, 234.

105. Teilhard used the phrase "Brain of brains" in his essay "The Formation of the Noosphere," in *Future of Man*, 166. To him, a collective "Brain" operated in similar ways to a single brain, "with its milliards of inter-connected nerve-cells" (166–67).

106. Teilhard, *Human Phenomenon*, 122–25, 172.

107. Teilhard explained "noosphere" often. Here I refer to his explanation of the origin of the term in *Heart of Matter*, 30–39. He said he based his understanding of the noosphere (first used by him in 1927) on the model of the "biosphere." Like the biosphere, ideas about the noosphere emanated from discussions with Le Roy and Vernadsky. He thought his idea bore some resemblance to psychologist Carl Jung's "collective unconsciousness." In a letter Teilhard wrote Swan on May 16, 1934, he encouraged her to read Jung's article, "Does the World Stand on the Verge of Spiritual Rebirth?" saying, "The ideas, substantially, are curiously akin to the mine [*sic*]"; *Letters of Teilhard de Chardin and Lucile Swan*, 15.

108. Crediting Julian Huxley for the phrase, he said that "we are *nothing else than evolution become conscious of itself*"; Teilhard, *Human Phenomenon*, 154; Teilhard, *Phenomenon of Man*, 221; Teilhard, "Cosmic Life," 37. See also, for example, Teilhard, *Human Phenomenon*, 197.

109. Teilhard, "Cosmic Life," 32.

110. For the Omega Point, the last phase in his evolutionary schema, the ongoing creative hand of God brings all into harmony; see *Phenomenon of Man*, 257–72.

111. Appleton-Weber, "Introduction," in Teilhard, *Human Phenomenon*, xix; Teilhard, *Oeuvres*, quote on 10:122.

112. Teilhard as quoted in Lukas and Lukas, *Teilhard*, 274, 340–41.

113. Teilhard to Father Janssens, October 12, 1951, in *Letters from a Traveller*, 43.

114. Citation awarded to Teilhard in June 1947 by the French; see King, *Spirit of Fire*, 191.

115. Lukas and Lukas, *Teilhard*, 227.

116. Pope Pius XII, *Humani Generis: Concerning Some False Opinions Which Threaten to Undermine the Foundations of Catholic Doctrine*, Washington, D.C., National Catholic Welfare Conference, quoted in Birx, *Pierre Teilhard de Chardin's Philosophy of Evolution*, xi.

117. Jacques Maritain, "Teilhard de Chardin and Teilhardism," *U.S. Catholic* 33 (1967): 9–10; and Birx, *Pierre Teilhard de Chardin's Philosophy of Evolution*, xiv.

118. Cardinal Feltin, *Documentation Catholique* 58 (1961): 1523, as quoted in E. L. Bone, "Teilhard," in *New Catholic Encyclopedia* (New York: McGraw-Hill, 1967), 14: 978.

119. Inspired by his notion of convergence, universal drive for love, and union through love, Flannery O'Connor plays with convergence between races, generations, and time; Flannery O'Connor, "Everything That Rises Must Converge," first printed in *New World Writing* 19 (1961) and included in her collected works, *The Complete Stories* (New York: Farrar, Straus and Giroux, 1979) and *Everything That Rises Must Converge* (New York: Farrar, Straus and Giroux, 1965). For O'Connor's interpretation of Teilhard, start with her review of Teilhard's *Phenomenon of Man*, which appeared in a local diocesan newspaper, *The Bulletin*, on February 20, 1960, and reprinted in *Presence of Grace and Other Book Reviews*, comp. Leo J. Zuber, ed. Carter W. Martin (Athens: University of Georgia Press, 1983). See also Richard Giannone, *Flannery O'Connor and the Mystery of Love* (Urbana: University of Illinois Press, 1989), 154–60; 212–13; and Miles Orvell, *Flannery O'Connor: An Introduction* (Jackson: University Press of Mississippi, 1991), 20.

120. Patricia Le Fevere, "Thousands Acclaim Jesuit's Global Vision," *National Catholic Reporter*, April 22, 2005, 9–10; and Thomas L. King, "Teilhard Makes Christianity Most Exciting Thing on the Block," *National Catholic Reporter*, April 22, 2005, 8, 10, Thant quote on p. 10. See also Woodstock Forum with James Salmon, S.J., Nicole Schmitz-Moormann, Philip Hefner, and Harris Wofford, "Teilhard de Chardin and His Relevance for Today," *Woodstock Report* 82 (June 2005), Georgetown University http://woodstock.georgetown.edu/resources/articles/Teilhard-de-Chardin-His-Relevance-for-Today.html (accessed December 2, 2008), for more information on Sargent Shriver's and Harris Wofford's engagement with Teilhard.

121. Paolo Soleri, "Teilhard and the Esthetic," in *Teilhard and the Unity of Knowledge* ed. Thomas M. King and James F. Salmon. (New York: Paulist Press, 1983), 74–82. Soleri's work can be seen at his ongoing project of Arcosanti, Arizona. See also Paolo Soleri, *Arcology: The City in the Image of Man* (Cambridge, Mass.: MIT Press, 1969); Peter Blake, "Paolo Soleri's Visionary City," *Architectural Forum* 114 (March 1961): 111–18; Walter Karp, "Soleri: Designer in the Desert," *Horizon* 12 (1970): 30–39; Tevere J. McFayden, "The Abbot of Arcosanti: Praised and Damned, Architect Paolo Soleri Carves Out His Dream in the Desert," *Horizon* 23 (1980): 54–61; and Georgi Stanishev, "Soleri's Laboratory." *World Architecture* 21 (1993): 58–63.

122. Kenneth E. Boulding wrote: "We can think of the stock of knowledge, or as Teilhard de Chardin called it, the 'noosphere,' and consider this as an open system, losing knowledge through aging and death and gaining it through birth and education and the ordinary experience"; "The Economics of the Coming Spaceship Earth" (1966), in *Collected Papers*, ed. Fred R. Glahe and Larry D. Singell, 6 vols. (Boulder: Colorado Associated University Press, 1971–85), 1:383–94, quote on 386, and reprinted in Anil Markandya and Julie Richardson, eds., *Environmental Economics: A Reader* (New York: St. Martin's Press, 1992,), 27–35, quote on 29.

123. Brandon Carter first proposed the anthropic principle in 1974 in *Confrontation of Cosmological Theories with Observation*, ed. M. S. Longair (Dordrecht:

Reidel, 1974). Others developed the notion, arguing both weak and strong variations. The strong variation contends that the world could not have been structured otherwise; it must have been created for human life, while the weak does not find it to be necessarily so. Physicist Freeman Dyson concurred with the anthropic principle in *Disturbing the Universe* (New York: Harper and Row, 1979): "The more I examine the universe and the details of its architecture, the more I find that the universe in some sense must have known we were coming" (250). For a history of the theory, as well as a discussion of Teilhard's ideas as they relate to the principle, see John D. Barrow and Frank J. Tipler, *The Anthropic Cosmological Principle* (Oxford: Clarendon Press, 1986). For further readings on the anthropic principle in its various manifestations, see F. Bertola, ed., *The Anthropic Principle: Proceedings of the Second Venice Conference on Cosmology* (Cambridge: Cambridge University Press, 1993). See also Errol E. Harris, *Cosmos and Anthropos: A Philosophical Interpretation of the Anthropic Cosmological Principle* (Atlantic Highlands, New Jersey: Humanities Press International, 1991); and Ian Barbour, "Experiencing and Interpreting Nature in Science and Religion," *Zygon* 29 (December 1994): 457–87, especially 465–67; see Barrow and Tipler, *The Anthropic Cosmological Principle*, 195–205; and Harris, *Cosmos and Anthropos*, 74, 85–87, for three who give credit to Teilhard for influencing the development of these ideas.

124. Marshall McLuhan, *The Medium Is the Massage* (New York: Bantam Books, 1967); and McLuhan, *The Gutenberg Galaxy: The Making of Typographic Man* (New York: New American Library, 1962); Marshall McLuhan and Bruce R. Powers, *The Global Village: Transformations in World Life and Media in the 21st Century* (New York: Oxford University Press, 1989). See Tom Wolfe, "Digibabble, Fairy Dust, and the Human Anthill," *Forbes ASAP*, special edition, October 4, 1999, 213–27, quote on 216. See also Thomas W. Cooper, "The Medium Is the Mass: Marshall McLuhan's Catholicism and catholicism," *Journal of Media and Religion* 5 (August 2006): 161–73.

125. Ralph Abraham, Frank Jas, and Willard Russell, *The Web Empowerment Book: An Introduction and Connection Guide to the Internet and the World-Wide Web* (Santa Clara, Calif.: TELOS, 1995), 12, quote on 29. See also Ralph Abraham, *Chaos, Gaia, Eros* (San Francisco: HarperSanFrancisco, 1995). Many have suggested Teilhard's prediction of the Internet, and there are Web sites that promote the use of the internet as a tool to build the future and the "global brain." See, for example, many articles on the *Principia Cybernetica Web* http://pespmc1.vub.ac.be/DEFAULT. html, starting with Francis Heylighen, "The Social Superorganism and its Global Brain," in *Principia Cybernetica Web* ed. Francis Heylighen, Cliff Joslyn, and Valentin Turchin (Brussels, Belgium: Principia Cybernetica, 2000) http://pespmc1.vub.ac. be/SUPORGLI.html (accessed December 29, 2009). See also Ingrid H. Shafer, "A Global Ethic for the Global Village," *Journal of Ecumenical Studies* 42 (Summer 2007): 440–53.

126. Thomas Mary Berry, *The Dream of the Earth* (San Francisco: Sierra Club, 1988); and Berry, "Teilhard in the Ecological Age," *Teilhard Studies* 7 (Fall 1982): 1–33. For Thomas Berry's beliefs, see the foreword to Dorothy Maclean, *To Honor the Earth* (San Francisco: HarperSanFrancisco, 1991); for the influence of Teilhard and Carson in his life, see the foreword to Anne Marie Dalton, *A Theology for the Earth: The Contributions of Thomas Berry and Bernard Lonergan* (King Edward, Ottawa: University of Ottawa Press, 1999), vi–viii.

127. Minna Cassard, as quoted in McCulloch, *Short History of the American Teilhard Association*, 13.

128. Ralph Burhoe and Harlow Shapley founded IRAS in 1954 to create a new religion based on the rationality of modern science. Like Teilhard, both experienced anxiety after the war and hoped to offer a spiritual interpretation of science. All three wanted to take into account evolutionary theories and new scientific cosmological understandings, but Teilhard spoke more out of his Catholic faith, whereas Shapley accepted a pantheistic worldview and Burhoe held a Unitarian perspective. Still, the three found common cause in their hopes of marrying science and religion. Gilbert tells the interesting story of IRAS in *Redeeming Culture*, 273–95.

129. Two issues of the journal *Zygon*, from September and December 1968, were devoted to Teilhard; in 1995, an issue commemorating thirty years of *Zygon* was dedicated to him.

130. Julia Van Denack, "Evolution Is God's Method of Creation," *American Biology Teacher* 35 (April 1973): 216–18. The Swiss theologian Joseph Kopp wrote a primer to *The Phenomenon of Man* in 1964 that Van Denack and others found helpful for deciphering Teilhard's message. See Joseph Kopp, *Teilhard de Chardin: A New Synthesis of Evolution* (Glen Rock, N.J.: Paulist Press, 1964).

131. Theodosius Dobzhansky, "Nothing in Biology Makes Sense Except in the Light of Evolution," *American Biology Teacher* 35 (March 1973): 125–29. For the Dobzhansky quote, see Van Denack, "Evolution Is God's Method," 216.

132. Rome moved to "rehabilitate" Teilhard in a letter from the Vatican in 1981. The letter praised Teilhard's contributions and character and stood in stark contrast to the monitum of 1962; see a reprint of the letter in the *Teilhard Review* 16 (1981): 4–5. In 1987, Pope John Paul II called a conference at the Vatican on the relationship between science and religion to encourage more integration between the two; see the papal message and responses collected in Robert J. Russell, William R. Stoeger, and George V. Coyne, eds., *John Paul II on Science and Religion: Reflections on the New View from Rome* (Rome: Vatican Observatory Publications, 1990).

133. Jay Dolan, *The American Catholic Experience: A History from Colonial Times to the Present* (Garden City, N.Y.: Doubleday, 1985), 384–454; Mark Oppenheimer, *Knocking on Heaven's Door: American Religion in the Age of the Counterculture* (New Haven, Conn.: Yale University Press, 2003), 61–94; and Porterfield, *Transformation of American Religion*, 69–87.

134. Thomas A. Tweed, ed., *Retelling U. S. Religious History* (Berkeley: University of California Press, 1997), 82–84; Porterfield, *Transformation of American Religion*.

135. Ted Peters, "Science and Theology: Toward Consonance," in *Science and Theology*, ed. Ted Peters. (Boulder, Colo.: Westview Press, 1998), 20–21.

136. Brian Swimme and Thomas Berry suggest that the universe is the epistemological base for New Age religion. "Our new sense of the universe is itself a type of revelatory experience," they wrote, asserting that the natural environment "is the primary economic reality, the primary educator, the primary governance, the primary technologist, the primary healer, the primary presence of the sacred, the primary moral value"; Swimme and Berry, *The Universe Story: From the Primordial Flaring Forth to the Ecozoic Era—A Celebration of the Unfolding of the Cosmos* (San Francisco: HarperSanFrancisco, 1992), 255. This passage is also quoted in Peters, "Science and Theology," 21.

137. Marilyn Ferguson, *The Aquarian Conspiracy: Personal and Social Trans-formations in the 1980s* (Los Angeles: Tarcher, 1980). For another history of New Age religion, see Phillip Charles Lucas, *The Odyssey of a New Religion: The Holy Order of MANS from New Age to Orthodoxy* (Bloomington: Indiana University Press, 1995).

138. Galt MacDermot, Gerome Ragni, and James Rado, *Hair: The American Tribal Love-rock Musical* (New York: Pocket Books, 1969).

139. Ferguson, *Aquarian Conspiracy*, 420. See also the preface to David H. Lane, *The Phenomenon of Teilhard: Prophet for a New Age* (Macon, Ga.: Mercer University Press, 1996). This book offers a critical view of Teilhard's thought and influence on the New Age movement. Lane misunderstands Teilhard's thought as pantheistic rather than panentheistic, but then so too do many New Age followers.

140. Ursula King, "Science and Mysticism: Teilhard de Chardin in Religious Thought Today," *Teilhard Review* 19 (Spring 1984): 10. See also Lane, *The Phenomenon of Teilhard*, x.

141. Robert Muller as quoted in Lane, *The Phenomenon of Teilhard*, 6.

142. See, for example, Robert Muller, *The Robert Muller School: World Core Curriculum Manual* (Arlington, Tex.: Robert Muller School Publishing, 1986). The manual received certification from UNESCO. See Lane, *The Phenomenon of Teilhard*, 128n160. For an overview of Muller, see Lane, *The Phenomenon of Teilhard*, 126–35.

143. King, "The Milieux Teilhard Left Behind," 95, as quoted in Lane, *The Phenomenon of Teilhard*, 135–36.

144. For the history of the Omega Institute, see its Web site at http://www.eomega.org/omega/about/history/ (accessed December 14, 2008).

145. Jean Huston, "The New World Religion," *Tarrytown Letter*, June/July 1983, 5, as quoted in Lane, *The Phenomenon of Teilhard*, 137.

146. Chardin, "Cosmic Life," 48–49.

147. Walter Truett Anderson, *The Upstart Spring: Esalen and the American Awakening* (Reading, Mass.: Addison-Wesley, 1983), 111. See also an example of Teilhard's influence on humanistic psychologists, Frank T. Severin, "The Humanistic Psychology of Teilhard de Chardin," in *Challenges of Humanistic Psychology*, ed. James F. T. Bugental (New York: McGraw-Hill, 1967), 151–60.

CHAPTER 5

1. Abraham H. Maslow, *Toward a Psychology of Being*, 2nd ed. (Princeton, N.J.: Van Nostrand, 1968), v.

2. Ibid., appendix B, 221.

3. Mary Harrington Hall, "A Conversation with the President of the American Psychological Association Abraham H. Maslow," *Psychology Today* 2 (1968): 54. For Maslow's biography, see Edward Hoffman, *The Right to Be Human: A Biography of Abraham Maslow* (Los Angeles: Tarcher, 1988); Willard B. Frick, *Humanistic Psychology: Interviews with Maslow, Murphy, and Rogers* (Columbus, Ohio: Merrill, 1971); Frank Goble, *The Third Force: The Psychology of Abraham Maslow* (New York: Grossman, 1970); International Study Project and Bertha G. Maslow, comp., *Abraham Maslow: A Memorial Volume* (Monterey, Calif.: Brooks/Cole, 1972); Richard Lowry, *A. H. Maslow: An Intellectual Portrait* (Monterey, Calif.: Brooks/Cole, 1973);

and Colin Wilson, *New Pathways in Psychology: Maslow and the Post-Freudian Revolution* (New York: Taplinger, 1972), 129–48.

4. Hall, "Conversation with Maslow," 54.

5. Ibid., 35.

6. Maslow, as quoted in Hoffman, *Right to Be Human*, 6.

7. Maslow, as quoted in Ibid., 9.

8. Walter Truett Anderson, *The Upstart Spring: Esalen and the American Awakening* (Reading, Mass.: Addison-Wesley, 1983), 67.

9. Ricardo B. Morant, "In Memoriam to Abraham H. Maslow," in Maslow, *Memorial Volume*, 26.

10. Maslow, as quoted in Hoffman, *Right to Be Human*, 9.

11. Maslow, as quoted in Ibid., 2.

12. Maslow, as quoted in Ibid., 11.

13. Maslow, as quoted in Ibid., 3.

14. Hoffman, *Right to Be Human*, 4.

15. Maslow, as quoted in Ibid., 5.

16. Maslow, as quoted in *Memorial Volume*, 113.

17. Abraham H. Maslow, *Motivation and Personality*, 2nd ed. (New York: Harper and Row, 1970), 164.

18. Abraham H. Maslow, *Religions, Values, and Peak-Experiences* (Columbus: Ohio State University Press, 1964), vii.

19. Maslow, *Toward a Psychology of Being*, iv.

20. For Watson's three essays on behaviorism, see "What the Nursery Has to Say about Instincts," "Experimental Studies on the Growth of the Emotions," and "Recent Experiments on How We Lose and Change Our Emotional Equipment," in *Psychologies of 1925: Powell Lectures in Psychological Theory*, ed. Carl Murchison, 2nd ed. (Worcester, Mass.: Clark University Press, 1927), 1–82. Watson outlined behaviorism in what has come to be called the "Behaviorist's Manifesto" in "Psychology as the Behaviorist Views It," *Psychological Review* 20 (1913): 158–77.

21. Abraham H. Maslow, *The Journals of A. H. Maslow*, ed. Richard Lowry, 2 vols. (Monterey, Calif.: Brooks/Cole, 1979), 1:164.

22. Maslow in a 1968 interview, as quoted in Frick, *Humanistic Psychology*, 19.

23. Maslow, *Journals*, 1:277–78.

24. Watson's famous statement read in full: "Give me a dozen healthy infants, well-formed, and my own specified world to bring them up in and I'll guarantee to take any one at random and train him to become any type of specialist I might select—a doctor, lawyer, artist, merchant-chief and, yes, even into beggar-man and thief, regardless of his talents, penchants, tendencies, abilities, vocations and race of his ancestors"; in Watson, "What the Nursery Has to Say about Instincts," 10. For his views on race, see Ibid., 10–11. For his thoughts on physical punishment, see Watson, "Experimental Studies on the Growth of the Emotions," 40–41; and Watson, "Recent Experiments on How We Lose and Change Our Emotional Equipment," 72.

25. Hoffman pinpoints Maslow's attraction to Sumner's thought in *Right to Be Human*, 29–31, 34.

26. William Graham Sumner, *Folkways: A Study of the Sociological Importance of Usages, Manners, Customs, Mores, and Morals* (New York: Ginn, 1940), 254, and quoted in Hoffman, *Right to Be Human*, 31.

27. Maslow, as quoted in Hoffman, *Right to Be Human*, 31. For Maslow's "peak experience" while reading Sumner and his vow to make a contribution in philosophy, psychology, and anthropology, see Maslow, as quoted in *Memorial Volume*, 81.

28. Maslow, as quoted in Wilson, *New Pathways in Psychology*, 137.

29. Maslow, quoted in Hall, "Conversation with Maslow," 37; also cited in Hoffman, *Right to Be Human*, 34.

30. For an overview of Maslow's college education, see Hoffman, *Right to Be Human*, chaps. 2–4. Maslow published his dissertation in articles; see, for example, A. H. Maslow, "The Role of Dominance in the Social and Sexual Behavior of Infra-human Primates: Observations at Vilas Park Zoo," *Journal of Genetic Psychology* 48 (1936): 261–77; and Maslow, "The Role of Dominance in the Social and Sexual Behavior of Infra-human Primates: II. An Experimental Determination of the Behavior Syndrome of Dominance," *Journal of Genetic Psychology* 48 (1936): 278–309; both reprinted in A. H. Maslow, *Dominance, Self-Esteem, Self-Actualization: Germinal Papers of A. H. Maslow*, ed. Richard J. Lowry (Monterey, Calif.: Brooks/Cole, 1973), 3–46.

31. Maslow, *Journals*, 1:93; Maslow, *Memorial Volume*, 15; Hoffman, *Right to Be Human*, 47–48.

32. Abraham Maslow delivered an informal lecture, "The Taboo of Tenderness: The Disease of Valuelessness," at Brandeis in 1965 and published it as "Humanistic Science and Transcendent Experiences," *Journal of Humanistic Psychology* 5 (1965): 223; see also Hoffman, *Right to Be Human*, 66–68, 278–79.

33. Charles E. Rosenberg, "The Tyranny of Diagnosis: Specific Entities and Individual Experience," *Milbank Quarterly* 80 (2002): 237–60. See also Christopher Lawrence and George Weisz, eds., *Greater Than the Parts: Holism in Biomedicine, 1920–1950* (New York: Oxford University Press, 1998).

34. For a discussion of this cultural critique and the resurgence of humanism at this time, see James A. Farrell, *The Spirit of the Sixties: The Making of Postwar Radicalism* (New York: Routledge, 1997), especially 111–25; Dwight Macdonald quoted on 123 and 292n42. For Mumford's quote, see Lewis Mumford, "Atom Bomb: Miracle or Catastrophe," *Air Affairs* 2 (July 1948): 328; and Farrell, *Spirit of the Sixties*, 125. This essay and others in which Mumford speaks out against nuclear weapons may be found in his book *In the Name of Sanity* (New York: Harcourt, Brace, 1954).

35. Alan Alda, as quoted in "A MASH Note for Docs," *Time*, May 28, 1979, http://www.time.com/time/magazine/article/0,9171,947321,00.html (accessed August 2, 2008).

36. Phyllis H. Mattson notes Maslow's contribution to the holistic health movement in *Holistic Health in Perspective* (Palo Alto, Calif.: Mayfield, 1982), 69, 88–89.

37. Maslow, "Humanistic Science and Transcendent Experiences," 224.

38. Watson, "Psychology as the Behaviorist Views It," 158–77, quote on 158; and John B. Watson, *Behaviorism*, rev. ed. (Chicago: University of Chicago Press, 1930), quote on v.

39. Maslow, as quoted in Hall, "Conversation with Maslow," 54. For Maslow's publications on dominance and sexuality in women, see the following: "Dominance-feeling, Personality, and Social Behavior in Women," *Journal of Social Psychology* 10

(1939): 3–39; "A Test for Dominance-feeling (Self-esteem) in College Women," *Journal of Social Psychology* 12 (1940): 255–70; *The Social Personality Inventory: A Test for Self-esteem in Women* (with manual) (Palo Alto, Calif.: Consulting Psychologists Press, 1942); "The Dynamics of Psychological Security-Insecurity," *Character and Personality* 10 (1942): 331–44; and "Self-esteem (dominance-feeling) and Sexuality in Women," *Journal of Social Psychology* 16 (1942): 259–94; all reprinted in *Dominance, Self-Esteem, Self-Actualization*, 49–136.

40. Maslow, as quoted in Wilson, *New Pathways in Psychology*, 141.

41. Maslow, as quoted in Hoffman, *Right to Be Human*, 74.

42. Alfred Kinsey engaged Maslow in a series of conversations in the 1940s and briefly drew him back to the study of sexuality. In 1945 the two collaborated on a research project, but the complete study was never published because, according to Maslow, Kinsey grew angry with the results, denied Maslow access to some of the findings, and refused to publish the data. For an overview of the study and the falling out between Maslow and Kinsey, see Hoffman, *Right to Be Human*, 167–70. See also Salvatore R. Maddi and Paul T. Costa, *Humanism in Personalogy: Allport, Maslow, and Murray* (Chicago: Aldine, 1972), 143–44. Maslow eventually did publish the records he had, noting the flaws that he saw in the study; "Volunteer-error in the Kinsey Study," *Journal of Abnormal and Social Psychology* 47 (1951): 259–62.

43. Maslow, as quoted in Hoffman, *Right to Be Human*, 138–39; Ann (b. 1938); Ellen (b. 1940).

44. For Wertheimer's influence on Maslow, see Hoffman, *Right to Be Human*, 90–94; and D. Brett King and Michael Wertheimer, *Max Wertheimer and Gestalt Theory* (New Brunswick, N.J.: Transaction, 2005), 299–304.

45. Michael Wertheimer, "Gestalt Theory, Holistic Psychologies and Max Wertheimer," *Personale Psycholgie* 5 (1983): 43, and as quoted in Wayne Viney and D. Brett King, *A History of Psychology: Ideas and Context*, 2nd ed. (Boston: Allyn and Bacon, 1998), 346; see all of chap. 15 for an introduction to Gestalt psychology. See Wolfgang Köhler's account of his psychology, "Gestalt Psychology," in *Schools of Psychology*, ed. David L. Krantz (New York: Appleton-Century-Crofts, 1969), 69–86.

46. Frederick S. Perls, Ralph E. Hefferline, and Paul Goodman, *Gestalt Therapy: Excitement and Growth in the Human Personality* (New York: Dell, 1951).

47. Ehrenfels published his remarks in "On Gestalt Qualities," in Richard Avenarius's *Quarterly for Scientific Philosophy*. For a translation and Ehrenfels's debts to Austrian and German philosophy, see *Foundations of Gestalt Theory*, trans. and ed. Barry Smith (Munich: Philosophia Verlag, 1988), 82–117. Ehrenfels also drew from the Scottish Common Sense school, particularly Thomas Reid, who suggested that complex ideas are apprehended as meaningful wholes; see Thomas H. Leahey, *A History of Psychology: Main Currents in Psychological Thought* (Upper Saddle River, N.J.: Prentice Hall, 1997), 136–38, 209. The German poet Goethe came to similar conclusions as expressed in his organic view of nature; see Mitchell G. Ash, *Gestalt Psychology in German Culture, 1890–1967: Holism and the Quest for Objectivity* (New York: Cambridge University Press, 1995), 85–86. Ash provides a good study of the precursors to Gestalt psychology and the problem of the whole and part in philosophy.

48. Max Wertheimer put forth this argument in 1912 in an article entitled "Experimental Studies on the Perception of Movement" ["Experimentelle studien

über das Sehen von Bewegung," *Zeitschrift für Psychologie* 61 (1912): 151–265]. For an overview of the "phi phenomenon" experiments, the initial experiments Wertheimer conducted with Koffka and Köhler, see Viney and King, *History of Psychology*, 346–47. Wertheimer's fascination in psychology lay more in the realm of cognition rather than perception; see his book *Productive Thinking*, ed. Michael Wertheimer (Chicago: University of Chicago Press, 1982), for his application of gestalt ideas to thinking. He argued that productive thinking or creative thinking (the "aha"-type) is based on an ability to grasp structural organization.

49. "There are wholes," Wertheimer wrote, "the behavior of which is not determined by that of their individual elements, but where the part-processes are themselves determined by the intrinsic nature of the whole"; Max Wertheimer, "Gestalt Theory," in *A Source Book of Gestalt Psychology*, ed. Willis D. Ellis, 3rd ed. (London: Routledge, 1950), 2.

50. King and Wertheimer, *Max Wertheimer and Gestalt Theory*, 300.

51. Maslow, *Journals*, 1:164–66, quote on 166. See also Hoffman, *Right to Be Human*, 106–10, for Goldstein's influence on Maslow.

52. Wolfgang Köhler, *Gestalt Psychology* (New York: Liveright, 1929). See Köhler's famous study on apes, where he determined that apes solve problems by examining the whole situation first and then rearranging the parts to achieve a goal. For example, to gain access to a banana that was higher than a chimpanzee could jump, Köhler found that if boxes lay within the area, then the chimps would use the boxes to reach the banana. See *The Mentality of Apes*, translated from the 2nd rev. ed. by Ella Winter (New York: Vintage, 1959). For Gestalt influences on Maslow, see Hoffman, *Right to Be Human*, chap. 6.

53. Ash, *Gestalt Psychology in German Culture*, ix.

54. Comparing physics and Gestalt psychology exposes a cross-fertilization of ideas between disciplines. Wertheimer was a close friend of Einstein's, and Köhler was a student of Planck's. Both Wertheimer and Köhler studied field physics and relativity theory, and Goldstein emphasized the importance of the role, context, and frame of reference of the observer.

55. Michael Wertheimer, as quoted in Leahey, *History of Psychology*, 210. The quote was taken from "Max Wertheimer: Gestalt Prophet," Presidential Address to Division 26 (History), annual meeting of the American Psychological Association. Toronto, Canada, August 31, 1978.

56. Abraham H. Maslow, *The Psychology of Science: A Reconnaissance* (New York: Harper and Row, 1966), 151.

57. Maslow, *Motivation and Personality*, ix.

58. In this way, Köhler placed himself in the same camp as Edmund Husserl (1859–1938), the German philosopher and founder of phenomenology. Human beings, Husserl said, require a special science. His answer was phenomenology, an examination of consciousness from the subject's viewpoint. For a short review, see Viney and King, *History of Psychology*, 407–8. Husserl called it the "science of inner-experience, subjectivity and the mental"; *Phenomenological Psychology*, trans. John Scanlon (The Hague: Nijhoff, 1977).

59. Maslow, *Psychology of Science*, xiii–xiv.

60. Maslow, *Journals*, 1:278.

61. Maslow, *Psychology of Science*, 15–16.

62. Abraham H. Maslow, *The Farther Reaches of Human Nature* (New York: Viking, 1971), 4.

63. Maslow, as quoted in Hoffman, *Right to Be Human*, 42.

64. Maslow, "Synergy in the Society and in the Individual," in *Farther Reaches of Human Nature*, 200. See also his chapter "Personality and Patterns of Culture," in *Psychology of Personality*, ed. Ross Stagner (New York: McGraw-Hill, 1937), 445–53.

65. Ruth Benedict, *Patterns of Culture* (1934; reprint, Boston: Houghton Mifflin, 1959), 46. See p. 51 for her suggestion that anthropology should heed Gestalt psychology; other quotes on 47, 48, 50.

66. Margaret Mead, *Ruth Benedict* (New York: Columbia University Press, 1974), 49.

67. Abraham H. Maslow and Bela Mittelmann, *Principles of Abnormal Psychology: The Dynamics of Psychic Illness* (New York: Harper and Row, 1941).

68. Maslow, *Motivation and Personality*, xii–xiii.

69. Maslow, "A Theory of Human Motivation," in *Motivation and Personality*, 46. This piece was first published in *Psychological Review* 50 (1943): 370–96.

70. "Higher Ceilings for Human Nature" was Maslow's working title for *Motivation and Personality*; for Goldstein, see ix.

71. See "Self-Actualizing People: A Study of Psychological Health" in *Motivation and Personality*, 149–80, list on 152.

72. Hall, "Conversation with Maslow," 56; and Maslow, *Journals*, 1:62 and 2:762.

73. Maslow, *Motivation and Personality*, 46.

74. Maslow, *Journals*, 1:626–27.

75. Maslow, *Farther Reaches of Human Nature*, 25.

76. Maslow, *Toward a Psychology of Being*, 160–61.

77. Maslow, *Farther Reaches of Human Nature*, 45. Maslow later qualified his use of the acorn-oak analogy. It was a "poor choice of figures of speech, of analogies, because it is programmed.... It just leads to the notion of something growing all by itself without any effort"; Maslow as quoted in Frick, *Humanistic Psychology*, 23. Part of this struggle reflected his position that "instinct-like" qualities had some determination over human development, but he was not willing to say it *controlled* human growth. "Growth toward self-actualization and full-humanness is made possible by a complex hierarchy of 'good preconditions'"; Maslow, *Motivation and Personality*, xxv.

78. Maslow, *Toward a Psychology of Being*, 160–61.

79. Ibid., 193.

80. Maslow first explained his hierarchy of needs in "A Dynamic Theory of Human Motivation," *Psychological Review* 50 (1943): 370–96. He revised and included it in *Motivation and Personality* under the title "A Theory of Human Motivation."

81. Maslow, *Toward a Psychology of Being*, 25.

82. Maslow, *Motivation and Personality*, 51.

83. Maslow, as quoted in *Memorial Volume*, 80.

84. Maslow, *Motivation and Personality*, 19.

85. Maslow, *Toward a Psychology of Being*, 83.

86. Maslow, *Motivation and Personality*, appendix B, 299.

87. Maslow, *Psychology of Science*, 11.

88. Ibid., 12.

89. Maslow, *Motivation and Personality*, appendix B, 297.

90. Science was never neutral, in Maslow's estimation; it was always value-laden. For his views, see especially chap. 12 in *Psychology of Science*.

91. Maslow, *Farther Reaches of Human Nature*, 75.

92. Ibid.

93. Maslow, *Psychology of Science*, quote on 63.

94. Ibid., 96.

95. Ibid., 103–4.

96. Hoffman, *Right to Be Human*, 224–25.

97. Abraham Maslow, *Future Visions: The Unpublished Papers of Abraham Maslow*, ed. Edward Hoffman (Thousand Oaks, Calif.: Sage, 1996), 13; Frick, *Humanistic Psychology*, 35; and Henry Geiger, introduction to *Farther Reaches of Human Nature*, xviii.

98. For this famous debate, see Carl R. Rogers and B. F. Skinner, "Some Issues Concerning the Control of Human Behavior," *Science* 124 (November 30, 1956): 1057–66; B. F. Skinner, *About Behaviorism* (New York: Vintage, 1976); Skinner, *Walden Two* (New York: Macmillan, 1948); Carl R. Rogers, *Client Centered Therapy: Its Current Practice, Implications, and Theory* (1953; New York: Trans-Atlantic, 1995). For Rogers and Skinner at Esalen, see George Leonard, *Walking on the Edge of the World* (Boston: Houghton Mifflin, 1988), 176–77.

99. Most place Maslow alongside Gordon Allport, Carl Rogers, Rollo May, and James Bugental as the chief founders of humanistic psychology, though many contributed. For histories of humanistic psychology, turn to Roy José DeCarvalho, *The Founders of Humanistic Psychology* (New York: Praeger, 1991); Donald Moss, ed., *Humanistic and Transpersonal Psychology: A Historical and Biographical Sourcebook* (Westport, Conn.: Greenwood Press, 1999), especially Moss's chapter, "Abraham Maslow and the Emergence of Humanistic Psychology," 24–37; and Viney and King, *History of Psychology*, 401–19. For overviews of the history of psychology, see Ellen Herman, *The Romance of American Psychology: Political Culture in the Age of Experts* (Berkeley: University of California Press, 1995); and Michael Wertheimer, *A Brief History of Psychology*, 3rd ed. (New York: Holt, Rinehart and Winston, 1987). For the placement of psychology in the American religious tradition and for sketches of psychological movements and actors, see Eugene Taylor, *Shadow Culture: Psychology and Spirituality in America* (Washington, D.C.: Counterpoint, 1999), especially chaps. 11–13.

100. Maslow, *Toward a Psychology of Being*, 97. He continued to discuss what he means by full humanness in this book; see his definition and list on pages 156–57.

101. Farrell, *Spirit of the Sixties*, 203–12.

102. Maslow, "The Creative Attitude," in *Farther Reaches of Human Nature*, 69–71.

103. Maslow, *Toward a Psychology of Being*, especially chaps. 6 and 7: "Cognition of Being in the Peak-Experiences" and "Peak-Experiences as Acute Identity-Experiences"; Maslow, *Religions, Values, and Peak Experiences*, quote on 59. See also Maslow, *Motivation and Personality*, 164. For a nineteenth-century comparison, turn to Ralph Waldo Emerson's description of his transcendental experience: "All mean egotism vanishes. I become a transparent eye-ball; I am nothing; I see all; the currents of the Universal Being circulate through me. I am part or parcel of God"; found in "Nature," in *Essays and Lectures: Ralph Waldo Emerson* (New York: Literary Classics of the U.S., 1983), 10.

104. Maslow, as quoted in *Memorial Volume*, 51–52, quote on 51.

105. Though intrigued with the possibility of using psychedelic drugs to trigger peak experiences, Maslow never took drugs or advocated their use. He did become friends with LSD researcher Timothy Leary and enjoyed discussing his work (Maslow's daughter Ellen was Leary's research assistant); Hoffman, *Right to Be Human*, 265–66. Multiple journal entries in 1968 and 1969 signal Maslow's increasing displeasure with Esalen and many in the youth movement who he thought acted selfishly and wanted instant gratification.

106. Frick, *Humanistic Psychology*, 35–36; and Maslow, *Future Visions*, 13.

107. Maslow, *Psychology of Science*, xiii–xvii.

108. Maslow, *Toward a Psychology of Being*, iii–iv.

109. For Maslow's early disillusionment with Marxism, see Wilson, *New Pathways in Psychology*, 180; and Hoffman, *Right to Be Human*, 15–16, 22–23, 45–46. In the 1960s, he condemned socialism for its "dichotomous" thinking of dividing the world between capitalists and socialists and for what he perceived as the Marxian tendency to ascribe only the "profit motive" to capitalists. Mostly, however, he lumped Marxism with Freudianism and rejected them because of their negative image of humanity. He read it as a fundamental contradiction to his humanistic philosophy. In his *Journals*, he offered an occasional critique of Marxism, oftentimes in response to articles or books he had read. For example, he attacked the works of Michael Harrington, Paul Goodman, and Herbert Marcuse. For a sampling, see Maslow, *Journals*, 2:843–52. In contrast, he linked his own thinking with that of the economist Walter Weisskopf, whom he felt had a more complex and accurate picture of human motivation in economics. Weisskopf and Maslow were both part of an academic values institute; see Hoffman, *Right to Be Human*, 230–32, for a brief account of this institute. See a sampling of their papers with respect to this institute in *New Knowledge in Human Values*, ed. Abraham Maslow (New York: Harper and Brothers, 1959). Weisskopf shared Maslow's holistic attitudes and would be a good study of the ways holistic thought influenced economic studies. See his books *The Psychology of Economics* (Chicago: University of Chicago Press, 1955), and *Alienation and Economics* (New York: Dutton, 1971). He held to "a philosophical anthropology with a holistic, encompassing image of man and human existence"; *Alienation and Economics*, 7.

110. Hoffman, *Right to Be Human*, 227–30.

111. Maslow, as quoted in *Memorial Volume*, 64–65, quote on 65; and Maslow *Journals*, 2:803.

112. Hoffman, *Right to Be Human*, 308–9.

113. Maslow, *Toward a Psychology of Being*, 6.

114. Maslow, as quoted in *Memorial Volume*, 59, 47.

115. Maslow, *Toward a Psychology of Being*, 6.

116. Maslow, *Farther Reaches of Human Nature*, 19.

117. Maslow, *Toward a Psychology of Being*, appendix B, 221.

118. For a definition of "synergy," see the *Oxford English Dictionary*, 2nd ed. (Oxford: Clarendon Press, 1991), 17:479–80. See also my chapter on Fuller in this book for a discussion of synergy.

119. Benedict's concept of synergy is not well known, for she did not publish anything on it. For Maslow's recollection of Benedict's use of the term and his own

conceptualization, see "Further Notes on the Psychology of Being," *Journal of Humanistic Psychology* 4 (1964): 45–58; and "Synergy in the Society and in the Individual," in *Farther Reaches of Human Nature*, 199–211; also printed in the *Journal of Individual Psychology* 20 (November 1964): 153–64. Maslow worked from lecture notes Benedict used for classes at Bryn Mawr College in 1941. Using them twenty-five years later to develop his own interpretation, he admitted that he could not tell which were her thoughts and which his: "I have made use of this concept through the years in various ways, and there has been a kind of fusion"; *Farther Reaches of Human Nature*, 203, quotes in text on 202. He printed Benedict's notes posthumously; Abraham H. Maslow and John J. Honigmann, "Synergy: Some Notes of Ruth Benedict," *American Anthropologist* 72 (1970): 320–33.

120. Maslow, *Motivation and Personality*, 179.

121. Maslow, *Farther Reaches of Human Nature*, 209.

122. Maslow's report to the Social Science Research Council, which supported his fieldwork; quoted in Hoffman, *Right to Be Human*, 127–28. The experience led him to denounce cultural relativism as he decided that "every human being comes at birth into society not as a lump of clay to be molded by society, but rather as a structure which society may warp or suppress or build upon. He concluded that first, his subjects were human beings, and only secondly, Blackfoot." Later Maslow grew more and more hostile to cultural relativism. At one point he wrote: "A total cultural determinism is still the official orthodox doctrine of many or most of the social scientists and anthropologists. This doctrine not only denies intrinsic and higher motivations, but comes perilously close sometimes to denying human nature itself"; Maslow, as quoted in *Memorial Volume*, 23.

123. Maslow, *Farther Reaches of Human Nature*, 204.

124. Though he expressed it a bit awkwardly, Maslow defined synergy as holistic: "Synergy is more holistic, and the more holistic is more synergic. (By contrast with atomistic, which is nonsynergic and which must be.) The more holistic a structure is operationally, that is, the more mutual interdependence there is, the better the communication, etc., etc., the more the team has to rely on each other—for instance as in a basketball team—the more synergic everything will be"; *Eupsychian Management: A Journal* (Homewood, Ill.: Irwin, 1965), 98.

125. Maslow, *Farther Reaches of Human Nature*, 213.

126. For his thoughts on "jungle world-views," see Abraham Maslow, "The Authoritarian Character Structure," *Journal of Social Psychology* 18 (1953): 401–11.

127. Maslow, *Farther Reaches of Human Nature*, 208.

128. Frank Manuel, as quoted in *Memorial Volume*, 9. Manuel was also a student of utopian thought; see Frank Manuel and Fritzie P. Manuel, *Utopian Thought in the Western World* (Cambridge, Mass.: Belknap Press, 1979); and an edited work, *Utopias and Utopian Thought* (Boston: Houghton Mifflin, 1966).

129. Maslow, *Motivation and Personality*, 277. In *Farther Reaches of Human Nature*, Maslow defined eupsychia as "a society which was specifically designed for improving the self-fulfillment and psychological health of all people" (78), and he admitted that his utopia was "a selected subculture" (214).

130. Maslow, "Politics Three," in Rollo May, Carl Rogers, and Abraham Maslow, *Politics and Innocence: A Humanistic Debate* (Dallas, Tex.: Saybrook, 1986), 90;

"Politics 3" was based on Maslow's journal entries and published posthumously in *Journal of Humanistic Psychology* 17 (1977): 5–20.

131. Maslow, as quoted in *Memorial Volume,* 113.

132. Ibid., 81.

133. Maslow, *Farther Reaches of Human Nature,* 19.

134. Benedict Anderson, *Imagined Communities: Reflections on the Origin and Spread of Nationalism,* rev. ed. (London: Verso, 1991).

135. Maslow explained his stance in *Future Visions,* 61–63.

136. Maslow, *Toward a Psychology of Being,* 237–40.

137. For the beginnings of humanistic psychology, see DeCarvalho, *Founders of Humanistic Psychology;* and Anthony Sutich, "The Founding of Humanistic and Transpersonal Psychology: A Personal Account" (Ph.D. diss., Humanistic Psychology Institution, 1976). The group started as the American Association of Humanistic Psychologists, but it dropped "American" from the name in 1969. DeCarvalho reports that the group always had an international focus, but in the McCarthy era, its members feared being seen as subversive and hence included "American" in the title; *Founders of Humanistic Psychology,* 12. Sutich worked with Maslow to form the journal and the association. He served as the editor until 1968 and then founded the *Journal of Transpersonal Psychology.* Sutich was largely self-trained in psychology but was well connected to many in the psychological world. For his story, see Taylor, *Shadow Culture,* 170–73. The Humanistic Psychology Archive in the Special Collections of University of California, Santa Barbara Davidson Library, houses a vast array of primary materials on humanistic psychology. Reprints of many Maslow papers are held there, as are papers, audiotapes, and videotapes. of multiple humanistic psychologists.

138. DeCarvalho, *Founders of Humanistic Psychology,* 10–11.

139. For Buhler's comments, see "Human Life as a Whole as a Central Subject of Humanistic Psychology," in Bugental, *Challenges of Humanistic Psychology,* 83–91, quote on 83.

140. DeCarvalho, *Founders of Humanistic Psychology,* 11.

141. Christopher M. Aanstoos, Ilene Serlin, and Thomas Greening, "History of Division 32 (Humanistic Psychology) of the American Psychological Association," in *Unification through Division: Histories of the Divisions of the American Psychological Association,* ed. Donald A. Dewsbury, vol. 5 (Washington, D.C.: American Psychological Association, 1999), 10–12, http://www.apa.org/divisions/Div32/pdfs/history.pdf (accessed September 1, 2008).

142. Carl Rogers, as quoted in Calvin Tomkins, "New Paradigms," *New Yorker,* January 5, 1976, 42. Rogers described the encounter experience, his intent in using it as a psychotherapist, and its proliferation in "The Process of the Basic Encounter Group," in *Challenges of Humanistic Psychology,* ed. James F. Bugental (New York: McGraw-Hill, 1967), 261–78. Kurt Lewin, a Gestalt psychologist, experimented with small groups to promote personal growth, learning, and leadership training at MIT. Psychologists running the groups encouraged honest communication between group members in order to improve relations and to help people work effectively in group situations. More democratic than the psychoanalytic methods involving the doctor and patient, these group encounters encouraged all the members to play a key role in their own and others' learning. Rogers especially developed a nondirective therapist approach that directly challenged psychoanalysis and behaviorism. "Client-

centered therapy" gave "clients" (not patients) a direct role in their treatment. He encouraged self-knowledge and introspection. Like Maslow, Rogers believed that human beings had an "actualizing tendency." He joined the Western Behavioral Sciences Institute (WBSI), based in La Jolla, California, in the 1960s.

143. Maslow spoke about "Bodhisattvas" on several occasions. See, for example, *Journals*, 1:624, for the quote. For his chastisement of Esalen, see Maslow, *Journals*, 2:827; see also Hoffman, *Right to Be Human*, 288–93.

144. For Maslow's influence on management, see Hoffman, *Right to Be Human*, 275, 285–86, 326, 315–17. In the 1970s, management historians judged Maslow to be one of the most influential contributors to business and management ideas and practice in the last 200 years; Daniel A. Wren and Robert D. Hay, "Management Historians and Business Historians: Differing Perceptions of Pioneer Contributors," *Academy of Management Journal* 20 (September 1977): 470–76. His ideas remained relevant at the end of the twentieth century, and his daughter Ann Kaplan reprinted *Eupsychian Management* under the new title *Maslow on Management* (New York: Wiley, 1998).

145. Betty Friedan, *The Feminine Mystique* (New York: Norton, 1963). For Friedan's reliance on Maslow, see Hoffman, *Right to Be Human*, 274; Daniel Horowitz, *Betty Friedan and the Making of the Feminist Mystique: The American Left, the Cold War, and Modern Feminism* (Amherst: University of Massachusetts Press, 1998). Helen Gurley Brown, author of *Sex and the Single Girl*, also relied on notions of self-actualization to forward her ideals of womanhood; see Jennifer Scanlon, *Bad Girls Go Everywhere: The Life of Helen Gurley Brown* (New York: Oxford University Press, 2009), 94–111; and Micki McGee, *Self-Help, Inc.: Makeover Culture in American Life* (New York: Oxford University Press, 2005), 39–43.

146. Casey Hayden and Mary King, "Sex and Caste: A Kind of Memo," *Liberation*, April 1966, Mary King's Web site, http://www.maryking.info/Mary-King-Sex-and-Caste-Memo.html (accessed September 30, 2008). The memo has been reprinted in multiple anthologies as well. For Farrell's discussion of the memo, see *Spirit of the Sixties*, 235.

147. Marty Jeezer, *Abbie Hoffman: An American Rebel* (New Brunswick, N.J.: Rutgers University Press, 1992), 22–25. Abbie Hoffman's wife, Sheila Hoffman, read *The Feminine Mystique*, which also influenced Abbie and Sheila's social protests; see Marty Jeezer, *Abbie Hoffman: An American Rebel* (New Brunswick, N.J.: Rutgers University Press, 1992), 34, 50. See also Farrell, *Spirit of the Sixties*, 206–7. The San Francisco *Oracle*, a Haight-Ashbury psychedelic newspaper, also lauded Maslow's ideas; see Stan Russell, "Maslow's Model Mutant," *Oracle of Southern California* 2 (April–May 1967): 10, and as noted in Howard Brick, *Age of Contradiction: American Thought and Culture in the 1960s* (Ithaca, N.Y.: Cornell University Press, 2000), 115, 212.

148. Abraham Maslow, "A Philosophy of Psychology," in *Personal Problems and Psychological Frontiers*, ed. Johnson E. Fairchild (New York: Sheridan House, 1957), 225–44, quote on 226–27.

149. Ibid., quote on 225. Maslow defined psychologists as "all the people who are interested in developing a truer, a clearer, a more empirical conception of human nature, and only such people. That excludes some professors of psychology and many psychiatrists" (227–28).

150. Maslow, as quoted in *Memorial Volume*, 100.

151. Maslow, *Toward a Psychology of Being*, iii.

152. Bugental, *Challenges of Humanistic Psychology*, vii. For Gestalt therapy, see Joel Latner, *The Gestalt Therapy Book: A Holistic Guide to the Theory, Principles, and Techniques of Gestalt Therapy as Developed by Frederick S. Perls and Others* (New York: Julian Press, 1973). See also Bastin J. Parangimalil, *Toward Integral Holism in Psychology* (New Delhi: Inter-India Publications, 1989), for an embrace of Maslow's holistic psychology.

153. Maslow, "What Is the Essence of Human Nature?" in *Future Visions*, 86.

154. Maslow, *Psychology of Science*, 2.

155. Robert Abzug, "Rollo May: Philosopher as Therapist," *Association for Humanistic Psychology Perspective Magazine*, April/May 2003, http://www.ahpweb.org/pub/perspective/may03/may03cover.html (accessed August 27, 2008).

156. I thank historian Wendy Plotkin for her review of the number of new and reprinted books about Jung in *Books in Print* (2007); she recorded a jump from five books on the psychologist in the 1950s to fifty-five in the 1970s; Wendy Plotkin, e-mail to author, September 1, 2007.

CHAPTER 6

1. For an earlier version of this chapter, please see Linda Sargent Wood, "Contact, Encounter, and Exchange at Esalen: A Window onto Late Twentieth-Century American Spirituality," *Pacific Historical Review* 77 (August 2008): 453–87. For the quote, see George Leonard, "Encounters at the Mind's Edge," *Esquire*, June 1985: 308.

2. Michael Murphy, Esalen fund-raising letter, c. 1982, MSS 8, File "Esalen Papers," Box 1, Humanistic Psychology Archive, University of California, Santa Barbara (hereafter cited as Esalen MSS). At another time he said, "Our original idea was to create a forum for social scientists, educators, religious leaders and others to explore the human potential"; Murphy, "Esalen: Where Man Confronts Himself," *Stanford Alumni Almanac* (May 1968), 7, File "Esalen Papers," Box 2, Esalen MSS.

3. For Esalen's history, see Walter Anderson, *The Upstart Spring: Esalen and the American Awakening* (Reading, Mass.: Addison-Wesley, 1983); Alice Kahn, "Esalen at 25," *Los Angeles Times Magazine*, December 6, 1987; Jeffrey J. Kripal, *Esalen: America and the Religion of No Religion* (Chicago: University of Chicago Press, 2007); Jeffrey J. Kripal and Glenn W. Shuck, eds., *On the Edge of the Future: Esalen and the Evolution of American Culture* (Bloomington: Indiana University Press, 2005); Leonard, "Encounters at the Mind's Edge"; Eugene Taylor, *Shadow Culture: Psychology and Spirituality in America* (Washington, D.C.: Counterpoint, 1999), 235–60; and Calvin Tomkins, "New Paradigms," *New Yorker*, January 5, 1976, 30–51.

4. Murphy, "Esalen: Where Man Confronts Himself," 6.

5. Stuart Miller, quoted in Anderson, *Upstart Spring*, 192. See Miller's account in his book *Hot Springs: The True Adventures of the First New York Jewish Literary Intellectual in the Human Potential Movement* (New York: Viking, 1971).

6. See, for example, Jeffrey J. Kripal, "From Emerson to Esalen: America's Religion of No Religion," *Chronicle of Higher Education* 53 (April 13, 2007), B6; Kripal, *Esalen*; Kripal and Shuck, *On the Edge of the Future*; Taylor, *Shadow Culture*;

and Don Lattin, *Following Our Bliss: How the Spiritual Ideals of the Sixties Shape Our Lives Today* (San Francisco: HarperSanFrancisco, 2003).

7. Catherine Albanese, "Exchanging Selves, Exchanging Souls: Conflict, Combination, and American Religious History," in *Retelling U. S. Religious History*, ed. Thomas A. Tweed (Berkeley: University of California Press, 1997), 200–226, quote on 223.

8. Conservative evangelicals, under various leaders such as James Dobson, Jerry Falwell, Richard Land, and Pat Robertson, made their presence felt particularly in the presidential elections of Ronald Reagan and George W. Bush; they wielded considerable political and cultural power in the last decades, influencing both domestic and international policy. At the same time, Protestantism as a whole registered fewer numbers and lost some of its cultural authority. The Methodist Church, for example, claimed 11 million members in 1965. By 2005, membership dropped to 8.5 million. Overall, mainline church membership fell 24 percent from 1960 to 2003. While these changes defined Protestantism, Catholicism held steady. Since 1965, about one-quarter of the U.S. population has professed Catholicism. For evangelical influence on politics and denominational statistics, see Walter Russell Mead, "God's Country?" *Foreign Affairs* 85 (September/October 2006), 24–43. For evangelicalism and Christianity in America, see Christian Smith, *American Evangelicalism: Embattled and Thriving* (Chicago: University of Chicago Press, 1998); Clyde Wilcox and Carin Larson, *Onward Christian Soldiers: The Christian Right in American Politics* (Boulder, Colo.: Westview Press, 2006); and Damon Linker, *The Theocons: Secular America under Siege* (New York: Doubleday, 2006). For Protestant decline, see Amanda Porterfield, *The Transformation of American Religion: The Story of a Late-Twentieth-Century Awakening* (New York: Oxford University Press, 2001). For Catholic numbers, see "Frequently Requested Catholic Church Statistics," Center for Applied Research in the Apostolate (CARA), Georgetown University, 2006, http://cara.georgetown.edu/bulletin/index.htm (accessed September 14, 2007). For additional information on America's religious population, see Thomas A. Tweed and Stephen Prothero, eds., *Asian Religions in America: A Documentary History* (New York: Oxford University Press, 1999); Edwin S. Gaustad and Leigh E. Schmidt, *A Religious History of America: The Heart of the American Story from Colonial Times to Today* (SanFrancisco: HarperSanFrancisco, 2004); and Mark Oppenheimer, *Knocking on Heaven's Door: American Religion in the Age of the Counterculture* (New Haven, Conn.: Yale University Press, 2003).

9. For the 20 percent figure, see Robert Fuller, *Spiritual but Not Religious: Understanding Unchurched America* (New York: Oxford University Press, 2001), 4. For the quote, see Tamar Frankiel, "Ritual Sites in the Narrative of American Religion," in Tweed, *Retelling U. S. Religious History*, 81.

10. For contemporary spirituality and its history, see Catherine L. Albanese, ed., *American Spiritualities: A Reader* (Bloomington: Indiana University Press, 2001); William Clebsch, *American Religious Thought: A History* (Chicago: University of Chicago Press, 1973); Sarah M. Pike, *New Age and Neopagan Religions in America* (New York: Columbia University Press, 2004); Amanda Porterfield, *Feminine Spirituality in America: From Sarah Edwards to Martha Graham* (Philadelphia: Temple University Press, 1980); Porterfield, *Transformation of American Religion*; Leigh E.

Schmidt, *Restless Souls: The Making of American Spirituality* (San Francisco: HarperSanFrancisco, 2005); Taylor, *Shadow Culture*; Tweed, *Retelling U.S. Religious History*; and Robert Wuthnow, *After Heaven: Spirituality in America since the 1950s* (Berkeley: University of California Press, 1998).

11. See, for example, Kripal, "From Emerson to Esalen"; Kripal and Shuck, *On the Edge of the Future*; Taylor, *Shadow Culture*; and Lattin, *Following Our Bliss*.

12. Oral history interview with Michael Murphy by author, July 8, 1999, San Rafael, California, in author's possession.

13. Glenn W. Shuck, "Satan's Hot Springs: Esalen in the Popular Evangelical Imagination," in Kripal and Shuck, *On the Edge of the Future*, 268–85.

14. Murphy's grandfather purchased 375 acres; Esalen sits on 52 of those acres now, 25 of which are open to guests. The rest of the land is held in a family trust. Jackie Krentzman, "In Murphy's Kingdom," *Stanford Magazine*, January/February 1998, http://www.stanfordalumni.org/news/magazine/1998/janfeb/articles/murphy.html (accessed November 22, 2006); and the Esalen Web site, http://www.esalen.org/info/faq/faq1.html#locate (accessed November 22, 2006). See the Esalen Web site for a virtual tour of the place: http://www.esalen.org/place/tour/tourwide/vrframes.htm (accessed March 25, 2008). See also Anderson, *Upstart Spring*, 45–54. For Price, see Barclay James Erickson, "The Only Way Out Is In: The Life of Richard Price," in Kripal and Shuck, eds., *On the Edge of the Future*, 148.

15. Sandra Sizer Frankiel, *California's Spiritual Frontiers: Religious Alternatives in Anglo-Protestantism, 1850–1910* (Berkeley: University of California Press, 1988), 126.

16. Henry Miller and Michael Murphy, as quoted in Tom McNichol, "To Sur; With Love," *Washington Post*, March 15, 1998, travel section. An entourage of Bohemian artists followed Miller, adding to those who had lived around Carmel, including Mary Austin, Sinclair Lewis, and Jack London. Other religious groups built sanctuaries nearby: the New Carmel Highlands convent; the Camaldoli hermitage at Lucia (1958); and one of the first Zen Buddhist training monasteries in the United States at Tassajara Springs (1964). Anderson, *Upstart Spring*, 18. Anthropologist Alfred Kroeber claimed in his *Handbook of California Indians* (Washington, D.C.: Government Printing Office, 1925) that the Esselen tribe had been eradicated, but the group survives in small numbers. Especially since the 1990s, under the leadership of Tom Little Bear Nason, the Esselen people (more than 100) have revitalized through tribal meetings, the building of the first Esselen roundhouse in centuries, and calls for federal recognition; Dolan H. Eargle Jr., *Native California Guide: Weaving the Past and Present* (San Francisco: Trees Company Press, 2000), 158–59, 192–93; Gary S. Breschini and Trudy Haversat, *The Esselen Indians of the Big Sur Country: The Land and the People* (Salinas, Calif.: Coyote Press, 2004); Esselen Tribe of Monterey, California, home page 2005, http://esselen.com/index.html (accessed November 11, 2005); and the Ohlone/Costanoan Esselen Nation Web site for tribal history and current information about this indigenous group, May 5, 2004, http://www.esselennation.com/ (accessed November 11, 2005).

17. Thompson, as quoted in Kripal, *Esalen*, 95.

18. Esalen Catalog (Summer–Fall 1964) advertised Frederick Perls's session on Gestalt therapy at $46 per weekend; Anderson, *Upstart Spring*, 96. The fall 1970 catalog offered five- to seven-day workshops for about $250, two-week workshops for

about $450, and four-week programs for around $800; for Esalen catalogs from 1968 to 1991, see Esalen MSS. For the "country club" quote, see Anderson, *Upstart Spring*, 146. For living expenses in San Francisco in the 1960s, see the U.S. Department of Commerce, Bureau of the Census, *The Statistical Abstracts of the United States* (Washington, D.C.: Government Printing Office, 1961–1970), http://www.census.gov/prod/www/abs/statab.html (accessed October 8, 2007).

19. Alan Watts, *In My Own Way: An Autobiography, 1915–1965* (New York: Pantheon, 1972), 218; Anderson, *Upstart Spring*, 54, 68.

20. Abraham Maslow, *Motivation and Personality*, 2nd ed. (New York: Harper and Row, 1970), 46.

21. Michael Murphy, quoted by Gordon Wheeler, "Spirit and Shadow: Esalen and the Gestalt Model," in Kripal and Shuck, *On the Edge of the Future*, 183.

22. Michael Murphy, quoted in Taylor, *Shadow Culture*, 243.

23. Author's interview with Murphy. Murphy counted six Joan Baez festivals held at Esalen.

24. Frederick S. Perls, *Ego, Hunger, and Aggression: The Beginning of Gestalt Therapy* (New York: Random House, 1969); Perls, *In and Out of the Garbage Pail* (Lafayette, Calif.: Real People Press, 1969); Perls, *Gestalt Therapy Verbatim* (Lafayette, Calif.: Real People Press, 1969); and Frederick S. Perls, Ralph E. Hefferline, and Paul Goodman, *Gestalt Therapy: Excitement and Growth in the Human Personality* (New York: Dell, 1951). For Frederick Perls's biography, see Martin Shepard, *Fritz* (New York: Saturday Review Press, 1975); and Anderson, *Upstart Spring*, 89–100; for an insightful discussion of Gestalt psychology, Perls's practice of it, and its influence on Esalen, see Wheeler, "Spirit and Shadow."

25. Perls delivered this statement in a paper titled "Workshop vs. Individual Therapy" at the American Psychological Association convention in New York City in September 1966. See also Frederick S. Perls, *Gestalt Is: A Collection of Articles about Gestalt Therapy and Living*, ed. John O. Stevens (Moab, Utah: Real People Press, 1975), 15; see also Perls, quoted in Anderson, *Upstart Spring*, 98, 326.

26. Murphy, "Esalen: Where Man Confronts Himself," 7.

27. Leonard, "Encounters at the Mind's Edge," 309. Michael Murphy, oral history by Jack Gaines, May 14, 1973, MSS 10, File "Mike Murphy," Box 1, Jack Gaines and Fritz Perls Collection, 1968–1981, Humanistic Psychology Archives, Davidson Library, University of California, Santa Barbara.

28. Albanese, "Exchanging Selves, Exchanging Souls," 203. For a history of some of the topics covered and people who have visited Esalen, see "History" at the Esalen Web site, http://www.esalen.org/air/esalen_initiativesfoldr/esalen_initiatives1.shtml (accessed March 25, 2008).

29. Stuart Miller, quoted in Leonard, "Encounters at the Mind's Edge," 308.

30. Murphy, "Esalen: Where Man Confronts Himself," 6.

31. Author's interview with Murphy.

32. Michael Murphy and James Hickman, "The Soviet-American Exchange Program," Esalen Catalog (September 1981), Esalen MSS. The Esalen Center for Theory and Research continues to sponsor a wide array of projects; see the Esalen Web site, http://www.esalenctr.org/display/aboutmenu.cfm (accessed November 22, 2006). For a newspaper account of the Soviet exchange, see Don Lattin, "Esalen Institute's Ties with Soviet Philosophy Project," *San Francisco Chronicle*, November

6, 1990. In the author's interview with Murphy, the founder stressed Esalen's social engagement and vision. Kripal tells of the connections with the Soviet Union in *Esalen*, 393–99.

33. Leonard has written about meeting Murphy and his Esalen involvement in George Leonard, *Walking on the Edge of the World* (Boston: Houghton Mifflin, 1988), 163–67, quote on 167; see also Anderson, *Upstart Spring*, 116.

34. For characterizations of Esalen as narcissistic, see Peter Marin, "The New Narcissism," *Harper's* 251 (October 1975): 45–46; and Tom Wolfe "The Me Decade and the Third Great Awakening," in *The Purple Decades: A Reader* (New York: Farrar, Straus and Giroux, 1982), 278; this piece was first published in *New York Magazine*, August 23, 1976, 26–40.

35. Murphy, quoted in Dirk Dunbar, "Eranos, Esalen, and the Ecocentric Psyche: From Archetype to Zeitgeist," *Trumpeter* 20 (2004): 32.

36. Baez tried to persuade Murphy and Price in the early 1960s to adopt more of a political focus; Anderson, *Upstart Spring*, 290. For an intriguing account of the beginnings of the student movement at Berkeley, see Marty Jeezer, *Abbie Hoffman: An American Rebel* (New Brunswick, N.J.: Rutgers University Press, 1992), 37–40.

37. Before offering political solutions, the Port Huron Statement declared, "*Human relationships* should involve fraternity and honesty.... Personal links between man and man are needed, especially to go beyond the partial and fragmentary bonds of function that bind men only as worker to worker, employer to employee, teacher to student.... Loneliness, estrangement, isolation describe the vast distance between man and man today. These dominant tendencies cannot be overcome by better personal management, nor by improved gadgets, but only when a love of man overcomes the idolatrous worship of things by man"; "The Port Huron Statement," as quoted in Todd Gitlin, *The Sixties: Years of Hope, Days of Rage* (New York: Bantam Books, 1987), 106–8.

38. For the Pacific Rim as an idea and a place of cross-cultural exchange, see Timothy Gray, *Gary Snyder and the Pacific Rim: Creating Counter-cultural Community* (Iowa City: University of Iowa Press, 2006), 4–20.

39. See Haridas Chaudhuri, "Western Theology and Eastern Mysticism," Cultural Integration Fellowship home page, 1996, at http://www.culturalintegration.org/article1.html (accessed August 22, 2006); the CIF home page for a short description of its history and purpose, 1999, http://www.culturalintegration.org/about.html#location (accessed August 22, 2006); and the "American Academy of Asian Studies to the California Institute of Integral Studies," David Ulansey's home page, http://www.well.com/user/davidu/aaas-ciis.html (accessed November 24, 2002).

40. For biographies of Murphy and Price, see Anderson, *Upstart Spring*; Jeffrey Kripal, "Reading Aurobindo from Stanford to Pondicherry: Michael Murphy and the Tantric Transmission (1950–1957)," in Kripal and Shuck, *On the Edge of the Future*, 99–131; and Erickson, "The Only Way Out Is In," 132–64. See also Kripal, *Esalen*, especially 47–82.

41. Michael Murphy, transcript of oral history interview by David E. Russell (University of Southern California Oral History Program, c. 1987), MSS 8, File "Esalen Papers," Box 2, Humanistic Psychology Archives, Davidson Library, University of California, Santa Barbara.

42. Frederic Spiegelberg called himself a "refugee theologian" because he felt he had fled both the political system of Nazi Germany and the traditions of Christianity; Spiegelberg, quoted in Michael Lumish, "American Academy of Asian Studies and the Quest for Authentic Identity" (paper presented at the annual conference of the Western History Association, Phoenix, Arizona, October 16, 2005); and Frederic Spiegelberg, *Living Religions of the World* (Englewood Cliffs, N.J.: Prentice-Hall, 1956), 17–18.

43. Alan Watts published Spiegelberg's first essay, "The Religion of Non-Religion," when he was the editor of the Buddhist Lodge journal, *Buddhism in England*; Watts, *In My Own Way*, 116.

44. Aurobindo Ghose, *The Life Divine* (New York: Greystone Press, 1949); and Ghose, *The Future Evolution of Man* (1963; Twin Lakes, Wis.: Lotus Press, 2002), 3. Michael Lumish describes Spiegelberg's trip to Aurobindo's ashram. When he was granted only five seconds with the master, Spiegelberg's initial anger at feeling slighted abated when he came face-to-face with the mystic. In a 1964 visit to Esalen, Spiegelberg told his audience that Aurobindo "saw me, or rather not really me, because he had a strange focusing of his eyes which seemed to penetrate me and look somehow at, shall we say, that *atman*, at the true self that was my real being." Those five seconds, Spiegelberg felt, were "infinitely more inspiring and powerful than I could ever have expected"; Lumish quoting Frederic Spiegelberg, "India and the Saints," audiotape, Esalen Institute, Big Sur, 1964, in Lumish, "American Academy of Asian Studies." See also Kripal, "Reading Aurobindo from Stanford to Pondicherry," 99–131; and Leonard, *Walking on the Edge of the World*, 165–66.

45. James Plaugher, a student in one of Spiegelberg's Buddhism's courses, writes about a time when Spiegelberg started a class by saying, "I just finished *The Phenomenon of Man* by Teilhard de Chardin," then switched his planned lecture to a disquisition on Teilhard's vision; "The American Academy of Asian Studies," Ulansey's Web site, http://www.well.com/user/davidu/aaas/html (accessed January 14, 2002).

46. Murphy said he started reading Teilhard in 1961; interview with the author. Michael Murphy, as quoted in Tomkins, "New Paradigms," 31. For an example of how Teilhard used the phrase, see Pierre Teilhard de Chardin, *The Phenomenon of Man*, trans. Bernard Wall (New York: Harper and Row, 1959), 221.

47. For Gainsborough's quote, see "The American Academy of Asian Studies," Ulansey's Web site, http://www.well.com/user/davidu/aaas.html (accessed January 14, 2002). See also Lumish, "American Academy of Asian Studies."

48. Watts believed the AAAS suffered because its financial backers and its teachers were at "cross purposes," one promoting a graduate degree and the other seeking the "transformation of consciousness"; *In My Own Way*, 245–47, quote on 245; see also Lumish, "American Academy of Asian Studies."

49. Murphy oral history interview by Russell.

50. Michael Murphy, *Golf in the Kingdom* (New York: Viking, 1972).

51. "The body came into [Esalen life] immediately," Murphy said; Tomkins, "New Paradigms," 50–51.

52. Anderson, *Upstart Spring*, 31; Kripal, *Esalen* 60.

53. Kripal, "Reading Aurobindo from Stanford to Pondicherry," 107.

54. Porterfield, *Transformation of American Religion*, 141.

55. Erickson, "The Only Way Out Is In," 139.

56. For Price's experience, see Wade Hudson, "An Interview with Dick Price," conducted in April 1985 Esalen Web site, http://www.esalen.org/air/essays/dick_price.htm (accessed November 4, 2005); Anderson, *Upstart Spring*, 36–43; and Erickson, "The Only Way Out Is In," 144–46.

57. Price interview with Hudson, April 1985.

58. For Murphy's appreciation of J. D. Salinger's characters, see Anderson, *Upstart Spring*, 33.

59. Michael McClure, *Scratching the Beat Surface* (San Francisco: North Point Press, 1982), quote on 12.

60. William Everson had already declared his pacifism during World War II by becoming a conscientious objector. Instead of serving in the military, he served time at Waldport, one of the military work camps organized for conscientious objectors during World War II. At Waldport, he linked hands with other artists, and their work anticipated the San Francisco Renaissance. Everson noted this in "William Everson (Brother Antoninus)," in *San Francisco Beat: Talking with the Poets*, ed. David Meltzer (San Francisco: City Lights Books, 2001), 25–30. For the San Francisco Renaissance and the Beat generation, see James Campbell, *This Is the Beat Generation: New York–San Francisco–Paris* (Berkeley: University of California Press, 2001); Michael Davidson, *San Francisco Renaissance: Politics and Community at Mid-Century* (New York: Cambridge University Press, 1991); Gray, *Gary Snyder and the Pacific Rim*; Michael Schumacher, *Dharma Lion: A Critical Biography of Allen Ginsberg* (New York: St. Martin's Press, 1992); Steven Watson, *Birth of the Beat Generation: Visionaries, Rebels, and Hipsters, 1944–1960* (New York: Pantheon, 1995); Gary Snyder, *Earth House Hold: Technical Notes and Queries to Fellow Dharma Revolutionaries* (New York: New Directions, 1969); Kenneth Rexroth, *An Autobiographical Novel* (New York: New Directions, 1991); Watts, *In My Own Way*, quote on 264.

61. Gary Snyder, as quoted in "Gary Snyder," Meltzer, *San Francisco Beat*, 291.

62. Stephen Mahoney, "The Prevalence of Zen," *Nation*, November 1, 1958, 311; and quoted in Anderson, *Upstart Spring*, 37. See Watts, *In My Own Way*; Watts, *Psychotherapy: East and West* (New York: Vintage, 1961), Watts, *The Spirit of Zen: A Way of Life, Work, and Art in the Far East* (New York: Grove Press, 1960); and Watts, *This Is It and Other Essays on Zen and Spiritual Existence* (New York: Collier, 1967).

63. For a selection of Watts's radio addresses, see Alan Watts, *Zen and the Beat Way* (Boston: Tuttle, 1997); see also Matthew Lasar, *Pacifica Radio: The Rise of an Alternative Network* (Philadelphia: Temple University Press, 2000); and Jeff Land, *Active Radio: Pacifica's Brash Experiment* (Minneapolis: University of Minnesota Press, 1999). For audio files and transcripts, see the Pacifica Radio Archives: A Living History, http://www.pacificaradioarchives.org/projects/restoredaudio/index.html (accessed August 22, 2006).

64. Upon his death, a commemoration of Alan Watts was printed in the Esalen Catalog (April–June 1974), Esalen MSS. The article summarized his activities with the center and concluded, "He was our gentlest and most joyous teacher" (2).

65. Watts, *In My Own Way*, 261.

66. Snyder, as quoted in Meltzer, *San Francisco Beat*, 281. For Snyder's Buddhism and role in the San Francisco Renaissance, see Gray, *Gary Snyder and the Pacific Rim*.

67. Kyger, as quoted in Meltzer, *San Francisco Beat*, 127.

68. Although the 1893 Parliament chiefly promoted Protestant Christianity, a charismatic Indian, Swami Vivekananda, captivated the Parliament's crowds. He stayed in the United States for several years, attracted a small following, and laid the foundation for the Vedanta Society. Other swamis followed, and Vedanta communities formed along the East Coast and West Coast. See Tomkins, "New Paradigms," 32; Carl T. Jackson, *Vedanta for the West: The Ramakrishna Movement in the United States* (Bloomington: Indiana University Press, 1994); and Timothy Miller, "Notes on the Prehistory of the Human Potential Movement: The Vedanta Society and Gerald Heard's Trabuco College," in Kripal and Shuck, *On the Edge of the Future*, 80–98. For more on the World's Parliament of Religions, see Richard Hughes Seager, *The World's Parliament of Religions* (Bloomington: Indiana University Press, 1995); and his edited collection of Parliament speeches, Seager, ed., *The Dawn of Religious Pluralism: Voices from the World's Parliament of Religions, 1893* (LaSalle, Ill.: Open Court, 1993). See also Eric J. Ziolkowski, ed., *A Museum of Faiths: Histories and Legacies of the 1893 World's Parliament of Religions* (Atlanta, Ga.: Scholars Press, 1993). Gerald Heard did more than write about his beliefs. From 1942 to 1947, he ran Trabuco College, a spiritual retreat and educational center, in southern California. For more on Heard's experiment and influence on Price and Murphy, see Anderson, *Upstart Spring*, 12–13; Kripal, *Esalen*, 86, 91; Miller, "Notes on the Prehistory of the Human Potential Movement"; and David King Dunaway, *Huxley in Hollywood* (New York: Harper and Row, 1989), especially 171–72.

69. For Buddhism in America, see Rick Fields, *How the Swans Came to the Lake: A Narrative History of Buddhism in America* (Boston: Shambhala, 1986); Porterfield, *Transformation of American Religion*, chap. 4; Richard Hughes Seager, *Buddhism in America* (New York: Columbia University Press, 1999); and Thomas A. Tweed, *The American Encounter with Buddhism, 1844–1912: Victorian Culture and the Limits of Dissent* (Bloomington: Indiana University Press, 1992). For the San Francisco Zen Center, see its Web site, http://www.sfzc.org/ (accessed August 23, 2006). Steven Tipton has explored the draw to Zen practices in the San Francisco area in the 1960s in *Getting Saved from the Sixties: Moral Meaning in Conversion and Cultural Change* (Berkeley: University of California Press, 1982), chap. 3; for the beginnings of the East-West House and Gia-Fu Feng's contribution to Esalen's beginnings, see Anderson, *Upstart Spring*, 42, 63.

70. Leonard, *Walking on the Edge of the World*, 118, emphasis in original.

71. Aldous Huxley, "Human Potentialities," University of California, San Francisco Medical Center lecture, 1960, quoted in Anderson, *Upstart Spring*, 10–11.

72. Michael Murphy, quoted in Leonard, *Walking on the Edge of the World*, 198.

73. LSD-25 (lysergic acid diethylamide) was first synthesized in 1943 by Albert Hofmann, a Swiss chemist. See Jay Stevens, *Storming Heaven: LSD and the American Dream* (New York: Atlantic Monthly Press, 1987), especially chaps. 4–6. For a history of LSD research by an Esalen regular, see Stanislov Grof, *LSD Psychotherapy* (San Bernardino, Calif.: Borgo, 1986). For Aldous Huxley's drug experimentation, see Aldous Huxley, *The Doors of Perception and Heaven and Hell* (New York: Harper and Row, 1956); Dunaway, *Huxley in Hollywood*, especially 285–97; and Milton H. Erickson, "A Special Inquiry with Aldous Huxley into the Nature and Character of Various States of Consciousness," in *Altered States of Consciousness*, ed. Charles

T. Tart (San Francisco: HarperSanFrancisco, 1990), 58–93. For additional information on the discovery of LSD, its use by science, the government, and the counterculture, see Martin A. Lee and Bruce Shlain, *Acid Dreams: The CIA, LSD, and the Sixties Rebellion* (New York: Grove Press, 1985). See also David Farber, "The Intoxicated State/Illegal Nation: Drugs in the Sixties Counterculture," in Braunstein and Doyle, *Imagine Nation*, 17–40.

74. For a summation of George Leonard's speech and quotes, see Taylor, *Shadow Culture*, 236. For works by Leonard, see *Education and Ecstasy* (New York: Delacorte Press, 1968); *The Transformation: A Guide to the Inevitable Changes in Humankind* (New York: Delacorte Press, 1972); *The Ultimate Athlete: Re-visioning Sports, Physical Education and the Body* (New York: Viking, 1975); *Mastery: The Keys to Long-Term Success and Fulfillment* (New York: Dutton, 1991); and George Leonard and Michael Murphy, *The Life We Are Given: A Long-Term Program for Realizing the Potential of Body, Mind, Heart, and Soul* (New York: Putnam, 1995).

75. Thomas Berry has written on Buddhism, Hinduism, ecology, and American culture; see, for example, Thomas Berry, *The Dream of the Earth* (San Francisco: Sierra Club Books, 1988); and his book with physicist Brian Swimme, *The Universe Story: From the Primordial Flaring Forth to the Ecozoic Era—A Celebration of the Unfolding of the Cosmos* (San Francisco: HarperSanFrancisco, 1992). Swimme has articulated a view of the universe as living, intelligent, and self-organizing. He was at Esalen in 1985 for a conference titled "Critical Questions about New Paradigm Thinking," Esalen History, Esalen Center Web site, http://www.esalenctr.org/display/aboutpage.cfm?ID=13 (accessed February 22, 2007).

76. Evangelical author Douglas R. Groothuis condemned Murphy, Esalen, and the human potential movement for undue reliance on the self, consciousness-altering, and faith in evolution. He argued, "Whether Darwin realized it or not, the mystical goal of the theory of evolution he championed has always been to become 'God,'" a thought anathema to an evangelical Christian. See Douglas R. Groothuis, *Unmasking the New Age* (Downer's Grove, Ill.: InterVarsity Press, 1986), 20, and quoted in Shuck, "Satan's Hot Springs," 273–74.

77. Watts, *In My Own Way*, 247.

78. Kahn, "Esalen at 25," 42.

79. Michael Murphy, *Jacob Atabet: A Speculative Fiction* (Millbrae, Calif.: Celestial Arts, 1977). Kripal analyzes this work in *Esalen*, 291–300.

80. Gary Zukav, *The Dancing Wu Li Masters: An Overview of the New Physics* (New York: Morrow, 1979). For Zukav's participation in the conference, see "Esalen History," Esalen Center Web site, http://www.esalenctr.org/display/aboutpage.cfm?ID=4 (accessed February 22, 2007).

81. Kripal discusses quantum theory and its influence on alternative religion; *Esalen*, 309–12. He points especially to the pivotal role of Berkeley physicist Henry Stapp in the university's discussions, even while Stapp was not happy with the popular versions.

82. Fritjof Capra, *The Tao of Physics: An Exploration of the Parallels between Modern Physics and Eastern Mysticism* (New York: Random House, 1975); Capra, "The Role of Physics in the Current Change of Paradigms," in *The World View of Contemporary Physics*, ed. Richard F. Kitchener (Albany: State University of New York Press, 1988), 144–55; and Capra, *The Web of Life*. See also Kripal, *Esalen*, 302–7. For other holistic

notions in physics, see David Bohm, *Wholeness and the Implicate Order* (London: Routledge, 1980).

83. Alan Watts, *The Joyous Cosmology: Adventures in the Chemistry of Consciousness* (New York: Pantheon, 1962); Gregory Bateson, *Mind and Nature: A Necessary Unity* (New York: Dutton, 1979); and Bateson, *Steps to an Ecology of Mind: Collected Essays in Anthropology, Psychiatry, Evolution, and Epistemology* (New York: Ballantine, 1972); Blake, as quoted in Kripal, *Esalen*, 307–8. Kripal details Capra's journey in these same pages.

84. Kripal, *Esalen*, 314.

85. Maslow, as quoted in Edward Hoffman, *The Right to Be Human: A Biography of Abraham Maslow* (Los Angeles: Tarcher, 1988), 66–67.

86. Leonard, *Walking on the Edge of the World*, 322.

87. White blamed Christian attitudes of human superiority toward nature for the ecological crisis and proposed an alternative Christian ethos of equality between human beings and nature; Lynn White, "The Historical Roots of Our Ecological Crisis," *Science* 155 (March 10, 1967): 1203–7. See also John Passmore, *Man's Responsibility for Nature* (New York: Scribner, 1974). For a short literature review, see Eric Katz, "Ethics and Philosophy of the Environment: A Brief Review of the Major Literature," *Environmental History Review* 15 (Summer 1991): 79–86.

88. Quotes found in Esalen Catalog (1971), Esalen MSS. The first lecture was titled "Ecological Crisis: Religious Cause and Religious Solution."

89. Esalen Catalog (1970), Esalen MSS.

90. Charlene Spretnak was invited to Esalen for two conferences in 1993 and 1994 titled "Ecopsychology: Theory and Practice," Esalen Web site, http://www.esalen.org/air/esalen_initiativesfoldr/esalen_initiatives3.shtml (accessed November 1, 2006). She has written numerous books, including *Lost Goddesses of Early Greece: A Collection of Pre-Hellenic Myths* (Berkeley: Moon Books, 1978); *States of Grace: The Recovery of Meaning in the Postmodern Age* (San Francisco: HarperSanFrancisco, 1991); and *The Spiritual Dimension of Green Politics* (Santa Fe, N.M.: Bear, 1986). See also Theodore Roszak, Mary E. Gomes, and Allen D. Kanner, eds., *Ecopsychology: Restoring the Earth, Healing the Mind* (San Francisco: Sierra Club Books, 1995). For a lucid overview of the spiritual in environmentalism, see Thomas R. Dunlap, *Faith in Nature: Environmentalism as Religious Quest* (Seattle: University of Washington Press, 2004).

91. For these conferences, see the Esalen Web site, http://www.esalen.org/air/esalen_initiativesfoldr/esalen_initiatives2.shtml (accessed November 1, 2006).

92. Kripal and Shuck, "Introducing Esalen," in *On the Edge of the Future*, 2.

93. Tomkins, "New Paradigms," 35.

94. Price, as quoted in Erickson, "The Only Way Out Is In," 157.

95. The research supported Price's suspicions that the medical treatment he had received was not effective in helping the mentally ill. All patients were treated humanely, but one group was given drugs (phenothiazines), and the other group was given a placebo. In a three-year follow-up, patients without drugs showed more clinical improvement. For a report of this study, see Julian Silverman, "The Agnews Project," Esalen Catalog (Fall 1970); Anderson, *Upstart Spring*, 217–19; and Erickson, "The Only Way Out Is In," 150–52. See also Michael Murphy's obituary for Julian Silverman at Esalen's Web site, http://www.esalen.org/air/essays/julian_silverman.htm (accessed October 22, 2007).

96. Esalen Catalog (March–April 1973), Esalen MSS.

97. Kripal, *Esalen*, 172.

98. For a discussion of Buddhism's acceptance and Americanization at this time, see Porterfield, *Transformation of American Religion*, chap. 4; and Tweed and Prothero, *Asian Religions in America*.

99. Sylvester Graham (1794–1851) advocated an alternative health system predicated on healthy, moral living and healthy eating, thus tying moral and spiritual health to physical health. See Stephen Nissenbaum, *Sex, Diet, and Debility in Jacksonian America: Sylvester Graham and Health Reform* (Westport, Conn.: Greenwood Press, 1980), 46–49; James C. Whorton, *Crusaders for Fitness: The History of American Reformers* (Princeton, N.J.: Princeton University Press, 1982); and Whorton, *Nature Cures: The History of Alternative Medicine in America* (New York: Oxford University Press, 2002), 85–89.

100. Aldous Huxley, for one, was taken with the Alexander approach; Anderson, *Upstart Spring*, 11; quote found in Esalen Catalog (January–March 1974), Esalen MSS.

101. Stewart C. Easton, *Rudolf Steiner: Herald of a New Epoch* (Hudson, N.Y.: Anthroposophic Press, 1980).

102. Kripal, *Esalen*, 241–46. See, for example, Kenneth Pelletier, *Mind as Healer, Mind as Slayer: A Holistic Approach to Preventing Stress Disorders* (Boston: Allen and Unwin, 1977); and Andrew Weil, *Health and Healing: Understanding Conventional and Alternative Medicine* (Boston: Houghton Mifflin, 1983).

103. For Esalen's influence on complementary medicine, see Wheeler, "Spirit and Shadow," 184–85; Esalen Center for Theory and Research Web site, http://www.esalenctr.org/display/aboutpage.cfm?ID=17; Kripal, *Esalen*, 241–46; and Kripal and Shuck, "Introduction," *On the Edge of the Future*, 3.

104. Esalen Catalog (March–April 1973) and Esalen Catalog (October–December 1974), both in Esalen MSS.

105. Murphy, *Golf in the Kingdom*; and Michael Murphy, *The Future of the Body: Explorations into the Further Evolution of Human Nature* (Los Angeles: Tarcher, 1992). See also Murphy's book with parapsychologist Rhea White, *In the Zone: Transcendent Experience in Sport* (New York: Penguin, 1995); and Murphy, *The Kingdom of Shivas Irons* (New York: Broadway Books, 1997). For Murphy's work with Leonard, start with Leonard and Murphy, *The Life We Are Given*, and visit their Web site, ITP International, at http://www.itp-life.com/ (accessed October 22, 2007). For a discussion of Murphy's link between sports and spirit, see also Anderson, *Upstart Spring*, 257–60; and Kripal, *Esalen*, 270–86.

106. The women's movement made significant contributions to understandings of the body. As social reformers pushed for women's rights and feminist theorists shifted the focus of history, sociology, religion, and other disciplines to the role of women in society and the social structures and values that affected personal and political practices, they called attention to gender and body awareness. For a helpful synthesis of the women's movement, body awareness, and gender consciousness, see Porterfield, *Transformation of American Religion*, 163–98.

107. Phyllis H. Mattson, *Holistic Health in Perspective* (Palo Alto, Calif.: Mayfield, 1982), 70. Historian Wendy Plotkin conducted a search of *Books in Print Professional, 2007* and found that books with the word "acupuncture" in the title jumped from fewer

than ten in the 1960s to a little more than fifty in the 1970s to close to eighty in the 1980s. Her results were based on books in and out of print and included reprints and new editions of older books. Wendy Plotkin, e-mail to author, September 1, 2007.

108. Mattson, *Holistic Health in Perspective*, 10.

109. Anthony Weston, "On the Body in Medical Self-Care and Holistic Medicine," in *The Body in Medical Thought and Practice*, ed. Drew Leder (Dordrecht, Netherlands: Kluwer Academic Publishers, 1992), 81. For a discussion of the differences between holistic medicine and more traditional systems, see Stephen Lyng, *Holistic Health and Biomedical Medicine: A Countersystem Analysis* (Albany: State University of New York Press, 1990).

110. Hoffman, *Right to Be Human*, 306–7, quote on 306.

111. Julian Silverman, as quoted in Kripal, *Esalen*, 461.

112. Leonard, *Walking on the Edge of the World*, 274.

113. Anderson reports in *Upstart Spring* the Leonard introduced himself to Cobbs after he read about Cobbs's experience with racism in the newspaper. Cobbs and his wife had moved into an all-white neighborhood in San Francisco and experienced difficulties. Leonard persuaded *Look* magazine to run an article on their experience; *Upstart Spring*, 162. For Leonard's account, see Leonard, *Walking on the Edge of the World*, 265–74, 322–26.

114. Price Cobbs, as quoted in Leonard, *Walking on the Edge of the World*, 274; and Anderson, *Upstart Spring*, 164.

115. Anderson, *Upstart Spring*, 195; and Leonard, *Walking on the Edge of the World*, 324–28.

116. For some parallels between the Great Awakening and the Esalen experience, see Anderson, *Upstart Spring*, 7–8; and Wolfe, "The Me Decade."

117. Michael Murphy (via Murphy's assistant Joseph Kearns) e-mail message to author, February 12, 2008.

118. Catherine Albanese, *A Republic of Mind and Spirit: A Cultural History of American Metaphysical Religion* (New Haven, Conn.: Yale University Press, 2006). See also Albanese, *Nature Religion in America: From the Algonkian Indians to the New Age* (Chicago: University of Chicago Press, 1990). For Esalen's tie to past metaphysical religions and the romantic movement, see Kripal, "From Emerson to Esalen"; and Kripal, *Esalen*.

119. Author's interview with Murphy.

120. Michael Murphy, "Esalen Institute Statement of Purpose," and 2006 catalogs downloaded at Esalen Institute Web site, http://www.esalen.org/air/essays/purpose.shtml (accessed November 21, 2006). See also Esalen Catalog (May–October 1998) and Esalen Catalog (May–October 1999), in author's possession, for other examples of similar workshops.

121. Leonard, *Walking on the Edge of the World*, 381.

122. Albanese, "Exchanging Selves, Exchanging Souls," 223.

EPILOGUE

1. R. Buckminster Fuller, *Operating Manual for Spaceship Earth* (New York: Dutton, 1963), 59, and Fuller, *Critical Path* (New York: St. Martin's Press, 1981), 169.

2. Abraham H. Maslow, *Motivation and Personality*, 2nd ed. (New York: Harper and Row, 1970), xi.

3. Martin Luther King Jr., *Strength to Love*, New York: Harper and Row, 1963, quote on 3; see also 55, 120.

4. For this discussion see the introduction to this book and the literature cited in n. 55.

5. The literature is voluminous. See, for example, Nathan Hatch, *The Democratization of American Christianity* (New Haven, Conn.: Yale University Press, 1989); R. Laurence Moore, *Selling God: American Religion in the Marketplace of Culture* (New York: Oxford University Press, 1994); and Jon Butler, *Awash in a Sea of Faith: Christianizing the American People* (Cambridge, Mass.: Harvard University Press, 1990).

6. James Gilbert, *Redeeming Culture: American Religion in an Age of Science* (Chicago: University of Chicago Press, 1997), 19.

7. For this new spirituality, see earlier discussions and notes in this book. See especially Thomas A. Tweed, ed., *Retelling U.S. Religious History* (Berkeley: University of California Press, 1997); Amanda Porterfield, *The Transformation of American Religion: The Story of a Late-Twentieth-Century Awakening* (New York: Oxford University Press, 2001); and Robert Fuller, *Spiritual but Not Religious: Understanding Unchurched America* (New York: Oxford University Press, 2001).

8. Phil Nelson, "Environment and Establishment: A Student Letter," *National Parks and Conservation Magazine* 44 (1970): 11–12, quote on page 11.

9. Mark Davidson, *Uncommon Sense: The Life and Thought of Ludwig von Bertalanffy (1901–1972), Father of General Systems Theory*, foreword by R. Buckminster Fuller, introduction by Kenneth E. Boulding (Los Angeles: Tarcher, 1983), 21–22.

10. Duke University Center for Integrative Medicine's Web site, http://dukehealth.org/health_services/integrative_medicine.asp (accessed January 22, 2002). Judy Packer-Tursman, "Georgetown's Alternative Course," *Washington Post*, October 2, 2001, health section, and Arizona Center for Integrative Medicine, University of Arizona, http://integrativemedicine.arizona.edu/about/definition.html (accessed January 10, 2009).

11. Acupuncture, the stimulation of precise points on the body, is a holistic treatment that originated in China thousands of years ago. It is based upon the Taoist concept of yin and yang and the belief that the body is controlled by a vital force or energy. Illness is understood as an imbalance or blockage of energy. Acupuncture's rising acceptance in America coincided with President Richard Nixon's visitto China and the opening of relations between the United States and China in the 1970s. One story, as Phyllis Matson reports, specifically caught American interest. Forced to undergo an emergency appendectomy in Peking, political columnist James Reston reported that the use of acupuncture alleviated his pain. Increased interest might also be noted in the number of articles printed on the subject. Prior to 1972, the *Index Medicus* listed only foreign articles that pertained to acupuncture, and these were few in number. After 1972, thirty-two American articles were cited; seven of these appeared in the *Journal of the American Medical Association*. See Phyllis H. Mattson, *Holistic Health in Perspective* (Palo Alto, Calif.: Mayfield, 1982), 62; James Reston, "Now, About my Operation in Peking," *New York Times*, July 26, 1971, 1, 6; E. Grey Diamond, "Acupuncture Anesthesia: Western Medicine

and Chinese Traditional Medicine," *Journal of the American Medical Association* 218 (1971): 1558–63.

12. Whole Foods Web site, http://www.wholefoodsmarket.com/company/index. php (accessed December 20, 2008).

13. Martin Luther King Jr., "A Christmas Sermon on Peace," in *A Testament of Hope: The Essential Writings and Speeches of Martin Luther King, Jr.*, ed. James Melvin Washington (San Francisco: HarperSanFrancisco, 1986), 257; see also Martin Luther King Jr., *The Trumpet of Conscience* (New York: Harper and Row, 1967), 67–78, and Martin Luther King Jr., "I See the Promised Land," in *Testament of Hope*, 279–86, quote on 280.

14. David Brower, *For Earth's Sake: The Life and Times of David Brower* (Salt Lake City, Utah: Gibbs Smith, 1990), 214.

15. Donald Worster, "The Ecology of Order and Chaos," *Environmental History Review* 14 (Spring/Summer 1990): 1–18, quote on page 9.

16. Charles A. Reich, *The Greening of America* (New York: Random House, 1970), 13. See also Mattson, *Holistic Health in Perspective*, 39–43.

17. Albert Gore, *Earth in the Balance: Ecology and the Human Spirit*, rev. ed. (Boston: Houghton Mifflin, 2000), quote on 367.

18. Kyle Longley, *Senator Albert Gore, Sr.: Tennessee Maverick* (Baton Rouge: Louisiana State University Press, 2004), 152.

19. "Gore Addresses Environmental Issues at Campaign Stop in Springdale," CNN Transcripts (August 12, 2000), http://archives.cnn.com/TRANSCRIPTS/0008/12/se.01.html (accessed October 30, 2007).

20. Gore's introduction, in Rachel Carson, *Silent Spring* (New York: Mariner Books, 1994), xx.

21. Gore, *Earth in the Balance*, 12.

22. In addition to calling Teilhard "one of the greatest theologians of the 20th century," Gore added: "There is almost a sensual longing for communion with others who have a large vision. The immense fulfillment of a friendship between those engaged in furthering the evolution of consciousness has a quality impossible to describe." Both quotes in Albert Gore, "That's Not Too Much to Ask," excerpt from speech at the Human Rights Campaign Gala (March 25, 2006), *In Los Angeles Magazine*, http://www.inlamag.com/904/opeds/904_oped1.html (accessed October 30, 2007); Jordan Fisher-Smith interview with Albert Gore, "Environmentalism of the Spirit: An Interview with Senator Al Gore," *EnviroLink Network*, http://arts. envirolink.org/interviews_and_conversations/AlGore.html (accessed October 29, 2007); originally published in *Orion* (Summer 1992).

23. President George H. W. Bush, as quoted by Michiko Kakutani, "Al Gore Revisits Global Warming, with Passionate Warming and Pictures," *New York Times Books of the Times* (May 23, 2006), *New York Times*, http://www.nytimes. com/2006/05/23/books/23kaku.html?ex=1306036800&en=aa3b3a80cef4cc07&ei=5088&partner=rssnyt&emc=rss (accessed October 30, 2007). See also Albert Gore's reference to wearing the term with honor in his introduction to *Silent Spring*. For Gore's celebrity status, see William Booth, "Al Gore, Rock Star," *Washington Post*, February 25, 2007, A01; and *Washington Post*, http://www.washingtonpost.com/wp-dyn/content/article/2007/02/24/AR2007022401586.html (accessed October 30, 2007).

24. Jo Becker and Barton Gellman, "Leaving No Tracks," *Washington Post*, June 27, 2007, A01, http://blog.washingtonpost.com/cheney/chapters/leaving_no_tracks/index.html (accessed October 1, 2007), and Julia Preston, "Environmental Laws Waived to Press Work on Border Fence," *New York Times*, October 23, 2007; http://www.nytimes.com/2007/10/23/us/23fence.html?_r=1&oref=slogin (accessed November 1, 2007).

Bibliography

ARCHIVAL SOURCES

Association for Humanistic Psychology Records. Humanistic Psychology Archive. Davidson Library, University of California, Santa Barbara, California.

James F. T. Bugental Papers. Humanistic Psychology Archive. Davidson Library, University of California, Santa Barbara, California.

Rachel Carson Letters and Papers. Rachel Carson Council, Chevy Chase, Maryland.

Rachel Carson Papers. Beinecke Library, Yale University, New Haven, Connecticut.

Esalen Institute Collection. Humanistic Psychology Archive. Davidson Library, University of California, Santa Barbara, California.

R. Buckminster Fuller Papers. Department of Special Collections. Stanford University Green Library. Stanford, California. [Originally housed at the R. Buckminster Fuller Institute, Sebastopol, California.]

Jack Gaines–Fritz Perls Collection. Humanistic Psychology Archive. Davidson Library, University of California, Santa Barbara, California.

Martin Luther King Papers Project. Martin Luther King, Jr., Research and Education Institute. Stanford University. http://mlk-kpp01.stanford.edu/index.php/king-papers/index.

Abraham Maslow Papers. Humanistic Psychology Archive. Davidson Library, University of California, Santa Barbara, California.

Carl R. Rogers Collection. Humanistic Psychology Archive. Davidson Library, University of California, Santa Barbara, California.

Charlotte Selver Papers. Humanistic Psychology Archive. Davidson Library, University of California, Santa Barbara, California.

Pierre Teilhard de Chardin Letters. Lauinger Library, Georgetown University, Washington, D.C.

Alan Watts Papers. Humanistic Psychology Archive. Davidson Library, University of California, Santa Barbara, California.

SELECTED WORKS BY RACHEL CARSON, R. BUCKMINSTER FULLER, MARTIN LUTHER KING JR., ABRAHAM MASLOW, AND PIERRE TEILHARD DE CHARDIN

Rachel Carson

Carson, Rachel. *Always Rachel: The Letters of Rachel Carson and Dorothy Freeman, 1952–1964*. Edited by Martha Freeman. Boston: Beacon Press, 1995.

———. *The Edge of the Sea*. New York: Signet, 1955.

———. *Lost Woods: The Discovered Writing of Rachel Carson*. Edited by Linda Lear. Boston: Beacon Press, 1998.

———. *The Sea around Us*. Rev. ed. New York: Oxford University Press, 1961.

———. *Sense of Wonder*. New York: Harper and Row, 1965.

———. *Silent Spring*. Boston: Houghton Mifflin, 1962.

———. *Under the Sea Wind*. New York: Simon and Schuster, 1941.

———. "Undersea." *Atlantic Monthly*, September 1937, 322–25.

R. Buckminster Fuller

Fuller, R. Buckminster. *Buckminster Fuller to Children of Earth*. Garden City, N.Y.: Doubleday, 1972.

———. *Critical Path*. New York: St. Martin's Press, 1981.

———. *Education Automation: Freeing the Scholar to Return to His Studies*. Carbondale: Southern Illinois University Press, 1962.

———. *4D Timelock*. 1928. Reprint, Corrales, N.M.: Lama Foundation, 1970.

———. *Grunch of Giants*. New York: St. Martin's Press, 1983.

———. *I Seem to Be a Verb*. With Jerome Agel and Quentin Fiore. New York: Bantam Books, 1969.

———. *Ideas and Integrities: A Spontaneous Autobiographical Disclosure*. Edited by Robert W. Marks. Englewood Cliffs, N.J.: Prentice-Hall, 1963.

———. *Intuition*. Garden City, N.Y.: Doubleday, 1972.

———. *Inventions: The Patented Works of R. Buckminster Fuller*. New York: St. Martin's Press, 1983.

———. *Nine Chains to the Moon*. New York: Lippincott, 1938. Reprint, Carbondale: Southern Illinois University Press, 1963.

———. *No More Secondhand God*. Garden City, N.Y.: Doubleday, 1963.

———. *Operating Manual for Spaceship Earth*. New York: Dutton, 1963.

———. "Prime Design." *Bennington College Bulletin*, May 1960.

———. *Synergetics: Explorations in the Geometry of Thinking*. In collaboration with E. J. Applewhite. New York: Macmillan, 1975.

———. *Synergetics 2: Further Explorations in the Geometry of Thinking*. In collaboration with E. J. Applewhite. New York: Macmillan, 1979.

———. "Turning Points: You Do Not Belong to You. You Belong to the Universe." *Quest*, November/December 1979, 104.

———. *Utopia or Oblivion*. New York: Bantam Books, 1969.

———. *The World Game: Integrative Resource Utilization Planning Tool*. Carbondale: Southern Illinois University Press, 1971.

Fuller, R. Buckminster, and Anwar S. Dil. *Humans in Universe*. New York: De Gruyter, 1983.

Martin Luther King Jr.

King, Martin Luther, Jr., "The American Dream." Commencement address at Lincoln University, June 6, 1961, Pennsylvania. Reprinted in *Negro History Bulletin* 31 (May 1968): 10–15.

———. *The Autobiography of Martin Luther King, Jr.* Edited by Clayborne Carson. New York: Intellectual Properties Management in Association with Warner Books, 1998.

———. "The Ethical Demands for Integration." *Religion and Labor* 6 (May 1963): 1, 3–4, 7–8.

———. "Facing the Challenge of a New Age." *Phylon* 28 (April 1957): 24–34.

———. "A Gift of Love." *McCall's*, December 1966, 146–47.

———. "Love, Law, and Civil Disobedience." *New South* 16 (December 1961): 3–11.

———. Martin Luther King Jr., "Nobel Peace Prize Acceptance Speech 1964," *Les Prix Nobel*. Edited by Göran Liljestrand. [Nobel Foundation], Stockholm, 1965, NobelPrize.org, http://nobelprize.org/nobel_prizes/peace/laureates/1964/king-acceptance.html (accessed December 29, 2009).

———. "Nonviolence: The Only Road to Freedom." *Ebony*, October 1966, 27–30.

———. "Our Struggle." *Liberation* 1 (April 1956): 3–6.

———. *The Papers of Martin Luther King, Jr.* Edited by Clayborne Carson et al. 6 vols. Berkeley: University of California Press, 1992–2007.

———. "Pilgrimage to Nonviolence." *Christian Century* 77 (April 13, 1960): 439–41.

———. *The Strength to Love*. New York: Harper and Row, 1963.

———. *Stride toward Freedom: The Montgomery Story*. New York: Harper, 1958.

———. *A Testament of Hope: The Essential Writings and Speeches of Martin Luther King, Jr.* Edited by James Melvin Washington. San Francisco: HarperSanFrancisco, 1986.

———. *The Trumpet of Conscience*. New York: Harper and Row, 1967.

———. *Where Do We Go from Here: Chaos or Community?* New York: Harper and Row, 1967.

Abraham H. Maslow

Maslow, Abraham H. "The Authoritarian Character Structure." *Journal of Social Psychology* 18 (1953): 401–11.

———. *Dominance, Self-Esteem, Self-Actualization: Germinal Papers of A. H. Maslow*. Edited by Richard J. Lowry. Monterey, Calif.: Brooks/Cole, 1973.

———. "Dominance-Feeling, Personality, and Social Behavior in Women." *Journal of Social Psychology* 10 (1939): 3–39.

———. "The Dynamics of Psychological Security-Insecurity." *Character and Personality* 10 (1942): 331–44.

———. "Eupsychia: The Good Society." *Journal of Humanistic Psychology* 1 (1961): 1–11.

————. *Eupsychian Management: A Journal.* Homewood, Ill.: Irwin, 1965.

————. *The Farther Reaches of Human Nature.* New York: Viking, 1971.

————. "Further Notes on the Psychology of Being." *Journal of Humanistic Psychology* 4 (1964): 45–58.

————. *Future Visions: The Unpublished Papers of Abraham Maslow.* Edited by Edward Hoffman. Thousand Oak, Calif.: Sage, 1996.

————. "'Higher' and 'Lower' Needs." *Journal of Psychology* 25 (1948): 433–36.

————. "Higher Needs and Personality." *Dialectica* 5 (1951): 257–64.

————. "Humanistic Science and Transcendent Experiences." *Journal of Humanistic Psychology* 5 (1965): 219–27.

————. *The Journals of A. H. Maslow.* Edited by Richard Lowry. 2 vols. Monterey, Calif.: Brooks/Cole, 1979.

————. *Maslow on Management.* New York: Wiley, 1998.

————. *Motivation and Personality.* 2nd ed. New York: Harper and Row, 1970.

————, ed. *New Knowledge in Human Values.* New York: Harper and Brothers, 1959.

————. "Personality and Patterns of Culture." In *Psychology of Personality,* edited Ross Stagner, 445–53. New York: McGraw-Hill, 1937.

————. "A Philosophy of Psychology." In *Personal Problems and Psychological Frontiers,* ed. Johnson E. Fairchild, 225–44. New York: Sheridan House, 1957.

————. *The Psychology of Science: A Reconnaissance.* New York: Harper and Row, 1966.

————. *Religions, Values, and Peak-Experiences.* Columbus: Ohio State University Press, 1964.

————. "Self-esteem (Dominance-feeling) and Sexuality in Women." *Journal of Social Psychology* 16 (1942): 259–94.

————. *The Social Personality Inventory: A Test for Self-esteem in Women.* With manual. Palo Alto, Calif.: Consulting Psychologists Press, 1942.

————. "Some Educational Implications of the Humanistic Psychologies." *Harvard Educational Review* 38 (1968): 685–96.

————. "Synanon and Eupsychia." *Journal of Humanistic Psychology* 7 (1967): 28–35.

————. "Synergy in the Society and in the Individual." *Journal of Individual Psychology* 20 (November 1964): 153–64.

————. "A Test for Dominance-feeling (Self-esteem) in College Women." *Journal of Social Psychology* 12 (1940): 255–70.

————. "A Theory of Meta-motivation: The Biological Rooting of the Value-life." *Journal of Humanistic Psychology* 7 (1967): 93–127.

————. *Toward a Psychology of Being.* 2nd ed. Princeton, N.J.: Van Nostrand, 1968.

————. "Volunteer-error in the Kinsey Study." *Journal of Abnormal and Social Psychology* 47 (1951): 259–62.

Maslow, Abraham H., and John J. Honigmann. "Synergy: Some Notes of Ruth Benedict." *American Anthropologist* 72 (1970): 320–33.

Maslow, Abraham H., and Bela Mittelmann. *Principles of Abnormal Psychology: The Dynamics of Psychic Illness.* New York: Harper and Row, 1941.

May, Rollo, Carl Rogers, Abraham Maslow, et al. *Politics and Innocence: A Humanistic Debate.* Dallas, Tex.: Saybrook, 1986.

Pierre Teilhard de Chardin

Teilhard de Chardin, Pierre. *The Appearance of Man*. London: Collins, 1965.

————. *Building the Earth*. Translated by Noel Lindsay and Norman Denny. London: Chaplin, 1965.

————. *Building the Earth and the Psychological Conditions of Human Unification*. Introductory essay by John Kobler. Foreword by Max H. Begouen. New York: Avon Books, 1969.

————. *Christianity and Evolution*. Translated by René Hague. New York: Harcourt Brace Jovanovich, 1971.

————. *Divine Milieu*. Translated by Bernard Wall. New York: Harper and Row, 1965.

————. *The Future of Man*. Translated by Norman Denny. New York: Harper and Row, 1964.

————. *Heart of Matter*. Translated by René Hague. New York: Harcourt Brace Jovanovich, 1978.

————. *Human Energy*. Translated by J. M. Cohen. New York: Harcourt Brace Jovanovich, 1969.

————. *The Human Phenomenon*. Translated by Sarah Appleton-Weber. Portland, Ore.: Sussex Academic Press, 1999. [See also Teilhard, *The Phenomenon of Man*.]

————. *Hymn of the Universe*. Translated by Gerald Vann. New York: Harper and Row, 1969.

————. *Letters from a Traveller*. Translated by René Hague. London: Collins, 1962.

————. *The Letters of Teilhard de Chardin and Lucile Swan*. Edited by Thomas M. King, S.J., and Mary Wood Gilbert. Washington, D.C.: Georgetown University Press, 1993.

————. *Letters to Léontine Zanta*. Introductions by Robert Garric and Henri de Lubac. Translated by Bernard Wall. London: Collins, 1969.

————. *Letters to Two Friends: 1926–1952*. New York: New American Library, 1967.

————. *The Making of a Mind: Letters from a Soldier-Priest, 1914–1919*. Translated by René Hague. New York: Harper and Row, 1965.

————. *Oeuvres de Teilhard de Chardin*. Edited by Karl Schmitz-Moormann and Nicole Schmitz-Moormann. 23 vols. Paris: Editions du Seuil, 1955–76.

————. *L'Oeuvre Scientifique*. 10 vols. Freiburg im Breisgau: Walter-Verlag Olten, 1971.

————. *On Love and Happiness*. Translated by René Hague. San Francisco: Harper and Row, 1984.

————. *The Phenomenon of Man*. Translated by Bernard Wall. New York: Harper and Row, 1959. [See also Teilhard, *The Human Phenomenon*.]

————. *Science and Christ*. Translated by René Hague. New York: Harper and Row, 1968.

————. *Toward the Future*. Translated by René Hague. New York: Harcourt Brace Jovanovich, 1975.

————. *Writings in Time of War*. Translated by René Hague. New York: Harper and Row, 1968.

OTHER SOURCES

Aanstoos, Christopher M., Ilene Serlin, and Thomas Greening. "History of Division 32 (Humanistic Psychology) of the American Psychological Association." In

Unification through Division: Histories of the Divisions of the American Psychological Association, ed. Donald A. Dewsbury, 10–12. Vol. 5 Washington, D.C.: American Psychological Association, 1999. http://www.apa.org/divisions/Div32/pdfs/history.pdf (accessed September 1, 2008).

Abraham Maslow: A Memorial Volume. Compiled by International Study Project and Bertha Maslow. Monterey, Calif.: Brooks/Cole, 1972.

Abraham, Ralph. *Chaos, Gaia, Eros: A Chaos Pioneer Uncovers the Three Great Streams of History.* San Francisco: HarperSanFrancisco, 1994.

Abraham, Ralph, Frank Jas, and Willard Russell. *The Web Empowerment Book: An Introduction and Connection Guide to the Internet and the World-Wide Web.* Santa Clara, Calif.: TELOS, 1995.

Abzug, Robert H. *Cosmos Crumbling: American Reform and the Religious Imagination.* New York: Oxford University Press, 1994.

———. "Rollo May: Philosopher as Therapist." *Association for Humanistic Psychology Perspective Magazine*, April/May 2003, http://www.ahpweb.org/pub/perspective/may03/may03cover.html (accessed August 27, 2008).

Adams, Henry. *The Education of Henry Adams.* Edited by Ernest Samuels. Boston: Houghton Mifflin, 1973.

Adorno, Theodor, and Max Horkheimer. *The Dialectic of the Enlightenment.* New York: Herder, 1972.

Akin, William E. *Technocracy and the American Dream: The Technocrat Movement, 1900–1941.* Berkeley: University of California Press, 1977.

Alexander, Jon. *American Personal Religious Accounts, 1600–1980: Toward an Inner History of America's Faiths.* New York: Edwin Mellen, 1983.

Albanese, Catherine L., ed. *American Spiritualities: A Reader.* Bloomington: Indiana University Press, 2001.

———. *Nature Religion in America: From the Algonquin Indians to the New Age.* Chicago: University of Chicago Press, 1990.

———. *A Republic of Mind and Spirit: A Cultural History of American Metaphysical Religion.* New Haven, Conn.: Yale University Press, 2006.

Aldersey-Williams, Hugh. "The Rise and Fall of Dymaxion Man." *World Architecture* 39 (1995): 138–41.

Alimchandani, C. R. "Art and Technology: A Holistic Approach to Design." *Architecture and Design* 8 (March–April 1991): 73–76.

Alastair, Gordon. "True Green: Lessons from 1960s'–70s' Counterculture Architecture." *Architectural Record* 196 (April 2008): 42.

Aller, Catherine. *The Challenge of Pierre Teilhard de Chardin.* New York: Exposition Press, 1964.

Alster, Kristine. *The Holistic Health Movement.* Tuscaloosa: University of Alabama Press, 1989.

Ambrose, Stephen E. *Nixon: The Education of a Politician, 1913–1962.* New York: Simon and Schuster, 1987.

———. *Rise to Globalism.* New York: Penguin, 1983.

Anderson, Benedict. *Imagined Communities: Reflections on the Origin and Spread of Nationalism.* Rev. ed. London: Verso, 1991.

Anderson, Terry H. *The Movement and the Sixties.* New York: Oxford University Press, 1996.

Anderson, Walter Truett. *The Upstart Spring: Esalen and the American Awakening.* Reading, Mass.: Addison-Wesley, 1983.

Anderton, Frances. "Dome Sweet Dome." *Architectural Review* 193 (November 1993): 66–67.

Ansbro, John J. *Martin Luther King, Jr.: The Making of a Mind.* Maryknoll, N.Y.: Orbis Books, 1982.

Applewhite, E. J. *Cosmic Fishing.* New York: Macmillan, 1985.

Architectural Design 37 (February 1967).

Ash, Mitchell G. *Gestalt Psychology in German Culture, 1890–1967: Holism and the Quest for Objectivity.* New York: Cambridge University Press, 1995.

Ashihara, Yoshinobu. *The Aesthetic Townscape.* Cambridge, Mass.: MIT Press, 1983.

Atcheson, Richard. "Big Sur: Coming to My Senses." *Holiday,* March 1968, 18.

"Baby Tooth Survey Launched in Search of Data on Strontium-90." *Nuclear Information* 24 (December 1958): 1–5.

Baer, Steve. *Dome Cookbook.* Corrales, N.M.: Lama Foundation, 1968.

———. *Zome Primer.* Albuquerque, N.M.: Zomeworks Corporation, 1970.

Bagby, Rachel L. "Building the Green Movement," *Women of Power* 9 (Spring 1988): 14.

Bailey, Liberty Hyde. *The Holy Earth.* New York: Scribner's, 1915.

———. *The Nature-Study Idea.* New York: Doubleday, 1903.

Baldwin, J. *Bucky Works: Buckminster Fuller's Ideas for Today.* New York: Wiley, 1996.

Baldwin, Lewis V. "The Minister as Preacher, Pastor, and Prophet: The Thinking of Martin Luther King, Jr." *American Baptist Quarterly* 7 (1988): 79–97.

———. *There Is a Balm in Gilead: The Cultural Roots of Martin Luther King, Jr.* Minneapolis, Minn.: Fortress Press, 1991.

———. *To Make the Wounded Whole: The Cultural Legacy of Martin Luther King, Jr.* Minneapolis, Minn.: Fortress Press, 1992.

Banham, Reyner. *Age of the Masters: A Personal View of Modern Architecture.* New York: Harper and Row, 1975.

Barbour, George B. *In the Field with Teilhard de Chardin.* New York: Herder and Herder, 1965.

Barbour, Ian. "Experiencing and Interpreting Nature in Science and Religion." *Zygon* 29 (December 1994): 457–87.

———. *When Science Meets Religion: Enemies, Strangers, or Partners?* San Francisco: Harper, 2000.

Barlow, Connie. *Green Space, Green Time: The Way of Science.* New York: Springer-Verlag, 1997.

Barrow, John D. *The Artful Universe.* Oxford: Clarendon Press, 1995.

Barrow, John D., and Frank J. Tipler. *The Anthropic Cosmological Principle.* Oxford: Clarendon Press, 1986.

Barzun, Jacques. *Classic, Romantic, and Modern.* New York: Anchor Books, 1961.

Bateson, Gregory. *Mind and Nature: A Necessary Unity.* New York: Dutton, 1979.

———. *Steps to an Ecology of Mind: Collected Essays in Anthropology, Psychiatry, Evolution, and Epistemology.* New York: Ballantine, 1972.

Bauersfeld, Walter. *Projection Planetariums and Shell Construction.* London: Institute of Mechanical Engineers, 1957.

Baum, Rudy. "Rachel Carson." *Chemical and Engineering News* 85, no. 23 (2007): 5.

Becker, Jo and Barton Gellman. "Leaving No Tracks." *Washington Post*, June 27, 2007, A01, http://blog.washingtonpost.com/cheney/chapters/leaving_no_tracks/index. html (accessed October 1, 2007).

Belgrad, Daniel. *The Culture of Spontaneity: Improvisation and the Arts in Postwar America*. Chicago: University of Chicago Press, 1998.

Benedict, Ruth. *Patterns of Culture*. 1934. Reprint, Boston: Houghton Mifflin, 1959.

Ben-Eli, Michael. "Buckminster Fuller Retrospective." *Architectural Design* 42 (1972): 746–73.

Bercovitch, Sacvan. *The American Jeremiad*. Madison: University of Wisconsin Press, 1978.

Berger, Peter. *The Sacred Canopy*. Garden City, N.Y.: Doubleday, 1967.

Bergson, Henri. *Creative Evolution*. Translated by Arthur Mitchell. 1911. Reprint, London: Macmillan, 1960.

———. *The Two Sources of Morality and Religion*. Translated by R. Ashley Audra and Cloudesley Brereton, with the assistance of W. Horsfall Carter. 1935. Reprint, Notre Dame, Ind.: University of Notre Dame Press, 1977.

Berry, Thomas Mary. *The Dream of the Earth*. San Francisco: Sierra Club, 1988.

———. "Teilhard in the Ecological Age." *Teilhard Studies* 7 (Fall 1982): 1–33.

Bertalanffy, Ludwig von. *General Systems Theory: Foundations, Development, Applications*. New York: Braziller, 1968.

Bertola, F., ed. *The Anthropic Principle: Proceedings of the Second Venice Conference on Cosmology*. Cambridge: Cambridge University Press, 1993.

Beston, Henry. *The Outermost House*. New York: Viking, 1928.

Bethune, Brian. "Was Rachel Carson Wrong?" *Maclean's* 120, no. 21 (2007): 42–43.

Birx, H. James. *Interpreting Evolution: Darwin and Teilhard de Chardin*. Buffalo, N.Y.: Prometheus Books, 1991.

———. *Pierre Teilhard de Chardin's Philosophy of Evolution*. Springfield, Ill.: Thomas, 1972.

Biskind, Morton S. "Public Health Aspects of the New Insecticides." *American Journal of Digestive Diseases* 20 (November 1953): 331–41.

Biskind, Morton S. and William Coda Martin. "The Use of Citrus Flavonoids in Infections II." *American Journal of Digestive Diseases* 22 (February 1955): 41–45.

Black, Davidson, Pierre Teilhard de Chardin, C. C. Young, and W. C. Pei. "Fossil Man in China: The Choukoutien Cave Deposits with a Synopsis of Our Present Knowledge of the Late Cenozoic in China." *Memoirs, Geological Survey in China* 11 (1933): 1–166.

Blake, Peter. "Bucky Fuller's Artifacts." Review of *the Artifacts of R. Buckminster Fuller*. Edited by James Ward. *Interior Design* 56 (September 1985): 316–17.

———. *God's Own Junkyard: The Planned Deterioration of America's Landscape*. New York: Holt, Rinehart and Winston, 1964.

———. "Paolo Soleri's Visionary City." *Architectural Forum* 114 (March 1961): 111–18.

Bloom, William. *Holistic Revolution: The Essential New Age Reader*. London: Penguin, 2000.

Blum, John Morton. *Years of Discord: American Politics and Society, 1961–1974*. New York: Norton, 1991.

Bohm, David. *Wholeness and the Implicate Order*. London: Routledge, 1980.

Bone, E. L. "Teilhard." In *New Catholic Encyclopedia*. New York: McGraw-Hill, 1967, 14: 978.

Bonta, Marcia Myers. *Women in the Field: America's Pioneering Women Naturalists*. College Station: Texas A&M University Press, 1991.

Booth, William. "Al Gore, Rock Star." *Washington Post*, February 25, 2007, A01; and *Washington Post*, http://www.washingtonpost.com/wp-dyn/content/article/2007/02/24/AR2007022401586.html (accessed October 30, 2007).

Boulding, Kenneth E. "The Economics of the Coming Spaceship Earth." 1966. In *Collected Papers*, edited by Fred R. Glahe and Larry D. Singell, 1:383–94. 6 vols. Boulder: Colorado Associated University Press, 1971–85.

Boyer, Paul. *By the Bomb's Early Light: American Thought and Culture at the Dawn of the Atomic Age*. Chapel Hill: University of North Carolina Press, 1994.

———. *Fallout: A Historian Reflects on America's Half-Century Encounter with Nuclear Weapons*. Columbus: Ohio State University Press, 1998.

Bramwell, Anna. *Ecology in the 20th Century: A History*. New Haven, Conn.: Yale University Press, 1989.

Branch, Taylor. *At Canaan's Edge: America in the King Years, 1965–68*. New York: Simon and Schuster, 2006.

———. *Parting the Waters: America in the King Years, 1954–63*. New York: Simon and Schuster, 1988.

———. *Pillar of Fire: America in the King Years, 1963–65*. New York: Simon and Schuster, 1998.

Brand, Stewart, ed. *The Last Whole Earth Catalog: Access to Tools*. New York: Portola Institute and Random House, 1972.

———, *The Next Whole Earth Catalog: Access to Tools*. 2nd ed. New York: Random House, 1981.

———. "Understanding Whole Systems." In *The Last Whole Earth Catalog*, 3. New York: Random House, 1971.

———. *The Whole Earth Catalog: Access to Tools*. New York: Portola Institute and Random House, 1968.

Braun, Frederick Augustus. *Margaret Fuller and Goethe: The Development of a Remarkable Personality, Her Religion and Philosophy, and Her Relation to Emerson, J. F. Clarke, and Transcendentalism*. New York: Holt, 1910.

Brennan, Andrew. *Thinking about Nature*. Athens: University of Georgia Press, 1988.

Breschini, Gary S., and Trudy Haversat. *The Esselen Indians of the Big Sur Country: The Land and the People*. Salinas, Calif.: Coyote Press, 2004.

Brick, Howard. *Age of Contradiction: American Thought and Culture in the 1960s*. Ithaca, N.Y.: Cornell University Press, 2000.

Brightman, Edgar S. "Personalism." In *A History of Philosophical Systems*, ed. Vergilius Ferm, 340–52. New York: Philosophical Library, 1950.

———. "A Personalistic Philosophy of History." *Journal of Bible and Religion* 18 (January 1950): 3–10.

Brooke, John Hedley. *Science and Religion: Some Historical Perspectives*. New York: Cambridge University Press, 1991.

Brookman, David M. *Teilhard and Aurobindo: A Study in Religious Complementarity*. Bhubaneswar, India: Mayur Publications, 1988.

Brooks, Paul. *The House of Life: Rachel Carson at Work.* Boston: Houghton Mifflin, 1972.

Braunstein, Peter, and Michael William Doyle, eds. *Imagine Nation: The American Counterculture of the 1960s and 1970s.* New York: Routledge, 2002.

Brower, David. *For Earth's Sake: The Life and Times of David Brower.* Salt Lake City, Utah: Gibbs Smith, 1990.

Bowne, Borden Parker. "The Failure of Impersonalism." In *The Development of American Philosophy,* ed. Walter G. Muelder and Lawrence Sears, 278–90. Boston: Houghton Mifflin, 1940.

———. *Personalism.* 1908. Reprint, Norwood, Mass.: Plimpton Press, 1936.

Brush, Stephen G. "The Chimerical Cat: Philosophy of Quantum Mechanics in Historical Perspective." *Social Studies of Science* 10 (1980): 393–447.

Buckminster Fuller Institute. Sebastopol, California. November 1, 2002. http://www.bfi.org/.

"Bucky's Biggest Bubble." *Architectural Forum* 124 (June 1966): 74–79.

Bugental, James F. T., ed. *Challenges of Humanistic Psychology.* New York: McGraw-Hill, 1967.

Buhler, Charlotte. "Human Life as a Whole as a Central Subject of Humanistic Psychology." In *Challenges of Humanistic Psychology,* edited by James F. T. Bugental, 83–91. New York: McGraw-Hill, 1967.

Burgess, Eric. "Fuller Insists World Can End Poverty within 25 Years." *Christian Science Monitor,* August 13, 1969, 15.

Burns, Stewart, ed. *Daybreak of Freedom: The Montgomery Bus Boycott.* Chapel Hill: University of North Carolina Press, 1997.

Butler, Jon. *Awash in a Sea of Faith: Christianizing the American People.* Cambridge, Mass.: Harvard University Press, 1990.

Cage, John. "Choosing Abundance." *North American Review* 6 (1969): 9–17.

Callicott, J. Baird, and Michael P. Nelson, eds. *The Great New Wilderness Debate.* Athens: University of Georgia Press, 1998.

Campbell, James. *This Is the Beat Generation: New York–San Francisco–Paris.* Berkeley: University of California Press, 2001.

Cannon, Katie G. *Black Womanist Ethics.* Atlanta, Ga.: Scholars Press, 1988.

Capra, Fritjof. "The Role of Physics in the Current Change of Paradigms." In *The World View of Contemporary Physics: Does It Need a New Metaphysics?* edited by Richard F. Kitchener, 144–55. Albany: State University of New York Press, 1988.

———. *The Tao of Physics: An Exploration of the Parallels between Modern Physics and Eastern Mysticism.* New York: Random House, 1975.

———. *The Web of Life: A New Scientific Understanding of Living Systems.* New York: Anchor Books, 1996.

Carey, James W., and John J. Quirk. "The Mythos of the Electronic Revolution." *American Scholar* 39 (Spring 1970): 219–41; 39 (Summer 1970): 395–424.

Carlisle, Robert B. "The Birth of Technocracy: Science, Society, and Saint-Simonians." *Journal of the History of Ideas* 35 (1974): 445–64.

Carson, Clayborne, Peter Holloran, Ralph E. Luker, and Penny A. Russell. "Martin Luther King, Jr., as Scholar: A Reexamination of His Theological Writings." *Journal of American History* 78 (June 1991): 93–105.

Casanova, José. *Public Religions in the Modern World.* Chicago: University of Chicago Press, 1994.

Chapman, Roger E. "Review of Henry Nash Smith, *Virgin Land: The American West as Symbol and Myth.*" H-Ideas, H-Net Reviews, July 2000. http://www.h-net.msu.edu/reviews/showrev.cgi?path=7216964552182 (accessed June 10, 2008).

Chaudhuri, Haridas. "Western Theology and Eastern Mysticism." Cultural Integration Fellowship Web site, 1996. http://www.culturalintegration.org/article1.html (accessed August 22, 2006).

Checkland, Peter B. "Science and the Systems Paradigm." *International Journal of General Systems* 3 (1976): 127–34.

Cheever, John. *The Enormous Radio and Other Stories.* New York: Funk and Wagnalls, 1953.

Chetany, J. *The Future of Man according to Teilhard de Chardin and Aurobindo Ghose.* New Delhi: Oriental Publishers and Distributors, 1978.

Chi, Jung Yun, and Ruy Marcelo de Oliveira Pauletti. "An Outline of the Evolution of Pneumatic Structures." Faculty of Architecture and Urban Planning and the Polytechnic School of the University of São Paulo. http://www.lmc.ep.usp.br/people/pauletti/Publicacoes_arquivos/Chi-and-Pauletti.pdf (accessed July 11, 2008).

Churchman, Charles West. *The Systems Approach.* New York: Delacorte Press, 1968.

Clebsch, William. *American Religious Thought: A History.* Chicago: University of Chicago Press, 1973.

Clements, Frederic E. *Plant Succession.* Washington, D.C.: Carnegie Institution, 1916.

Close, Gloria W. R. *Buckminster Fuller: A Selected Bibliography of References in the D. H. Hill Library and the Design Library.* Monticello, Ill.: Council of Planning Librarians, 1977.

Cohen, Lizabeth. *A Consumers' Republic: The Politics of Mass Consumption in Postwar America.* New York: Vintage, 2003.

Cohen, Stuart E. *Chicago Architects.* Chicago: Swallow Press, 1976.

Cohen, Warren. *America in the Age of Soviet Power, 1945–1991.* New York: Cambridge University Press, 1993.

Commoner, Barry. *The Closing Circle: Nature, Man and Technology.* New York: Knopf, 1971.

———. "The Closing Circle: Nature, Man, and Technology," in *Thinking about the Environment: Readings on Politics, Property, and the Physical World,* eds. Matthew Alan Cahn and Rory O'Brien. New York: M.E. Sharpe, 161–66.

Comstock, Anna Botsford. *Handbook of Nature Study.* Ithaca, N.Y.: Cornell University Press, 1911.

Comte, Auguste. *Auguste Comte and Positivism: The Essential Writings.* Edited by Gertrud Lenzer. New Brunswick, N.J.: Transaction, 1998.

Cone, James H. "Black Theology in American Religion." *Journal of the American Academy of Religion* 53 (December 1985): 755–71.

———. "Martin Luther King: The Source for His Courage to Face Death." *Concilium* 183 (March 1983): 74–79.

———. "Martin Luther King, Jr., Black Theology–Black Church." *Theology Today* 15 (January 1984): 409–20.

Conkin, Paul K. *When All the Gods Trembled: Darwinism, Scopes, and American Intellectuals.* Lanham, Md.: Rowman and Littlefield, 1998.

Cooper, Thomas W. "The Medium Is the Mass: Marshall McLuhan's Catholicism and catholicism." *Journal of Media and Religion* 5 (August 2006): 161–73.

Le Corbusier. *Towards a New Architecture.* Translated by Frederick Etchells. New York: Praeger, 1946.

"Le Corbusier Citrohan House." *Digital Arts,* October 23, 2007. http://www.digitalarts.dk/2007/10/citrohan/ (accessed June 13, 2008).

Corn, Joseph J., and Brian Horrigan. *Yesterday's Tomorrows: Past Visions of the American Future.* New York: Summit Books, 1984.

Cort, David. "Darkness under the Dome." *Nation,* March 1, 1958, 187–88.

Cousins, Ewert H. *Hope and the Future of Man.* Philadelphia: Fortress Press, 1972.

Cousins, Norman. *Anatomy of an Illness as Perceived by the Patient.* New York: Norton, 1979.

———. "The Holistic Health Explosion." *Saturday Review,* March 31, 1979, 17–20.

Craige, Betty Jean. *American Patriotism in a Global Society.* SUNY Series in Global Politics. Albany: State University of New York Press, 1996.

———. *Eugene Odum: Ecosystem Ecologist and Environmentalist.* Athens: University of Georgia Press, 2001.

———. *Laying the Ladder Down: The Emergence of Cultural Holism.* Amherst: University of Massachusetts Press, 1992.

———. "Political Holism and the Pursuit of Peace." Speech at the Veterans for Peace convention, Arlington, Virginia, August 16, 1997. Center for Humanities and Arts, University of Georgia. http://www.cha.uga.edu/bjc/vfp.htm (accessed November 2, 2002).

———. *Reconnection: Dualism to Holism in Literary Study.* Athens: University of Georgia Press, 1988.

Crawford, Sheri F. "Arcosanti: An American Community Looking toward the Millennium." *Communal Societies* 14 (1994): 49–66.

Creese, Walter. "Fowler and the Domestic Octagon." *Art Bulletin* 28 (June 1946): 89–102.

Critchlow, Donald. *The Conservative Ascendancy: How the GOP Right Made Political History.* Cambridge, Mass.: Harvard University Press, 2007.

Cronon, William J. "A Place for Stories: Nature, History, and Narrative." *Journal of American History* 78 (March 1992): 1347–76.

———, ed. *Uncommon Ground: Toward Reinventing Nature.* New York: Norton, 1995.

Cuénot, Claude. *Teilhard de Chardin: A Biographical Study.* Translated by Vincent Colimore. Edited by René Hague. Baltimore: Helicon Press, 1965.

Curl, John. *Memories of Drop City: The First 1960s Hippie Commune and the Summer of Love.* Lincoln, Neb.: iUniverse Books, 2007. http://www.red-coral.net/DC_Chapter_1.html (accessed June 12, 2008).

Curtis, Susan. *A Consuming Faith: The Social Gospel and Modern American Culture.* Baltimore: Johns Hopkins University Press, 1991.

Curtis, William J. R. *Modern Architecture since 1900.* New York: Oxford University Press, 1982.

Dalton, Anne Marie. *A Theology for the Earth: The Contributions of Thomas Berry and Bernard Lonergan.* King Edward, Ottawa: University of Ottawa Press, 1999.

Darby, Henry E., and Margaret N. Rowley. "King on Vietnam and Beyond." *Phylon* 47 (1986): 43–50.

Darnton, Robert. *The Great Cat Massacre and Other Episodes in French Cultural History.* New York: Oxford University Press, 1986.

Darwin, Charles. *The Origin of Species.* 1859. Reprint, New York: Oxford University Press, 1996.

Daubenmire, Rexford F. *Plants and Environment: A Textbook of Plant Autecology,* 2nd ed. New York: Wiley, 1959.

Davidson, Mark. *Uncommon Sense: The Life and Thought of Ludwig von Bertalanffy (1901–1972), Father of General Systems Theory.* Foreword by R. Buckminster Fuller. Introduction by Kenneth E. Boulding. Los Angeles: Tarcher, 1983.

Davidson, Michael. *San Francisco Renaissance: Politics and Community at Mid-Century.* New York: Cambridge University Press, 1991.

Deats, Paul, and Carol Robb, eds. *The Boston Personalist Tradition in Philosophy, Social Ethics, and Theology.* Macon, Ga.: Mercer University Press, 1986.

DeCarvalho, Roy José. *The Founders of Humanistic Psychology.* New York: Praeger, 1991.

Deliman, Tracy, and John S. Smolowe, eds. *Holistic Medicine: Harmony of Body, Mind, Spirit.* Reston, Va.: Reston, 1982.

Deming, Barbara. *Prisons That Could Not Hold.* San Francisco: Spinsters Ink, 1985.

Desjardins, Joseph R. *Environmental Ethics: An Introduction to Environmental Philosophy.* Belmont, Calif.: Wadsworth, 1993.

Devall, Bill, and George Sessions. *Deep Ecology: Living as If Nature Mattered.* Salt Lake City, Utah: Peregrine Smith, 1985.

DeWolf, L. Harold. "Personalism in the History of Western Philosophy." *Philosophical Forum* 12 (1954): 29–51.

———. *A Theology of the Living Church.* Rev. ed. New York: Harper and Row, 1960.

Diamond, E. Grey. "Acupuncture Anesthesia: Western Medicine and Chinese Traditional Medicine." *Journal of the American Medical Association* 218 (1971): 1558–63.

Diamond, Irene and Gloria Feman Ornstein, eds. *Reweaving the World: The Emergence of Ecofeminism.* San Francisco: Sierra Club Books, 1990.

Diggins, John Patrick. *The Proud Decades: America in War and Peace, 1941–1960.* New York: Norton, 1988.

Dobbelaere, Karel. *Secularization: A Multi-dimensional Concept.* Beverly Hills, Calif.: Sage, 1981.

Dobzhansky, Theodosius. "Nothing in Biology Makes Sense Except in the Light of Evolution." *American Biology Teacher* 35 (March 1973): 125–29.

———. "Teilhard de Chardin and the Orientation of Evolution. A Critical Essay." *Zygon* 3 (September 1976): 242–58.

Dolan, Jay. *The American Catholic Experience: A History from Colonial Times to the Present.* Garden City, N.Y.: Doubleday, 1985.

———. "Immigrants and Their Gods: A New Perspective in American Religious History." *Church History* 57 (1988): 61–72.

"Domes House LA's Homeless." *Architecture* 83 (January 1994): 95.

Doss, Erika. "Imaging the Panthers: Representing Black Power and Masculinity, 1960s–1990s." *Prospects: An Annual of American Culture* 23 (1998): 483–516.

Douglass, Ann. "Periodizing the American Century: Modernism, Postmodernism, and Postcolonialism in the Cold War Context." *Modernism* 5 (1998): 71–98.

Du Bois, W. E. B. *The Souls of Black Folks*. 1903. Reprint, New York: Bantam Books, 1989.

Duberman, Martin. *Black Mountain: An Exploration in Community*. Garden City, N.Y.: Anchor Books, 1973.

Dunaway, David King. *Huxley in Hollywood*. New York: Harper, 1989.

Dunbar, Dirk. "Eranos, Esalen, and the Ecocentric Psyche: From Archetype to Zeitgeist." *Trumpeter* 20 (2004): 21–43.

Dunlap, Thomas R. *Faith in Nature: Environmentalism as Religious Quest*. Seattle: University of Washington Press, 2004.

Durkheim, Émile. *The Elementary Forms of the Religious Life*. New York: Free Press, 1965.

"The Dymaxion American." *Time*, January 10, 1964.

Dyson, Freeman. *Disturbing the Universe*. New York: Harper and Row, 1979.

Eargle, Dolan H., Jr. *Native California Guide: Weaving the Past and Present*. San Francisco: Trees Company Press, 2000.

"Earthonauts, USA." *L.A. Architect*, September 1993, 1.

Easton, Stewart C. *Rudolf Steiner: Herald of a New Epoch*. Hudson, N.Y.: Anthroposophic Press, 1980.

Edmondson, Amy C. *A Fuller Explanation: The Synergetic Geometry of R. Buckminster Fuller*. Boston: Birkhauser, 1987.

Edwards, Jonathan. *Images or Shadows of Divine Things*. Edited by Perry Miller. New Haven, Conn.: Yale University Press, 1948.

Ehrenfels, Christian von. "On Gestalt Qualities." In Richard Avenarius's *Quarterly for Scientific Philosophy*. English translation in *Foundations of Gestalt Theory*, translated and edited by Barry Smith, 82–117. Munich: Philosophia Verlag, 1988.

Ehrlich, Paul R. *The Population Bomb*. New York: Ballantine, 1968.

Ehrlich, Paul R., and Anne H. Ehrlich. *Population, Resources, Environment: Issues in Human Ecology*. San Francisco: Freeman, 1970.

Eisley, Loren. *The Immense Journey*. New York: Random House, 1946.

Elliot, Robert, ed. *Environmental Ethics*. New York: Oxford University Press, 1995.

Emerson, Ralph Waldo. "Nature." In *Essays and Lectures: Ralph Waldo Emerson*, 5–49. New York: Literary Classics of the U.S., 1983.

Erskine, Noel Leo. *King among the Theologians*. Cleveland, Ohio: Pilgrim Press, 1994.

Esalen Institute. Web site http://www.esalen.org/ (accessed November 2, 2002).

Etzioni, Amitai, ed. *New Communitarian Thinking: Persons, Virtues, Institutions and Communities*. Charlottesville: University of Virginia Press, 1995.

———. *The Spirit of Community: The Reinvention of American Society*. New York: Touchstone, 1993.

Farber, David. *The Age of Great Dreams: America in the 1960s*. New York: Hill and Wang, 1994.

Farrell, James J. *The Spirit of the Sixties: The Making of Postwar Radicalism*. New York: Routledge, 1997.

Ferguson, Marilyn. *The Aquarian Conspiracy: Personal and Social Transformations in the 1980s*. Los Angeles: Tarcher, 1980.

Fields, Rick. *How the Swans Came to the Lake: A Narrative History of Buddhism in America*. Boston: Shambhala, 1986.

Fine Art on the Web. Fine Arts Department, Boston College. Boston, Massachusetts. November 1, 2002. http://www.bc.edu/bc_org/avp/cas/fnart/Artweb.html.

Fisher-Smith, Jordan. "Environmentalism of the Spirit: An Interview with Senator Al Gore," *EnviroLink Network*, http://arts.envirolink.org/interviews_and_conversations/AlGore.html (accessed October 29, 2007); originally published in *Orion* (Summer 1992).

Fleming, Donald. "Roots of the New Conservation Movement." *Perspectives in American History* 6 (1972): 7–91.

Flewelling, Ralph Tyler. "Studies in American Personalism." *Personalist* 31 (Summer 1950): 229–44.

———. "This Thing Called Personalism." *Personalist* 28 (Summer 1947): 229–36.

Fodor, Jerry, and Ernest Lepore, eds. *Holism: A Consumer Update*. Amsterdam: Rodopi, 1993.

———. *Holism: A Shopper's Guide*. Cambridge, Mass.: Basil Blackwell, 1992.

Foley, Mary Mix. *The American House*. New York: Harper and Row, 1980.

Fowler, Orson. *The Octagon House: A Home for All*. 1853, Reprint, New York: Dover, 1973.

Fox, Stephen. *The American Conservation Movement: John Muir and His Legacy*. Madison: University of Wisconsin Press, 1981.

Frankiel, Sandra Sizer. *California's Spiritual Frontiers: Religious Alternatives in Anglo-Protestantism, 1850–1910*. Berkeley: University of California Press, 1988.

Franklin, Jimmie Lewis. "Review Essay: Autobiography, the Burden of Friendship, and Truth." *Georgia Historical Quarterly* 74 (Spring 1990): 84–98.

Frick, Willard B. *Humanistic Psychology: Interviews with Maslow, Murphy, and Rogers*. Columbus, Ohio: Merrill, 1971.

Friedan, Betty. *The Feminine Mystique*. New York: Norton, 1963.

Fuller, Robert. *Spiritual but Not Religious: Understanding Unchurched America*. New York: Oxford University Press, 2001.

"Fuller's Initial Concept for the U.S. Pavilion at Expo '67." *Domus* 464 (July 1968): 3.

Gabel, Medard, ed. *Energy, Earth and Everyone: A Global Strategy for Spaceship Earth*. San Francisco: Straight Arrow Books, 1975.

Gaddis, John. *Russia, the Soviet Union, and the United States: An Interpretive History*. 2nd ed. New York: McGraw-Hill, 1990.

Gaines, Jack. *Fritz Perls, Here and Now*. Millbrae, Calif.: Celestial Arts, 1979.

Galleni, Lodovico. "Relationships between Scientific Analysis and the World View of Pierre Teilhard de Chardin." *Zygon* 27 (June 1992): 153–66.

Garrow, David. *Bearing the Cross: Martin Luther King, Jr. and the Southern Christian Leadership Conference*. New York: Morrow, 1986.

———. "Martin Luther King, Jr., and the Spirit of Leadership." *Journal of American History* 74 (September 1987): 438–47.

———. "Martin Luther King, Jr.: Bearing the Cross of Leadership." *Peace and Change* 12 (Spring 1987): 1–12.

Gartner, Carol B. *Rachel Carson*. New York: Ungar, 1983.

Gaustad, Edwin S., and Leigh E. Schmidt. *A Religious History of America: The Heart of the American Story from Colonial Times to Today.* San Francisco: HarperSanFrancisco, 2004.

Gay, Peter. *The Enlightenment: An Interpretation.* 2 vols. New York: Norton, 1969.

Geertz, Clifford. *The Interpretation of Cultures: Selected Essays.* New York: Basic Books, 1973.

Ghose, Aurobindo. *The Future Evolution of Man.* Twin Lakes, Wis.: Lotus Press, 2002.

———. *The Life Divine.* New York: Greystone Press, 1949.

George, Henry. *Progress and Poverty.* 1879. Reprint. New York: Cosimo, 2005.

Giannone, Richard. *Flannery O'Connor and the Mystery of Love.* Urbana: University of Illinois Press, 1989.

Gigch, John P. Van. *Applied General Systems Theory.* 2nd ed. New York: Harper and Row, 1978.

Gilbert, James. *Another Chance: Postwar America, 1945–1968.* Philadelphia: Temple University Press, 1981.

———. *A Cycle of Outrage: America's Reaction to the Juvenile Delinquent in the 1950s.* New York: Oxford University Press, 1986.

———. "Many Modernisms." *Reviews in American History* 29 (2001): 264–70.

———. *Redeeming Culture: American Religion in an Age of Science.* Chicago: University of Chicago Press, 1997.

Giorgi, L. "Religious Involvement in a Secularised Society: An Empirical Confirmation of Martin's General Theory of Secularisation." *British Journal of Sociology* 43 (1992): 639–56.

Gitlin, Todd. *The Sixties: Years of Hope, Days of Rage.* New York: Bantam Books, 1987.

Gleason, Henry A. "The Individualistic Concept of the Plant Association." *Bulletin of the Torrey Botanical Club* 53 (1926): 7–26; and a later version of the article appeared in *American Naturalist* 111 (November–December 1977): 1119–44.

Goble, Frank. *The Third Force: The Psychology of Abraham Maslow.* New York: Grossman, 1970.

Golley, Frank Benjamin. *A History of the Ecosystem Concept in Ecology: More Than the Sum of the Parts.* New Haven, Conn.: Yale University Press, 1993.

Gordon, James, Dennis Jaffe, and David Bresler, eds. *Mind, Body, and Health: Toward an Integral Medicine.* New York: Human Sciences Press, 1984.

Gore, Albert. *Earth in the Balance: Ecology and the Human Spirit.* Rev. ed. Boston: Houghton Mifflin, 2000.

———. *An Inconvenient Truth: The Planetary Emergency of Global Warming and What We Can Do about It.* New York: Rodale, 2006.

Gore, Albert. "That's Not Too Much to Ask." Speech excerpt at the Human Rights Campaign Gala (March 25, 2006), In *Los Angeles Magazine*, http://www.inlamag.com/904/opeds/904_oped1.html (accessed October 30, 2007).

Gorrell, Donald K. *The Age of Social Responsibility: The Social Gospel in the Progressive Era, 1900–1920.* Macon, Ga.: Mercer University Press, 1988.

Gottlieb, Robert. *Forcing the Spring: The Transformation of the American Environmental Movement.* Washington, D.C.: Island Press, 1993.

Graebner, William S. *The Age of Doubt: American Thought and Culture in the 1940s.* Boston: Twayne, 1991.

Graham, Frank, Jr. *Since Silent Spring.* Boston: Houghton Mifflin, 1970.

Grant, Jacqueline, ed. *Perspectives on Womanist Theology.* Atlanta, Ga.: ITC Press, 1995.

Gray, Timothy. *Gary Snyder and the Pacific Rim: Creating Counter-cultural Community.* Iowa City: University of Iowa Press, 2006.

Greeley, Andrew. *Unsecular Man: The Persistence of Religion.* New York: Schocken Books, 1972.

Grof, Stanislov. *LSD Psychotherapy.* San Bernardino, Calif.: Borgo, 1986.

Groothuis, Douglas R. *Unmasking the New Age.* Downer's Grove, Ill.: InterVarsity Press, 1986.

Hagen, Joel B. *An Entangled Bank: The Origins of Ecosystem Ecology.* New Brunswick, N.J.: Rutgers University Press, 1992.

Halberstam, David. *The Fifties.* New York: Villard, 1993.

Hall, Mary Harrington. "A Conversation with the President of the American Psychological Association Abraham H. Maslow." *Psychology Today* 2 (1968): 35–57.

Hamilton, Malcolm B. *The Sociology of Religion: Theoretical and Comparative Perspectives.* New York: Routledge, 1995.

Hanley, Wayne. *Natural History in America from Mark Catesby to Rachel Carson.* New York: Quadrangle, 1977.

Haraway, Donna. *Simians, Cyborgs, and Women: The Reinvention of Nature.* New York: Routledge, 1991.

Harding, Sandra. *The Science Question in Feminism.* Ithaca, N.Y.: Cornell University Press, 1986.

———. *Whose Science, Whose Knowledge: Thinking from Women's Lives.* Ithaca, N.Y.: Cornell University Press, 1991.

Harding, Sandra, and Merrill Hintikka, eds. *Discovering Reality: Feminist Perspectives on Epistemology, Metaphysics, Methodology, and Philosophy of Science.* Dordrecht: Reidel, 1983.

Harris, Errol E. *Cosmos and Anthropos: A Philosophical Interpretation of the Anthropic Cosmological Principle.* Atlantic Highlands, New Jersey: Humanities Press International, 1991.

Harris, Mary Emma. *The Arts at Black Mountain College.* Cambridge, Mass.: MIT Press, 1987.

Harrison, Ruth. *Animal Machines: The New Factory Farming Industry.* London: Vincent Stuart, 1964.

Hartley, Elba. *Holistic Health: The New Medicine.* Cos Cob, Conn.: Hartley Productions, 1978.

Harvey, Mary Kersey. "Using a Plague to Fight a Plague." *Saturday Review,* September 29, 1962, 18.

Hatch, Alden. *Buckminster Fuller: At Home in the Universe.* New York: Dell, 1974.

Hatch, Nathan. *The Democratization of American Christianity.* New Haven, Conn.: Yale University Press, 1989.

Haught, John F. *The Cosmic Adventure: Science, Religion and the Quest for Purpose.* New York: Paulist Press, 1984.

Hayden, Casey, and Mary King. "Sex and Caste: A Kind of Memo." *Liberation,* April 1966, Mary King's Web site http://www.maryking.info/Mary-King-Sex-and-Caste-Memo.html (accessed September 30, 2008).

Hayden, Dolores. *Building Suburbia: Green Fields and Urban Growth, 1820–2000.* New York: Vintage, 2003.

———. *Seven American Utopias: The Architecture of Communitarian Socialism, 1790–1975.* Cambridge, Mass.: MIT Press, 1976.

Hays, Samuel P. *Beauty, Health, and Permanence: Environmental Politics in the United States, 1955–1985.* New York: Cambridge University Press, 1987.

———. *Conservation and the Gospel of Efficiency: The Progressive Conservation Movement, 1890–1920.* Cambridge, Mass.: Harvard University Press, 1959.

———. *Explorations in Environmental History: Essays.* Pittsburgh: University of Pittsburgh Press, 1998.

———. *A History of Environmental Politics since 1945.* Pittsburgh: University of Pittsburgh Press, 2000.

Hazlett, Maril. "'Woman vs. Man vs. Bugs': Gender and Popular Ecology in Early Reactions to *Silent Spring.*" *Environmental History* 9 (October 2004): 701–29. http://www.historycooperative.org/journals/eh/9.4/hazlett.html (accessed March 23, 2006).

———. "Voices from the Spring: *Silent Spring* and the Ecological Turn in American Health." In *Seeing Nature through Gender,* edited by Virginia Scharff, 103–28. Lawrence: University Press of Kansas, 2003.

Hefner, Philip. *The Promise of Teilhard: The Meaning of the Twentieth Century in Christian Perspective.* Philadelphia: Lippincott, 1970.

Herber, Lewis (Murray Bookchin). *Our Synthetic Environment.* New York: Knopf, 1962.

Herman, Ellen. *The Romance of American Psychology: Political Culture in the Age of Experts.* Berkeley: University of California Press, 1995.

Higginbotham, Evelyn Brooks. *Righteous Discontent: The Women's Movement in the Black Baptist Church, 1880–1920.* Cambridge, Mass.: Harvard University Press, 1993.

Hix, John. *The Glass House.* Cambridge, Mass.: MIT Press, 1974.

Hodgson, Godfrey. *America in Our Time: From World War II to Nixon—What Happened and Why.* Garden City, N.Y.: Doubleday, 1976.

Hoffman, Edward. *The Right to Be Human: A Biography of Abraham Maslow.* Los Angeles: Tarcher, 1988.

Horowitz, Daniel. *Betty Friedan and the Making of the Feminist Mystique: The American Left, the Cold War, and Modern Feminism.* Amherst: University of Massachusetts Press, 1998.

"How to Print a House, and Why." *Interiors* 113 (May 1954): 18–19.

Hudson, Wade. "An Interview with Dick Price." Esalen Web site, http://www.esalen.org/air/essays/dick_price.htm (accessed November 4, 2005).

Huggard, William A. "Whitman's Poem of Personalism." *Personalist* 28 (Summer 1947): 273–78.

Huggett, R. J. "Ecosphere, Biosphere, or Gaia? What to Call the Global Ecosystem." *Global Ecology and Biogeography* 8 (November 1999): 425–31.

Hughes, J. Donald. *Pan's Travail: Environmental Problems of the Ancient Greeks and Romans.* Baltimore: Johns Hopkins University Press, 1994.

Hughes, Thomas P. *American Genesis: A Century of Invention and Technological Enthusiasm, 1870–1970.* New York: Penguin, 1989.

Hull, David L. *The Metaphysics of Evolution.* Albany: State University of New York Press, 1989.

Huth, Hans. *Nature and the American: Three Centuries of Changing Attitudes.* Berkeley: University of California Press, 1957.

Huxley, Aldous. *The Doors of Perception and Heaven and Hell.* New York: Harper and Row, 1956.

Huxley, Julian. *Evolution: The Modern Synthesis.* London: Allen and Unwin, 1942.

Hynes, H. Patricia. "Ellen Swallow, Lois Gibbs and Rachel Carson: Catalysts of the American Environmental Movement." *Women's Studies International Forum* 8 (1985): 291–98.

———. *The Recurring Silent Spring.* New York: Pergamon Press, 1989.

Isserman, Maurice, and Michael Kazin. *America Divided: The Civil War of the 1960s.* New York: Oxford University Press, 2000.

Ivie, Stanley D. "Abraham Maslow: Utopian." *Vitae Scholasticae: The Bulletin of Educational Biography* 9 (1990): 37–52.

Jackson, Carl T. *Vedanta for the West: The Ramakrishna Movement in the United States.* Bloomington: Indiana University Press, 1994.

Jackson, Kenneth. *Crabgrass Frontier: The Suburbanization of the United States.* New York: Oxford University Press, 1985.

Jacobs, David. "An Expo Named Buckminster Fuller." *New York Times Magazine,* April 23, 1967.

Jameson, Fredric. *Postmodernism, or, the Culture of Late Capitalism.* Durham, N.C.: Duke University Press, 1991.

Jeezer, Marty. *Abbie Hoffman: An American Rebel.* New Brunswick, N.J.: Rutgers University Press, 1992.

Joseph, Brandon W. "Hitchhiker in an Omni-Directional Transport: The Spatial Politics of John Cage and Buckminster Fuller." *ANY* 17 (1997): 40–44.

Kahn, Alice. "Esalen at 25." *Los Angeles Times Magazine,* December 6, 1987.

Kahn, Lloyd, and others. *Domebook 1.* Los Gatos, Calif.: Pacific Domes, 1970.

———. *Domebook 2.* Los Gatos, Calif.: Pacific Domes, 1971.

Kahn, Lloyd, ed. *Shelter.* Bolinas, Calif.: Shelter Publications, 1973.

Kakutani, Michiko. "Al Gore Revisits Global Warming, with Passionate Warming and Pictures." *New York Times Books of the Times* (May 23, 2006), *New York Times,* http://www.nytimes.com/2006/05/23/books/23kaku.html?ex=1306036800&en=aa3b3a80cef4cc07&ei=5088&partner=rssnyt&emc=rss (accessed October 30, 2007).

Karp, Walter. "Soleri: Designer in the Desert." *Horizon* 12 (1970): 30–39.

Katz, Eric. "Ethics and Philosophy of the Environment: A Brief Review of the Major Literature." *Environmental History Review* 15 (Summer 1991): 79–86.

Keller, Evelyn Fox. *A Feeling for the Organism: The Life and Work of Barbara McClintock.* New York: Freeman, 1983.

———. "The Gender/Science System: Or, Is Sex to Gender as Nature Is to Science?" *Hypatia* 2, no. 3 (Fall 1987): 37–50.

———. *Reflections on Gender and Science.* New Haven, Conn.: Yale University Press, 1986.

Keller, Evelyn Fox, and Helen E. Longino, eds. *Feminism and Science.* New York: Oxford University Press, 1996.

Kelly, Barbara M. *Expanding the American Dream: Building and Rebuilding Levittown.* Albany: State University of New York Press, 1993.

Kennedy, John F. "Inaugural Address, Washington, D.C., January 20, 1961." Papers of John F. Kennedy: President's Office Files, January 20, 1961–November 22, 1963. John F. Kennedy Library, National Archives and Records Administration. John F. Kennedy Presidential Library and Museum Historical Resources. http://www.jfklibrary.org/Historical+Resources/Archives/Reference+Desk/Speeches/JFK/003POF03Inaugural01201961.htm (accessed January 22, 2009).

Kenner, Hugh. *Bucky: A Guided Tour of Buckminster Fuller.* New York: Morrow, 1973.

Kevles, Daniel J. *The Physicists.* New York: Vintage, 1979.

King, Coretta Scott. *My Life with Martin Luther King, Jr.* New York: Holt, Rinehart and Winston, 1969.

King, D. Brett and Michael Wertheimer. *Max Wertheimer and Gestalt Theory.* New Brunswick, N.J.: Transaction, 2005.

King, Thomas L. "Teilhard Makes Christianity Most Exciting Thing on the Block." *National Catholic Reporter,* April 22, 2005, 8, 10.

King, Ursula. "Science and Mysticism: Teilhard de Chardin in Religious Thought Today." *Teilhard Review* 19 (Spring 1984): 10.

———. *Spirit of Fire: The Life and Vision of Teilhard de Chardin.* New York: Orbis, 1996.

———. "Teilhard's Reflections on Eastern Religions Revisited." *Zygon* 30 (March 1995), 47–72.

———. *Towards a New Mysticism: Teilhard de Chardin and Eastern Religions.* New York: Seabury Press, 1980.

King, Ynestra. *What Is Ecofeminism?* New York: Ecofeminist Resources, 1990.

Kirk, Andrew. "Appropriating Technology: The Whole Earth Catalog and Counterculture Environmental Politics." *Environmental History* 6 (July 2001): 374–94.

———. *Counterculture Green: The Whole Earth Catalog and American Environmentalism.* Lawrence: University Press of Kansas, 2007.

Knudson, Albert C. *The Doctrine of God.* New York: Abingdon Press, 1930.

———. *The Philosophy of Personalism: A Study in the Metaphysics of Religion.* 1927. Reprint, New York: Abingdon Press, 1969.

Köhler, Wolfgang. *Gestalt Psychology.* New York: Liveright, 1929.

———. *The Mentality of Apes.* Translated from the second revised edition by Ella Winter. New York: Vintage, 1959.

Kolbe, Frederick C. *A Catholic View of Holism: A Criticism of the Theory Put Forward by General Smuts in His Book, Holism and Evolution.* New York: Macmillan, 1928.

Kooning, Elaine de. "Dymaxion Artist." *Art News,* September 1952, 14–17.

Kopelman, L., and J. Moskop. "The Holistic Health Movement: A Survey and Critique." *Journal of Medicine and Philosophy* 6 (1981): 209–35.

Kopp, Joseph. *Teilhard de Chardin: A New Synthesis of Evolution.* Glen Rock, N.J.: Paulist Press, 1964.

Kraft, R. Wayne. *The Relevance of Teilhard.* Notre Dame, Ind.: Fides Publishers, 1968.

Krantz, David L., ed. *Schools of Psychology.* New York: Appleton-Century-Crofts, 1969.

Krausse, Joachim. "The Miracle of Jena." *World Architecture* 20 (November 1992): 46–53.

Krausse, Joachim, and Claude Lichtenstein, eds. *Your Private Sky: R. Buckminster Fuller, The Art of Design Science.* Baden, Germany: L. Müller, 1999.

Kreisberg, Jennifer Cobb. "A Globe, Clothing Itself with a Brain." *Wired.* June 1995. http://www.wired.com/com/wired/archive/3.06/teilhard.html (accessed January 21, 2010).

Krentzman, Jackie. "In Murphy's Kingdom." *Stanford Magazine,* January/February 1998, http://www.stanfordalumni.org/news/magazine/1998/janfeb/articles/murphy.html (accessed November 22, 2006).

Kripal, Jeffrey J. *Esalen: America and the Religion of No Religion.* Chicago: University of Chicago Press, 2007.

———. "From Emerson to Esalen: America's Religion of No Religion." *Chronicle of Higher Education* 53 (April 13, 2007), B6.

Kripal, Jeffrey J., and Glenn W. Shuck, eds. *On the Edge of the Future: Esalen and the Evolution of American Culture.* Bloomington: Indiana University Press, 2005.

Kroeber, Alfred. *Handbook of California Indians.* Washington, D.C.: Government Printing Office, 1925.

Krutch, Joseph Wood. *The Best Nature Writing of Joseph Wood Krutch.* Salt Lake City: University of Utah Press, 1995.

———. *The Measure of Man: On Freedom, Human Values, Survival and the Modern Temper.* London: Redman, 1956.

Kuhn, Thomas S. *The Structure of Scientific Revolutions.* Chicago: University of Chicago Press, 1962.

Kutchins, Fred. "The Elite Feature Interview: 'Inquiring for Buckminster Fuller.'" *Chicago's Elite* 2 (November–December 1977): 1–3.

Kwinter, Sanford. "Fuller Themselves." *ANY* 17 (1997): 62.

Land, Jeff. *Active Radio: Pacifica's Brash Experiment.* Minneapolis: University of Minnesota Press, 1999.

Lane, David H. *The Phenomenon of Teilhard: Prophet for a New Age.* Macon, Ga.: Mercer University Press, 1996.

Lanpo, Jia, and Huang Weiman. *The Story of Peking Man: From Archaeology to Mystery.* Beijing: Foreign Languages Press; Hong Kong: Oxford University Press, 1990.

Lapp, Ralph E. *The Voyage of the Lucky Dragon.* New York: Harper, 1958.

Lasar, Matthew. *Pacifica Radio: The Rise of an Alternative Network.* Philadelphia: Temple University Press, 2000.

Lasch, Christopher. *The Culture of Narcissism: American Life in an Age of Diminishing Expectations.* New York: Norton, 1977.

Latner, Joel. *The Gestalt Therapy Book: A Holistic Guide to the Theory, Principles, and Techniques of Gestalt Therapy as Developed by Frederick S. Perls and Others.* New York: Julian Press, 1973.

Lattin, Don. "Esalen Institute's Ties with Soviet Philosophy Project," *San Francisco Chronicle,* November 6, 1990.

———. *Following Our Bliss: How the Spiritual Ideals of the Sixties Shape Our Lives Today.* San Francisco: HarperSanFrancisco, 2003.

Lawrence, Christopher, and George Weisz, eds. *Greater Than the Parts: Holism in Biomedicine, 1920–1950.* New York: Oxford University Press, 1998.

Lawson, Steven F. "Freedom Then, Freedom Now: The Historiography of the Civil Rights Movement." *American Historical Review* 96 (April 1991): 456–71.

Leahey, Thomas H. *A History of Psychology: Main Currents in Psychological Thought.* Upper Saddle River, N.J.: Prentice Hall, 1997.

Lear, Linda. *Rachel Carson: Witness for Nature.* New York: Henry Holt, 1997.

Leder, Drew, ed. *The Body in Medical Thought and Practice.* Dordrecht, Netherlands: Kluwer Academic Publishers, 1992.

Lee, Martin A., and Bruce Shlain. *Acid Dreams: The CIA, LSD, and the Sixties Rebellion.* New York: Grove Press, 1985.

LeFevere, Patricia. "Thousands Acclaim Jesuit's Global Vision." *National Catholic Reporter,* April 22, 2005, 9–10.

Lenin, Vladimir I. "Summary of Dialectics." In *The Collected Works of Vladimir Lenin.* 2nd English ed., 38:220–22. Moscow: Progress Publishers and Foreign Languages Press, 1965. http://www.marxists.org/archive/lenin/works/1914/cons-logic/summary.htm (accessed October 22, 2007).

Leonard, George. *Education and Ecstasy.* New York: Delacorte Press, 1968.

———. "Encounters at the Mind's Edge." *Esquire,* June 1985, 306–16.

———. *Mastery: The Keys to Long-Term Success and Fulfillment.* New York: Dutton, 1991.

———. *The Transformation: A Guide to the Inevitable Changes in Humankind.* New York: Delacorte Press, 1972.

———. *The Ultimate Athlete: Re-visioning Sports, Physical Education and the Body.* New York: Viking, 1975.

———. *Walking on the Edge of the World.* Boston: Houghton Mifflin, 1988.

Leonard, George, and Michael Murphy. *The Life We Are Given: A Long-Term Program for Realizing the Potential of Body, Mind, Heart, and Soul.* New York: Putnam, 1995.

Leopold, Aldo. *A Sand County Almanac, and Sketches Here and There.* New York: Oxford University Press, 1968.

Lewis, Martin W., and Karen E. Wigen. *The Myth of Continents: A Critique of Metageography.* Berkeley: University of California Press, 1997.

Linker, Damon. *The Theocons: Secular America under Siege.* New York: Doubleday, 2006.

Loeb, Arthur L. *Space Structures: Their Harmony and Counterpoint.* Reading, Mass.: Addison-Wesley, 1976.

Longair, M. S., ed. *Confrontation of Cosmological Theories with Observation.* Dordrecht: Reidel, 1974.

Longley, Kyle. *Senator Albert Gore, Sr.: Tennessee Maverick.* Baton Rouge: Louisiana State University Press, 2004.

Lovelock, James. *The Age of Gaia: A Biography of Our Living Earth.* New York: Norton, 1988.

———. *Gaia: A New Look at Life on Earth.* Oxford: Oxford University Press, 1979.

Lowenberg, June. *Caring and Responsibility: The Crossroads between Holistic Practice and Traditional Medicine.* Philadelphia: University of Pennsylvania Press, 1989.

Lowry, Richard. *A. H. Maslow: An Intellectual Portrait.* Monterey, Calif.: Brooks/Cole, 1973.

Lubac, Henri de. *The Eternal Feminine: A Study on the Poem by Teilhard de Chardin.* Translated by René Hague. New York: Harper and Row, 1971.

————. *Teilhard de Chardin: The Man and His Meaning*. Translated by René Hague. New York: Hawthorn Books, 1965.

Lucas, Phillip Charles. *The Odyssey of a New Religion: The Holy Order of MANS from New Age to Orthodoxy*. Bloomington: Indiana University Press, 1995.

Luce, Henry R. "The American Century." *Life*, February 17, 1941, 61–65.

Luckmann, Thomas. *Invisible Religion*. New York: Macmillan, 1967.

Lukas, Mary, and Ellen Lukas. *Teilhard*. Garden City, N.Y.: Doubleday, 1977.

Lumish, Michael. "American Academy of Asian Studies and the Quest for Authentic Identity." Paper presented at the annual conference of the Western History Association, Phoenix, Arizona, October 16, 2005.

Lutts, Ralph H. "Chemical Fallout: Rachel Carson's *Silent Spring*, Radioactive Fallout, and the Environmental Movement." *Environmental History Review* 9 (Fall 1985): 210–25.

————. *The Nature Fakers: Wildlife, Science, and Sentiment*. Golden, Colo.: Fulcrum, 1990.

Lyng, Stephen. *Holistic Health and Biomedical Medicine: A Countersystem Analysis*. Albany: State University of New York Press, 1990.

Lyotard, Jean-François. *The Postmodern Condition: A Report on Modernity*. Minneapolis: University of Minnesota Press, 1984.

Lytle, Mark Hamilton. *Gentle Subversive: Rachel Carson, Silent Spring, and the Rise of the American Environmental Movement*. New York: Oxford University Press, 2007.

MacCormack, Carol, and Jack Monger. *The Blossoming of a Holistic World View*. Landenberg, Pa.: Quaker Universalist Fellowship, 1992.

MacDermot, Galt, Gerome Ragni, and James Rado. *Hair: The American Tribal Love-rock Musical*. New York: Pocket Books, 1969.

Maclean, Dorothy. *To Honor the Earth*. San Francisco: Harper and Row, 1991.

Macy, Christine, and Sarah Bonnemaison, eds. *Architecture and Nature: Creating the American Landscape*. New York: Routledge, 2003.

Maddi, Salvatore R., and Paul T. Costa. *Humanism in Personalogy: Allport, Maslow, and Murray*. Chicago: Aldine, 1972.

Maher, Neil. "Neil Maher on Shooting the Moon." *Environmental History* 9 (July 2004): 526–31.

Mahoney, Stephen. "The Prevalence of Zen." *Nation*, November 1, 1958.

"Main Street Goes to Moscow." *Newsweek*, July 20, 1959.

Makowski, Z. S. "A Survey of Recent Three Dimensional Structures." *Architectural Design* 36 (January 1966): 10–41.

Malthus, Robert. *An Essay on the Principle of Population as It Affects the Future Improvement of Society*. 1798 Reprint. New York: A. M. Kelley, 1965.

"'A Man of the Century': Richard Buckminster Fuller, Royal Gold Medallist 1968." *Royal Institute of British Architects Journal* 75 (August 1968): 341–43.

Manuel, Frank. *Utopias and Utopian Thought*. Boston: Houghton Mifflin, 1966.

Manuel, Frank E., and Fritzie P. Manuel. *Utopian Thought in the Western World*. Cambridge, Mass.: Belknap Press, 1979.

Marcuse, Herbert. *One-Dimensional Man: Studies in the Ideology of Advanced Industrial Society*. Boston: Beacon Press, 1964.

Marin, Peter. "The New Narcissism." *Harper's*, October 1975, 45–56.

Maritain, Jacques. "Teilhard de Chardin and Teilhardism." *U.S. Catholic* 33 (1967): 9–10.

Markandya, Anil, and Julie Richardson, eds. *Environmental Economics: A Reader.* New York: St. Martin's Press, 1992.

Marco, Gino J., Robert M. Hollingworth, and William Durham, eds. *Silent Spring Revisited.* Washington, D.C.: American Chemical Society, 1987.

Marks, Robert W. "The Breakthrough of Buckminster Fuller." *New York Times Magazine,* August 23, 1959.

———. *The Dymaxion World of Buckminster Fuller.* New York: Reinhold, 1960.

Marsh, George Perkins. *Man and Nature.* New York: Scribner, 1864.

Martin, David. *A General Theory of Secularization.* New York: Harper and Row, 1978.

———. *The Religious and the Secular.* New York: Schocken Books, 1969.

Martin, John H. "Saints, Sinners and Reformers: The Burned-Over District Re-visited." *Crooked Lake Review* 137 (Fall 2005): http://www.crookedlakereview.com/books/saints_sinners/martin12.html.

Martin, Reinhold. "Crystal Balls." *ANY* 17 (1997): 35–39.

———. "Forget Fuller?" *ANY* 17 (1997): 14–15.

Martin Luther King, Jr., Papers Project. "The Student Papers of Martin Luther King, Jr.: A Summary Statement on Research." *Journal of American History* 78 (June 1991): 23–40.

Marty, Martin E. *Modern American Religion.* 3 vols. Chicago: University of Chicago Press, 1987–96.

———. "The Tradition of the Church in Health and Healing." *Second Opinion* 13 (1990): 48–73.

Marty, Martin E., and R. Scott Appleby, eds. *Fundamentalisms Observed.* Chicago: University of Chicago Press, 1994.

Marx, Leo. *The Machine in the Garden: Technology and the Pastoral Ideal in America.* London: Oxford University Press, 1964.

"A MASH Note for Docs." *Time,* May 28, 1979.

Matson, Floyd. *The Broken Image: Man, Science, and Society.* New York: Braziller, 1964.

Mattson, Phyllis H. *Holistic Health in Perspective.* Palo Alto, Calif.: Mayfield, 1982.

May, Elaine Tyler. *Homeward Bound: American Families in the Cold War Era.* New York: Basic Books, 1988.

May, Lary, ed. *Recasting America: Culture and Politics in the Age of Cold War.* Chicago: University of Chicago Press, 1989.

May, Rollo, Carl Rogers, and Abraham Maslow. *Politics and Innocence: A Humanistic Debate.* Dallas, Tex.: Saybrook, 1986.

Mays, Benjamin E. *The Negro's God as Reflected in His Literature.* New York: Russell and Russell, 1938.

McCay, Mary A. *Rachel Carson.* New York: Twayne, 1993.

McClure, Michael. *Scratching the Beat Surface.* San Francisco: North Point Press, 1982.

McCulloch, Winifred. *A Short History of the American Teilhard Association.* Chambersburg, Pa.: American Teilhard Association, 1979.

McFayden, Tevere J. "The Abbot of Arcosanti: Praised and Damned, Architect Paolo Soleri Carves Out His Dream in the Desert." *Horizon* 23 (1980): 54–61.

McGee, Micki. *Self-Help, Inc.: Makeover Culture in American Life.* New York: Oxford University Press, 2005.

McHale, John. "Buckminster Fuller." *Architectural Review* 120 (July 1956): 12–20.

———. *R. Buckminster Fuller.* New York: Braziller, 1962.

———. "Richard Buckminster Fuller" *Architectural Design* 31 (July 1961): 290–319.

McIntosh, Robert P. *The Background of Ecology: Concept and Theory.* Cambridge: Cambridge University Press, 1985.

———. "H. A. Gleason's 'Individualistic Concept' and Theory of Animal Communities: A Continuing Controversy." *Biological Reviews* 70 (1995): 317–57.

McLoughlin, William G. *Revivals, Awakenings, and Reform: An Essay on Religion and Social Change in America, 1607–1977.* Chicago: University of Chicago Press, 1977.

McLuhan, Marshall. *The Gutenberg Galaxy: The Making of Typographic Man.* New York: New American Library, 1962.

———. *The Medium Is the Message.* New York: Bantam Books, 1967.

McLuhan, Marshall, and Bruce R. Powers. *The Global Village: Transformations in World Life and Media in the 21st Century.* New York: Oxford University Press, 1989.

McNichol, Tom. "To Sur; with Love." *Washington Post,* March 15, 1998, Travel.

Mead, Margaret. *Ruth Benedict.* New York: Columbia University Press, 1974.

Mead, Walter Russell. "God's Country?" *Foreign Affairs* 85 (September/October 2006), 24–43.

Meller, James, ed. *The Buckminster Fuller Reader.* London: Jonathan Cape, 1970.

Mellor, Mary. *Feminism and Ecology.* New York: Polity Press, 1997.

Melosi, Martin V. *Coping with Abundance: Energy and Environment in Industrial America.* Philadelphia: Temple University Press, 1985.

Meltzer, David, ed. *San Francisco Beat: Talking with the Poets.* San Francisco: City Lights Books, 2001.

Merchant, Carolyn. *The Death of Nature: Women, Ecology, and the Scientific Revolution.* San Francisco: Harper and Row, 1980.

———. *Earthcare: Women and the Environment.* New York: Routledge, 1995.

Midgley, Mary. *Science as Salvation: A Modern Myth and Its Meaning.* New York: Routledge, 1992.

Miller, John P. *The Holistic Curriculum.* Toronto: Ontario Institute for Studies in Education, 1993.

Miller, Keith D. *Voice of Deliverance: The Language of Martin Luther King, Jr. and Its Sources.* New York: Free Press, 1992.

Miller, Perry. *The Life of the Mind in America.* New York: Harvest, 1965.

Miller, Stuart. *Hot Springs: The True Adventures of the First New York Jewish Literary Intellectual in the Human Potential Movement.* New York: Viking, 1971.

Miller, Timothy, ed. *America's Alternative Religions.* Albany: State University of New York Press, 1995.

———. "Drop City: Historical Notes on the Pioneer Hippie Commune." *Syzygy: Journal of Alternative Religion and Culture* 1 (Winter 1992): 22–23.

———. *The Quest for Utopia in Twentieth-Century America.* Syracuse, N.Y.: Syracuse University Press, 1998.

———. "Roots of Communal Revival 1962–1966." The Farm Web site. http://www.thefarm.org/lifestyle/root2.html (accessed July 17, 2007).

———. *The 60s Communes: Hippies and Beyond.* Syracuse, N.Y.: Syracuse University Press, 1999.

Minter, David. "The Puritan Jeremiad as a Literary Form." In *The American Puritan Imagination: Essays in Revaluation*, edited by Sacvan Bercovitch, 45–55. New York: Cambridge University Press, 1974.

Minton, Tyree Goodwin. "The History of the Nature-Study Movement and Its Role in the Development of Environmental Education." Ph.D. diss., University of Massachusetts, 1980.

Mooney, Christopher, S. J. *Teilhard de Chardin and the Mystery of Christ.* New York: Harper and Row, 1966.

Moore, R. Lawrence. *Selling God: American Religion in the Marketplace of Culture.* New York: Oxford University Press, 1994.

"More Talks with the Russians—Part I." *Saturday Review*, September 26, 1964, 30.

Morgan, Edmund S. *American Slavery, American Freedom: The Ordeal of Colonial Virginia.* New York: Norton, 1975.

Moss, Donald, ed. *Humanistic and Transpersonal Psychology: A Historical and Biographical Sourcebook.* Westport, Conn.: Greenwood Press, 1999.

Muir, John. *My First Summer in the Sierra.* Boston: Houghton Mifflin, 1911.

Muller, Robert. *The Robert Muller School: World Core Curriculum Manual.* Arlington, Tex.: Robert Muller School Publishing, 1986.

Mumford, Lewis. "Atom Bomb: Miracle or Catastrophe." *Air Affairs* 2 (July 1948): 326–45.

———. *In the Name of Sanity.* New York: Harcourt, Brace, 1954.

———. *Technics and Civilization.* New York: Harcourt, Brace, and World, 1934.

Murchison, Carl, ed. *Psychologies of 1925: Powell Lectures in Psychological Theory.* 2nd ed. Worcester, Mass.: Clark University Press, 1927.

Murphy, Michael. *The Future of the Body: Explorations into the Further Evolution of Human Nature.* Los Angeles: Tarcher, 1992.

———. *Golf in the Kingdom.* New York: Viking, 1972.

———. *Jacob Atabet: A Speculative Fiction.* Millbrae, Calif.: Celestial Arts, 1977.

———. *The Kingdom of Shivas Irons.* New York: Broadway Books, 1997.

Murphy, Michael, and Rhea White. *In the Zone: Transcendent Experience in Sport.* New York: Penguin, 1995.

Murphy, Priscilla Coit. *What a Book Can Do: The Publication and Reception of Silent Spring.* Amherst: University of Massachusetts Press, 2005.

Muschamp, Herbert. "Critic's Notebook: When Design Huffed and Puffed, Then Went Pop." *New York Times*, June 18, 1998.

Myrdal, Gunnar. *An American Dilemma: The Negro Problem and Modern Democracy.* New York: Harper and Row, 1944.

Naess, Arne. *Ecology, Community and Lifestyle: Outline of an Ecosophy*, trans. and ed. David Rothenberg. Cambridge: Cambridge University Press, 1989.

———. "The Shallow and the Deep, Long-Range Ecology Movement. A Summary." *Inquiry* 16 (Spring 1973): 95–100.

Naka, F. Robert, and William W. Ward. "Distant Early Warning Line Radars: The Quest for Automatic Signal Detection." *Lincoln Laboratory Journal* 12 (2000): 181–204. Lincoln Laboratory, Massachusetts Institute of Technology. http://www.ll.mit.edu/news/journal/pdf/vol12_no2/12_2distantearly.pdf (accessed July 13, 2007).

Nash, George. *The Conservative Intellectual Movement in America since 1945*. 2nd ed. 1976; Wilmington, Del.: Intercollegiate Studies Institute, 2006.

Nash, Linda. *Inescapable Ecologies: A History of Environment, Disease, and Knowledge*. Berkeley: University of California Press, 2006.

Nash, Roderick. *Wilderness and the American Mind*. Rev. ed. New Haven, Conn.: Yale University Press, 1973.

Naylor, Gillian. *Bauhaus*. London: Studio Vista, 1968.

Nelson, Phil. "Environment and Establishment: A Student Letter." *National Parks and Conservation Magazine* 44 (1970): 11–12.

Newman, M. W. "Bucky." *Inland Architect* 27 (September/October, 1983): 4–5.

Nissenbaum, Stephen. *Sex, Diet, and Debility in Jacksonian America: Sylvester Graham and Health Reform*. Westport, Conn.: Greenwood Press, 1980.

Nordenson, Guy J. P. "Notes on Bucky: Patterns and Structure." *ANY* 17 (1997): 54–55.

Norwood, Vera. "Heroines of Nature: Four Women Respond to the American Landscape." *Environmental Review* 8 (1984): 34–56.

———. *Made from This Earth: American Women and Nature*. Chapel Hill: University of North Carolina Press, 1993.

Numbers, Ronald. *Darwinism Comes to America*. Cambridge, Mass.: Harvard University Press, 1998.

Nye, David. *American Technological Sublime*. Cambridge, Mass.: MIT Press, 1996.

Oates, Stephen B. "The Intellectual Odyssey of Martin Luther King." *Massachusetts Review* 22 (1981): 301–20.

———. *Let the Trumpet Sound: The Life of Martin Luther King, Jr.* New York: Harper and Row, 1982.

Obst, Lynda Rosen, ed. *The Sixties: The Decade Remembered Now, by the People Who Lived It Then*. New York: Random House/Rolling Stone Press, 1977.

O'Connor, Flannery. "Everything That Rises Must Converge." *New World Writing* 19 (1961). Reprinted in *The Complete Stories*. New York: Farrar, Straus and Giroux, 1979, and *Everything That Rises Must Converge*. New York: Farrar, Straus and Giroux, 1965.

———. *Presence of Grace and Other Book Reviews*. Compiled by Leo J. Zuber. Edited and with an introduction by Carter W. Martin. Athens: University of Georgia Press, 1983.

Odum, Eugene P. *Ecology and Our Endangered Life-Support Systems*. Sunderland, Mass.: Sinauer Association, 1993.

———. *Fundamentals of Ecology*. Philadelphia: Saunders, 1953.

———. "Introductory Review: Perspective of Ecosystem Theory and Application." In *Ecosystem Theory and Application*, edited by Nicholas Polunin. New York: Wiley, 1986, 1–11.

Oelschlaeger, Max. *The Idea of Wilderness: From Prehistory to the Age of Ecology*. New Haven, Conn.: Yale University Press, 1991.

———, ed. *Postmodern Environmental Ethics*. Albany: State University of New York Press, 1995.

Olson, Ken, and Al Miller. "What Do you Know about the Geodesic Dome?" *Better Homes and Gardens*, June 1, 1957.

O'Neill, William. *American High: The Years of Confidence, 1945–1960.* New York: Free Press, 1986.

Opie, John, and Norbert Elliot. "Tracking the Elusive Jeremiad: The Rhetorical Character of American Discourse." In *The Symbolic Earth: Discourse and Our Creation of the Environment,* edited by James C. Cantrill and Christine L. Oravec, 9–35. Lexington: University Press of Kentucky, 1996.

Oppenheimer, Mark. *Knocking on Heaven's Door: American Religion in the Age of the Counterculture.* New Haven, Conn.: Yale University Press, 2003.

Orvell, Miles. *Flannery O'Connor: An Introduction.* Jackson: University Press of Mississippi, 1991.

Oved, Yaacov. *Two Hundred Years of American Communes.* New Brunswick, N.J.: Transaction, 1988.

Packer-Tursman, Judy. "Georgetown's Alternative Course." *Washington Post,* October 2, 2001, health section.

Palmer, Clare. *Environmental Ethics.* Santa Barbara, Calif.: ABC-CLIO, 1997.

———. *Environmental Ethics and Process Thinking.* Oxford: Clarendon Press, 1998.

Pappas, Theodore. *Plagiarism and the Culture War: The Writings of Martin Luther King, Jr., and Other Prominent Americans.* Tampa, Fla.: Hallberg, 1998.

Parangimalil, Bastin J. *Toward Integral Holism in Psychology.* New Delhi: Inter-India Publications, 1989.

Passmore, John. *Man's Responsibility for Nature.* New York: Scribner, 1974.

Patterson, James T. *Grand Expectations: The United States, 1945–1974.* New York: Oxford University Press, 1996.

Patterson, Orlando. *Slavery and Social Death: A Comparative Study.* Cambridge, Mass.: Harvard University Press, 1982.

Pauling, Linus. *Vitamin C and the Common Cold.* San Francisco: Freeman, 1970.

Pawley, Martin. *Buckminster Fuller.* London: Trefoil Publications, 1990.

Pearce, Peter. *Structure in Nature Is a Strategy for Design.* Cambridge, Mass.: MIT Press, 1978.

Pelletier, Kenneth. *Mind as Healer, Mind as Slayer: A Holistic Approach to Preventing Stress Disorders.* Boston: Allen and Unwin, 1977.

Pells, Richard H. *The Liberal Mind in a Conservative Age: American Intellectuals in the 1940s and 1950s.* New York: Harper and Row, 1985.

Pepper, Stephen C. *World Hypotheses: A Study in Evidence.* Berkeley: University of California Press, 1942.

Perls, Frederick S. *Ego, Hunger, and Aggression: The Beginning of Gestalt Therapy.* New York: Random House, 1969.

———. *Gestalt Is: A Collection of Articles about Gestalt Therapy and Living.* Edited by John O. Stevens. Moab, Utah: Real People Press, 1975.

———. *Gestalt Therapy Verbatim.* Lafayette, Calif.: Real People Press, 1969.

———. *In and Out of the Garbage Pail.* Lafayette, Calif.: Real People Press, 1969.

Perls, Frederick S., Ralph E. Hefferline, and Paul Goodman. *Gestalt Therapy: Excitement and Growth in the Human Personality.* New York: Dell, 1951.

Peters, Ted, ed. *Science and Theology: The New Consonance.* Boulder, Colo.: Westview Press, 1998.

Petruska, Clarkson, and Jennifer Mackewn. *Fritz Perls.* Newbury Park, Calif.: Sage, 1993.

Pickering, Andrew. *The Mangle of Practice: Time, Agency, and Science*. Chicago: University of Chicago Press, 1995.

Pickett, S. T. A., and Richard S. Ostfeld. "The Shifting Paradigm in Ecology." In *A New Century for Natural Resources Management*, edited by Richard L. Knight and Sarah F. Bates, 261–78. Washington, D.C.: Island Press, 1995.

Pike, Sarah M. *New Age and Neopagan Religions in America*. New York: Columbia University Press, 2004.

Polkinghorne, Donald. *Methodology for the Human Sciences: Systems of Inquiry*. Albany: State University of New York Press, 1983.

Popko, Edward. *Geodesics*. Detroit, Mich.: School of Architecture, University of Detroit, 1968.

Porterfield, Amanda. *Feminine Spirituality in America: From Sarah Edwards to Martha Graham*. Philadelphia: Temple University Press, 1980.

———. *The Transformation of American Religion: The Story of a Late-Twentieth-Century Awakening*. New York: Oxford University Press, 2001.

Posner, Gerald L. *Killing the Dream: James Earl Ray and the Assassination of Martin Luther King, Jr*. New York: Random House, 1998.

Possony, Stefan T., ed. *Lenin Reader*. Chicago: Henry Regnery, 1966.

Poynter, Jane. *The Human Experiment: Two Years and Twenty Minutes inside Biosphere 2*. New York: Thunder's Mouth Press, 2006.

Price, Cedric. "Buckminster Fuller, 1895–1983." *Architectural Review* 174 (August 1983): 4.

Price, Jennifer. *Flight Maps: Adventures with Nature in Modern America*. New York: Basic Books, 2000.

Principia Cybernetica Web. Edited by Francis Heylighen, Cliff Joslyn, and Valentin Turchin. Brussels, Belgium: Principia Cybernetica, 2002. http://pespmc1.vub.ac.be/DEFAULT.html (accessed December 29, 2009).

Preston, Julia. "Environmental Laws Waived to Press Work on Border Fence." *New York Times*, (October 23, 2007); http://www.nytimes.com/2007/10/23/us/23fence.html?_r=1&oref=slogin (accessed November 1, 2007).

Proctor, Robert N. *Cancer Wars: How Politics Shapes What We Know and Don't Know about Cancer*. New York: Basic Books, 1995.

"R. Buckminster Fuller Talks about Transparency." *House Beautiful*, September 1968, 92–94.

Rabbit, Peter. *Drop City*. New York: Olympia Press, 1971.

Raines, Howell. *My Soul Is Rested: The Story of the Civil Rights Movement in the Deep South*. New York: Putnam, 1977.

Rapaport, Brooke Kamin, and Kevin L. Stayton. *Vital Forms: American Art and Design in the Atomic Age, 1940–1960*. Brooklyn: Brooklyn Museum of Art, 2001.

Raschke, Carl A. "The Human Potential Movement." *Theology Today* 33 (October 1976): 253–62.

Rathbun, John W. "Martin Luther King: The Theology of Social Action." *American Quarterly* 20 (1968): 38–53.

Rauschenbusch, Walter. *Christianity and the Social Crisis*. New York: Macmillan, 1907.

Ray, James Earl. *Who Killed Martin Luther King, Jr.? The True Story by the Alleged Assassin*. 2nd ed. New York: Marlowe, 1997.

Reice, Seth R. "Nonequilibrium Determinants of Biological Community Structure." *American Scientist* 82 (September–October 1994): 424–35.

Reich, Charles A. *The Greening of America.* New York: Random House, 1970.

Reisser, Paul C., Teri J. Reisser, and John Weldon. *The Holistic Healers: A Christian Perspective on New-Age Health Care.* Downers Grove, Ill.: InterVarsity Press, 1983.

Reston, James. "Now, About my Operation in Peking." *New York Times,* July 26, 1971, 1, 6.

Reuther, Rosemary Radford. *Ecology and Feminism.* Poughkeepsie, N.Y.: Vassar College, 1989.

———. *Gaia and God: An Ecofeminist Theology of Earth Healing.* San Francisco: HarperSanFrancisco, 1992.

Rexroth, Kenneth. *An Autobiographical Novel.* New York: New Directions, 1991.

———. "The Dragon and the Unicorn." In *The Collected Longer Poems.* New York: New Directions, 1968.

Richards, M. V. *Toward Wholeness: Rudolf Steiner Education in America.* Middletown, Conn.: Wesleyan University Press, 1980.

Richert, Clark. Personal Web site. http://www.clarkrichert.com/dropcity (accessed June 10, 2008).

Riesman, David. *The Lonely Crowd: A Study of the Changing American Character.* New Haven, Conn.: Yale University Press, 1950.

Robertson, Donald. *Mind's Eye of Richard Buckminster Fuller.* New York: Vantage Press, 1974.

Rogers, Carl R. *Client Centered Therapy: Its Current Practice, Implications, and Theory.* New York: Trans-Atlantic, 1995.

———. "Toward a More Human Science of the Person." *Journal of Humanistic Psychology* 25 (1985): 7–24.

Rogers, Carl R. and B. F. Skinner. "Some Issues Concerning the Control of Human Behavior." *Science* 124 (November 30, 1956): 1057–66.

Rome, Adam. *The Bulldozer in the Countryside: Suburban Sprawl and the Rise of American Environmentalism.* New York: Cambridge University Press, 2001.

———. "Give Earth a Chance: The Environmental Movement and the Sixties." *Journal of American History* 90 (September 2003): 525–54.

Romney, Hugh. "The Hog Farm." *Realist* 86 (November–December 1969): 18.

Rosenberg, Charles E. "Holism in Twentieth-Century Medicine." In *Greater Than the Parts: Holism in Biomedicine, 1920–1950,* edited by Christopher Lawrence and George Weisz, 335–56. New York: Oxford University Press, 1998.

———. "The Tyranny of Diagnosis: Specific Entities and Individual Experience." *Milbank Quarterly* 80 (2002): 237–60.

Rossiter, Margaret. *Women Scientists in America.* 2 vols. Baltimore: Johns Hopkins University Press, 1982–95.

Roszak, Theodore. *From Satori to Silicon Valley: San Francisco and the American Counterculture.* San Francisco: Don't Call It Frisco, 1986.

———. *The Making of a Counter Culture: Reflections on the Technocratic Society and Its Youthful Opposition.* Garden City, N.Y.: Doubleday, 1969.

———. *Person/Planet: The Creative Disintegration of Industrialization.* Garden City, N.Y.: Anchor/Doubleday, 1978.

———. *Unfinished Animal: The Aquarian Frontier and the Evolution of Consciousness*. New York: Harper and Row, 1975.

———. *Where the Wasteland Ends: Politics and Transcendence in a Postindustrial Society*. London: Faber and Faber, 1972.

Roszak, Theodore, Mary E. Gomes, and Allen D. Kanner, eds. *Ecopsychology: Restoring the Earth, Healing the Mind*. San Francisco: Sierra Club Books, 1995.

Rothenberg, David. *Is It Painful to Think? Conversations with Arne Naess*. Minneapolis: University of Minnesota Press, 1993.

———, ed. *Wisdom of the Open Air: The Norwegian Roots of Deep Ecology*. Minneapolis: University of Minnesota Press, 1992.

Rothman, Hal K. *The Greening of a Nation? Environmentalism in the United States since 1945*. Orlando, Fla.: Harcourt Brace, 1998.

Roy, Lindy. "Geometry as a Nervous System." *ANY* 17 (1997): 24–27.

Rubin, Charles T. *The Green Crusade: Rethinking the Roots of Environmentalism*. New York: Free Press, 1994.

Russell, Edmund P., III. "'Speaking of Annihilation': Mobilizing for War against Human and Insect Enemies, 1914–1945." *Journal of American History* 82 (March 1996): 1505–29.

Russell, Franklin. "Man at War with Nature." *Horizon* 10, no. 3 (1968): 16–39.

Russell, Robert J., William R. Stoeger, and George V. Coyne, eds. *John Paul II on Science and Religion: Reflections on the New View from Rome*. Rome: Vatican Observatory Publications, 1990.

Russell, Stan. "Maslow's Model Mutant." *Oracle of Southern California* 2 (April–May 1967): 10.

Ruttner, Jared. "Arcosanti: A City in the Image of Man." *Mankind* 6 (1980): 16–21.

Sadler, Simon. "Drop City Revisited." *Journal of Architectural Education* 59 (February 2006): 5–14.

Sahli, Nancy. "Smashing: Women's Relationships before the Fall." *Chrysalis* 8 (Summer 1979): 17–27.

Salmon, J. Warren. *Alternative Medicines: Popular and Policy Perspectives*. New York: Tavistock, 1984.

———. "The Holistic Alternative to Scientific Medicine: History and Analysis." *International Journal of Health Services* 10 (1980): 133–47.

Samuelson, Robert J. *The Good Life and Its Discontents: The American Dream in the Age of Entitlement, 1945–1995*. New York: Times Books, 1995.

Sandage, Scott A. "A Marble House Divided: The Lincoln Memorial, the Civil Rights Movement, and the Politics of Memory, 1939–1963." *Journal of American History* 80 (June 1993): 153–67.

Scanlon, Jennifer. *Bad Girls Go Everywhere: The Life of Helen Gurley Brown*. New York: Oxford University Press, 2009.

Schiebinger, Londa L. *The Mind Has No Sex? Women in the Origins of Modern Science*. Cambridge, Mass.: Harvard University Press, 1989.

Schindler, George, Jr. "It Didn't Begin with Earth Day: The Green Momentum Was Building Long before 1970." *E: The Environmental Magazine* 6 (March/April 1995): 32.

Schmidt, Carl F. *The Octagon Fad*. New York: Schmidt, 1958.

Schmidt, Leigh E. *Restless Souls: The Making of American Spirituality*. San Francisco: HarperSanFrancisco, 2005.

Schmitz-Moormann, Karl. "Teilhard de Chardin, Theologian of an Evolutionary Creation." *Insights: The Magazine of the Chicago Center for Religion and Science* 8 (October 1996): 5–12.

———. "Teilhard de Chardin's View on Evolution." In *Evolution and Creation*, edited by Svend Anderson and Arthur Peacocke, 162–69. Aarhus, Denmark: Aarhus University Press, 1987.

———. *Theology of Creation in an Evolutionary World*. Cleveland, Ohio: Pilgrim Press, 1997.

Schumacher, E. F. *Small Is Beautiful: Economics as If People Mattered*. New York: Harper and Row, 1973.

Schumacher, Michael. *Dharma Lion: A Critical Biography of Allen Ginsberg*. New York: St. Martin's Press, 1992.

Schutz, Will. *Profound Simplicity*. New York: Bantam, 1979.

Scott, Alison M., and Christopher D. Geist, eds. *The Writing on the Cloud: American Culture Confronts the Atomic Bomb*. Lanham, Md.: University Press of America, 1997.

Scott, Felicity D. "Acid Visions." *Grey Room* 23 (Spring 2006): 22–39. http://magazines.documenta.de/frontend/article.php?IdLanguage=1&NrArticle=1739 (accessed July 31, 2008).

Seager, Richard Hughes. *Buddhism in America*. New York: Columbia University Press, 1999.

———, ed. *The Dawn of Religious Pluralism: Voices from the World's Parliament of Religions, 1893*. LaSalle, Ill.: Open Court Press, 1993.

———. *The World's Parliament of Religions*. Bloomington: Indiana University Press, 1995.

Seale, William. *Domes of America*. San Francisco: Pomegranate, 1994.

Secrest, Clark. "No Right to Be Poor': Colorado's Drop City." *Colorado Heritage*, Winter 1998, 14–21.

Segal, Howard P. *Technological Utopianism in American Culture*. Chicago: University of Chicago Press, 1985.

Settanni, Harry. *Holism—A Philosophy for Today: Anticipating the Twenty-first Century*. New York: Peter Lang, 1990.

Shafer, Ingrid H. "A Global Ethic for the Global Village." *Journal of Ecumenical Studies* 42 (Summer 2007): 440–53.

Shapiro, Stewart B. *The Place of Confluent Education in the Human Potential Movement: A Historical Perspective*. Lanham, Md.: University Press of America, 1998.

———. "The UCSB Confluent Education Program: Its Essence and Demise." *Journal of Humanistic Psychology* 37 (1997): 80–105.

Sharp, Dennis. "Buckminster Fuller: A Tribute." *Architectural Journal* 23 (December 14, 1995): 20–25.

Shepard, Martin. *Fritz*. New York: Saturday Review Press, 1975.

Sherrington, Charles Scott. *The Integrative Action of the Nervous System*. New Haven, Conn.: Yale University Press, 1906.

Shyrock, Richard H. *The Development of Modern Medicine: An Interpretation of the Social and Scientific Factors Involved*. Madison: University of Wisconsin Press, 1980.

Sieden, Lloyd Steven. *Buckminster Fuller's Universe: An Appreciation.* New York: Plenum Press, 1989.

Sierra Club. "Sierra Club History." February 26, 2003. http://www.sierraclub.org/history/timeline.asp (accessed August 20, 2004).

Singal, Daniel Joseph. "Towards a Definition of American Modernism." *American Quarterly* 39 (1987): 7–26.

Sitkoff, Harvard. *The Struggle for Black Equality, 1954–1980.* New York: Hill and Wang, 1981.

Skinner, B. F. *About Behaviorism.* New York: Vintage, 1976.

———. *Walden Two.* New York: Macmillan, 1948.

Skyttner, Lars. *General Systems Theory: Ideas and Applications.* River Edge, N.J.: World Scientific, 2001.

Smith, Baldwin E. *The Dome: A Study in the History of Ideas.* Princeton, N.J.: Princeton University Press, 1978.

Smith, Barry, ed. and trans. *Foundations of Gestalt Theory.* Munich: Philosophia Verlag, 1988.

Smith, Christian. *American Evangelicalism: Embattled and Thriving.* Chicago: University of Chicago Press, 1998.

Smith, Donald H. "An Exegesis of Martin Luther King, Jr.'s Social Philosophy." *Phylon* 31 (1970): 89–97.

Smith, Henry Nash. *Virgin Land: The American West as Symbol and Myth.* Cambridge, Mass.: Harvard University Press, 1950.

Smith, Kenneth L., and Ira G. Zepp Jr., *Search for the Beloved Community: The Thinking of Martin Luther King, Jr.* Valley Forge, Pa.: Judson Press, 1974.

Smith, M. B. "'Silence, Miss Carson!' Science, Gender, and the Reception of *Silent Spring.*" *Feminist Studies* 27 (Fall 2001): 733–52.

Smithline, Arnold. *Natural Religion in American Literature.* New Haven, Conn.: College and University Press, 1966.

Smith-Rosenberg, Carol. *Disorderly Conduct: Visions of Gender in Victorian America.* New York: Oxford University Press, 1985.

Smuts, Jan Christaaen. *Holism and Evolution.* New York: Macmillan, 1926.

Snyder, Gary. *Earth House Hold: Technical Notes and Queries to Fellow Dharma Revolutionaries.* New York: New Directions, 1969.

Snyder, Robert, ed. *R. Buckminster Fuller—An Autobiographical Monologue/Scenario.* New York: St. Martin's Press, 1980.

Soleri, Paolo. *Arcology: The City in the Image of Man.* Cambridge, Mass.: MIT Press, 1969.

———. "How Things Look to Me." *Stolen Paper Review* 1 (1963): 37.

———. "Teilhard and the Esthetic." In *Teilhard and The Unity of Knowledge,* edited by Thomas M. King and James F. Salmon, 74–82. New York: Paulist Press, 1983.

Speaight, Robert. *The Life of Teilhard de Chardin.* New York: Harper and Row, 1967.

Speaight, Robert, Robert V. Wilshire, and J. V. Langmead Casserly. *Teilhard de Chardin: Re-mythologization.* Chicago: Argus, 1970.

Spiegelberg, Frederic. *Living Religions of the World.* Englewood Cliffs, N.J.: Prentice-Hall, 1956.

Spretnak, Charlene. *Lost Goddesses of Early Greece: A Collection of Pre-Hellenic Myths.* Berkeley, Calif.: Moon Books, 1978.

———. *The Spiritual Dimension of Green Politics*. Santa Fe, N.M.: Bear, 1986.

———. *States of Grace: The Recovery of Meaning in the Postmodern Age*. San Francisco: HarperSanFrancisco, 1991.

Stalker, Douglas, ed. *Examining Holistic Medicine*. Buffalo, N.Y.: Prometheus Books, 1985.

Stanishev, Georgi. "Soleri's Laboratory." *World Architecture* 21 (1993): 58–63.

Stansell, Christine. *American Moderns: Bohemian New York and the Creation of a New Century*. New York: Holt, 2001.

Stark, Rodney, and William Sims Bainbridge. *The Future of Religion*. Berkeley: University of California Press, 1985.

Steiner, Rudolf. *Education of the Child in the Light of Anthroposophy*. Translated by G. Adams and M. Adams. London: Rudolf Steiner Press, 1976.

Steinkraus, Warren E. "Martin Luther King's Personalism and Non-Violence." *Journal of the History of Ideas* 34 (1973): 97–111.

Sterling, Philip. *Sea and Earth: The Life of Rachel Carson*. New York: Crowell, 1970.

Stevens, Jay. *Storming Heaven: LSD and the American Dream*. New York: Atlantic Monthly Press, 1987.

Strohecker, James, ed. *Alternative Medicine: The Definitive Guide*. Puyallup, Wash.: Future Medicine, 1994.

Sumner, William Graham. *Folkways: A Study of the Sociological Importance of Usages, Manners, Customs, Mores, and Morals*. New York: Ginn, 1940.

Susman, Warren I. *Culture as History: The Transformation of American Society in the Twentieth Century*. New York: Pantheon, 1984.

Sutich, Anthony. "The Founding of Humanistic and Transpersonal Psychology: A Personal Account." Ph.D. diss., Humanistic Psychology Institution, 1976.

Svihus, Richard H. "On Healing the Whole Person: A Perspective." *Western Journal of Medicine* 131 (1979): 478–88.

Swimme, Brian, and Thomas Berry. *The Universe Story: From the Primordial Flaring Forth to the Ecozoic Era—A Celebration of the Unfolding of the Cosmos*. San Francisco: HarperSanFrancisco, 1992.

Tart, Charles T., ed. *Altered States of Consciousness*. San Francisco: HarperSanFrancisco, 1990.

Taussig, Helen B. "The Thalidomide Syndrome." *Scientific American* 207 (August 1962): 29–35.

Taylor, Bob Pepperman. *Our Limits Transgressed: Environmental Political Thought in America*. Lawrence: University Press of Kansas, 1992.

Taylor, Eugene. *Shadow Culture: Psychology and Spirituality in America*. Washington, D.C.: Counterpoint, 1999.

Taylor, Harold. "Inside Buckminster Fuller's Universe." *Saturday Review*, May 2, 1970, 56–57, 69–70.

Terra, Helmut de. *Memories of Teilhard de Chardin*. London: Scientific Book Club, 1964.

Thomson, John Arthur. *The System of Animate Nature*. Gifford Lectures 1915–1916. 2 vols. New York: Holt, 1920.

Thoreau, Henry David. *The Major Essays of Henry David Thoreau*, edited by Richard Dillman. Albany, N.Y.: Whitston, 2001.

Tierney, John. "Fateful Voice of a Generation Still Drowns Out Real Science." *New York Times*, June 5, 2007, Health and Fitness, 1.

Tipton, Steven. *Getting Saved from the Sixties: Moral Meaning in Conversion and Cultural Change*. Berkeley: University of California Press, 1982.

Tobias, Michael, ed. *Deep Ecology*. San Marcos, Calif.: Avant Books, 1988.

Tomkins, Calvin. "Architecture: Umbrella Man." *Newsweek*, July 13, 1959, 84–87.

———. "New Paradigms." *New Yorker*, January 5, 1976, 30–51.

———. "Profiles: In the Outlaw Area." *New Yorker*, January 8, 1966, 35ff.

Trachtenberg, Alan. *Brooklyn Bridge: Fact and Symbol*. Chicago: University of Chicago Press, 1965.

———. *The Incorporation of America: Culture and Society in the Gilded Age*. New York: Hill and Wang, 1982.

Trego, Charlotte. "Drop City: New Life for Old Cars." *Architectural Forum* 127 (September 1967): 74–75.

Turner, Fred. *From the Counterculture to the Cyberculture: Stewart Brand, the Whole Earth Network, and the Rise of Digital Utopianism*. Chicago: University of Chicago Press, 2006.

Turner, Frederick Jackson. *The Frontier in American History*. New York: Holt, 1920.

Twain, Mark. *A Connecticut Yankee in King Arthur's Court*. New York: Charles L. Webster, 1889.

Tweed, Thomas A. *The American Encounter with Buddhism, 1844–1912: Victorian Culture and the Limits of Dissent*. Bloomington: Indiana University Press, 1992.

———, ed. *Retelling U. S. Religious History*. Berkeley: University of California Press, 1997.

Tweed, Thomas A., and Stephen Prothero, eds. *Asian Religions in America: A Documentary History*. New York: Oxford University Press, 1999.

Twombly, Robert. *Power and Style: A Critique of Twentieth-Century Architecture in the United States*. New York: Hill and Wang, 1995.

Ulansey, David. Home page. http://www.well.com/user/davidu/index.html (accessed January 29, 2010).

U.S. Department of Commerce, Bureau of the Census. *The Statistical Abstracts of the United States*. Washington, D.C.: Government Printing Office, 1961–1970, http://www.census.gov/prod/www/abs/statab.html (accessed Oct. 8, 2007).

"The U.S. in Moscow: Russia Comes to the Fair." *Time*, August 3, 1959.

Van Denack, Julia. "Evolution Is God's Method of Creation." *American Biology Teacher* 35 (April 1973): 216–18.

Veblen, Thorstein. "Prophets of Technocracy Tell How Industry Might Be Ruled." *Science Newsletter* 23 (January 28, 1933): 52, 62.

Viney, Wayne, and D. Brett King. *A History of Psychology: Ideas and Context*. 2nd ed. Boston: Allyn and Bacon, 1998.

Vliet, Willem Van. *Encyclopedia of Housing*. Thousand Oaks, Calif.: Sage, 1998.

Voorhees, James. *Dialogue Sustained: The Multi-level Peace Process and the Dartmouth Conference*. Washington, D.C.: United States Institute of Peace, 2002.

Voyd, Bill. "Funk Architecture." In *Shelter and Society*, edited by Paul Oliver, 156–64. New York: Praeger, 1969.

Waddell, Craig, ed. *And No Birds Sing: Rhetorical Analyses of Rachel Carson's Silent Spring*. Carbondale: Southern Illinois University Press, 2000.

Walker, Lester. *American Shelter: An Illustrated Encyclopedia of the American Home*. Woodstock, N.Y.: Overlook Press, 1981.

Wallerstein, Immanuel. "Modernization: Requiescat in Pace." In *The Capitalist World Economy, 132–37.* Cambridge: Cambridge University Press, 1979.

Wang, Jessica. *American Science in an Age of Anxiety: Scientists, Anticommunism, and the Cold War.* Chapel Hill: University of North Carolina Press, 1999.

Ward, Barbara. *Spaceship Earth: The Impact of Science on Society.* New York: Columbia University Press, 1966.

Ward, James, ed. *The Artifacts of R. Buckminster Fuller.* 4 vols. New York: Garland, 1985.

Warshofsky, Fred. "Meet Bucky Fuller, Ambassador from Tomorrow." *Reader's Digest,* November 1969, 199–206.

Watson, John B. *Behaviorism.* Rev. ed. Chicago: University of Chicago Press, 1930.

———. "Psychology as the Behaviorist Views It." *Psychological Review* 20 (1913): 158–77.

Watson, Steven. *Birth of the Beat Generation: Visionaries, Rebels, and Hipsters, 1944–1960.* New York: Pantheon, 1995.

Watts, Alan. *In My Own Way: An Autobiography, 1915–1965.* New York: Pantheon, 1972.

———. *The Joyous Cosmology: Adventures in the Chemistry of Consciousness.* New York: Pantheon, 1962.

———. *Psychotherapy: East and West.* New York: Vintage, 1961.

———. *The Spirit of Zen: A Way of Life, Work, and Art in the Far East.* New York: Grove Press, 1960.

———. *This Is It and Other Essays on Zen and Spiritual Existence.* New York: Collier Books, 1967.

———. *Zen and the Beat Way.* Boston: Tuttle, 1997.

Weart, Spencer R. *Nuclear Fear: A History of Images.* Cambridge, Mass.: Harvard University Press, 1988.

Weber, Max. *From Max Weber,* edited by H. H. Gerth and C. W. Mills. New York: Oxford University Press, 1946.

Weil, Andrew. *Health and Healing: Understanding Conventional and Alternative Medicine.* Boston: Houghton Mifflin, 1983.

Weisskopf, Walter. *Alienation and Economics.* New York: Dutton, 1971.

———. *The Psychology of Economics.* Chicago: University of Chicago Press, 1955.

Werner, Craig. *A Change Is Gonna Come: Music, Race, and the Soul of America.* New York: Plume, 1999.

Wertheimer, Max. "Gestalt Theory." In *A Source Book of Gestalt Psychology,* edited by Willis D. Ellis, 1–11. 3rd ed. London: Routledge, 1950.

———. *Productive Thinking,* edited by Michael Wertheimer. Chicago: University of Chicago Press, 1982.

Wertheimer, Michael. *A Brief History of Psychology.* 3rd ed. New York: Holt, Rinehart and Winston, 1987.

———. "Gestalt Theory, Holistic Psychologies and Max Wertheimer." *Personale Psychologie* 5 (1983): 5, 32–49.

Wertz, Frederick J. "The Role of the Humanistic Movement in the History of Psychology." *Journal of Humanistic Psychology* 38 (1988): 42–70.

West, Cornel. *The Cornel West Reader.* New York: Basic Civitas Books, 1999.

Wetzteon, Ross. *Republic of Dreams: Greenwich Village: The American Bohemia, 1910–1960.* New York: Simon and Schuster, 2003.

"What the Russians Will See." *Look*, July 21, 1959, 52–54.

White, Fred D. "Rachel Carson: Encounters with the Primal Mother." *North Dakota Quarterly* 59 (Spring 1991): 184–97.

White, Lynn, Jr. "The Historical Roots of Our Ecological Crisis." *Science* 155 (March 10, 1967): 1203–7.

White, Richard. "Environmental History, Ecology, and Meaning." *Journal of American History* 76 (March 1990): 1111–16.

Whitfield, Stephen J. *The Culture of the Cold War*. Baltimore: Johns Hopkins University Press, 1991.

"Who Was David Brower," David Brower Center. http://www.browercenter.org/node/17 (accessed July 14, 2008).

Whorton, James C. *Before Silent Spring: Pesticides and Public Health in Pre-DDT America*. Princeton, N.J.: Princeton University Press, 1974.

———. *Crusaders for Fitness: The History of American Health Reformers*. Princeton, N.J.: Princeton University Press, 1982.

———. *Nature Cures: The History of Alternative Medicine in America*. New York: Oxford University Press, 2002.

Whyte, William H. *The Organization Man*. New York: Simon and Schuster, 1956.

Wickberg, Daniel. "What Is the History of Sensibilities? On Cultural Histories, New and Old." *American Historical Review* 112 (June 2007): 660–84.

Wiebenson, Dora. "The Two Domes of the Halle au Blé in Paris." *Art Bulletin* 54 (June 1973): 262–79.

Wieman, Henry Nelson. "Theocentric Religion." In *Contemporary American Theology: Theological Biographies*, edited by Vergilius Ferm, 339–52. New York: Round Table Press, 1932.

Wiener, Norbert. *The Human Use of Human Beings: Cybernetics and Society*. Boston: Houghton Mifflin, 1954.

Wilcox, Clyde, and Carin Larson. *Onward Christian Soldiers: The Christian Right in American Politics*. Boulder, Colo.: Westview Press, 2006.

Wilkes, Joseph A., ed. *AIA Encyclopedia of Architecture: Design, Engineering, and Construction*. 5 vols. New York: Wiley, 1988.

Wilson, Bryan. *Religion in a Secular Society*. London: Watts, 1966.

———. "Secularization: The Inherited Model." In *The Sacred in a Secular Age*, edited by Phillip E. Hammond, 9–20. Berkeley: University of California Press, 1985.

Wilson, Clyde. "Brave Old World." *Inland Architect* 35 (July–August 1991): 72.

Wilson, Colin. *New Pathways in Psychology: Maslow and the Post-Freudian Revolution*. New York: Taplinger, 1972.

Wilson, Sloan. *The Man in the Gray Flannel Suit*. New York: Simon and Schuster, 1955.

Winthrop, John. *The Journal of John Winthrop, 1630–1649*, edited by Richard S. Dunn, James Savage, and Laetitia Yeandle. Cambridge, Mass.: Harvard University Press, 1996.

Wofford, Clare and Harris Wofford. *India Afire*. New York: J. Day, 1951.

Wolfe, Thomas. "Digibabble, Fairy Dust, and the Human Anthill." *Forbes ASAP*, special edition, October 4, 1999, 213–27.

———. *The Electric Kool-Aid Acid Test*. New York, Bantam, 1969.

———. *From Bauhaus to Our House*. New York: Farrar, Straus and Giroux, 1981.

———. "The Me Decade and the Third Great Awakening." In *The Purple Decades: A Reader*. New York: Farrar, Straus and Giroux, 1982.

Woodcock, John. "The Garden in the Machine: Variations on Spaceship Earth." *Michigan Quarterly Review* 18 (Spring 1979): 308–17.

Woodstock Forum with James Salmon, S.J., Nicole Schmitz-Moormann, Philip Hefner, and Harris Wofford (April 11, 2005). "Teilhard de Chardin and His Relevance for Today." *Woodstock Report* 82 (June 2005). Georgetown University. http://woodstock.georgetown.edu/resources/articles/Teilhard-de-Chardin-His-Relevance-for-Today.html (accessed June 2, 2008).

Worster, Donald. "The Ecology of Order and Chaos." *Environmental History Review* 14 (Spring/Summer 1990): 1–18.

———. *Nature's Economy: A History of Ecological Ideas*. 2nd ed. New York: Cambridge University Press, 1994.

———. *A Passion for Nature: The Life of John Muir*. New York: Oxford University Press, 2008.

———. "The Pathless Way: John Muir and American Wilderness." Review of *The Pathless Way: John Muir and American Wilderness*, by Michael P. Cohen. *Environmental Ethics* 10 (1998): 268–69.

Wren, Daniel A., and Robert D. Hay. "Management Historians and Business Historians: Differing Perceptions of Pioneer Contributors." *Academy of Management Journal* 20 (September 1977): 470–76.

Wright, Robert. *Nonzero: The Logic of Human Destiny*. New York: Pantheon, 2000.

Wrobel, David. *The End of American Exceptionalism: Frontier Anxiety from the Old West to the New Deal*. Lawrence: University Press of Kansas, 1993.

Wuthnow, Robert. *After Heaven: Spirituality in America since the 1950s*. Berkeley: University of California Press, 1998.

Yarwood, Doreen. *A Chronology of Western Architecture*. London: Batsford, 1987.

Young, Perry Deane. *God's Bullies: Native Reflections on Preachers and Politics*. New York: Holt, Rinehart and Winston, 1982.

Youngblood, Gene. "World Game: The Artist as Ecologist." *Arts/Canada* 27 (August 1970): 42–49.

Zaehner, Robert C. *Evolution in Religion: A Study in Sri Aurobindo and Pierre Teilhard de Chardin*. Oxford: Clarendon Press, 1971.

Zepp, Ira G., Jr. *The Social Vision of Martin Luther King, Jr.* Brooklyn: Carlson, 1989.

Zevi, Bruno. *The Modern Language of Architecture*. New York: De Capo Press, 1994.

Ziolkowski, Eric J., ed. *A Museum of Faiths: Histories and Legacies of the 1893 World's Parliament of Religions*. Atlanta, Ga.: Scholars Press, 1993.

Zukav, Gary. *The Dancing Wu Li Masters: An Overview of the New Physics*. New York: Morrow, 1979.

Zung, Thomas T. K., ed. *Buckminster Fuller: Anthology for the New Millennium*. New York: St. Martin's Press, 2001.

Index